AMELIA EARHART

Doris L. Rich

AMELIA

EARHART

A BIOGRAPHY

Smithsonian Institution Press

Washington and London

This book was edited by Therese Boyd and designed by Alan Carter.
Library of Congress Cataloging-in-Publication Data
Rich, Doris L.
    Amelia Earhart : a biography / by Doris L. Rich.
       p.   cm.   Foreword by Jeana Yeager.
    Bibliography: p.
    Includes index.
    Summary: A biography of the famous aviatrix who disappeared in the South
Pacific on an around-the-world flight attempt in 1937.
    ISBN 0-87474-836-4
       1. Earhart, Amelia, 1897–1937.   2. Air pilots—United States—Biography.
[1. Earhart, Amelia, 1897–1937.   2. Air pilots.]   I. Title.
TL540.E3R53   1989
629.13'092—dc20   89-32181
British Library Cataloguing-in-Publication Data ia available.

A paperback reissue (ISBN 1-56098-725-1) of the original cloth edition.

⊗ The paper used in this publication meets the minimum requirements of the
American National Standard for Permanence of Paper for Printed Library Materials
Z39.48-1984.

Manufactured in the United States of America

03 02 01 00 99 98 97   5 4 3 2

For Stanley
and our children
Christopher, Lawrence, and Deborah

CONTENTS

*Note numbers are not used in this book. Instead, as a pleasurable convenience to the reader, notes are printed at the back of the book and are identified by page number and an identifying phrase or quotation from the text.

FOREWORD

I am often asked whether Amelia Earhart was one of my childhood idols.

The simple answer is no. I grew up very much a loner, very quiet, and I never had anyone that I consciously modeled my *self* after. But I was always ready to reach out and live my fantasies, to explore my own capabilities, to challenge myself—and to this extent I believe that many young people have been touched by her example and spirit.

For many years, however, I was more interested in horses than aircraft. I obtained my pilot's license at the age of twenty-six primarily so that I could fly helicopters, which reminded me of the dragonflies I had admired as a child. My full absorption in the world of aviation did not transpire until I met Dick Rutan in 1980 and joined in the design and testing of experimental aircraft. We soon began setting records for speed and distance, as we pursued the dream of building and flying the first aircraft capable of circling the world nonstop without refueling.

That dream—which was realized by the flight of *Voyager* in December 1986—certainly reminded us of Amelia and her own courageous attempt at an around-the-world flight. But it was not until I received a copy of this book's manuscript that I had actually read an account of her life. The similarities between her goals and enthusiasms and my own are almost spooky—similarities such as a love for horses, a competitive interest in setting records, and an inherent stubbornness. A lot of the other ingredients of her life—the long hours, the physical exhaustion—also strike familiar chords.

This book tells us of a gifted woman's lessons in dreaming and work and determination. Her achievements were worth all the physical discomforts and dangers she endured in seizing that one rare chance offered to so few: to be the *first*.

Jeana Yeager
Nipomo, California

ACKNOWLEDGMENTS

Much of the material in this book came from special collections and the archives of the following libraries and organizations: National Archives, Library of Congress, Martin Luther King Library and Society of Woman Geographers, all in Washington, D.C.; Arthur and Elizabeth Schlesinger Library, Radcliffe College; Ninety-Nines, Inc.; J. B. Carruthers Aviation Collection, Harvey Mudd College; Charles Dawson History Center of Harrison, New York; West Virginia and Regional History Collection, West Virginia University Library; Special Collections, Purdue University Libraries; Archives of Contemporary History, University of Wyoming; Cochran Papers, Dwight D. Eisenhower Library; Oral History Collection, Butler Library, Columbia University in the City of New York; Aero Club of France; North Hollywood Amelia Earhart Regional Library; Zonta International; Swarthmore College Peace Collection; and the Office of Public Information, Lockheed California Company.

In all of them, staff members were invariably patient and helpful. I wish to thank in particular Kenneth Dowden, Thomas Branigar, Dr. Virginia Purdy, Edythe Caro, Loretta Gragg, Eleanor Mitchell, Dr. David Kuhner, Jeri Nunn, Robert C. Ferguson, Roy A. Blay, Herbert Bowen, Ginger BeVard, Marian Holt, Helen Bergan, Emmett D. Chisum, Eunice E. Spackman, and Lynn Durkee.

I spent most of the first three years of my six years of research at the library of the National Air and Space Museum of the Smithsonian Institution. The staff members who gave me guidance and encouragement, as well as information, include Phil Edwards, Larry Wilson, Robert Dreeson, Frank Piatropaoli, Peter Suthard, and Mary Pavlovich. I thank them all.

I am grateful for the interviews given me, especially by Amelia's sister, Muriel Earhart Morrissey; by Amelia's stepson, David Binney Putnam, and his daughter, Sally Putnam Chapman; and by Margaret Haviland Lewis, Donna Kinner Hunter, Winfield Kinner, Jr., and Marian Stabler. The late pilot-author Don Dwiggins gave me the papers of Paul Mantz, and Richard Sanders Allen, identification of all of Earhart's planes.

Others who gave me interviews were: Capt. Ralph Barnaby, USN (Ret.), Mrs. James E. Bassett, Jr., Melba Gorby Beard, Albert Bresnick, Jessie B. Chamberlin, Harvey C. Christen, Marie Christiansen, Phyllis Fleet Crary, Harkness Davenport, R. E. G. Davies, Susan Dexter, Shirley Dobson-Gilroy, Lucille Emch, Col. Vincent Ford, USAF (Ret.), Paul Garber, Eddie Gorski, Mrs. James G. Haizlip, Mrs. Clifford Henderson, Charles Hill, Terry Gwynne-Jones, Charles LeBoutillier, John L. Maddux, Jim Montijo, Edna Whiting Nisewaner, Elise von R. Owen, Frank Pine, Paul Rafford, Ogden Reid, Whitelaw Reid, Pat H. V. Riley, Vivian Maatta Sims, Neta Snook Southern, Clair C. Stebbins, Nancy Hopkins Tier, Evelyn "Bobbi" Trout, Mrs. Robert W. Trump, Maj. Gen. Leigh Wade, USAF (Ret.), Dr. Max Ward, Bradford Washburn, Fay Gillis Welles, Patrick Welsh, Edna Gardner Whyte, Bernard Wiesman, Margaret and Benson Workman, C. L. Zakhartchenko and Lt. Cmdr. Thomas Zinavage, USN (Ret.).

Information through correspondence came from Virginia L. Ames, Mrs. Bernt Balchen, Michelle Birnbaum, Eleanor Merrick Bissell, Pam Blittersdorf, Doris Brell, Jane Dow Bromberg, Mrs. Robert C. Canavello, Masataka Chihaya, Anne F. Cooper, Louise Van Dyne Cotterman, Emma Encinas DeGuitierrez, Jack Elliott, Elizabeth Braun Ernst, Doris H. Farr, Harold C. Field, Herbert O. Fisher, Ella May Frazer, Eddie Fritts, Betty Huyler Gillies, R. J. Hyland, David Jones, Susan Kiner, Valerie F. Levitan, Anne Morrow Lindbergh, Ellen C. Masters, Clinton and Marian Morrison, Carole Osborne, Ben R. Rich, Dorothy Schaeffer, Richard G. Strippel, Anne Saunders, Nicholas Meredith Turner, Charles and Anne Thielen, W. M. Tegerdine, and Margaret Warren.

I am deeply indebted to Claudia M. Oakes, Curator of Aeronautics at the Air and Space Museum of the Smithsonian Institution; to Jacqueline Hubbard, author and friend; and to Ann Elmo, my agent; all of whom read the manuscript and made helpful suggestions. My thanks also to my life-long friend, Capt. Roger Pineau, USNR (Ret.), to Chris Prouty Rosenfeld, Nonna Cheatham, Luree Miller, Susan Dexter, and Julia Dean for their interest and support, and to Felix C. Lowe, Ruth Spiegel, and Therese Boyd for editorial guidance.

Finally, I could not have completed this work without the constant help of my husband, Stanley Rich, who took time from his own interests to become reader, editor, secretary, chauffeur, and an expert baker of frozen meat pies in motel ovens.

PART ONE

TAXIING

CHAPTER ONE

A Double Life

On a bitterly cold winter day in 1904, seven-year-old Amelia Mary Earhart stood at the top of a hill near her grandparents' house in Atchison, Kansas. Her blue-grey eyes surveyed the icy street descending to a crossroad below. Muriel, her four-year-old sister and co-owner of the new sled given them at Christmas, watched silently as Amelia knelt in the snow and carefully laid the tow rope over the top of the sled before picking it up. She ran forward a few steps, then fell on the sled for a perfect "belly-slammer" start. By mid-hill she had gained the speed she wanted, the road beneath the sled flashing by her eyes. Watching from above, Muriel saw a wagon drawn by a horse with blinders emerge from the side street. The hill was too icy for a turn; the driver of the cart, whose ears were covered by a woolen cap, was deaf to Amelia's warning cries. Just when collision seemed inevitable, Amelia put her head down, and sled and rider shot under the horse's belly. A moment later the grinning, triumphant speedster stood in the deserted road, waving up at Muriel.

On the way home Muriel was warned that Grandmother Otis should not hear of the incident. Grandmother did not approve of girls "belly-slamming." Years later Amelia claimed, "that condemned tomboy method saved my life . . . had I been sitting up, either my head or the horse's ribs would have suffered in contact—probably the horse's ribs."

There was no mention of the possibility of contact with the horse's legs. Luck was ignored, the method idealized.

Their grandmother also disapproved of the "bloomers" worn by the Earhart girls, apparel promoted by their mother's sister, Margaret, who was an admirer of feminist Amelia Jenks Bloomer. Even Amelia harbored reservations about it. "We wore them Saturdays to play in and though we felt terribly 'free and athletic,' we also felt somewhat as outcasts among the little girls who fluttered about us in their skirts."

Amelia Otis, the black-gowned, corseted matriarch of an affluent Victorian household, was not to be ignored. The first time she caught Amelia leaping the wrought iron fence enclosing the Otis yard, the old woman told her, "Ladies don't climb fences, child. Only boys do that. Little girls use the gate." From that time on Amelia looked before she leaped, although she was certain that if she had been a boy her grandmother would have thought the shortcut "entirely natural." If her thoughts seem mundane in the late 1980s, they were revolutionary at the time, when rules of female conduct bewildered and annoyed an adventurous, active little girl.

On the day of the sled ride, when Amelia walked up the hill to the corner of North Terrace and Santa Fe streets, she could see the spacious white wood and brick Victorian house against the darkening winter sky. It was home to her for nine months of each year, the house in which she was born. Her grandfather, Alfred E. Otis, had had it built for his bride, Amelia Harres Otis, in 1861 when Kansas became a state, at a time when Indian raiders still threatened the lives of Kansas farmers, and an endless stream of trappers, traders, miners, and homesteaders crossed the new state on their way west. In it Amelia Otis had borne six children, one of whom was Amy Otis Earhart, Amelia's mother.

Amy was twenty-three when she came to Atchison for the birth of her first child, Amelia, a healthy, nine-pound girl born on July 24, 1897. The young mother's first pregnancy had been terminated by a cable-car accident in Kansas City where she lived with her husband, Edwin Stanton Earhart. Pregnant again a few months later, Amy returned to her parents' home in Atchison for her "confinement" and remained until the child was baptized on October 10. The baby was named Amelia for her maternal grandmother and Mary for her paternal grandmother, Mary Wells Earhart. A few days after the baptism, mother and child returned to Kansas City, twenty-two miles south of Atchison.

At seven and a half months, Amelia was photographed in the arms of her Aunt Margaret. Wide-eyed and plump, the child looked much like any other healthy infant of that age with one exception. Her hand, resting on Margaret's sleeve, was neither chubby nor grasping, but fully extended, the fingers unusually long and slim.

The picture was taken at the Otis home where Amelia was to spend much of her childhood. The house stood on a bluff four hundred feet above the muddy, turgid waters of the Missouri River. In the summer, tall shade trees shielded it from the blazing sun, their leaves casting a pale green glow over sparkling white clapboard siding. Leading to the long front porch with its four pairs of tall wooden pillars was a paved walk guarded by two stone dogs. The fence Amelia loved to jump enclosed house, trees, walk, dogs, neatly trimmed shrubbery, and a green lawn at the south side of the house where a wrought iron stag-at-bay stared off into the distance.

Long before she entered school Amelia was familiar with all eleven rooms of the house on the bluff. She explored the drawing room where frock-coated men sat in oversized chairs discussing politics and business. She watched tightly corseted women in long gowns with bustles and leg-o'-mutton sleeves drink tea in the living room with its Tiffany lamps and horsehair sofa. At Thanksgiving and Christmas the table in the stately dining room was set with fine china and silver that glistened in the light cast by a crystal chandelier and the flames from the open fireplace were reflected in the curved, stained-glass windows. After grace was said, Grandmother Otis would orchestrate the serving of the food dispatched by the cook through a serving window to waiting maids.

The house mirrored the values and achievements of Alfred Otis, chief warden of the Trinity Episcopal Church, lawyer, retired U.S. District Court Judge, and president of the Atchison Savings Bank. Of his six children, Amelia's mother, Amy, was his favorite. He had been bitterly disappointed when she married Edwin Earhart. Son of an impoverished Evangelical Lutheran minister who taught school, farmed, and carried out his ministry whenever and wherever he could, handsome, charming Edwin was raised in grinding poverty. He had worked for his education, shining shoes and building furnace fires and, later, tutoring less diligent students at the University of Kansas Law School. One of his pupils was Mark Otis, Amy's brother, who invited Edwin to Atchison for Amy's six-teenth birthday party, also the occasion of her formal presentation to society. For Amy and Edwin, love occurred at first sight, but marriage did not. Five years passed before Edwin could meet the Judge's minimal requirement—a monthly salary of fifty dollars in the claims department of the Rock Island Railroad's office in Kansas City. The Judge provided a house in that city, furnished.

When Amelia reached school age, she was enrolled in the school her mother had attended, the College Preparatory School in Atchison; she lived with her grandparents while her parents remained in Kansas City. The headmistress, Sarah Walton, reported that Amelia "deduces the correct answer to complex arithmetic problems but hates to put down the steps by which she arrived at the results."

Amelia was seldom intentionally disobedient but her impatience led to frequent clashes with authority. A gifted speaker, she annoyed the headmistress by arriving too late for an annual school contest in which she was to share with a classmate the complete recitation of an Horatian ode. When the headmistress demanded an explanation, Amelia said that she had promised to exercise a horse every day for some friends of her grandparents and thought she could ride first and get back in time to take over the second half of the ode. Too late to compete for the prize that would have been hers, Amelia said she was glad she knew all of the poem anyway.

On another occasion Amelia displayed that same reluctance to consult her elders before taking action. She was playing with her friend, Kathy Dolan, when she noticed a horse tied in front of a delivery cart parked down Second Street. The animal, Amelia told Kathy, was uncomfortable, its check rein tied much too high. She immediately crossed the street and lowered the rein just as the angry driver appeared. His scolding was accepted in stony silence.

Although often impatient, Amelia could be very tenacious. One afternoon she took a .22-caliber rifle her father had given her for Christmas and went to hunt rats in her grandfather's barn. When she wounded one, she spent hours searching for it to deliver the *coup de grâce*. It was long after dinner before she succeeded and returned to the house. Her grandfather confiscated the gun, a penalty she accepted without protest. Charley, the Otis's handyman, observed that once "Meelie" decided to do something she would do it, regardless of the punishment.

Amelia was the undisputed leader of the neighborhood children. She decided who would be pitcher, catcher, or batter in any baseball game. She taught a younger neighbor, Mary Elizabeth Campbell, to ride a bike and lent her her roller skates. She invited Mary Elizabeth and Kathy to lunch on a private railroad car that Edwin Earhart was allowed to use even though he was merely an employee of the company's claims department. The two girls were awed by the luxury of the appointments and the service by a white-jacketed Filipino.

Amelia's favorite games were played with Muriel and their two cousins, Lucy and Kathryn Challis, known as "Tootie" and "Katch," who lived next door. Amelia wrote the scripts and they played out these adventures in an old carriage stored in the barn. In one, "The Pursuit of the Hairy Men," the girls were pioneers traveling to an imaginary place. When attacked, the carriage became mired in mud or a wheel came off and the horses stampeded. While pursued, the girls would lash the horses and bang away with make-believe guns. Amelia sometimes chose actual places, all of them exotic. Africa was her favorite, the rivers Nile and Niger sufficiently mysterious, the Taureg and Swahili peoples satisfactorily ferocious.

Every summer Amelia went to Kansas City, a twenty-two-mile journey into a different world. She left the house directed by her wealthy, generous, but somewhat reserved grandfather for a second household headed by her idol—her tall, handsome, witty, loving father. Edwin Earhart was all of these, but he lacked the self-confidence and drive of his father-in-law. Bored and unhappy in his ill-paid job at the railroad, he was certain he had found a faster, easier road to fame and fortune by means of an invention, a holder for signal flags at the rear of railroad cars. In May of 1903, when Amelia was almost six, he left for Washington to secure a patent, financing the trip with money needed for property taxes on the Kansas City house. While he was in Washington, Amy received two messages in the mail. The first was the bill for delinquent taxes. The second, a letter from Edwin, revealed that a man from Colorado had filed a patent on an identical holder two years before. Assuring her he would be home soon, Edwin added, "I must recount a feeling which I experienced as I walked past the glorious buildings which house our lawmakers and the great legal minds of the Supreme Court. I felt that I shall some day mount those marble steps in an official capacity or never again. Who knows?"

For Edwin, already forty-seven years old, it would be "never again." Amy was both angry and frightened. To marry him she had defied the father she loved, endured a delay of five years before the marriage, and after a few idyllic months, suffered a miscarriage. The house in Kansas City was a gift from her father. Money was a constant worry to her and the social status she had taken for granted was diminished by Edwin's failure to earn a living. This latest defeat threatened to leave them bankrupt. To pay the taxes Edwin sold several valuable law books given him by his father-in-law, a sale inadvertently revealed to Otis by the buyer. The Judge was convinced that Edwin Earhart was a hopeless failure as a businessman, a husband, and a father.

Unaware of her father's difficulties, Amelia spent a happy summer. In the late afternoons she waited for him to come home and play cowboys and Indians, which he did with gusto. During the day she explored unknown territory, cutting across the neighbors' backyards. She planted a flower garden and, when a neighbor's chickens invaded it, she designed a chicken trap from an empty orange crate with a hinged lid. When it worked she felt "like a big game hunter."

The following summer, when Amelia was seven, Edwin made one hundred dollars from legal work done outside the office. He promptly spent it all on a family excursion to the World's Fair in St. Louis. The roller coaster with its serpentine track climbing and plunging, its cars filled with screaming, laughing passengers, fascinated Amelia. As soon as they returned to Kansas City, she began to build one of her own, aided by Muriel, neighborhood playmate Ralphie Morton, and her Uncle Carl, Amy's brother.

They hauled lumber from a tool shed behind the house and nailed wooden tracks from the ridge pole of the shed down to the lawn below. A cart was constructed with buggy wheels to fit the tracks, which were greased with lard, and the cart was dragged up to the roof where Amelia lay on it, her feet held by Muriel until she gave the signal to let go. The first run ended in a crash landing, cart and rider hitting the ground well off the tracks. Amelia called for additional track for a more gradual descent. With this in place, the second run was a success. It was, Amelia said, "just like flying."

Amelia was ten in the summer of 1907 when Edwin was transferred by the railroad company to Des Moines, Iowa. He took Amy with him and the girls went back to their grandparents in Atchison, to remain until living quarters could be found. They stayed until September of 1909, when they joined their parents in Des Moines. Without enough money to pay day school tuition for her daughters and worried by reports that pupils in the public school had lice, Amy hired a young widow, Florence Gardiner, to move in as governess. After Amelia and Muriel had endured a few months of French, poetry, music, and sampler stitching, their mother realized that the public school had to be accepted and Mrs. Gardiner was dismissed.

Amelia entered the seventh grade and Muriel the fourth, untroubled by fears of lice or the company of classmates less privileged than those of Atchison's College Preparatory School. That summer they spent a month in Worthington, Minnesota, where Amelia had her first automobile ride and went fishing, boating, and swimming. She also attended the Iowa State Fair, where she saw her first airplane, six years after the Wright brothers' flight at Kitty Hawk. She was not impressed. "It was a thing of rusty wire and wood. I was much more interested in an absurd hat made of an inverted peach basket which I purchased for fifteen cents," she said.

A year later, when Edwin became head of the claims department, the family moved to another, larger house and Amy hired a maid. She also supplemented the public school education of her daughters with informal lessons of her own. While preparing a chicken, she taught anatomy and she encouraged both girls to bring home garden toads, spiders, stones, and wood, all to be used in informal lessons.

Although Edwin had been promoted and the Earharts seemed to enjoy a very comfortable standard of living, there was never enough money to meet expenses. Amy had never learned to economize and Edwin did no better. He bought a set of Kipling's works for Amy on the installment plan, but after making the initial payment he had to ask Amy to meet the remaining ones out of her household funds. Past fifty, and ashamed that he could not provide a better living for his wife and children, Edwin began to drink.

In the fall of 1910 Amelia returned to school in Atchison, where she helped care for her ailing grandmother. Grandmother Otis died in February of 1912, leaving an inheritance of a half million dollars to her four living children, to be divided equally. Amy's share was left in trust for twenty years or until the death of Edwin Earhart. Humiliated by the Otises' obvious lack of trust in him, the handsome father whom Amelia adored became a surly, drunken stranger to her, a man who released his fury in repetitive, caustic criticism of the Otises, the railroad, and Amy's handling of household funds. Amy withdrew in silence, barely acknowledging his presence. Amelia and Muriel followed suit. The railroad fired him.

It was a year before Edwin found another job, this time as a clerk in St. Paul, Minnesota, in the freight office of the Great Northern Railway. The family moved in the spring of 1913 into a large but shabby rented house on Fairmont Street. A few days later a wealthy uncle of Amy's paid them a formal call, an opening, Amy assumed, for familial introductions to St. Paul society. Always aware of her social position as an Otis, she expected him to propose Amelia for membership in the skating club or arrange for her attendance at the sub-debutante cotillion. However, after he had made polite inquiries about the Otises of Atchison and sipped his tea, he took his hat, cane, and gloves and departed. The snub was yet another step in Amy's descent into unhappiness. It never occurred to her that if the man had offered what she wanted for Amelia, she still would not have had the money to pay for club fees or a wardrobe for her daughter.

Edwin continued to make sporadic efforts to overcome alcoholism but lapsed again and again. On one occasion he rushed home with news that he was to leave immediately for the site of a railroad accident and to act as legal representative for the company if any passengers chose to file suit. When Amelia went to his room to pack his suitcase, she found a bottle of whiskey hidden among his socks. Edwin found her angrily emptying the bottle into the kitchen sink. He raised his arm to hit her when Amy stopped him. Pale and shaken, he begged Amelia to forgive him and promised he would stay sober. He did for a while, until he realized that the company was not going to promote him from clerking to a place in the legal department.

That Christmas Amelia and Muriel decided to attend a Twelfth Night dance at the church Amy had joined. The two girls decorated the living room and agreed that they would invite the two boys who were expected to escort them home to come in for cocoa and cookies after the dance. Fathers were expected to bring their daughters to the party and Edwin had promised to do so, but he came home too late and very drunk. Amelia pulled down the holiday decorations, tore up the paper Christmas napkins, and threw out the marshmallows already in the cups, then stormed up the stairs to her room. She sat in bed reading until she heard the boys walk past the house, then turned out the light and put her head down on the pillow.

The flare-up at Christmas was Amelia's last. If there was to be no help from others she would manage on her own. In March of 1914 she wrote to one of her friends in Atchison, "Of course I'm going to B.M. [Bryn Mawr] if I have to drive a grocery wagon to accumulate the cash."

In the winter of 1915 Amelia learned about poverty firsthand, a lesson she would never forget. Half the rooms in the Fairmont Street house were closed off to save fuel. She and Muriel walked in the bitter Minnesota cold to save carfare. Edwin was hit by a car and medical bills added to Amy's worries. Amelia made Easter outfits for herself and Muriel, old blouses trimmed with new ribbon and skirts from silk curtains stored in the attic. Thread, ribbons, and buttons were bought with $3.40 earned by selling empty bottles she and Muriel found in the cellar. That fall, when Edwin heard about a job with the Burlington Railroad in Springfield, Missouri, he moved his family without any confirmation from the company. There was no permanent job, only a temporary one. They lived in a dingy boarding house for a month before Edwin gave up and went to Kansas City to live with his sister. Amy left for Chicago with Amelia and Muriel to stay with friends while she looked for rooms. She found some near the University of Chicago, the living room to be shared with two other women. Amelia enrolled in Hyde Park High School.

In the yearbook Amelia, no longer "Meelie" or "Millie," was now "A. E.—the girl in brown who walks alone." Her favorite color was brown, and she did remain aloof from her classmates, but not by choice. She was spurned because she had alienated most of her classmates. She attempted to have an incompetent English teacher who was deaf and rumored to be an aunt of the corrupt mayor removed from her post. The woman did not teach at all, but only sat at her desk and left her pupils to do whatever they wished during the daily fifty-minute lesson. A. E. drew up a petition demanding a change of instructor and asked her classmates to sign it. They not only refused, but tore it up, preferring their daily gratuitous recreational period. Disgusted, A. E. convinced the librarian that she had been assigned a paper that required her to spend every En-

glish period in the library and did not return to class for the entire se-
mester. The incident was a striking example of her stubborn adherence to
principle, one that would surface repeatedly in later years.

When she graduated, she refused to attend commencement exercises and instead left immediately with Amy and Muriel to meet Edwin in
Kansas City. He had discovered that Amy's brother, Mark, trustee for her
portion of the estate, had already lost fifteen thousand dollars of it in ill-
chosen investments. Amy contested the will and, when Amelia Otis's
physician testified that she was incompetent at its signing, the court ruled
against continuance of the trust. Once in possession of her capital, Amy
made Amelia and Muriel the first recipients of this bonanza. By September of 1916 Amelia was enrolled in the Ogontz School at Rydal, Pennsylvania, and Muriel entered St. Margaret's College, a Canadian preparatory
school in Toronto. While the Earhart girls might never again be wrapped
in the cozy blanket of social and economic security they knew as children
in Atchison, they were to be reinstated in the society familiar to their
mother—for as long as the money might last.

Amelia was ecstatic. By then an enthusiastic scholar of both arts and
sciences, she would be given the first-rate education she wanted. Leaving
home was an adventure, not a threat, because there had been no real
home for her for seven years. They were crucial years, from thirteen to
nineteen, in which she had learned that to depend on those she loved
could be disappointing, to confide too much in others might lead to humiliation, and to expect her standards of achievement or honesty to be
shared by her peers was naïve. Along with Amy's money came an inheritance of determination and a strict sense of honor. Edwin's gifts of wit,
intelligence, and imagination were also hers. The round-faced little girl of
eleven, in the crisp, white, high-collared dress, long blonde hair tied back
by a huge bow, that uninhibited, outspoken child from Atchison, had
grown up. In her place was a tall, very slender young woman who moved
with the grace of a dancer and spoke softly, almost hesitantly, with a de-
liberate thoughtfulness. The haunting gray eyes remained unchanged.
They were the eyes of a maverick.

CHAPTER TWO

Arrow without a Target

*I*n the fall of 1916 Amelia Earhart traveled by train from Kansas to Pennsylvania across a nation on the brink of entering a world war, a country beset by struggle between advocates and opponents of neutrality, universal sufferage, prohibition, "trust-busting," and organized labor. The "new girl" from Kansas arrived on the morning of October 3 at Ogontz School, then a few miles north of Philadelphia on what is now a campus of the Pennsylvania State University. Enrolling girls for elementary grades through what would now be junior college, Ogontz was owned and managed by one woman, Abby Sutherland.

Abby Sutherland did not record her first impression of Amelia but the new student promptly dispatched hers of the headmistress to Amy Earhart. Dr. Sutherland (the degree was an honorary one from Temple University) was "come up from the depths," Amelia wrote. "A hard cold woman." A few weeks later Amelia changed her mind. "She is a very brilliant woman, very impressive as she is taller than I." (At five feet, eight inches, Amelia was a tall woman for her generation.) Attending a Philadelphia Symphony concert with Miss Sutherland and four other students, Amelia thought her "so charming that I can't feel my first impression was correct altho I have watched her closely. She has had many chances at matrimony because she is brilliant but she passes them all by. She has read very widely and has very good ideas about a lot of things."

There were elements of truth in both Amelia's positive and negative assessments. Miss Sutherland was a strong-willed disciplinarian who had worked her way through normal school by teaching before she went to Radcliffe, where she was in the same class as Gertrude Stein and Helen Keller. Not brilliant but well read, she had a remarkable memory, quoting page after page of material on a given subject of discussion. She was a formidable person, literally as well as figuratively, and although her faculty had been exposed to her charm, which they admitted existed, they had also been subjected to imperious demands and unnecessary meddling in their work.

If Amelia was not intimidated by Miss Sutherland, most of her classmates were. One recalled, "We treated her like a queen. She looked like a queen. She was a big woman, very attractive and you never turned your back on her. When you left a room, you'd go up to her and you would bow and then you would bow out in a backward position."

At Ogontz there were no idle hands to do the devil's work, not under the regime established by Miss Sutherland. On weekdays Amelia rose at seven, participated in group prayer, and did setting-up exercises before breakfast at eight, which was followed by a walk until nine when classes began. After classes, which ended at two, she played hockey, basketball, or tennis until four, then went to study hall until five-thirty when she was allowed an hour in which to dress for dinner. Dinner was followed by more prayers, spelling lessons, and instruction in French or German. On Saturdays prayers and lectures occupied her until noon and two hours of exercise after lunch preceded more study until four o'clock. Sundays brought more prayers and another lecture. Saturday and Monday nights were free.

Although Ogontz was primarily an institution that prepared its students for further higher education, it also provided lessons in correct social behavior. Amelia described "a drawing room evening" in a letter to Amy: "Miss Pughsey's evening they call it. She has us walk bow sit stand shake hands etc. etc. . . . the funniest thing was sitting. She put a little chair out in the middle of this huge room and we all aimed at it and tried to *clammer* [sic] on it gracefully. It was a scream. One of the girls landed with her legs crossed, on the extreme edge. I got on but not with noticeable grace as there was no comment made." A decade later these lessons would serve her well at state dinners and receptions given by royalty.

At nineteen, Amelia was older than most of the students at Ogontz. With the exception of girls whose fathers were Army or Navy officers, many came from affluent American families, along with a few from Latin America or Europe. Lacking both the financial resources and stable family life enjoyed by the majority of her fellow students, Amelia showed none of the effects of previous poverty, her father's alcoholism, or the rift between her parents. After the first term, Miss Sutherland reported to Amy that her daughter's "charm of manner has made a warm place for herself in the hearts of schoolmates and teachers."

Among her new friends was a former student, Leonora Hassinger, who was visiting the school. "They are of a very fine family, the Hassingers of Birmingham. They come from New Orleans and Leonora is going to make her debut this winter altho she has been presented in Birmingham . . . she leaves tomorrow with her father for New York. . . . I may be able to go and visit her for one night at the Waldorf."

It is difficult to determine if Amelia had social ambitions or was only telling Amy what her mother wanted to hear. Ambitious or not, she faced the realities that Amy tried to avoid. At six hundred dollars a term, school fees left Amelia with very little for recreation or clothing, a fact she accepted cheerfully, hastening to reassure Amy that these needs could be met. "I can wear an old suit with a little alteration so it will be more reasonable. I hate to spend money for things I never will need or want. I bot a pair of Leonora's black high-heeled slippers. They fit me and I needed some. . . . She had only worn them since Wednesday a week ago." In another letter she told her mother, "Dearie, I don't need spring clothes so don't worry about sending me money. . . . I know you all need things more than I."

Her only reproach to Amy came over what she considered her mother's unnecessary correspondence with Miss Sutherland regarding Amelia's welfare. Addressing Amy as "Dear Hen," she wrote that letters "go thru the whole faculty and come to me and I just shrivel. I am not overdoing and all that is needed to bouncing health is plenty to eat and happiness. Consider me bursting, please."

In the summer of 1917 Amelia went back to Kansas City to join her parents and then to a camp in Michigan. Edwin accompanied her as far as Chicago. In spite of the anger and humiliation she had suffered from his drinking bouts, Amelia still loved him deeply. "Poppy was such a lamb last night I came near coming back with him," she wrote to Amy.

Any thought of returning to Kansas City was immediately dismissed on her arrival at Camp Grey, a few miles south of Holland, Michigan, on the Kalamazoo River. When Amy suggested that Muriel and a cousin join her there, Amelia protested vigorously. She liked being on her own, although she did not use this freedom to misbehave.

Amy did not need to worry about her daughter's conduct, either in speech or action on matters relating to sex. Amelia was a typical Victorian-born, shy, upperclass prude. Even to her mother she did not call menstruation by its proper name but alluded to "a tendency to be as quiet as possible which came upon me in Chicago—much to my joy as I can go swimming in a day or two for the rest of the time."

At the camp, for the first time in her life she met young men who were not neighbors or cousins and she seemed to enjoy it. There was Gordon Pollack, a twenty-three-year-old photographer whose father had been one of Theodore Roosevelt's Rough Rider staff and who was going to join the aviation corps. He took a series of portraits of her. There was another young man who was "very nice and sensitive and almost brilliant." He left camp before Amelia but suggested he return for a weekend to see her. By that time Amelia's friend Sarah Tredwell and Sarah's mother, who had been their chaperon, had returned to Chicago. Amelia wrote to Amy that she too would leave because "without Sarah I should not feel quite comfortable—it seeming as tho I might possibly be waiting for him and doing it purposely."

Guarding her purse as well as her reputation, she continued to account for every penny spent, as if she already knew that Amy had no more financial sense than Edwin and was living off capital that could not last forever. The train ticket from Chicago to the camp was $3.91, her board, $9.80 a week.

When she returned to Ogontz in the fall she was elected vice-president of the class and composed its motto, "Honor is the foundation of courage." One of five members of the board for the new honors system created by Miss Sutherland that year, Amelia clashed with the headmistress after the latter demanded the board include faculty members. It took courage to defy Miss Sutherland. At least one teacher, Elizabeth Vining, later tutor to the children of Japanese emperor Hirohito, resigned, unable to endure her autocratic ways. Others thought her cruel and discourteous. Amelia won that battle and was soon engaged in another when the headmistress attempted to place a number of her favorite students on the board. Amelia maintained that the board was elected by a vote of the school, for which, "I nearly had my head taken off when I told her the essence of true leadership was to have the girls behind you."

The true leader also crossed swords with a number of her classmates who objected to Miss Sutherland's banishing of sororities. When the sororities continued to meet secretly, Amelia protested. She was willing to fight Miss Sutherland's rules openly but refused to cheat. Although the matter proved to be a tempest in a teapot, Amelia was momentarily out of favor, feeling she had "lost all my friends or a good many for jumping on them so—as very few people understand what I mean when I go at length into the subtleties of moral codes." Very few people ever would.

Her rigid code of ethics may have temporarily bewildered or annoyed her classmates but her mischievous wit charmed them. On one evening when she was seated at Miss Sutherland's dinner table, looking the image of wide-eyed innocence, she asked the puritanical headmistress if she would please explain the meaning of Oscar Wilde's novel, *The Picture of Dorian Grey*.

The public Amelia, known at Ogontz as "Meelie" or "Butterball," was a recognized leader, wit, and scholar. The private Amelia remained "A. E.—the girl in brown who walks alone." She was not interested in the future most Ogontz girls assumed would be theirs—presentation to society followed by marriage. A clue to her thoughts lay in the scrapbook of newspaper clippings she kept in her desk:

> Mrs. Paul Beard, fire lookout at Harney Peak, South Dakota, is one of the few women workers in the Federal Forestry service.

> Breaking all precedents for this county, the Orange County Medical Association last night elected a woman as president of the organization. She is Dr. Bessie Raiche of Anaheim.

> Mrs. E. E. Abernathy is Oklahoma's only woman bank president.

> Helen H. Gardner, the first woman to hold the position of United States Civil Service Commissioner, says the simultaneous conducting of a home and job is difficult but not impossible.

Under the last item Amelia wrote, "Good girl, Helen!" The maverick had become a feminist, albeit a closet one.

For the Christmas holidays of 1917 Amelia went to Toronto to join

Muriel, a student at St. Margaret's College, and her peregrinating mother who was already there, staying at the St. Regis Hotel. Although the United States had entered the First World War the previous spring and Amelia had knitted sweaters and socks for the Red Cross at Ogontz, she saw her first war-wounded in Toronto. She was walking with Muriel on King Street when four young men on crutches, all of them amputees, passed them. Amelia looked in a store window until they had moved down the block, then turned to watch them. A week later she told her mother, "I'm not going back to graduate. I'm needed here. I've been taking instructions all this past week and I'm going to be a V.A.D. [nurse's aide]."

The decision was not surprising to those who knew her best. She had always acted on her beliefs. Her decisions were precipitate, made without consultation and, once made, acted upon. She knew help was needed. In the preceding nine months Canadian military hospitals had had to increase their capacity from 2,500 beds to more than 12,000. By April Amelia was posted to Spadina Military Hospital at the head of Spadina Avenue, not far from what is now the lower campus of the University of Toronto. Its 233 beds were occupied by soldiers with "ailments of the chest"—poison gas burns, shrapnel in the lungs, and tuberculosis.

The previous October she had sat for a graduation picture at Ogontz, in cap and gown, the cap partially covering her long, honey-blonde hair, her arresting eyes staring boldly into the camera lens. Six months later, in a second photograph taken on the balcony of Spadina Hospital, her slight figure was hidden in a long, shapeless uniform dress and a large kerchief covered her hair. Her face was thinner; the bone structure revealed the face of a mature woman.

The hospital, an imposing Victorian structure that had formerly been the Knox Theological College and more recently a barracks, was surrounded by streets lined with three-story houses and shops in a neighborhood reminiscent of nineteenth-century Europe. In this building, through whose open windows drifted the clang of milk tins at the nearby City Dairy Company and the clatter of street cars, Amelia was "on duty from seven in the morning until seven at night. . . . I spent a great deal of time in the diet kitchen and later in the dispensary, because I knew a little chemistry. Probably the fact that I could be trusted not to drink up the medical supply of whiskey counted more than the chemistry."

A teetotaler like Amelia was badly needed. The Canadian Army Medical Corps had just taken over management from civilians who, influenced by an indulgent public and press, had permitted a continuous flow of liquor to the thirsty patients.

In spite of the long hours on duty Amelia found time for the half-hour walk or ride on the streetcar to Muriel's school on Bloor Street. She saw some ice hockey games, played tennis, and rode horses rented from a stable. After Amelia conquered one fiery steed called "Dynamite" with an artful mix of carrots, sugar lumps, and a firm hand on the reins, the stable owner invited her to ride without charge. During one of those rides, she and Muriel were invited by three Royal Canadian Air Force pilots to come to the military airfield at Armour Heights to see the planes fly. Although she was not permitted to ride in them, Amelia returned to watch. She also went to an air show at the Canadian National Exposition grounds, where she stood her ground when a bored pilot began to "buzz" the spectators, making them run from the field. She knew it was dangerous but was fascinated by "the mingled fear and pleasure" she felt.

Most of her time was spent at the hospital, where her patients included men who had fought at Vimy Ridge and in the water-filled trenches of Passchendale. In her letters she concealed the distress she felt. In one to her father she wrote that she was working in the laboratory, keeping records, staining slides and doing "all kinds of tests on myself." She worked, she said, from nine to 4:45 at the lab, then in the diet kitchen to get out the evening meal. "I have Sunday morning off," she told him, "and cultivate the church habit I have had installed into me from youth up."

A year later she discussed the "church habit" in a letter to her mother, who suspected Amelia was no longer a devout Episcopalian. Amelia said that although she was frequently disillusioned by the uncharitable behavior of clergy and parishioners, "Don't think for an instant I would ever become an atheist . . . nor lose faith in the Church's teachings as a whole." The "whole" she spoke of was already becoming very unconventional for an Episcopalian. Fifteen years after that letter to Amy, when she was asked for her concept of God by Atlanta reporter Alice Renton Jennings, she said, "I think of God as a symbol for good—thinking good, identifying good in everybody and everything. This God I think of is not an abstraction, but a vitalizing, universal force, eternally present, and at all times available."

She needed all of this force to comfort her on November 11, 1918, when the Armistice was signed and the residents of Toronto took to the streets to celebrate. Flags flew everywhere while whistles blew and cheering, crying mobs circled bonfires in the streets. But Amelia, who counted as the cost of victory the battered bodies and twisted minds of her patients, didn't hear "a serious word of thanksgiving in all that hullabaloo." The feminist had become a pacifist.

Although she continued to work through the winter of 1918–19, during a worldwide influenza epidemic that claimed more lives than the war, by late January she was bedridden with a serious sinus infection. Without antibiotics, opening and drainage of the sinus cavities was the only treatment available. These "washings out," as she called them, were agonizing and only partially effective, leaving her a semi-invalid.

In February she left Toronto for Northampton, Massachusetts, to join Muriel who was taking preparatory courses for entrance to Smith College in the fall. That same year an American woman, Laura Brownell, became the first female pilot to be licensed by the Federation Aeronautique Internationale, and two Englishmen, Capt. John Alcock and Lt. A. W. Brown, made the first nonstop transatlantic flight. But Amelia seemed to have lost interest in airplanes and taken up two new pastimes. She bought a banjo and enrolled in an auto mechanics course. Muriel marveled over "the incongruity of the two activities . . . she was always so; artistic and impractical on the one hand and scientific and practical on the other."

For the summer Amy Earhart, who had left Edwin again, rented a cottage at Lake George, New York, a popular vacation spot for the well-to-do. There Amelia met their neighbors, Walter and Clara Stabler, and son Frank, who introduced her to other young people in their early twenties. Postwar sparks of "flaming youth" were spreading across the nation, foreshadowing the advent of mini-skirted "flappers" with bobbed hair who danced the Charleston and Shimmy and drank gin in speakeasies before hopping a train for the divorce courts of Reno. The flames failed to reach Lake George. Often incited by Amelia, her friends opted for innocent pranks, "kidnappings," and thefts of canoe oars and Victrola handles.

In mid-August Frank Stabler's twenty-three-year-old sister, Marian, arrived from New York City where she had been studying art at summer school. She first met Amelia, about whom her family had been writing letters all summer, aboard a lake side-wheeler, "a tall, very slim girl in a blue suit. . . . I was conscious of eyes wide apart, which seemed to be taking uncritical notes, a small nose, a wide mouth, slow Western speech, a serious expression. She was still very pale from the previous winter's illness, with circles under her eyes. Her hair was gold, wrapped around a small, well-shaped head and she wore no makeup. . . . She was an unusual combination of boyish straight-forwardness and a strangely poetic beauty which did not depend upon regularity of feature or perfection of bodily structure."

Later, Marian observed that Amelia's tennis game was good, her swimming competent, and her body that of a contortionist. She was able to "balance on her hands with her knees thrown up close to her chest" and "to curl all of her five feet, eight inches within the area of a sofa cushion with nothing hanging over the edges, and take a nap of indefinite length with no apparent discomfort."

After Marian's arrival, the earlier games of summer were abandoned for evenings in front of an open fire, reading poetry, popping corn, "talking nonsense," and composing parodies of popular songs. Amelia told Marian she had decided to enter Columbia University as a premedical student; in addition to a full program at Columbia, she planned to audit other courses at Teacher's College and Barnard, among these what she termed "a luxury course" in French literature.

That fall she found a room in a house with other students on Morningside Drive in New York City, and lived comfortably, if frugally, on an allowance from her mother. Her laboratory hours took most evenings, but on Thursdays she went to the Stablers' apartment for dinner, often followed by an evening with Marian at a concert heard from the steps of the second balcony of Carnegie Hall for a fifty-cent, standing-room ticket. On Sundays, for as long as the ferry at Dyckman Street could break through the ice, they crossed the Hudson River and hiked in the Palisades.

As their friendship developed, Marian noticed that Amelia was frequently exhausted, her face pale and drawn, dark circles under her eyes. Admonitions on the subject were ignored by Amelia. No matter how heavy her workload, she did whatever interested her. She discovered and explored hidden underground passageways that connected a number of university buildings; she climbed a stairway leading to the top of the library dome more than once for a view of New York at sunset. On one February morning she left a note on Marian's door. "I thot of the accompanying as I reached the second step in front of the library."

The "accompanying" was a graceful, skillfully rhymed translation of a French poem.

In addition to Marian, Amelia made another friend, Louise de Schweinitz, a history graduate of Smith College in 1918, taking science courses in preparation for entering medical school at Johns Hopkins. When she told Amelia she was considering marrying a fellow student, Daniel Darrow, but also wanted to get her medical degree, Amelia said she thought it wrong for Louise to give up *her* career while her fiancé went on with his. There were worse things, after all, than never getting married. "One of the worst would be being married to a man who tied you down," she said. "I'm not sold on marriage at all for myself. Of course, I'm not in love with anybody—yet."

Louise, who admired Amelia's "vivid personality" and was to be a lifelong friend, gave her ideas serious consideration. But she did marry Daniel and also finished medical school. Amelia, who offered advice to Louise on the pursuit of her vocation, had no idea what her own might be. At the close of the school year she was drifting again on a sea of doubt when Edwin Earhart, who had won his battle with alcoholism, asked both Amelia and her mother to join him in Los Angeles where he was practicing law. Amy, still in New England, needed surgery that she had elected to have done in Boston. Amelia countered with a suggestion that the operation be performed in Los Angeles so that both she and Muriel could spend the summer there looking after their mother.

To Muriel she wrote, "I'll see what I can do to keep Mother and Dad together until you finish college, Pidge, but after that I'm going to come back here and live my own life."

What that life might be she still did not know. Meanwhile, family duty provided a temporary goal. At twenty-three she assumed the role of the sensible member of an unstable family, although she may actually have been an immature, uncertain offspring returning to her parents for comfort and assurance. For whatever reason, she left Columbia for Los Angeles in May and moved into the large house on Fourth Street occupied by Amy, Edwin, and three young male boarders. Although Edwin was working again, the depletion of Amy's inheritance money and Muriel's continued attendance at Smith required the income from the boarders.

One of the young men was Samuel Chapman, a tall, dark engineer from New England, a Tufts College graduate who soon became Amelia's suitor. They played tennis, went to the theater, and spent evenings at home discussing literature. They also went to at least one meeting of the Industrial Workers of the World, known as the "Wobblies," the most radical of American labor unions. Although Amelia had told Amy she thought the Episcopal Church's membership and clergy "narrow," she was looking for what many present-day Christians call "social and economic justice." She wanted to hear what the I.W.W. proposed. If she remembered that her Grandfather Otis's cousin, Harrison Gray Otis, former editor of the *Los Angeles Times,* was killed in an I.W.W. bombing, it didn't deter her from attending. The meeting was raided by police, but Amelia and Sam escaped arrest.

Muriel, who was home for the summer from Smith, thought Sam an ideal suitor. "At Christmas he brought her a leather-bound set of [Joseph] Conrad. It pleased her very much and was a measure of the man." However, Muriel also observed that he would be a traditional husband, expecting Amelia to become a housewife and mother. There is no doubt that Amelia was very fond of Sam Chapman. She continued to see him for the next seven years, in Los Angeles and later in Boston.

If Amelia's fear of being "tied down" was the first deterrent to the match, an event of Christmas Day 1920 proved the ultimate one. On that day Edwin took her to the official opening of Earl Dougherty's new airfield in Long Beach at the corner of Willow Street and American Avenue (now Long Beach Avenue). Billed as a Winter Air Tournament and backed by the Aeronautical Club of Southern California, the show included races, aerobatics, and wing walking, all done by military personnel. For all of her secret feminist beliefs, she was too timid to inquire about lessons for fear that a woman wanting to fly would be considered hilarious, or so she claimed. In an era when emancipated women were widely regarded as freaks, subject to public ridicule, Amelia zealously guarded her privacy, even from family and friends. However, for a deeply desired goal, she could be both determined and shrewd. Her solution to the problem was to ask her father to inquire about the cost of lessons. It was a prudent approach, one that answered her question and might even make Edwin an unwitting supporter of her learning to fly.

Three days later he accompanied her to Rogers Field, an open space off Wilshire Boulevard in the then-suburbs of Los Angeles, and bought her a ticket for a ride. The pilot was Frank Hawks, who would later become nationally known for setting speed records. "As soon as we left the ground," Amelia said "I knew I myself had to fly." That same evening the twenty-three-year-old college dropout could no longer keep it a secret. "'I think I'd like to fly,' I told my family casually that evening, knowing full well I'd die if I didn't."

CHAPTER THREE

Linen Wings and a Leather Coat

*I*n 1921 Amelia Earhart was one of several thousand Americans who wanted to fly. Most were men, some already aviators, veterans of world war aerial combat. While a fortunate few remained in the armed forces, the majority were discharged when the military not only divested itself of surplus aviators but also of airplanes, sold for from three hundred to five hundred dollars. To release grounded aviators and cheap airplanes simultaneously was like throwing iron shavings at magnets. A nucleus of veterans with surplus airplanes was rapidly augmented by young admirers who became students, then partners of their teachers. The task of advancing aviation was left to them, for neither the government with its power nor private business with its capital viewed aviation as a practical means of transport.

While the public may have agreed with that assessment, a large segment of the same public was fascinated by the novelty of flight. A small number was willing to pay five dollars per person for a ten-minute flight to see "what it was like," and many more preferred to watch from the ground while the airborne risked their lives. During a decade of "barnstorming" and air circuses, pilots moved their worn, patched planes from the outskirts of one town to the next, renting farmers' fields as bases for a day or two and coaxing the curious into cockpits for a brief, often risky, ride. For paying viewers, pilots in their fragile craft of wood, linen, and wire staged mock aerial fights, skimmed upside down twenty-five feet off the ground, and ascended high into the sky for breathtaking dives, spins, and stalls. Their partners—some of them women—wingwalked, hung from struts, and took freefall parachute jumps. In Miami, one pilot flew into a vacant lot between two buildings one hundred feet apart, a strip of openended land that went back from the street for six hundred feet. His wife, who operated an aerial sightseeing service, sold tickets from a soapbox on the street. These barnstormers and stunters, along with military and airmail pilots, were the true believers in the future of aviation.

A number headed for Southern California where the mild climate diminished the single greatest threat to flight—bad weather. Attracted to the area by that same climate was a second group of visionaries, the moviemakers. The two groups shared more than a mutual interest in a beneficent climate. Their members were capital-poor gamblers in two high-risk, infant industries, men whose characteristics were similar and whose interests often converged. Cecil B. De Mille, who would make millions in the film industry, was also a pilot. Too old in 1917 for wartime flight training, he hired a pilot to teach him. When the Army still refused his services, he founded the Mercury Airline, bought a Junkers JL-6 that young Lt. Eddie Rickenbacker delivered to him in 1921, and attempted to schedule flights between San Diego and San Francisco. He lost money but never his interest in aviation. Charlie Chaplin's stepbrother, Sydney, was the founder of an aircraft company at Wilshire Boulevard and Fairfax Avenue. With ex-Army pilot Emory Rogers, Chaplin ran a regular service between Wilmington and Catalina Island, which also failed. Rogers bought Chaplin out, and it was at Rogers Field that Amelia took her first airplane ride with Frank Hawks on that December day in 1920.

On the first Monday of January in 1921, Amelia Mary Earhart appeared at Kinner Field accompanied by her father, who found the owner of the field, Winfield B. Kinner, working in the hangar. Bert Kinner, former streetcar motorman, farm machinery mechanic and Cadillac dealer from Magnolia, Minnesota, had come to Los Angeles five years before and opened an auto repair shop in which he built custom-made sports car bodies for Model-T Fords. A mechanical wizard with an eighth-grade education, Kinner built an airplane in 1919. When he finished it, he taught himself how to fly, then bought a field at the corner of Long Beach Boulevard and Tweedy Avenue, in a semirural area of cabbage patches, avocado fields, and palm trees. Facilities at the Kinner Aircraft and Motor

Corporation consisted of a single hangar with living quarters at the back, a hamburger stand, and a gas and repair station set along the edge of the unpaved, scruffy field.

Bert told Amelia to talk to his field manager, twenty-four-year-old Neta Snook, while he had a few words with Edwin Earhart. Neta, who had just finished a tiring day of flying sightseers over the bay, was walking in from her plane, an old Canuck that she had rebuilt in her father's workshop back in Ames, Iowa. "More silly people with silly questions," she thought, as she watched the tall, slim woman with long, golden braids wrapped around her head approach. The woman wore a brown suit with a silk scarf at the neck and white gloves. She looked like the elegant young women who went to the Frances Shimer Academy in Mount Carroll, Illinois. She spoke like one, too. "I want to fly," she told Neta, "and I understand you take students. My parents aren't in accord with my ambitions, but might reconsider if they found another woman in the business." Amelia was less than candid. *She* wanted to learn from a woman. Neta agreed to teach Amelia for one dollar a minute. Amelia said she would pay with Liberty Bonds. The first lesson was scheduled for the following day.

A third person who saw Amelia and her father at the field that day was Cora Brusse Kinner, Bert's thirty-five-year-old wife, who had stepped out of the house at the back of the hangar. Cora watched the Earharts, her hazel eyes scanning the young woman's white gloves, then the man's stiff-collared shirt and frock coat. A very odd couple for Kinner Field, Cora thought, where men wore oil-stained slacks or coveralls and Neta, the only other woman there, was covered from neck to ankle by greasy brown overalls, her hair tucked under a flying helmet, her hands grimy from tinkering with engines. Cora continued to watch the two visitors until they left Neta and walked toward the boulevard.

On the way home Edwin Earhart told Amelia he thought Bert Kinner was a "visionary and not too practical, but intelligent." For highly intelligent but far more impractical Edwin to make this assessment was ironic. When Bert Kinner had a vision, he pursued it until he realized it, no matter how difficult. He wanted to make some money for Cora and the children and he wasn't above hustling a few innocents to do it, but the primary goal was to create something new, something that worked. This restless man, fingers constantly running through black, wiry hair, piercing dark brown eyes intent on the job at hand, was the man farmers in

Minnesota called "the kid who could fix anything." To those who helped him, he was kind and generous. He saw nothing odd in a woman like Neta using his field for her Canuck. She knew planes. She pumped gas and fixed shocks. She earned her keep. Amelia Earhart couldn't have found a better place to learn to fly.

The next day Amelia, wearing riding breeches, laced boots, and a well-tailored jacket, met Neta at the field. She had taken the streetcar to the end of the line and walked the three miles to the field, a journey she would repeat time after time over the next two years. Under her arm was a book on aeronautics from the library. Neta, one of the first women to graduate from the Glenn Curtiss School for aviators, regarded it with approval. After a few minutes of explanation, Neta told her pupil to get in the front cockpit of her dual-controlled Canuck, a Canadian version of the JN-4 (or "Jenny"), a World War I army trainer. Its top speed was sixty miles an hour, its landing speed forty, the OX-5 engine's horse-power ninety.

During her first lesson Amelia learned how to taxi. By February she had logged four hours in the air and Neta called her "a natural." "There wasn't much for me to do. She just seemed to take over and do it, although she did have a tendency to bank more steeply than I did, and a great many times I had to shove the nose down because she held it too high."

The "natural" had another inclination Neta found worrying, one she would have expected if she had known the little girl who "belly-slammed" down that icy hill in Atchison. To land at Kinner Field it was necessary to clear two lines of high tension wires, eight feet apart, running along the side of Long Beach Boulevard. Amelia "would have gone between them if I didn't watch her all the time," Neta claimed.

Only a year Amelia's senior, Neta, who kept a firm hand on the dual controls and a stern eye on her adventurous pupil, was soon a friend and frequent guest at the Earharts'. Amelia liked her because she was a pleasant, intelligent contemporary, but the strongest bond was Neta's interest in aviation. Amelia had no time for idle conversation. Discussions were meant to raise and answer questions on matters of substance. When they failed to do so, she lost interest. At the airfield, where they cooked and shared meals with pilots and mechanics, Amelia "never wanted to dally long at what she called 'frivolous doings' if the weather was right for flying." If the weather was not right, she left the group and sat with her back against the hangar wall, reading a library book. While she read, Neta's Great Dane, Camber, a lumbering animal, coat covered with adobe dust, lay across her outstretched legs, waiting for the hand he knew would reach out after turning a page and scratch his ears.

Neta taught Amelia how to drive. Waving a twenty-dollar bill at her one day, Amelia announced, "This is the day I learn how to drive a car. . . . You rent it, because you have a license, then I'll drive it." The rented 1921 Model T Ford was not an easy car to drive. There were three foot pedals, one a planetary shift with high, medium, and low gears, depending on how near the floor boards it was pushed, a second for reverse, and a third for braking. On the dashboard were two hand levers, one for spark and throttle, and the second, a choke. Each time she stalled the car Amelia had to get out and crank it. Several hours later she was driving, with flair if not skill, missing the driveway when she returned it to the rental agency and ascending by way of the curb.

Both young women enjoyed the company of men. Neta's constant escort was William Southern. In addition to Sam Chapman, Amelia went out with other men, some who were friends of Southern's. On one occasion they were caught in a rainstorm two hundred miles from Los Angeles on their way back from the Tehachapi mountains where the two men had an interest in a mining claim. Although a separate cabin was offered the women, Amelia refused to spend the night.

If she seemed excessively prudish on that night, she surprised Neta on another when a black limousine pulled up in front of Neta's house in Huntington Park. Amelia was in the back, "sitting ramrod straight" beside an old man who wore a bowler hat and held a gold-headed cane. His legs were covered by a travel rug. Amelia introduced him as Powell Ramsdell, adding that he shared her interest in early Californian history. After Ramsdell left, she explained to Neta they had met when she helped his driver find some books on the subject in the library. Ramsdell offered her a ride home. "I took six books which were heavy, and with five blocks to walk, I thought I might as well. . . . He looked harmless."

Ramsdell's car began to appear frequently at Kinner Field. Cora Kinner, always blunt and staunchly respectable, disapproved of what seemed to her Amelia's thoughtless acceptance of the old man's attentions. Nor did Neta escape judgment. "He'd come out there every morning in his Cadillac. He was a sick guy. An old guy. Those girls got hold of him because he had lots of money to spend. . . . Those girls really took advantage. . . . I didn't like that."

Cora may have misjudged Amelia, who enjoyed the company of older men. Father figures would continue to appear in her life for she had never lost her deep love for Edwin, no matter what his faults. When younger, more attractive men asked her out she refused those who failed to interest her. She told Neta it was dishonest to let them spend their money on her for theater tickets or dinner. Nor did she think an escort was always an advantage. With her newly acquired knowledge of California's history and a smattering of Spanish, she wanted to explore what Neta thought were "out-of-the-way," dangerous areas of Los Angeles, areas her friend insisted necessitated the protection of male companions.

Neta frequently stayed overnight at the Earharts', sharing Amelia's room where they talked late into the night, covering the wide range of interests held by two typical, young, college-educated women. Topics included religion, philosophy, literature, music, films, clothing styles, and men. On one of those nights Neta asked Amelia what she thought of William Southern. After her customary pause and with a smile she said, "I think he has the mating instinct. His eyes . . . oh, his eyes are magnificently sullen. Are you sure you're ready to give up your career?" When Neta asked her why she thought that would be necessary, she replied, "Because you will. He's the kind who will insist on being boss."

Amelia's warning to Neta, like the one she had given her friend Louise a year before at Columbia, was not a conventional one. The new postwar "freedom" of American women was one of frivolity and sexuality. Skirts were shorter, cheeks rouged, corsets discarded. The Charleston replaced the waltz and "petting parties" were gaining acceptance, taking place on the new American sofa—the back seat of an automobile. But the liberation was one for men, making women more desirable as playmates or mates. While the Twentieth Amendment had given women the vote the previous year, census takers listed housewives as having "no occupation," and the "nonoccupation" of housewife was the primary goal of the vast majority of American women. Women who did not marry were referred to as "old maids." Many of the better educated worked as school teachers, librarians, or unpaid helpers in the households of their parents or married relatives. Those who achieved the status of college professors, doctors, or lawyers, however honored in their professional roles, were also "old maids" socially.

Already in her mid-twenties, past the age when most women married, Amelia ignored the prevailing opinion of single women. Instead, she added notes and clippings to her scrapbook. No profession or business was singled out. Her interest was clearly in the fact that no matter what had been accomplished, a woman had done it. She included the following:

Foreign Women Developing as Film Directors

Texas has a woman pistol shot champion, Miss Grace McClellan of Austin

Florence Egan and her Jazz Orchestra on Program from Examiner Studio Tonight

Miss Mithan Ardeshire Tata, B.A., of Bombay University, has been formally admitted to the practice of law in Great Britain. Miss Tata is the first woman of India to be admitted to the bar.

Woman Manages City. After April 15, Warrenton, Oregon, is to be managed by a woman, Miss R. E. Barrett . . . according to available records Miss Barrett is the only and first woman to direct a city's affairs.

Mrs. Lulu Eckles, President of the Women's Advertising Club, and advertising and sales manager of A. Hamburger & Sons, Inc., talks to Women's Personnel Club.

However great Amelia's admiration for career women and her aversion to home, hearth, husband, and children, she kept both well concealed. Except with Neta, she did not share her views on the potential of women in what was essentially a man's world. Her behavior was that of a conventional, well-bred young woman. She dressed with care and style, so much so that Waldo Waterman, one of the pilots who knew her at Kinner Field, remarked that while Neta wore coveralls and a helmet, "Amelia was usually dressed in jodphurs, or riding breeches and boots, yet looked thoroughly feminine, with a loose shirtwaist and tousled hair."

Another admirer was Winfield Kinner, Jr., an eleven-year-old schoolboy. However, neither her good looks nor penchant for daring but often poorly executed landings were what interested him. Initially it was her contortionist's skills, demonstrated to him by placing the entire palms of both hands on the ground without bending her knees. He was also impressed by what seemed to him considerable stoicism on the day she removed a small bandage from her cheek to show his mother the tiny tube used to drain the chronic abcess of the antrum which continued to plague her. For the most part Amelia was approved of by both men and women at the one place she most wanted to be—Kinner Field.

She began to cut her long, honey-blonde hair, inch by inch, probably because she disliked doing anything that attracted too much attention if it could be avoided. She also bought a leather coat.* The first time she wore it the men at the airfield exchanged remarks about the "dude aviator." The next time they saw it, it was wrinkled and oil-stained. The stains were easy to make, the wrinkles created by sleeping in it. Dressing as she did was not just youthful play-acting but evidence of her unerring instinct for making a physical statement of who and what she was. She was a woman *and* an aviator. The bobbed hair was thick and curly (with the aid of a curling iron), the jacket under the leather coat beautifully tailored and worn with a white silk blouse, a colorful scarf knotted at the neck.

By the time Muriel came home in the summer of 1921, Amelia was one of the airfield crowd, "regarded by many people as slightly crazy." She was invited to join them and did. "We shellacked the canvas wings, replaced struts . . . and when there was enough gasoline . . . took turns cruising over the bay and north a few miles along Malibu Beach."

After only two and a half hours of instruction in Neta's Canuck, Amelia had decided "life was incomplete unless I owned my own plane." The plane she wanted was one built by Bert Kinner. Originally a single-seater, it was cracked up in a test flight and rebuilt as a dual control ship to be used as a trainer. As usual, Amelia's problem was money. Already working as a clerk at the telephone company and one day a week at her father's office, she completed a course in commercial photography at the University of California and went into partnership with another young woman, Jean Bandreth. When the venture proved unprofitable, she bought an old Moreland truck and contracted to haul gravel for a construction company. Her father, who had taken her to her first air show, treated her to her first ride, and accompanied her to Kinner Field to arrange for lessons, had lost his initial enthusiasm and refused to help her buy the plane. It was Amy Earhart who came to the rescue, after a considerable delay that annoyed Cora Kinner. Bert had already agreed to let Amelia

---

*The leather jacket, which she wore on her solo transatlantic flight in 1932, is on display at the National Air and Space Museum in Washington, D.C.

have his small, rebuilt plane in exchange for his right to it as a demonstrator while he waited for Amy to pay up. Cora wryly observed that Amy had "too much money with a string around her sock, and Bert couldn't get her to take it out." The sock was finally opened on July 24, 1922, Amelia's twenty-fifth birthday. Cora said that Amy only paid on condition that Amelia "give up that truck and act like a lady."

The little plane, which Bert Kinner called the Airster, did not meet with Neta's approval, nor that of the other pilots who frequented the field. Neta said its seventeen-foot wing span made it "fly like a leaf in the air," that it lacked stability and was inclined to ground-loop if landed in a cross wind. She also noted that the third cylinder of its three-cylinder engine clogged frequently, dangerously reducing its already minimal sixty horsepower. Neta's advice was ignored by Amelia who had the plane painted yellow and named it the *Canary*. Bert's demonstration rights were again exchanged for hangar space and mechanical repairs and Neta volunteered to teach Amelia "all over again," giving her four more hours of instruction without charge.

There were accidents. Cora Kinner witnessed one. "Amelia set her little Kinner *Canary* down in my cabbage patch, but she walked away from it. She used to scare me to death." In another mishap Neta was with her. They had taken the Airster to the Goodyear Field, six miles from Kinner's, to see the huge, new Cloudster, designed by Donald W. Douglas, whose World Cruisers, flown by U.S. Army Service pilots, would circle the globe in 1924. On the return flight to Kinner Field, the *Canary*'s third cylinder failed immediately after takeoff. When Amelia tried to pull up over a grove of eucalyptus trees, the plane stalled and crashed into the trees, breaking the undercarriage and propeller. Neta crawled out of the wreckage and looked back to see if Amelia had been injured. She was standing by the plane, grinning and powdering her nose. They must look nice, she told Neta, when the reporters arrived.

The accidents may have upset her more than she admitted. When Neta told her she was ready to solo, she procrastinated. The same woman who had wanted to fly between two high tension wires eight feet apart and who "scared" Cora Kinner "to death," said she wanted more training. But solo she did. There is no official record of it but it was before December 15, 1921, not quite a year after her first lesson, because on that date she took and passed her trials for a National Aeronautic Association license.

The solo flight that preceded these trials had been a shaky one. "In taking off for the first time alone," she wrote, "one of the shock absorbers broke, causing the wing to sag just as I was leaving the ground. I didn't know just what had happened, but I did know something was wrong and wondered what I had done. The mental agony of starting the plane had just been gone through and I was suddenly faced with the agony of stopping it." After repairs were made she took off again, only to make "a thoroughly rotten landing."

Two days after her NAA trials she flew in an exhibition at the Sierra Airdrome in Pasadena. The official program listed the tenth event as the "Pacific Coast Ladies Derby, An Exhibition by Miss Amelia Earhart in her Kinner Airster and Miss Aloyfia [sic] McKlintock in her Laird Swallow." Coming in for a landing the same troublesome spark plug that had failed before did it again. "Luckily I was over the field. . . . Otherwise I might have made my landing in a treetop."

In spite of joking about looking nice for the reporters after the crash at Goodyear Field, Amelia did not like exhibition flying. "The moment I flew up the field I began to feel like a clown, although happily there were two of us females to divide the honors and odium." What the retiring, often secretive Amelia really wanted was to be alone and aloft, flying for her own pleasure. But publicity provided airplanes and the money needed to maintain them and she took what she could get.

In May of 1922 Bert Kinner put out a flyer advertising the Airster. Headed "A Lady's Plane as Well as a Man's—read what Miss Earhart has to say after flying a KINNER AIRSTER two years," a letter from Amelia followed:

> After flying my Kinner Airster for two years, it is a real pleasure to state that the performance has at all times been beyond my expectations.
>
> In placing my order with you for one of the new models I am taking advantage of the recently improved refinements but am glad to know that you have retained those fundamental characteristics that have always placed the Kinner Airster high in my regard.

Scrupulously honest in other matters, Amelia stretched the truth for that Airster, and for a newer one she hoped to get from Kinner. She did not mention the fact that the third cylinder was too often "beyond her expectations." Her claim that she had owned the Airster for two years was a false one. The letter was dated May 20, 1922, a time when she was still at Columbia University. It would be six months before her first airplane ride as a passenger, and when she wrote the letter her mother had not yet completed paying for the plane.

Three months later, on August 8, 1922, a Los Angeles newspaper ran a story along with a two-column picture of her in leather coat and goggles, headed "Air Student-Aviatrix to 'Drop In' for Study":

> Vassar College is primed for its thrill of thrills. Some sunny day next fall a large and dusty airplane is due to pull a near-tailspin over its exclusive campus and descending, to disgorge Miss Amelia Earhart, Los Angeles society girl student-aviatrix.
>
> "I just dropped in," she'll tell the faculty. "to take a post-graduate course. . . .
>
> "It's my greatest present ambition," said the winsome Miss Earhart yesterday. "I don't crave publicity or anything, but it seems to me it would be the greatest fun to fly across the continent. I think I'll do it."
>
> Miss Earhart is popular in society circles here. She is the daughter of Attorney Edwin S. Earhart, 1334 West Fourth Avenue.

The story is a typical tabloid fabrication of that era but there is no record of Amelia's objecting to it.

The same month the story appeared, Amelia changed instructors. Neta Snook's flying career ended as Amelia had predicted it would. Married to William Southern and expecting her first child, Neta sold her Canuck and turned her student over to John G. "Monte" Montijo, proprietor of a flying school across the road from Kinner's, on Long Beach Boulevard. The arrangement was a good one for Amelia. Pleased to have a woman teacher when she was a beginner, she was ready for aerobatic instruction from an expert. Monte Montijo was a former Army flier, barnstormer, and stuntman for Goldwyn Studios, a sturdy, broad-shouldered man with a handsome sun-bronzed face, his dark eyes beneath arched eyebrows commanding attention. One of the best pilots in the region and, like most, barely making a living, he flew for a local oil man, gave lessons to students and, to augment these meager earnings, ran a restaurant with his wife, Alta.

Amelia was an eager, attentive student. After seven hours of lessons, she soloed for him. "She handled the ship like a veteran," he said, "and made a perfect takeoff and landing." When she took more lessons in advanced aeronavigation and aerobatics, "after each flight she wanted to know what the mechanical action of each movement was and she showed a keen interest in motors."

Her confidence greatly enhanced by Monte's training, Amelia set her first flying record on October 22, 1922, at an air meet at Rogers Field. Edwin brought Muriel, who had dropped out of Smith College and was teaching at Huntington Beach, but neither of them knew what Amelia intended to do. She had asked a representative of the Aero Club of Southern California to seal a barograph in her Airster. In an open cockpit, with no oxygen supply, on her second attempt she climbed to fourteen thousand feet through fog and sleet before the Airster's motor began to falter. Fearing a stall, she kicked the little plane into a tailspin, bringing it out only after she dropped beneath the fog line at three thousand feet. When one of the older pilots asked her what she thought might have happened if the fog had reached ground level she was embarrassed, but not enough to regret making the record, which was acknowledged by the Aero Club.

Her approach to this first record would be repeated again and again. She was secretive about her plan to set it and insisted on calling it an attempt at "a calibration of the ceiling" (for that particular aircraft) instead of admitting she was trying to set an altitude record. She was meticulous in arranging for the barograph to prove what she had done but showed far less concern about the capabilities of the plane or her own safety.

Seven months after her "calibration of the ceiling" at Rogers Field, nine weeks before her twenty-sixth birthday, on May 15, 1923, she received a license from the Federation Aeronautique Internationale, the international aviation organization of which the American National Aeronautic Association was a member. She was the sixteenth woman in the world to receive one.

CHAPTER FOUR

Ceiling Zero but Lifting

*I*n 1924, less than nine months after she received her FAI license, Amelia Earhart was hospitalized for another sinus operation. She was not only ill, she was broke. Almost twenty-seven, she had spent the last three years racing on a treadmill of multiple, menial jobs to pay for flying. It was a matter, she said, of "no pay, no fly and no work, no pay." Her only financial help had come from her mother, who gave her the money for the little Airster from the sale of the Otis house in Atchison.

Amy Earhart had been spending capital as well as income ever since she gained control of her inheritance. By 1921 her capital had shrunk from more than sixty thousand dollars to twenty thousand dollars, at a time when a ten-room house could be built for ten thousand dollars. She decided to recoup her losses by investing in a gypsum mine managed by Peter Barnes, a young friend of Sam Chapman's. It was a foolish venture, one in which both Edwin and Amelia became involved.

Edwin bought a used truck for Barnes. When it broke down he asked Amelia's friend, Lloyd Royer, a master mechanic at Bert Kinner's, for his advice. Amelia told Royer not to bother. "I think," she said, "that Dad imagines all mechanically inclined gentlemen *like* to play with broken-down automobiles." The broken-down automobile was only one of the many misfortunes suffered by Barnes as he struggled to get all the gypsum he could out of the old mine before the rainy season began in February or March.

In January of 1922 Barnes told the Earharts that production had fallen behind schedule and asked for their help. Amelia and Edwin took the train to Las Vegas, where Barnes met them and drove them to the mine site. Amelia shoveled gypsum into one of the two trucks Barnes had and Edwin lifted sandbags to shore up the approach to a small bridge over a gulley that the trucks had to cross. While they worked, a rainstorm swept over the area, creating flash-flood waters that rushed down the gulley, washing away its banks. Amelia, Edwin, and two of Barnes's friends who were helping load gypsum escaped over the bridge in one truck, but when Barnes followed in the second, the bridge collapsed and he was trapped in the overturned cab. Amelia wrote to Muriel at Smith College: "There is no way I can soften the blow for you. We have to take these things as they come. Peter is drowned, the mine irreparably flooded and all of Mother's investment gone."

During the next two years all the Earharts' efforts to keep the family together and solvent failed. Muriel had to leave Smith at the end of her third year and take a teaching job in Huntington Beach. Amy Earhart gave up her attempt at reconciliation with Edwin and asked him for a divorce. By spring of 1924 both she and Muriel decided to return to New England where the latter had enrolled in summer school at Harvard. Amelia proposed to join her mother and sister there by flying the Airster to Boston. For once Amy flatly countermanded one of Amelia's plans with one of her own—Amelia could drive her to Boston and Amy would pay travel expenses. Amelia accepted the offer.

Before she left California Amelia sold the Airster to a novice flyer who crashed the first time he took it up, killing himself and his passenger, a young university student. Cora Kinner said, "The kid must have frozen to the stick . . . we had to pry his hands away from it . . . It looked like a bombing . . . fire all over the boulevard." Amelia thought the accident tragic but unnecessary, the result of ignorance and overconfidence on the part of the pilot.

With the money from her sale of the ill-fated Airster Amelia bought a car—not a cheap, practical Model T Ford like one Kinner lent her, but a 1922 Kissel Kar. A beautiful vehicle with a convertible top, big nickel headlamps, and a long, low, yellow body with black fenders, the car was the equivalent of a modern-day Alfa Romeo. The Kissel was named the *Yellow Peril* by its new owner, whose penchant for beauty preempted the threat of unemployment and unpaid bills. More aware of economic reality than Amy, Amelia was still her mother's daughter, a member of the impoverished gentry. At Ogontz she copied a poem by "Moslin [sic] Eddin Saudi, Mohmmadan [sic] Sheik and Persian Poet":

> If thou of fortune be bereft
> And in thy store be but two loaves left—sell one,
> Buy hyacinthe to find thy soul.

The Kissel was her hyacinthe.

When she packed up for the trip east she took an odd collection of books and notes. One small notebook contained notes from her photography class at the University of California, Los Angeles, along with her thoughts on two widely different subjects:

> Crossing a track while driving is much easier diagonally, i.e., so that each wheel strikes the raised surface at a different time—thus distributing and neutralizing the shocks. I think some kind of shock absorber could be devised on this principle. (Drawings later)

> Sowing wild oats is putting cracks in the vase of our souls which can never be obliterated or sealed by love. As GBS [George Bernard Shaw] says, "Virtue does not consist in abstaining from vice but in not desiring it."

The engineer and moralist also showed an interest in economic justice, copying this poem in another book:

Stupidity Street

> I saw with open eyes
>   Singing birds sweet
> Sold in the shops
>   For people to eat
> Sold in the shops of Stupidity Street.
>
> I saw in a vision
>   the worm in the wheat
> And in the shops nothing
>   For people to eat;
> Nothing for sale in Stupidity Street.

Ralph Hodgson

Amelia and Amy left Hollywood on a bright May day. Barely recovered from one operation and knowing another would be necessary as soon as she reached Boston, Amelia was determined to see something on the way. She drove to the Sequoia National Park, then to Yosemite and Crater Lake in early June. When Amy asked if they were ever going east, her daughter said, "Not until we reach Seattle." After Seattle she drove to Banff, Alberta, and Lake Louise before crossing Calgary's prairie land on her way to Yellowstone National Park where they arrived June 30. The seven-thousand-mile trip to Boston took six weeks. Two weeks later Amelia entered Boston General Hospital for more surgery. After her release she joined Amy and Muriel in Medford, a suburb of Boston, where Muriel was teaching at Lincoln Junior High.

The house Amy rented at 47 Brooks Street was a large, turn-of-the-century, two-storied structure. The neighborhood, so near the crowded, urban center of Boston, was very like the one Amelia had lived in as a child in Atchison. Its large houses were set back from the street with shrubs and flowerbeds in the front yard and vegetable gardens at the rear. Tall trees arched over streets where children played and friendly dogs roamed without leash or owner. Unlike the Ford and Chevrolet sedans parked in nearby drives, the *Yellow Peril* left the neighborhood children awe-stricken.

While she recuperated, Amelia set about trying to raise money to pay some of her bills. In August she wrote to Lloyd Royer, who was building a plane with Monte Montijo at Kinner's new field in Glenwood. Royer had sold the old Moreland truck for her, left from the Earharts' ill-fated mining venture, but the buyer was slow in paying. "I certainly wish the gentleman would come across," she wrote. "I need the money."

In another letter to Royer she referred to an airplane motor she had left with Bert Kinner: "As long as I have that motor, I'll have days when I just couldn't sell it. Either I'll have to let him [Kinner] sell it soon at any price or let you [Royer] take it and pull down the motor and fix it. Then we'll think about building a plane for it."

Before Amelia could think about another plane, Amy offered her the money for a second year at Columbia University and Amelia accepted, returning there in September of 1924. She renewed her friendship with Marian Stabler, who had become an insurance statistician after abandoning efforts to make a living as an artist. "This time she lived poorly,"

Marian said, "and went without everything but essentials, in order to maintain the Kissel car, which she loved like a pet dog."

Marian thought her old friend looked pale and tired. Her bobbed hair had darkened, its sheen dulled by illness and repeated use of a curling iron. Yet whenever she seemed near total exhaustion Amelia would take a twenty-minute nap and awaken completely rested. She was never too tired to discuss art, science, poetry, religion, or politics, but told Marian nothing of a personal nature. Not until years later, when she heard it from a Hollywood reporter, did Marian learn that Edwin Earhart was an alcoholic.

Marian's parents had moved from their Manhattan apartment to a big house in Great Neck, Long Island, where their childrens' friends came in droves from the city for dinner and dancing to records in the living room or a game of deck tennis on the porch. One of the regulars, Elise von R. Owen, a music student who was living "on a nickel a day" in the city, was fascinated by Amelia's powers of concentration. After dinner she would withdraw from the crowd to a desk at the far end of the room where she studied, ignoring the noise of records and conversation. But she turned on the radio beside the desk to listen to classical music, which she told Elise helped her to concentrate.

Elise was not the only one to be impressed by Marian's tall, quiet friend. On a night when Amelia and Marian were at a party given by a woman artist, another guest, the art director of an advertising agency, kept watching Amelia, who was sitting on the floor by the fire. The next time he asked the hostess to do an illustration for the agency he said, "I want a figure that's really lovely. Someone like that Amelia Earhart."

Amelia's second year at Columbia was her last. Amy could no longer afford the tuition. After the three-time college dropout returned to Boston, she wrote to Marian: "No, I did not get into MIT [Massachusetts Institute of Technology] as planned, owing to financial difficulties. No, I'm not coming back to New York, much, ah, much as I would like doing it. When I leave Boston, I think I'll never go back." In the fall of 1925 she found work of a sort, teaching English to foreign students for a University of Massachusetts extension program. Her wages for this part-time work were barely enough to pay for meals and gas for the Kissel.

Sam Chapman who had followed her back east and was working at the Boston Edison Company offered her an alternative to this hand-to-mouth existence when he proposed again. Not long after he returned, Amelia met Marian in the Boston train station, where they sat at the lunch counter waiting for Marian's connection. It was one of the few occasions on which Amelia confided in anyone about her emotional reactions. "I don't want to marry him," she said. "I don't want to marry anyone."

She looked away from Marian and sighed. "There's something the matter with me, Marian. I went to a doctor and he's giving me pills. He said he's going to be able to make me fall in love. I can't. I just don't want to." She slowly turned her head and looked into Marian's eyes, a sly grin widening into a broad smile. "But I'm taking my pills!"

The pills didn't work, at least not for Sam. He thought perhaps his working schedule was objectionable and offered to change jobs. Amelia was not flattered; she was irritated. "I don't want to tell Sam what he should do," she told Muriel. "He ought to know what makes him happiest, and then do it, no matter what other people say. I know what I want to do and I expect to do it, married or single!" Sam continued to see Amelia but he still disapproved of working wives, while the woman he loved referred to marriage as "living the life of a domestic robot."

It was evident from the clippings and notes Amelia kept adding to her scrapbook that she had not given up her hopes for a career:

> A woman has now broken into the Royal College of Veterinary Surgeons. She is Miss Aleen Cust, sister of Sir Charles Cust, equerry to the King.

> I note women are employed as testers in a French automobile factory—proving equal or superior to men.

> One of the youngest trust busters is Miss Crena Sellers, now on the staff of U.S. Attorney Buckner here. She graduated from Yale Law School last September.

The supporter of careers for women looked for additional work for herself and found it in October, another part-time job, this one at Denison House, a settlement house in a Boston neighborhood of rundown tenements occupied by immigrants, most of whom were Chinese, Armenian, or Syrian and whose children were to be her charges. At first she captivated the children with her beautiful car in which she often gave them rides. But her obvious patience and affection for them soon aroused a deeper admiration. More companion than mother, Amelia played games with them, bandaged their playground wounds, taught them English, and visited their often chaotic and always impoverished homes. When Marian visited her once at Denison House she noticed Amelia's "tenderness for children, even the occasionally smelly little children of the settlement." Amelia assured her, "Chinese are an *adorable* people. You can't realize it until you really know them."

However, the surrogate big sister was also a serious and dedicated social worker. Forty years before Operation Headstart, she decided that "social service should be preventative rather than curative" and defined the ultimate goal of social work with children as giving them "a sound education." Only with education could they "make adjustments to poverty, illness, illiteracy or any other morbid condition."

At Denison House she was certain she had discovered a vocation and a career. The work was a practical expression of her basic beliefs, learned and accepted as a child. It was not enough to talk about social justice and charity. One must act. The children in her care needed help and she had the experience to give it. The former nurse could teach basic hygiene. The former office clerk could type. The scholar could write up reports and the teacher of English to foreign adults could teach it to their children. The Ogontz student had enough social poise to gain the approval of a board of directors. The aviator had already raised funds for the house by flying over Boston one spring day dropping leaflets for a benefit carnival to be held in Waltham. Already a friend and protégée of the director, Marion Perkins, in October Amelia became a fulltime staff member, moved into living quarters at the settlement house, and was elected secretary of the board.

Although Amelia worked five days a week at Denison House, she spent her weekends pursuing her "hobby" of flying. She had joined the local chapter of the National Aeronautic Association soon after her arrival in Boston. When her old friend and mentor, Bert Kinner, was looking for a sales outlet for his planes, one of the people he met in California was Harold T. Dennison of Quincy, Massachusetts, who was developing a commercial airport on land near the present-day Naval Reserve Air Base at Squantum. At Kinner's suggestion, Dennison asked Amelia to become both Kinner's sales representative at Dennison Airport and one of its stockholders. She accepted both offers and somehow scraped up the money for a few shares of stock.

In a newspaper report on the airport's official opening, July 2, 1927, Amelia is described as a director of Dennison Corporation, the only woman on the flying staff, as well as a social worker at Denison House and professor of English in the State Extension Service (she continued to teach until her full-time employment at Denison House). A few days before the opening Amelia wrote to Marian Stabler: "Though I haven't a real job for the summer [Marion Perkins did not hire her on a full-time basis until October] I am kept pretty busy doing things for Denison House and Dennison Airport. I am having a great time selecting hangings and furniture for the main hangar."

The quiet, reserved woman Bert Kinner had picked to demonstrate his plane became an articulate, persuasive salesperson at the airport. Kinner flew there from Los Angeles the first week in September in a new plane he had just built, one with five cylinders.* He left the plane at Dennison with Amelia as his demonstrator–sales representative.

Bert was still having trouble with cylinders, one of which broke down during Amelia's first demonstration. She wrote to him suggesting that he send some heavier ones for replacements and told him that a Boston man wanted to take the plane to New York to someone who could develop a *good* motor for it. She added: "May I report that you will make fittings that can't be criticized aerodynamically on the next ship? If you do I think the game is almost won."

On the same day Amelia wrote a second letter to Ruth Nichols, a woman flyer she had never met. A Wellesley graduate, Nichols was a member of the Junior League who played golf, tennis, hockey, and polo, and had driven automobiles, speed boats, and motorcycles. She had received her FAI license a year after Amelia and was later referred to by polar explorer Richard E. Byrd, along with Amelia, as one of the two who stood out among "a handful of women who shared in the hardships and perils of aviation pioneering."

After introducing herself as a fellow FAI licensee, Amelia wrote, "What do you think of the advisability of forming an organization composed of women who fly?" There followed a list of questions as to who might be eligible before she closed: "Personally, I am a social worker who flies for sport, and am on the board of directors of an aeronautical concern. I cannot claim to be a feminist, but do rather enjoy seeing women tackling all kinds of new problems—new for them, that is."

Amelia undoubtedly refused to "claim to be a feminist" because the

---

*The flight of thirty-five hundred miles took Kinner 16 days, from August 19 to September 3.

term was perjorative to the majority of Americans who thought of feminists as marching, shouting eccentrics who were frequently chained to fences or jailed by police. Perhaps the word suggested to Amelia an unattractive woman who did not like men. Although male aviators often regarded their female counterparts as lightweights in the profession, the women were aviators nonetheless, partners in a camaraderie that Muriel thought remarkable at Kinner Field. Without the men who built airplanes, Amelia could not pursue the "sport" of flying.

Pursue it she did, signing a contract for more lessons at twenty dollars an hour with Dennison Aviation Corporation on October 15, 1927. Notations on the contract show that she paid one hundred seventy-five dollars and logged four and two-thirds hours at unspecified dates. The remaining three hours due her are not accounted for. She had already written Kinner, asking him to estimate her total flying time in California, but seemed to do no better at keeping records of it in Boston.

In November she wrote Kinner again. There were potential buyers for his plane but she could not sell it until the motor had passed government tests. Meanwhile she worried about unscrupulous competitors: "What is to prevent anyone's taking the dimensions of the Airster and constructing a ship from them and marketing that ship? . . . I wonder if you are safe in letting your product out here in the east unless you have a very strong organization to protect it?"

Amelia had planned to go to California that summer to learn more about Kinner's new motor but her work with him was cut short by a telephone call in April. The caller was Capt. Hilton H. Railey, ex-Army pilot and public relations man. He wanted to know if she would fly the Atlantic. She suspected a publicity stunt, a followup on the solo flight of Charles A. Lindbergh less than a year before, but she agreed to an interview with Railey in his Boston office. She had to. If his offer was legitimate she—Amelia Earhart—would be the first woman to cross the Atlantic in an airplane.

Lindbergh's flight on May 20, 1927, had made him the most famous man in the world. There were four other crossings later that summer— Clarence Chamberlin and passenger Charles Levine from New York to Berlin; Commander Byrd, Bert Acosta, Bernt Balchen, and George Noville from New York to France; Edward Schlee and William Brock from Newfoundland to London; F. de Pinedo with del Prete and Zachetti from New Foundland to Portugal. None could challenge Lindbergh as

America's favorite hero who had just performed "the greatest feat of a solitary man in the records of the human race." The handsome, modest, twenty-five-year-old, ex–airmail pilot was the personification of an American dream. "Romance, chivalry, and self-dedication—here they were," author Frederick Lewis Allen wrote, "with the machinery of ballyhoo . . . ready and waiting to lift him up where everyone could see him."

A master of that machinery of ballyhoo was George Palmer Putnam, grandson of the founder of G. P. Putnam's Sons, publishers. It was Putnam who urged the new hero to write a postflight book, *We*, published by Putnam's Sons. It was Putnam who instigated Railey's call to Amelia Earhart. Putnam, who had also published Richard Byrd's polar story, *Skyward*, heard that Byrd had sold his Fokker trimotor plane to an Englishwoman who wanted to cross the Atlantic in it. The person who knew her identity was said to be a lawyer, David T. Layman.

Putnam went to Layman, who told him the buyer was a client, Amy Phipps Guest, heir to a Pittsburgh steel fortune and wife of the former British Air Minister, Frederick E. Guest. Putnam then asked Railey to check on the plane, which was at the East Boston Airport. If the story was true, he told Railey, they might "crash the gate" and manage the flight of the first woman to cross the Atlantic by plane.

Both men soon learned that Mrs. Guest's family had refused to let her make the flight and that she had decided she wanted another woman to try, provided her substitute were "the right sort of girl." Layman entrusted Putnam and Railey to find him one, a woman who was a flier (which Mrs. Guest was not), well educated, with a pleasing appearance and manners acceptable to the English as well as to the less demanding American public.

Railey asked a friend, Rear Adm. Reginald K. Belknap, if he knew of anyone who might qualify. Belknap did. "A thoroughly fine person," he said, whom he had seen at lectures sponsored by the Boston NAA. "I noticed her," he told Railey, "because she was always there and seemed so much in earnest. . . . She said she had been flying about four years then and was still doing a little at Dennison Airport." Her name, he said, was Amelia Earhart.

From the moment Amelia walked into his office Railey knew she was "the right sort of girl." "Her resemblance to Colonel Lindbergh was extraordinary. Most of all I was impressed by the poise of her boyish figure. Mrs. Guest had stipulated the person to whom she would yield must be 'representative' of American women. In Amelia Earhart I saw not only their norm but their sublimation."

Although Railey was certain she would be perfect, he explained that the decision would be made by others at a second interview in New York. When he asked her to keep the plan a secret, Amelia said she would have to ask her supervisor, Marion Perkins, for time off from Denison House but assured him that Miss Perkins could be trusted.

Miss Perkins gave her a two-week leave and a promise of confidentiality. To her family Amelia said nothing except that she was going to New York and would be staying with Marian Stabler. Nor did she confide in her hostess during the brief visit. Her thank you note written six weeks later said, "You may grant me pardon when you hear, in a little while, what all this mysterious business is. . . . Yes, my performance in New York was successful—at least, it gives me a chance at success of a kind."

For the interview Amelia went to the office of Putnam, who told his secretary to have her wait in the outer office. She made no effort to disguise her irritation when the handsome, forty-one-year-old, publisher-promoter came out to greet her. Nor was she overly impressed by the electric tension and instant charm directed at her by this tall, broad-shouldered man in the well-cut suit. There were four persons at the interview—Mrs. Guest's brother, John S. Phipps, Layman, Railey, and Putnam, who was already in charge of the project. After explaining that the trimotored Fokker was to be named *Friendship* as a symbol of goodwill between Mrs. Guest's native and adopted countries, the committee asked a battery of questions, Amelia said in her account of the meeting:

> Was I willing to fly the Atlantic?
> In the event of disaster would I release those in
> charge of of all responsibility?
> What was my education—if any?
> How strong?
> How willing?
> What flying experience?
> What would I do after the flight?

Amelia was told that Wilmer Stultz, test pilot for one of Byrd's planes, would be paid twenty thousand dollars to fly the Atlantic flight and the mechanic, Louis Gordon, five thousand. There would be no reward for her except for opportunities in aviation that she might be offered after a successful crossing. Fees for newspaper stories she wrote would be put back in the operating fund. Accepting those terms, Amelia made some requests of her own. She wanted to check the equipment and to meet the pilot. She also wanted to do some of the flying on the trip. Returning to Boston, she reported to Marion Perkins, "I found myself in a curious situation. If they did not like me at all or found me wanting in many respects, I would be deprived of the trip. If they liked me too well, they might be loath to drown me. It was, therefore, necessary for me to maintain an attitude of impenetrable mediocrity."

After the interview she said Putnam had escorted her to the train station. He talked all the way, telling her about his young son, David Binney Putnam, who had accompanied him on a trip to Greenland and written a book about it for juvenile readers. Amelia thought him an interesting man but was amused by how quickly he hustled her aboard the train without offering to pay for her return ticket.

Two days later she received a note and formal agreement from Mrs. Guest. Amelia was to be captain of the flight; her decisions, once aboard, to be final. Any money from royalties or advertising would be turned over to the operating fund.

Amelia signed the agreement and returned it promptly. She knew how dangerous the flight would be. Since Lindbergh's crossing the previous May, fourteen persons attempting the flight had been lost at sea, three of them women. The last, the Honorable Elsie Mackay, an Englishwoman accompanied by Capt. Walter Hinchcliffe, disappeared somewhere over the Atlantic within days of Amelia's interview in New York. A fourth woman, American Ruth Elder, accompanied by George W. Haldeman, had survived an unsuccessful attempt when they were plucked from the sea by the crew of a Dutch freighter three hundred miles northeast of the Azores.

Amelia's decision did not surprise Marion Perkins. Not long after she came to work for Perkins at Denison House Amelia gave Perkins a poem she had written, entitled "Courage."

Courage is the price that life exacts for granting peace.
The soul that knows it not, knows no release
From little things.

Knows not the livid loneliness of fear
Nor mountain heights where bitter joy can
Hear the sound of wings.

How can life grant us boon of living, compensate
For dull gray ugliness and pregnant hate
Unless we dare

The soul's dominion? Each time we make a choice, we pay
With courage to behold resistless day
And count it fair.

It was not a very good poem, almost sophomoric in its disdain for the mundane, but to Perkins and, later, to others who knew her, the poem was the essence of Amelia. She could not and would not live a conventional life. Her objectives were empyrean—to go where no one had gone and to do what no one had done. If to dare was to die, then she would die.

Once committed to the flight, she wrote a will listing her debts, mostly medical bills of a little over one thousand dollars, and her assets, one government bond, the Kissel Kar, and stock in Kinner Airplane and Dennison Airport companies. Amy was to receive anything remaining after settlement of Amelia's debts. Amelia closed the will with, "My regret is that I leave just now. In a few years I feel I could have laid by something substantial, for so many new things were opening for me."

She also wrote a letter to each of her parents, to be opened only if she were dead. To her father she said,

> Hooray for the grand adventure! I wish I had won, but it was worth while anyway. You know that.
> I have no faith we'll meet anywhere else, but I wish we might.
> Anyway, goodbye and good luck to you.

She omitted her doubts about heavenly reunions in the one to her mother:

> Even though I have lost, the adventure was worth while. Our family tends to be too secure. My life has really been very happy, and I didn't mind contemplating its end in the midst of it.

Amelia gave the letters to Sam Chapman, the only other person besides Marion Perkins in whom she confided her plans. The will was in a safety deposit box at Medford Bank, the key left with Sam. She also asked him to tell Amy and Muriel about the flight immediately after the *Friendship* left Boston.

To Hilton Railey she wrote, "I appreciate your forbearance in not trying to 'sell' the idea, and should like you to know I assume all responsibility for any risk involved." When Railey's wife, Julia, urged her to back out of the agreement just before the *Friendship* took off, Amelia replied, "No, this is the way I look at it. My family's insured; there's only myself to think about. And when a great adventure's offered you—you don't refuse it, that's all."

PART TWO

AIRBORNE

CHAPTER FIVE

Across the Atlantic

*I*n the spring of 1928 Amelia Earhart made two decisions. The first was to accept the offer of the *Friendship* flight, the second, to return to Denison House when it was over. "I'll be back for summer school," she told Marion Perkins. She made both decisions as independently as she had when she defied her Hyde Park classmates in Chicago, when she left Ogontz for a Toronto hospital, when she dropped out of Columbia University, and when she decided to be a pilot. But "the girl in brown who walks alone" was now locked in step with others who had converging interests and equally strong wills.

One was Cmdr. Richard Evelyn Byrd, USN, conqueror of the North Pole in 1926. The thirty-year-old Byrd, brother of Sen. Harry Byrd of Virginia, was described by a fellow officer as a great navigator, a competent pilot, a fine companion, but a "publicity hound." "The minute he got back from one thing and sat on his fanny for a week or two he commenced to get agitated. Wanted to do something else . . . good at raising money . . . equipment from the Navy, 'custodial loans' which the Navy never got back."

The ambitious, restless Byrd was both friend and client of G. P. Putnam who published his books and publicized his expeditions. Byrd not only agreed to secretly sell his trimotor Fokker to Mrs. Guest, he also offered to pick a crew for the enterprise, an offer Putnam welcomed. Although nominally captain of the *Friendship,* Amelia was not consulted. Byrd asked Wilmer "Bill" Stultz to be pilot. Stultz was a magnificent pilot. Only twenty-eight, he was already a veteran of both the Army and Navy air services. He had worked for Curtiss Export Company, delivering forty planes to Rio de Janeiro, where he taught the Brazilian air force pilots to fly them. From Curtiss he went to Anthony Fokker's firm as a test pilot and only one month before he accepted Byrd's offer as pilot of the *Friendship* he had flown Charles A. Levine and Mabel Boll to Havana. The wealthy Miss Boll, known to the public as the "Diamond Queen," told the press that she would sell all her diamonds to make a transatlantic flight and that Stultz had agreed to be her pilot. Either she misunderstood or Stultz had reneged before he accepted Byrd's offer. Stultz was also an alcoholic, not an unusual condition for test pilots of that era.

To assist Stultz as mechanic and copilot, Byrd chose Louis Edward "Slim" Gordon. A year younger than Stultz, Gordon was also a veteran of the Army Air Service. An additional pilot, Louis Gower, was put on standby by Byrd.

Byrd also chose three more members of the *Friendship* team, retired Navy Cmdr. E. P. Elmer as technical advisor, Capt. William Rogers of the International Mercantile Marine to make the flight charts, and Dr. James H. Kimball of the U.S. Weather Bureau in New York to provide weather advisories.

Although Byrd selected most of the personnel, real control of the *Friendship* flight was always Putnam's. The suave, handsome Putnam was everything he claimed to be to Amelia—author, editor, explorer, publisher, and friend of the famous. Putnam knew how to provide heroes to a hero-worshipping public. This time he had a potential heroine. Physically, this woman was the feminine equivalent of Lindbergh. Her tall, erect, slender figure, piercing blue-grey eyes, high forehead, firm chin, and Nordic coloring were a guarantee for a "Lady Lindy" image. She had the same shy smile and the same hesitation before speaking. In addition she was an intelligent, compassionate social worker who didn't smoke or drink, an unmarried woman with a reputation as unsullied as a Girl Scout's. If the *Friendship* crossing was successful Putnam was certain he could make Amelia Earhart a national heroine.

Secrecy and speed were essential to Putnam's plan. Amelia's crossing would have to be a surprise and she would have to be the first woman to do it. The plane sale was made through a go-between, millionaire

Donald Woodward of Le Roy, New York, owner-president of the Mechanical Science Corporation. The sale was registered on April 9, 1928, with the corporation as buyer.

Making Amelia the first woman to cross the Atlantic by airplane was more difficult. Two others were threatening to do it. The first was Mabel Boll, who had the use of Levine's *Columbia,* the plane in which he and Chamberlin had flown to Berlin in 1927, and who continued to badger Stultz about his alleged promise to be her pilot. The second challenger was Thea Rasche of Germany who announced on May 6 that she intended to make the flight from New York with Ernst Udet, a German war ace. A few days later Rasche said she would take off after June 10, as soon as weather permitted.

Along with the challenges of the "Diamond Queen" and the "Flying Fraulein," there was the chance that the public could become jaded from too many successful transatlantic flights. In mid-April two Germans and an Irishman had made a westbound flight from Dublin to Newfoundland. During May two Germans, an Englishman, two Frenchmen, a Pole, a Swede, and two Spaniards all announced plans for crossing from west to east. A prize of thirty thousand dollars was offered by the Belgians to the first airman to land at Oestand Farm from New York. Although Hollywood's biggest box-office hit of the year was William Wellman's *Wings,* if even half the aspiring transatlantic fliers made it, the public might well tire of aviation exploits.

In addition to the *Friendship* team, the only other persons who knew of Amelia's plans were Marion Perkins and Sam Chapman. Although Amelia would not marry Sam, she thought of him as part of her family and gave him the onerous task of telling her mother and sister her plan *after* the flight left Boston. Amelia told no one else and avoided being seen near the plane:

> I did not dare show myself around Boston airport where the ship was being worked on. Not once was I with the men on their test flights. . . . I actually saw the *Friendship* only once before the first attempted take-off. To have been detected in the picture would have brought premature publicity and swamped all concerned with thrill writers and curiosity seekers.

During April and May she carried on her customary schedule, working at Denison House and spending weekends at Dennison Airport. She kept up her correspondence, writing again to Ruth Nichols on April 24 about a women's flying organization. She suggested to Nichols that they be "autocratic about officers at first, in order to start something. One of us should be chairman, and a secretary and treasurer may be selected later."

Putnam's newest protégée was as aware as he of the uses of publicity. To increase support for the Boston NAA, she wrote to its secretary, Bernard Wiesman, that the chapter should receive all visiting fliers, offer speakers on aviation to clubs and schools, and ask department stores to feature aviation displays. "The mob should be thought of too," she wrote, "as it is or will be the support of the industry." The letter brought an immediate response. The nominating committee named her a vice-president, "the first woman chosen as an officer of the NAA anywhere in the country."

The *Friendship* was ready by early May, its wheels replaced by pontoons, its wings painted gold, spanning seventy-one feet, and its three two-hundred horsepower motors overhauled and tested. For the next three weeks the crew waited while one adverse weather report followed another. When conditions were good over the Atlantic, there was not enough wind for a takeoff from Boston Harbor. The clumsy, box-like aircraft was hobbled by the pontoons that Byrd insisted might save lives in the event of a forced landing at sea. But for takeoff the pontoons required wind-roughened waters. Without waves they induced suction like a coin on a flat, wet surface, holding down the aircraft with its heavy fuel load. Not until July 1 did meteorologist Kimball issue a really promising forecast.

On Friday, July 1, Amelia moved into a room at the Copley-Plaza Hotel. That night she wrote a letter to Muriel:

> Dear Snappy,
> I have tried to play for a large stake and if I succeed all will be well.
> If I don't I shall be happy to pop off in the midst of such an adventure. My only regret would be leaving you and mother stranded for a while.
> I haven't told you about the affair as I didn't want to worry mother, and she would suspect (she may now) if I told you. The whole thing came so unexpectedly that few knew about it. Sam will tell you the whole story. Please explain to mother. I couldn't stand the added strain of telling mother and you personally.
> If reporters talk to you, say you knew, if you like.
> Yours respectfully,
> Sister

P.S. I have made my will and placed my house in order. I have appointed a girl friend at Denison House administrator in case of my death.

Amelia was awakened at 3:30 on Sunday morning. She dressed for the flight in brown riding breeches, high, laced boots, a white silk blouse with a red kerchief tied at the neck, and her old leather coat, bought when she was learning to fly in California. Over all she wore a fur-lined flying suit, borrowed from Maj. Charles H. Woolley, an Air National Guard pilot who did not know why she had asked for it. With her she carried a camera given her by David Layman, field glasses from G. P., and a copy of Byrd's book, *Skyward,* which he asked her to give to Mrs. Guest. Assembled in the hotel lobby for a drive through the dark, wet streets to Boston Harbor's "T" Wharf were Bill Stultz, Commander Elmer, and Lou Gower, all accompanied by their wives; Slim Gordon and his fiancée, Ann Bruce; G. P., Marion Perkins, and J. E. "Jake" Coolidge, a Paramount News cameraman hired by G. P. No other reporters or photographers were present.

At the wharf a tugboat, *Sadie Rose,* took the party out to the *Friendship,* where Amelia, Stultz, Gordon, and Gower, who was to accompany the first three as far as Trepassey, Newfoundland, boarded the plane. Stultz took the pilot's seat, Amelia stood amidships between two auxiliary fuel tanks, and Gower went aft. Slim Gordon balanced on the pontoons while he started each of the three engines, then climbed into the copilot seat. The big ship taxied down the bay followed by the tug, but when Stultz gunned the motors and raced across the bay, it would not lift off. There was not enough wind to stir the waters and counteract the suction of the pontoons. Gower moved as far aft as possible, hoping his weight would raise the nose, and they tried again without success. On a third attempt they threw out six five-gallon tins of gasoline before Stultz taxied up to the tug and shouted that he thought he could make it with a few less pounds. Putnam and Elmer rowed over from the tug in a small boat and took Gower off. As Stultz turned into the wind for another try, the breeze freshened, the motors roared, and the *Friendship* was airborne.

A report of the takeoff stated, "Those on the tugboat who saw Miss Earhart at close range in her flying togs were amazed at her resemblance to Colonel Charles A. Lindbergh. 'Lady Lindy' was what one deckhand called her." The same story included a comment by a Norwegian artist, Brynjulf Strandenaes, who was in Boston the week before and who had done a portrait from life of Lindbergh. "She looks more like Lindbergh than Lindbergh himself," he told the reporter.

The *New York Times*'s man described her as tall and slim with a boyish face, a high forehead, level grey eyes, a firm chin, and very white teeth, which she displayed in a "quick, flashing Lindbergh smile." Her hair, he wrote, was yellow, bobbed, curly, and unruly.

The description was accurate except for her hair being darker than yellow and the writer failing to note a marked space between her two front teeth, so noticeable in black-and-white newspaper photographs that she soon took G. P.'s advice to smile with her lips closed. The shadow of Putnam's image-making fell over the whole story. Although an enterprising reporter could have found a deckhand as soon as the tug docked, even one who might say that she looked like Lindbergh, and that same reporter could also have elucidated a quote from the artist who painted Lindbergh, no reporters were aboard the tug. G. P. was there, however, to make it easier and G. P. was a personal friend of the *Times* publisher, Adolph Ochs.

Nevertheless, even G. P. could not create a "Lady Lindy" out of whole cloth. He could only direct attention to an attractive woman with a distinctive style, a slim figure, a beautiful smile, and a unique hair style. Colleagues who later grumbled that G. P. even invented the haircut that would soon cause instant recognition by millions of admirers were wrong. Bernard Wiesman noticed her hair the first time he met her in Boston two years before the flight. It was bobbed, dark blonde, curly, and unruly.

The departure of the *Friendship* was far more perilous than it appeared to the spectators. Just before the takeoff, the latch on the cabin door had broken and Amelia held it closed until Gordon left the copilot's seat and tied the handle to a heavy gasoline tin with a rope. When the big plane rose, the door, forced open by the wind, dragged the can across the deck. Amelia leapt on the tin and held it, rolling toward the open door and shouting for Gordon. He jumped up from his seat and dragged her back with the tin, then teetered on the door ledge, reaching out for the handle of the door. The plane banked, throwing him back into the cabin and slamming the door behind him. This time he tied it securely to a leather thong on the door frame. They were on their way at last, at 6:30 in the morning, heading up the New England coast, into a brilliant sun. Amelia sat on a gasoline tin keeping a log in a stenographer's notebook.

The heavily laden *Friendship* lumbered along at an average speed of

114 miles an hour, crossing over Fear Island near Nova Scotia by 8:55 A.M. The haze of the sun was swallowed up by grey clouds and fog so thick that thirty miles past Halifax, Stultz turned back and circled until, through a hole in the fog, he saw the Halifax Naval Air Station in Halifax Harbor. He landed there, moored near the station, and went ashore with Gordon for weather reports, leaving Amelia aboard the plane. Returning at 1:30 P.M. when the fog appeared to lift, Stultz took off again, but half-way to Trepassey he was forced to turn back to Halifax again.

They checked into a hotel in Dartmouth, where Stultz and Gordon again left Amelia while they went to a Chinese restaurant. There two reporters and a photographer found them sitting at a counter. Stultz said that, weather permitting, he would go on to Trepassey the next morning, take on more fuel, and leave immediately for Ireland. Back at the hotel Amelia refused to be interviewed. While reporters dogged Amelia's footsteps in Newfoundland and besieged Amy and Muriel Earhart in Boston, they were pleasing G. P. in New York. The New York Times four-column, front-page headline read, "Boston Girl Starts Atlantic Hop, Reaches Halifax, May Go On Today." The following day she shared another four-column, first-page headline with Sir Charles Kingsford-Smith and his crew on the Southern Cross who had just completed the longest nonstop flight ever made, from Honolulu to Fiji.

On Monday morning, twenty-four hours after the Friendship left Boston, Stultz took off from Halifax for Trepassey, reaching it at two in the afternoon. By this time the flight was worldwide news. Once ashore, Amelia again dodged reporters, walking to a nearby Roman Catholic convent where she visited with the nuns, while Stultz and Gordon returned to the ship to pump gas until sundown. Stultz said they would spend the night at the house of a local family and take off for Ireland at noon.

When reporters could not talk to Amelia they described her: "Miss Earhart's slightness of build was accentuated by the tight-fitting brown knickers [sic] and high-laced boots she wore when she stepped from the plane here. . . . Her close-cut, light hair was tousled by the wind, for she wore no hat." In New York G. P. gave the press the cable he had received from her: "Good trip from Halifax. Average speed 111 miles per hour. Motors running beautifully. Trepassey harbor very rough. . . . Everybody comfortably housed and happy."

It was the last time the crew of the Friendship would be comfortable or happy for the next thirteen days. During those days Amelia kept in constant touch with G. P. In Boston where she had seen him frequently, along with Railey and Byrd at the latter's house, she realized that the flight was only one of a dozen projects Putnam managed at any given moment. She could not resist teasing him about this, telling him a child's story about a shrewd cat named Simpkin who caught a mouse and because he was not hungry at the moment stored it under a teacup. Having a mouse available whenever he wanted one seemed such a good idea he thought it even better to catch and store more. Amelia told G. P. he was a "Simpkin" and it was to "Simpkin" she sent her messages. When he suggested she "turn in and have your laundering done" she answered, "No laundry because underwear all worn out and shirt lost to Slim at gin rummy."

Amelia's cheery cables disguised her growing anxiety. Within forty-eight hours of their landing at Trepassey she realized Stultz was an alcoholic. The only member of the crew competent enough to pilot the tri-motored Fokker and navigate the Atlantic, the restless, nervous Stultz began to drink. While Amelia played cards with Slim Gordon in the drafty, primitive house where they stayed, or went hiking with him whenever the gale-force winds abated, Stultz found solace in the bottle. He left it only to make dangerous and futile attempts to get the *Friendship* airborne.

Stultz made three attempts on June 6 and eight on June 12, four of them after discarding the movie camera, film, a large thermos, and all their extra clothing. He tried again the next day, dumping 135 gallons of gasoline to lighten the plane but he could not lift it off the choppy waves of the harbor. After this failure he decided to overhaul all three engines with Gordon but he beached the plane on a sand ledge and could not get it off until midnight when the tide rose. That same day Mabel Boll sent Amelia an invitation from Harbor Grace, another port in Newfoundland, where she had already arrived in the *Columbia,* suggesting that the *Friendship* return to Harbor Grace where smoother waters would make it easier to take off. Boll was inviting Amelia to a race with the *Columbia,* a plane Stultz knew was faster than the *Friendship*. The message provided yet another excuse for him to drink himself into a stupor.

On the night of June 16 Amelia took command of the flight. She was already legally the captain, authorized in writing "to have control of the plane . . . and of all its employees as if she were the owner."

The agreement had been written by lawyer Layman who cabled her on June 13: "Please send Putnam confidential report what goes on. Are you satisfied there? Can we help more here or there? Do you see his [Stultz's] messages?"

Amelia realized something would have to be done. She told Gordon her decision while she sat with him at the dining-room table, listening to Stultz up in his room, drunk and feverish with a cold, cursing as he paced up and down. If Gordon was willing, Amelia wanted to leave the next morning. The good-natured Gordon was willing. Stultz had so exasperated him that he was ready to take the next boat back to Boston unless Amelia took over.

They both knew the risks were appalling. Stultz had yet to lift the big plane off the bay waters. To do so he would have to cut back fuel to a dangerous minimum. Doc Kimball's latest message from New York warned of unstable weather conditions. But at seven the next morning, a Sunday, Amelia pounded on the door of the room shared by Gordon and Stultz. When Gordon opened the door she saw Stultz sprawled on the bed, snoring. Gordon pushed him under a cold shower, dressed him, and brought him back to Amelia, who forced him to drink cup after cup of hot coffee. An hour later he was downstairs, sober enough to eat breakfast. Amelia left the table long enough to send a cable to G. P. It read, "Violet. Cheerio! A.E." Violet was the code word for takeoff. When she returned she told reporters, "We are going today in spite of everything."

They left the boarding house with Amelia and Gordon steadying Stultz between them, walking him down the steep path to the wharf. Amelia helped load more gasoline into tanks while Gordon put Stultz and four extra tins of fuel aboard. An hour later, when Gordon climbed down onto a pontoon to start the engines the surly Stultz left him barely enough time to scramble back into the cabin before gunning the engines and taxiing out onto the harbor. Three times Stultz tried and failed to raise the heavy craft. Twice they dumped auxiliary fuel tins overboard. On the fourth attempt, the Fokker plowed through the water for two miles, rose slowly, dipped, steadied, and rose again, wobbling up through the fog, one water-drenched engine sputtering. They were on their way.

The captain of the *Friendship* retired amidships where she started the log with the time of departure—11:40 A.M. Not long after she spied a whiskey bottle lodged between a rib of the fuselage and Gordon's tool kit. Her impulse was to open the hatch and throw it out just as she had once poured her father's hidden supply down the sink, but she left the bottle where it was. Stultz might need it later.

Three hundred miles out of Trepassey the plane was enveloped by fog. Searching for a clearing, Stultz climbed into a snow squall. Without de-icing equipment, he was forced to take the ship down again, so quickly that Amelia slid across the deck and into the oil drums stored behind the seat. Regaining her place amidships Amelia watched him struggle to stay awake for the next one hundred miles until the weather cleared when he signaled for Gordon to take over, then fell asleep in his seat.

Seven hours out Amelia wrote in the log, "I am . . . kneeling here at the [chart] table gulping beauty. Radio contact. *Rexmore,* Britisher bound for New York." It was the last radio contact. Amelia dozed off after midnight until she was awakened by Gordon's voice calling for ships to "come in." None did. The radio was dead. They would have to depend on Stultz's navigational skills. They had been flying for sixteen hours and had four, possibly five, hours of fuel left.

At dawn Stultz came down through the clouds searching the cold, grey waters for a ship. At 6:30 they sighted the S.S. *America,* which Stultz circled while Amelia tied a message to two oranges and dropped it. She missed. Now on the emergency tank with about one hour's fuel remaining, Stultz sighted a fleet of fishing boats. Minutes later Amelia saw land, then a smokestack less than a mile off. Stultz circled what seemed to be a factory town on the coast and brought the ship in for a perfect landing. The *Friendship*'s flight across the international time zones of the Atlantic ended at Burry Port, Wales, where it was one o'clock in the afternoon of June 18, twenty hours and forty minutes after their departure from Trepassey. Its crew was 3,000 miles from Boston and 140 miles from Southhampton, where a vast crowd had gathered to see the first woman to cross the Atlantic in an airplane.

CHAPTER SIX

The Circus

O ne hour after the *Friendship* landed off the Welsh coast, Norman Fisher, the High Sheriff of Carmanthenshire, pulled his small dinghy alongside the big plane.

"Do ye be wanting something?" he asked the young woman in the fur-lined coverall who leaned out from the open hatch.

"We've come from America," she said. "Where are we?"

"Have ye now?" Fisher said. "Well, I'm sure we wish you welcome to Burry Port, Wales. I'll go see about getting ye mooring space for the flying machine and getting ye ashore."

Until the sheriff rowed out to them, no one in Burry Port seemed overly curious about the flying machine. Amelia had waved at a group of longshoremen loading coal on a freighter by the quay but, after waving back, they went back to work. The exhausted, short-tempered Stultz was threatening to run the *Friendship* right into the quay when Fisher arrived and offered to take one of the crew back to shore. Stultz went, leaving Amelia and Gordon on the plane.

From Burry Port, Stultz telephoned Hilton Railey in Southampton where he had been standing by for two weeks. Stultz called at 2:45. Three hours later Railey and Allen Raymond of the *New York Times* arrived in Burry Port. By then two thousand people—almost the entire population of the town—had heard about "the girl flyer" and were waiting on the dock to see Amelia. When she stepped ashore she was literally assaulted by "men, women, and children who tried to touch her flying suit, shake her hand or get her autograph." Railey and Raymond, along with three policemen and the sheriff, locked arms to form a circle around her and fought their way for one hundred yards to the nearest shelter, the office of the Fricker Metal Company.

Amelia was stunned. "The accident of sex," she said, had made her the star of "our particular sideshow." An hour later she was forced to run the gauntlet again surrounded by additional police mustered to escort her to a local hotel. She was angered and frightened by the shoving, clutching, grasping strangers and the reporter's questions about her personal life. At the hotel, Stultz and Gordon ate dinner and went to their rooms to sleep. Amelia, who was too upset to eat, still had to write the first of four stories on the flight that Putnam had promised to the *Times.*

An hour later, when Hilton Railey went to her room to collect the story along with messages for Amy, Muriel, and Marion Perkins, he was shocked to see how ill she looked. Her hands shook, her face was blotched and grey, and when he reached out to pat her shoulder, she flinched like a caged animal.

"Aren't you excited?" he asked.

"Excited? No," she said. "It was a grand experience but . . . Bill did all the flying—had to. I was just baggage."

In the story she gave to Railey she praised Stultz and Gordon but protested that she had never touched the controls of the *Friendship,* even though she had had five hundred hours of solo flying.

When Railey saw her the next morning after she had had six hours of sleep and her first hot bath since leaving Boston, she appeared to have forgotten her grievances of the previous night. On the brief flight from Burry Port to Southampton, she flew the *Friendship* at last, after Stultz invited her to take over the controls. At Southampton, where thousands waited to see her, she was met first by two women who could have been the subjects of her feminist scrapbook clippings of the previous decade. They were Mrs. Guest, who had bought the *Friendship* so that a woman could make the transatlantic flight, and Mrs. Foster Welch, the Lord Mayor of Southampton and first female sheriff of England.

For the remainder of the day, crowds gathered to see Amelia wherever she went. In Southampton, four mounted policemen struggled to hold back hundreds of eager autograph seekers who thrust bits of paper at her through the open windows of the Lord Mayor's Rolls Royce. During a fifty-mile drive to the Hyde Park Hotel in London, track fans returning from Ascot waved to her from their cars. More admirers gathered in the hotel lobby and on the sidewalk outside, pushing and jostling to catch a glimpse of her.

In her flower-banked room she sat on a sofa, barricaded behind a tea table while photographers' flashguns flared and reporters fired questions at her. Asked if she was afraid during the flight, she said, "Mr. Stultz is such an expert pilot that I never felt afraid." She cited Stultz again in an answer to the congratulatory telegram sent by President Calvin Coolidge: "The crew of the *Friendship* desire to express their deep appreciation of your Excellency's gracious message. Success entirely due to great skill of Mr. Stultz." When Byrd called from New York she told him, "The success is yours too, Commander, for it was your wonderful ship that brought us through."

George Palmer Putnam couldn't have produced better quotes if he had been there to dictate them to her. By the time she sent her second dispatch to the *Times* her first was on the front page under an eight-column, three-line head: "Amelia Earhart Flies Atlantic, First Woman to Do It; Tells Her Own Story of Perilous 21-Hour Trip to Wales; Radio Quit and They Flew Blind over Invisible Ocean."

On her first morning in London she awakened to an avalanche of editorial praise from American and foreign newspapers. As an aviator she was commended for her "unquenchable determination to go on attempting the hitherto unachieved, no matter how great the dangers" and for her intent "to render service to commercial aviation, not to make a sensation." As a woman she was acclaimed for "a feat none of her sex had accomplished, though many had attempted it." She had not failed "to bring home to everyone the fine spirit of audacity shown by her sex in this age."

Criticism was minimal, the most cutting in the *Church Times*: "The voyage itself . . . is a remarkable achievement made possible by the skill and courage of the pilot. . . . As the *Evening Standard* has properly pointed out, 'her [Amelia's] presence added no more to the achievement than if the passenger had been a sheep.'" In the French newspaper, *Liberté* the public received more criticism than Amelia: " . . . the palpitating interest of the world in these great adventures comes from the taste for agony and death which all humanity shares, from that dark frenzy which pushed the

Romans to watch the bloody spectacles of the arena." Deeply hurt by these comments the neophyte celebrity kept her feelings to herself and fibbed to reporters, " . . . from first to last my contact with the press has been thoroughly enjoyable."

That first day in London Amelia was besieged with invitations, business propositions, requests for autographs, cables of congratulations and even a proposal of marriage from a Kent farmer, "provided she was well off, financially." By mid-afternoon she was exhausted in spite of aid from Railey and two secretaries. Help arrived in the person of her sponsor, who had decided Amelia was not only a "suitable person" for the flight but charming enough to be a houseguest. Amelia was moved from the hotel to the Guests' Park Lane mansion, where shopkeepers were summoned to provide her with a wardrobe before she was dispatched in a chauffeured car on a restful, solitary ride around London. The limousine was a seven-passenger Lincoln from Ford of England, "placed at the disposal of Miss Earhart during her stay." Mr. Ford also sent her a congratulatory telegram from Detroit. In the ensuing eight days Amelia would be introduced to London society, have tea with Bernard Shaw, and dance with the Prince of Wales. She had entered the world of the rich and famous.

At dinner that night she met Lady Mary Heath who had recently flown an Avro Avian, a small, single-engine plane, from Cape Town to London—eight thousand miles. Mary Heath wanted to sell the plane. On June 26 Amelia bought it with credit extended by G. P., who already held Amelia's contract for a Putnam's Sons book on the *Friendship*'s flight.

On her second day at the Guests, her hostess took her shopping and introduced her to H. Gordon Selfridge, the American owner of a Mayfair department store. It marked the beginning of a continuing friendship with Selfridge and with his daughter, Violette, and her husband, Vicomte Jacques de Sibour, both of whom were avid pilots.

Next to befriend Amelia was one of the most influential women in England, Lady Nancy Astor. The former Nancy Langhorne of Virginia, she was the first woman to become a member of Parliament, a seat she held from 1919 until her retirement in 1945. Nancy Astor was not interested in aviation. She wanted to hear about Amelia's work at Denison House. Amelia was charmed by this beautiful, witty social activist and advocate of women's interests. A paradoxical feminist who disapproved of bobbed hair and bachelor girls, a divorcée before her marriage to Viscount Waldorf Astor, Amelia's new friend was a staunch supporter of marriage and family. She also sought pensions for women, employment of women on the police force, reform of legitimacy laws, and improved labor conditions for both sexes.

Lady Astor arranged a number of meetings with Amelia. At a luncheon given by the Women's Committee of the Air League of the British Empire she dropped her disapproval of bobbed hair and asked Amelia to remove her hat so the guests could see her "tousled golden curls." Lady Astor also took her friend to tea at the House of Commons and the Olympia horse show. "Everyone I have talked to in England thinks this girl is a great credit to womanhood and to her country," she told reporters. "She has charm, intelligence and above all, character." Amelia, who discounted mass admiration, was delighted.

On Wednesday, June 27, nine days after landing at Burry Port, Amelia was driven from Lady Astor's town house to Wimbledon to see America's greatest woman tennis player, Helen Wills, win a match. From there she went on to Southampton to sail on the next day for New York on the S.S. *Roosevelt* with Stultz and Gordon.

Amelia had seen very little of either of the two men while they were in England. Removed from his natural element—the air—a grounded Stultz was a drunken Stultz. He also made awkward statements to the press. On his first day in London he said that if he had to return to New York by sea he would insist it be on an American ship because he doubted the safety of foreign vessels. The sea-going English were not pleased. On another occasion Stultz inadvertently insulted the heir to the throne. After a flight with Gordon to Le Bourget in France, they were forced down on the return trip by gales on the coast and missed an appointment with the Prince of Wales.

Things were no better aboard the *Roosevelt*. Stultz was noticeably intoxicated for most of the voyage and Amelia feared he might endanger the continuation of what she perceived to be the *Friendship*'s mission. G. P. may have viewed the flight as a stunt in the creation of his new heroine-client but Amelia—saleswoman for Bert Kinner and part owner of Dennison Airport—was determined to use this opportunity to boost commercial aviation. After G. P. sent her his schedule of homecoming celebrations, Amelia confided her worries about Stultz to Harry Manning, the captain of the *Roosevelt*. "It's bad enough in London where people are tolerant," she told Manning, "but what will happen if I can't keep him sober for these New York affairs?"

Her worries were well-founded. Stultz would continue to drink his way through the festivities and was often absent or late. Less than a year later, while stunting, he was killed along with his two passengers in a crash at Roosevelt Field. He was drunk, flying a plane declared unsuitable for aerobatics by a board of inquiry investigating the accident.

Amelia's New York arrival was carefully choreographed by G. P. and directed by the city's colorful meeter and greeter, Grover B. Whalen. On the morning of July 6, Amelia stood on the promenade of the *Roosevelt* looking down at the launch *Macon* as it drew alongside the big ship. Whalen, in top hat and cutaway, followed by Byrd and his aide in full dress uniform, bounded up the gangplank while strains of "Home, Sweet Home" played by the New York Fire Department band blared across the harbor. Amelia was wearing a blue crepe suit and cream silk blouse, her hair hidden by a hideous cloche of feathers which fortunately did not hide her handsome face and blue-grey eyes. Stultz stood at her right, the collar of his suit riding up over a crumpled shirt, his necktie askew, his greying hair blowing in the wind and his blunt-featured face puffy with dissipation. On her left was Gordon, tall, thin, grinning, as relaxed as Stultz was tense.

Aboard the *Macon*, Amelia was led by G. P. and his wife, Dorothy Binney Putnam, to a cabin where reporters surrounded her. One noted that she not only looked like Lindbergh but she spoke like him, gazing straight at the questioner, then "giving a little shake of the head and a long, drawn-out, 'Well . . .'"

Among the women aviators invited aboard the *Macon* by G. P. was Ruth Nichols. Amelia recognized her from a newspaper photograph and immediately launched into an accolade for aviation country clubs, a project of Nichols's. After G. P. retrieved Stultz from his mother and a delegation of hometown friends, Amelia directed the reporters' queries to Stultz but his replies were cut short by an ear-splitting blast from the *Macon*'s siren. Fireboats pumped streams of water into the air, whistles blew and a crowd of five thousand clustered along the edge of Battery Park rushed toward Pier A where the *Macon* docked.

Amelia was seated between Stultz and Gordon on the backseat of an open car that made its way from the Battery up Broadway in a blizzard of tickertape and pages torn from telephone books and newspapers. Neither photographs nor newsreels can convey the emotions generated by a New York parade of the twenties or thirties. Like most Americans of the era, allegedly postwar disillusioned New Yorkers were actually fervent believers in vaguely defined concepts of "progress," "science," and "opportunity" (which only knocked once). They wanted heroes and heroines who expressed these mythical values. Amelia, whose earlier allusion to the "sideshow" was not amiss, was now in the center ring of an ebullient, electric circus of the street.

At City Hall, where the parade ended, Amelia's assertion that "most of the credit should go to Mr. Stultz," was greeted by a roar of approval. For the next fourteen hours, with time out for costume changes, Amelia was on display for her public. The closing event at midnight was an Olympic Fund benefit at the Palace Theater. When she offered a small flag carried on the *Friendship* for auction, Babe Ruth pushed the bids to three figures but auctioneer Charles Winninger, star of *Showboat,* secured the flag for $650, a sum equaling ten times that at present-day prices.

The sideshow continued for two more days with dawn to midnight appearances scheduled by G. P., who solved the problem of the elusive Stultz by insisting that all three of the *Friendship*'s crew stay at the Putnam house in Rye.

On the fourth day Amelia moved on to Boston. Waiting there was Amy, who had experienced a gamut of conflicting emotions—surprise, humiliation, worry, and, finally, pride. Although she was used to Amelia's penchant for sudden, secret decisions, when she was told that her daughter was on her way to Newfoundland in an attempt to cross the Atlantic by air, Amy had snapped, "I thought she had too much sense to try it."

Later she told Amelia her unfortunate comment was the result of learning the news from a reporter before Sam Chapman could deliver Amelia's explanation that "it was an experiment for me and it was better to spare you the worry until I started." When first informed of Amelia's safe arrival in Wales, Muriel was reported near collapse but Amy, "rigidly erect of carriage, determinedly unmoved in feature," showed no outward signs of the strain she must have been under. "Well," she said, "now that it's all over I'll have a chance to catch up on my mending."

While Amy, who had not seen her daughter in six weeks, waited in an office at the airport, Amelia was delayed on the field, first by the reception committee, then by Stultz and Gordon who had wandered off into the crowd as soon as they arrived in a second plane. Amelia, her arms filled with flowers, was taken at last to Amy, who rushed to embrace both daughter and flowers. "Amelia!" she cried. "Darling!" Amelia murmured before the door was closed, leaving them alone. This intense, if brief, display of affection would be the most overt Amelia ever gave anyone in public.

After leaving Amy, Amelia had only a moment in which to greet Muriel and Marion Perkins before she was hustled into the official car. Although her mother, her sister, and her friend attended all the events of that day, there was never time for any real conversation. At the end of the day Amelia drove Amy and Muriel back to Medford in the yellow Kissel Kar but returned immediately to the Ritz Carlton in Boston. The young NAA secretary, Bernard Wiesman, was one of the friends who went to call on her there late that night. "She was just the same," Wiesman said, "hadn't changed at all."

Wiesman was wrong. Amelia was just the same to all those who shared her interest in aviation. But the flight with its ensuing opportunities and obligations left her with less time for and different interests than those of her family and friends at Denison House. The next day in Medford she told Amy and Muriel that she could not resume her social work until she finished the book for G. P., who also assured her that she could make money giving lectures. The money was important to Amelia. She wanted it to maintain a plane, to buy books and clothes, to send Amy a monthly allowance, to live comfortably with bills paid and money in the bank.

Also relegated to the status of old friend—one to be seen infrequently in the future—was Sam Chapman. Before Amelia left Boston she spent an hour with him in her hotel room in what one reporter called "a secret tryst." It was no such thing. From that time on, Chapman was never again referred to as Amelia's sweetheart or fiancé.

After forty-eight hours in Boston, Amelia returned to New York to make a nationwide broadcast on NBC from Madison Square Garden. A week later she was on the road again for official welcomes from Altoona and Williamsburg, Pennsylvania, on her way to Chicago and Toledo, and Pittsburgh on the way back. In Chicago, Stultz disappeared again, just before the parade was to begin. Gordon was sent to look for him but failed to return. Amelia was so angry that she refused to ride along in the open touring car until G. P. solved the problem by sitting in for Stultz, blithely signing Stultz's name for autograph seekers. Maj. Reed Landis, World War I ace and former classmate of Amelia's at Hyde Park High, took Gordon's place. The deception went unnoticed. The crowd was there to see Amelia.

In every city she visited, Amelia's schedule permitted almost no rest or privacy. By the time she reached Pittsburgh, one observer noticed that although she smiled at the cheering crowds she seemed "daunted by the sea of faces," and acted as if she wanted to escape. She was exhausted. She hated the mindless adulation of strangers and shrank from their touch. Nevertheless, she finished the tour like the professional G. P. wanted her to be. The sideshow seemed the only solution to the old problem of "no pay—no fly" and Amelia wanted to fly. If George Palmer Putnam piped the right tune, she was willing to dance.

CHAPTER SEVEN

The Hustler's Apprentice

*I*n the fall of 1928 Charles LeBoutillier, who was living in New York City's Greenwich Village, saw Amelia Earhart peering under the open hood of a car parked near Greenwich House on Barrow Street. "It was a beautiful car—looked like a Stutz Bearcat—and she took care of it herself," he said.

"I knew who she was," added LeBoutillier, a friend and former Harvard classmate of Boston NAA secretary Bernard Wiesman. "I'd seen her at the Boston airport after her Atlantic flight with her arms full of flowers. She was living in an apartment in the Village that fall, in that settlement house. I think most of the people in the neighborhood knew who she was but nobody took much notice. She ate in a cafe with a courtyard—one a lot of us went to—and someone said she liked to talk about Edna St. Vincent Millay's poetry. She didn't seem different from us—just an ordinary person." The relative anonymity Amelia was enjoying would not last much longer. George Palmer Putnam's campaign to make her one of America's most famous women was already in its fifth month.

On July 24—her thirty-first birthday—when Amelia returned to New York from her five-city homecoming tour, G. P. brought her directly from Grand Central to the Putnam house in Rye, where he put her to work on the book she had promised to write. Even before she left Boston on the *Friendship,* he had decided that, if she survived, Amelia's story might prove as popular as Lindbergh's and Byrd's had been for G. P. Putnam's Sons. While she was still at Trepassey he had wired: "For occupation might write skeleton thousand word story thus far Halifax Trepassey with names details to enlarge here after you underway."

By Putnam employing all the names and details he had collected from Amelia, with a good deal of editorial direction on his part, the book was finished in three weeks—in time for the shrewd Putnam to take advantage of the free publicity generated by the flight and subsequent homecoming hoopla. Amelia worked in the library of the sixteen-room, six-bath, Spanish mission–style house, which had been designed by G. P. and built in 1925. She dedicated the book to her hostess Dorothy Binney Putnam, "under whose roof-tree this book was written."

G. P.'s wife was an attractive, intelligent woman, the daughter of a Pittsburgh millionaire,* who had met her husband at a Sierra Club outing in New England soon after her graduation from Vassar College. They married in 1911 in Bend, Oregon. The twenty-four-year-old bridegroom, editor of the town's newspaper, was elected mayor of Bend a year later. They remained in Oregon until G. P. was commissioned a lieutenant in the Army in 1917. After the war he joined the family firm and by 1925 had moved into the house in Rye with Dorothy and their two sons, David Binney and George Palmer, Jr.

Dorothy Putnam was a popular hostess whose guests included opera stars, authors, artists, and explorers. During their seventeen-year marriage, her wide-ranging interests were frequently not shared by G. P., who had been known to come home late and stomp upstairs to bed without speaking to her guests. However, G. P.'s latest protégée and his wife liked each other. Dorothy described Amelia as "an educated and cultivated person with a fine, healthy sense of humor."

As soon as the book was finished, Amelia told G. P. she wanted to fly the Avro Avian she had purchased from Lady Heath to the West Coast and back. Although G. P. had paid for the plane and it was registered in his name, Amelia knew it was an investment made to convince the public and the press that she was a genuine aviator with a plane of her own. She also knew that he expected to decide when and where she flew it. She was asking him for permission to fly as she pleased and without any scheduled appearances en route. G. P. agreed because he had already

*Her father, Edward Binney, was the manufacturer of Crayola crayons.

learned that, although she followed his instructions most of the time, when she did set a goal of her own it was almost impossible to make her abandon it. He was also confident that by this time, wherever she went, she would be recognized and pursued by reporters. To make certain she was, two days before she left, he broke his promise to keep her trip a secret.

As secretive as always, Amelia wrote to Marian Stabler that she would be at the Putnams' in Rye until the first of September, when she actually intended to leave a week earlier. During a brief visit to her mother in Boston, she said to Amy that she *might* fly to the West Coast but gave her no date. The vague announcement was made to save Amy from the embarrassment she had suffered over not knowing about the Atlantic flight until reporters told her. Amy immediately told Muriel. Amelia then scolded her mother for telling Muriel. "I don't want her to spread the news," she wrote, "and I fear she will." In the same letter she suggested that Amy refer reporters to her or G. P., but added that Amy could tell them she knew her daughter's plans but did not want to reveal them.

On August 29, the first day of her trip, Amelia cracked up the Avian at Pittsburgh. She was taxiing across Rogers Field when the wheels of the little biplane dropped into an unmarked ditch, throwing it on its side in a ground-loop, which damaged the propeller, lower wing, and landing gear. She reacted to this crackup just as she had all those in the past and those she would have in the future. She was annoyed when questioned about it, unimpressed that she had been spared injury or death, and acted as if the incident might be obliterated if people would stop talking about it. When one newsman asked her about it a week later she said that in her ten years of flying she had never been in an accident like the one he described: "All they had to do was pull mine [her plane] out and it was ready to take up," she told him.

The plane was not ready to take up. G. P., who had accompanied her to Pittsburgh, returned to New York to make certain a second Avro Avian was flown to Pittsburgh to provide spare parts for the damaged machine. She was delayed for forty-eight hours.

By September 3, Amelia reached Scott Field near St. Louis, where she was recognized by a young woman who immediately commandeered her as a houseguest and insisted she attend a country club dance that night. Amelia, who had very little money and liked to dance, accepted.

The local hotel cost more and offered even less privacy. Her next hostess was Mrs. John Hay, a young Army wife in Muskogee, Missouri, who thought herself "the luckiest woman in all the universe" to have Amelia for a guest. Mrs. Hay said that Amelia sent a wire to her mother and "to some man, too, but of course I didn't listen to find out who he was." Although G. P. had broken his promise to keep the trip a secret, Amelia kept hers to notify him of her whereabouts at every stop on the way.

Her hostess admired Amelia's luggage, given her in England, and her clothes—all wrinkleproof and "just darling"—but she was ambiguous about Amelia's appearance. "She was really sort of homely, but she was nice to look at and I imagine she'd be pretty if she weren't so brown." In midwestern America, suntans were not yet fashionable, being more an indication of life on the farm than a winter in Miami.

Misfortune dogged Amelia for the remainder of the flight. She was forced down at Lovington, New Mexico, and again at Pecos, Texas, where she made an emergency landing on the main street after the plane developed valve trouble. She waited five days in Pecos for spare parts, then was forced down at an isolated ranch outside Douglas, Arizona, after the climb over the mountains overheated the engine. At Yuma, eager volunteers who offered to push her plane to the end of the field for takeoff upended the aircraft, bending the propeller. Amelia removed it, hammered it back into shape, reinstalled it, and left for Glendale, California, where she arrived on September 13.

The National Air Exhibition at Mines Field in Los Angeles was in its fifth day when Amelia showed up after a night's sleep at the Biltmore Hotel. This annual event was aviation's "Barnum and Bailey Show of Shows" with crowds of fifty to seventy-five thousand attending daily to watch the world's best aviators perform. When Amelia was introduced from the announcers' stand, she received a standing ovation. Two days later, Hollywood columnist Louella Parsons wrote that a movie company filming the aviation show failed to attract the attention of spectators who were more interested in getting "a glimpse of Colonel Lindbergh and Amelia Earhart."

While she waited for the Avian to be overhauled in Los Angeles, Amelia called on Bert and Cora Kinner. Cora, who had never forgotten "how she treated that old man," was still not impressed by Amelia. After Amelia told her she was tired of banquet hall chicken and longed for some of Cora's delicious pork chops, Cora fixed them, but grumbled later, "I didn't want to bother with her, but she had her pork chops all right."

That same week Amelia flew as a passenger to San Francisco, where she paid a visit to the Army's 381st Aero Squadron at Cressey Field. The squadron made her an honorary major and presented her with the silver pilot's wings of the U.S. Air Service. She obviously prized this gift more than any other she had received and wore the wings frequently for the rest of her life—even on formal gowns.

On the return flight east the Avian's motor died on her one hundred miles south of Salt Lake City. Making a dead-stick landing in a rutted field, she nosed the little plane over. This time, replacement parts required a ten-day wait in Salt Lake City. While she was there she gave speeches to the high school girls' assembly and the directors of the Community Chest, was taken to see copper mines and canyons, and was entertained by more than a dozen eager hosts. In an interview at the home of her principal hosts, the P. C. Schramms, she said she would gladly break another propeller to lengthen her visit to Utah. Wherever she stopped, she assured the residents that their town or city was a wonderful place in which she would like to stay longer. If her compliments were good copy for the local paper, they were also basically truthful. Amelia was an inquisitive, undemanding, and tireless tourist.

At her next stop, in Omaha, after a play she went backstage to talk to the stars, Lou Tellegen and Eve Casanova. She asked Casanova how she kept such a beautiful complexion and said hers was so sunburned and weatherbeaten that she was ashamed of it. Although she soon stopped talking about it in public, Amelia did think her skin was unattractive and that her figure was ruined by thighs that were too heavy. Slacks or floor-length evening gowns would hide the latter defect, but flying left her no escape from exposure to sun and wind. Her face was frequently sunburned, freckled, and sometimes peeling.

In Omaha she gave her only display of temper on the trip, after she discovered that there were no attendants at the airfield, her plane had not been serviced, and someone had folded back the wings the wrong way. Instead of criticizing the airfield attendants, she turned her ire on souvenir hunters. "Why they even cut pieces of the fabric from the wings of your machine," she complained, "and then ask you to autograph them! Some day a souvenir hound will carry off a vital part and there will be a crash," she told a reporter.

The flying vacation ended on October 13 in New York when G. P. presented her with a schedule of future engagements designed to boost sales of her book, *Twenty Hours Forty Minutes: Our Flight in the "Friendship,"* released a month earlier. In spite of brisk sales and generally flattering reviews, the book was not very interesting. Other than entries from Amelia's diary, it was a dull summary of the problems of commercial aviation and a plea for more support from the government and the public. The last chapter did show a flair for self-deprecating humor, a talent Amelia was already using to great advantage in speeches and interviews. In one account of her difficulties with photographers, she described a visit to Hyde Park High School where a cameraman, trying to include a group of students in the picture with her, asked her to step forward onto a grand piano that was level with the stage. In a note to her, a friend who saw the picture asked, "*How* did you get on the piano?" Amelia was certain her friend had pictured her making "scandalizing progress through the west, leaping from piano to piano."

Amelia did not complain about the heavy schedule of engagements made for her by G. P. He had financed the Avian for her, her first plane since she was forced to sell the Kinner Airster four years earlier. She had already collected other rewards. For appearing on the NBC broadcast in an auto show at Madison Square Garden, she had been presented with a blue Chrysler roadster. For her endorsement of a fur-lined, leather "Amelia Earhart Flying Suit," a Fifth Avenue department store gave her one. She had no intention of "wearing it up and down Fifth Avenue," as the advertisement claimed, but she had learned from G. P. that there could be considerable gain in enduring such foolishness.

However, G. P. made a mistake in advising her to accept fifteen hundred dollars for endorsing a brand of cigarettes with Stultz and Gordon. *McCall's* magazine, which had offered her a job, hastily withdrew the offer after an ominous number of former admirers, who believed that nice women did not smoke, wrote letters of protest. Amelia did not, in fact, smoke but Stultz and Gordon had needed the money and the tobacco company refused to use the advertisement without her name. Amelia countered by giving the entire sum to Byrd's upcoming South Pole expedition. Soon after, William Randolph Hearst's magazine, *Cosmopolitan,* came to her rescue with a job as aviation editor.

Her first article appeared in the November edition. Entitled "Try Flying," it was a dull rehash of material from her book. More interesting was the introduction of the magazine's newest columnist by O. O. McIntyre who called Amelia "a real American girl"—the answer to the problem of decadent, young American women indulging in everything from gin-guzzling to "harlotry." McIntyre claimed Amelia had already become "a symbol of new womanhood" that would be emulated by thousands of young girls. In time, his effusive accolade would prove to be true.

Amelia liked answering her mail, but dreaded writing the column, and made at least one attempt to hire a ghostwriter. During a week spent taking membership pledges for the American Red Cross at a table in Arnold Constable's Fifth Avenue store, Amelia met Ella May Frazer, a young freelance writer who introduced herself after she saw that Amelia sat alone, unrecognized by the shoppers. "She was the most *natural* woman in the world," Frazer said, "and didn't try to draw attention to herself—even as a saleswoman for the Red Cross." When Frazer returned several times during the week, Amelia told her that she dreaded the program proposed by *Cosmopolitan* in which she was to fly to a dozen cities in the next twelve months, writing an article on each flight and giving a lecture to a women's club in each city. She said it was impossible to take notes while flying, and once she landed there was always a group waiting for her, then a speech to make that same day. If Frazer would come with her, Amelia said, to take notes and do the writing, then she could fly and give the lectures. But first she would have to give Frazer a test flight to make certain she liked flying.

Frazer had not told Amelia that she was four months pregnant, nor had she informed her husband about Amelia's job offer. When she consulted her obstetrician he told her flying would be too dangerous in her condition and her husband absolutely forbade it. "Telling Amelia was terrible," she said. "She was very disappointed but she did say that she liked me and felt that we could have been a wonderful pair to do this." Eventually Amelia persuaded the magazine's editor to abandon the plan.

To supplement her income from endorsements, book royalties, and the magazine column, Amelia gave lectures, work that would eventually bring in the greater part of her earnings. G. P. helped her to become an accomplished performer. After assessing her appearance, voice, and personality, he asked for changes where he thought they were needed. He approved of her "natural" hairstyle, so artfully bleached and curled, so carefully disarranged, and of her posture, her expressive hands, and her low-pitched, musical voice. He thought she had excellent taste in clothes but called her hats "a public menace" and told her to wear one only when necessary and then only one with a small brim.

He taught her how to talk into a microphone, to point at a screen without turning her back to the audience, and to avoid lowering her voice at the end of a sentence. He also advised her on posing for photographers. At first the flare of flashguns had caught her pigeon-toed, her hands frozen at her sides, her wide smile revealing a marked space between her two upper front teeth. G. P. told her to close her lips when she smiled. Although she never liked being photographed, she learned to pose like a professional model.

After she returned from her cross-country flight, Putnam dispatched her on a round of lectures, including one in New Haven at a college aeronautical club conference hosted by Yale University, and another in Detroit where five hundred members of the Detroit Adcraft and Women's Advertising clubs packed the dining room of the Detroit-Leland Hotel to hear her speak. She was on her way to becoming a star of the nation's lecture circuit, the principal means by which celebrities could be seen before the advent of television.

G. P. continued to notify the press of her every move. In December she attended the International Civil Aeronautics Conference in Washington, which was followed by a celebration at Kitty Hawk, North Carolina, of the twenty-fifth anniversary of the Wright brothers' first flight. Although she was not an official delegate she was one of two hundred guests invited to go by sea on the steamer, *District of Columbia*. Three thousand others had to find their own transportation. In a letter to her mother Amelia wrote: "I was considered important enough to be the guest of the government so I am riding and eating free. . . . It's the kind of junket you'd like and had I any idea I was going I should have arranged for your coming."

Amy was fortunate to have missed it. The celebration was plagued by fog, rain, and transportation breakdowns but when the monument at Kill Devil Hill was unveiled on December 17, Amelia was right where G. P. wanted her to be—standing between Orville Wright and Sen. Hiram Bingham, president of the NAA.

A week later Amy went to the apartment in Greenwich House to spend the Christmas holiday of 1928 with her daughter. When Amelia bought two tickets to take her mother on an air tour over the city, her purchase was reported in New York newspapers. Amelia Earhart was still "news." In six months she had flown across the country and back, visited more than thirty cities, and given at least one hundred speeches and twice as many interviews. For the first time in her life she believed it might be possible to fly and earn a decent living.

CHAPTER EIGHT

The Vega

*B*y January of 1929 Amelia Earhart had become the best-known woman pilot in America. G. P. had made her famous but she never forgot that she had been nothing more than a passenger on the *Friendship*. Amelia wanted to fly—to go faster, higher, or farther than any woman (and if possible, any man) had ever gone before. She needed a plane designed to do it—a big powerful aircraft. Her choice was the Lockheed Vega. It took her six months to get it but a week before her thirty-second birthday she owned one.

During the first half of that year she made paid public appearances in twelve cities. Whatever her fees for these visits, she certainly earned them. For a typical one in Rochester, New York, in January her schedule included breakfast with the committee meeting the train at eight o'clock; an inspection of the airport and two airplane plants before noon; a luncheon and speech for the Advertising Club; a trip to nearby LeRoy, New York, where Donald W. Woodward who had purchased the *Friendship* had put the plane on display; tea with a LeRoy couple and dinner with members of the Rochester Automobile Dealers Association. Her speech at dinner was followed by an auto show at which she was cornered by a pushing, shoving crowd until she was rescued by two policemen and four association members who escorted her from the building. She returned to

New York on the ten o'clock train after fourteen hours of continuous public scrutiny.

Her lectures were a great success, although her audiences were more interested in her than in what she said. Amelia *was* the message. If anyone came expecting a coarse or odd person, perhaps even a lesbian (what sort of woman would challenge an ocean and suggest that other women become aviators?), they were disappointed. A woman who saw her in Detroit remembered her fifty years later as "a slender figure in grey chiffon with coral beads. Her smile and her gracious femininity were unforgettable, but what she said I don't recall."

Although audiences were more impressed by her presence than her message, Amelia was soon expounding her beliefs in the future of aviation, including jobs for women, mechanical training for girls as well as boys, world peace, and social and economic justice for everyone.

She continued to deny she was a feminist but insisted women had been handicapped as pilots by their lack of training, which men were given in the armed forces. "Not," she added, "that I am advocating our entrance into the army." She resented the lack of cost-free training but her pacifist convictions were as strong as ever. Before accepting an offer to speak to the Ohio Federation of Women's Clubs in April, she wrote to an NAA official asking that he check a rumor that one of the speakers was going to give an anti-pacifist address. He answered that the woman objected only to claims that the airplane was a deadly weapon, intended to incite hostilities. He also reminded Amelia that she would be speaking in support of civil aviation to the representatives of one hundred thousand women. She spoke.

Amelia's enthusiastic advocacy brought her a job offer from transportation czar Clement M. Keyes. Keyes, who was creating a transcontinental air-mail service with the Pennsylvania and Santa Fe railroads, hired Amelia as assistant to the general traffic manager of the new line. He also hired Lindbergh as chief technical adviser and began to refer to his newly created Transcontinental Air Transport as "the Lindbergh line." Amelia's job was to promote flying on TAT to women who were afraid to fly and discouraged their husbands from doing so. It was ideal for her. Headquarters were in New York, travel with the line was free, and she could continue to lecture and write, using the material she gathered along the way. Lindbergh and Amelia shared the spotlight during inaugural ceremonies on July 7—he in Glendale, California, and she in New York City, where she commissioned the TAT's flagship, the *City of New York*, then boarded the train with the passengers for TAT's first flight west.

The trip, which cost as much as one on the Concorde does now, was not an easy one. Because night travel by air was still very dangerous, the travelers were taken by train from New York to Columbus, Ohio, before boarding their first plane the next morning. The aircraft stopped at Indianapolis, St. Louis, Kansas City, Wichita, and Waynoka, Oklahoma. At Waynoka, passengers again took a night train, this time to Clovis, New Mexico. On the second morning of their journey, they boarded a second plane at Clovis, which stopped at Albuquerque, Winslow, and Kingman, Arizona, and finally, forty-nine hours later, at Glendale. The west-to-east flight followed this itinerary in reverse.

Lindbergh flew the first TAT plane east from Glendale as far as Winslow. At Winslow, he and his bride of six weeks, Anne Morrow Lindbergh, waited for Amelia's plane to arrive. From there the Lindberghs accompanied Amelia back to Glendale. Anne met Amelia for the first time in Winslow. Ten years Amelia's junior, the daughter of the ambassador to Mexico, Dwight W. Morrow, and the wife of the most famous man in America, Anne Lindbergh was even more reserved than Amelia and far more distressed by the relentless pursuit of newsmen and curious crowds. Anne liked Amelia. In a letter to her parents a few days later, when all three were houseguests of one of the future founders of TWA, Jack Maddux, she wrote that Amelia was "*very* likeable and very intelligent and nice and amusing."

Amelia was an enthusiastic, sometimes brazen salesperson for the new line. She told the crowd that met the plane at Glendale that transcontinental travel had become "a matter of a weekend." Four days later, she invited the mayor of Los Angeles to take an airplane ride with her. When he declined, she asked if his wife would like to ride. He replied that his wife was in bed as the result of an automobile accident. Amelia suggested that if his wife had ridden in a plane she might not have been injured. The mayor must have been annoyed but the press gave Amelia more free publicity for TAT.

Amelia's boss, traffic manager H. B. Clement, said that her job was to advise the line on comforts for women traveling by air, a task that required "the mind of a woman." The feminist who loathed the concept of "the mind of a woman" and who longed to see "the sex line washed out of aviation" was working for a blatantly sexist organization. Why? Too many years of near poverty? An aging mother in need of additional support? No other jobs in aviation? The chance to become a colleague of the men who financed, built, and flew the best airplanes in the world? Amelia did it for all these reasons and one more—the money to buy a battered, secondhand Lockheed Vega. The plane was in the hangar of Air Associates, Incorporated, the eastern distributors for Lockheed Aircraft Corporation. With its two-hundred-horsepower Wright Whirlwind engine, the Lockheed Vega was built for speed and distance and considered a difficult plane to handle. But during the previous six months, Amelia had been preparing for this as best she could.

In February of 1929 she took lessons in a Ford trimotor at Newark Municipal Airport from Colonial Transport pilot Edward Weatherdon. On March 3 she nosed over her Avian on a muddy field in New York, but just five days later she took and passed her tests for a commercial transport license in Brownsville, Texas. At least one reporter filed a story on the accident in New York, but none noticed what she did in Brownsville. That day all eyes were on Lindbergh, who was making an inaugural flight from Mexico City through Brownsville to New York. When thirty thousand fans stormed fences and broke through police lines, Lindbergh refused to leave his plane or to permit his passengers to do so until the crowd backed off. Eventually, his face flushed with anger, he was taken from the plane to a waiting car. It was not surprising that the only notice taken of Amelia was by one reporter who wrote that "she took a few flights around the field."

On March 27, the Aviation Bureau of the Department of Commerce wired her that her papers from the Brownsville examiner had not been received but that she had passed all tests. Her license was issued the next day. The number was 5716. Amelia became the fourth woman to hold a transport license after Phoebe Omlie, Ruth Nichols, and Lady Mary Heath.

No matter what her commitments she was always eager to fly. Most of the time she used the only plane she had, the Avian, although she had had two forced landings before the end of March. The first was en route from New York to Washington when engine failure brought her down at Philadelphia. The second occurred when hail during a violent thunderstorm threatened to split the propeller. She landed in a cornfield near Utica, New York, waded through the mud to a farmhouse and telephoned for a truck to haul the plane to town, then invited Muriel who was teaching in Utica to have dinner with her.

Whenever she was offered another airplane to fly, she accepted. After being "manhandled" by fans at an air show in Buffalo the night of March 26, she flew for most of the next day in several airplanes that were new to her, among them a new trainer intended for the army by its maker, Maj. R. H. Fleet, head of Consolidated Aircraft. She was accompanied by Fleet's test pilot, Leigh Wade, veteran World War aviator and later a major general in the Air Force. Wade had been pilot of the *Boston,* one of the three Army Air Service planes in the first round-the-world flight in 1924. The trainer he was demonstrating for Fleet was designed with "neutral stability," to respond to any change on the controls, good or bad, on the part of the student pilot. When Amelia took off into a strong southwest wind, Wade braced himself to take over quickly in case she made a mistake. She did not. "She was a born flier," he said, "with a delicate touch on the stick."

After taking the plane through a series of maneuvers Amelia looked back at Wade and laughed, pointing first in one direction, then in another. She was lost. She had been so intent on studying the controls and feeling the responses of the aircraft that she had no idea where they were.

A few years later, Wade saw what he thought was another demonstration of Amelia's instinctive skill when he watched her take off from Clover Field in Santa Monica. As her Vega headed toward the trees at the end of the runway, he saw intermittent puffs of black smoke in its wake, evidence of a badly misfiring motor. With the aircraft nearing stall point Amelia eased it up gently over the trees, circled the field, and landed. "There," Wade said, "was a pilot."

At least one colleague disagreed. Elinor Smith, holder of the women's solo endurance record who learned to fly when she was twelve years old, thought Amelia was an incapable amateur. Amelia came to New Castle, Delaware, while Smith was there for the trials of a new plane designed by Giuseppe Bellanca in which she intended to set a second record. Bellanca's test pilot, George Haldeman, invited Amelia to go up with him and Smith. Smith claimed later that as soon as Amelia took the controls "our big, calm bird suddenly lurched out of control." Amelia asked to go up again without Haldeman. When Smith took her up the second time, the same thing happened. They "slipped and skidded all over the sky," she said.

Smith's recollections of the incident were written a half century after a bitter dispute with George Palmer Putnam, long after the deaths of both Putnam and Amelia. She claimed that he had tried to hire her to fly Amelia's plane for her in the Women's Air Derby of 1929 and when she refused his offer he said that he would see to it that she never flew again professionally. It seems likely that Smith's differences with G. P. might have colored her view of Amelia's ability and it seems unlikely that Amelia could have been so inept when she had just passed the tests for her transport license.

Certainly the two women disagreed on the attributes of the Lockheed Vega. Smith said the Vega "had all the glide potential of a boulder falling off a mountain." That was after she bought one in 1931 for a transatlantic flight she hoped to make but cracked it up at Garden City four months later. Amelia, who thought the Vega was a great plane, never changed her mind. In 1933 she bought the same Vega Smith had cracked up from a subsequent owner and set three records in it.

While she looked for a Vega that was old (and cheap) Amelia flew whatever she was offered, including gliders in Michigan and, in May, a single-engine amphibian as copilot with Ralph DeVore. The flight was a near disaster. They were taking a Keystone Loening Air Yacht on an inaugural flight from Cleveland to Detroit when a fog forced them down on Lake Erie. They had no radio, so while the plane tossed on five-foot waves for almost three hours, search parties were organized ashore and newsboys were on the streets selling "extras" on the plane's disappearance. When the fog lifted, DeVore made it to the Detroit terminal. For most of the return trip, Amelia piloted the plane and pronounced the flight "a great lark," a phrase more suited to an Ogontz debutante than a working pilot.

Until July, most of Amelia's flying was in the Avian, which she took on the lecture and air show circuit whenever weather permitted. She also attempted to fly to Boston in it for Muriel's marriage to Albert Morrissey in West Medford on June 29, but was grounded by weather and missed the rehearsal. She made it in time for the ceremony, at which she was the maid of honor, then informed the officiating minister that she thought it would take more courage to marry than it took to cross the Atlantic in a plane.

There is no record of whether she talked first to someone at Air Associates in New York about buying the Vega or waited until she visited the Burbank plant of Lockheed while she was in California for TAT. She bought it in July—serial number 10, the tenth Vega built by Lockheed, registered to her as NC6911. The plane, which had been a demonstrator for a year and had been leased to New York's Mayor Walker, was reported to be in poor condition.

Amelia took possession on July 20, ten days before the bill of sale was completed, and went to Chatauqua, New York, where an audience of five thousand packed the amphitheater to hear her speak. She did not fly the Vega but took along a pilot, Lt. O. L. Stephens, either because she was not yet the legal owner or because she was still uncertain about her ability to land it on the fourteenth hole of the golf course like Stephens did. Years later, she told the great speed flier and test pilot Ben Howard that the first time she took the Vega up alone, the altimeter failed to function and with poor visibility she had to estimate how low she could safely fly by using a combination of readings from the fuel mixture control and carburetor response dials, a solution Howard thought ingenious and sensible.

She had to wait another two weeks after her return from Chatauqua before she could spend much time in the Vega. G. P. had scheduled other appearances, including a publicity stunt at Block Island off the coast of Rhode Island on July 23. Part owner of a submarine along with its inventor, Simon Lake, and a third man, Putnam had tried and failed to sell Lake's concept of an air pressure escape compartment to the Navy. Before he sold his rights to the ship, G. P. decided to use it for some free publicity for Amelia. He arranged for Amelia and Dorothy Putnam to swim out of the escape compartment of the submarine to the surface. Both women wore bathing suits but Dorothy looked a lot more attractive than Amelia, who was too thin. Amelia also donned a diver's suit and descended thirty-five feet to the bottom of the harbor where she remained for fifteen minutes. Unfortunately two St. Louis aviators, Forest O'Brine and Dale Johnson, broke the world's endurance record the same day, relegating Amelia's dive to the inside pages.

She also had work to do for TAT on the West Coast. This time she took Amy along. She was back in New York by August 3 for a national network broadcast to Richard Byrd at the South Pole. She finished at midnight and left the next morning with Lieutenant Stephens for Los Angeles where they arrived on August 7.*

When Amelia brought the plane to the Lockheed plant for an inspection flight, Wiley Post, the test pilot, said it was unfit to fly. Lockheed offered her a replacement, serial number 36, registered as NC31E. The trade was arranged by Carl B. Squire, the new general manager of Lockheed, which had just been purchased by a holding company, Detroit Aircraft Corporation. Lockheed was currently building a new plane for Lindbergh, the Lockheed Sirius,† and with Amelia in another Lockheed, Squire could claim as customers the public's king and queen of the air.

One year after the instant fame resulting from her transatlantic flight, Amelia was ready for another exploit. The fires of that fame needed refueling; the lecture circuit, new material; and Amelia, proof that she was more than an attractive, lucky pilot with a shrewd manager. The best opportunity offered her that summer of 1929 was the first cross-country women's air derby. Amelia took it.

---

* A week later Stephens was killed in a crash near Clovis, New Mexico. The thirty-eight-year-old Army man was flying a new plane he planned to use in the National Air Races at Cleveland when the vent for his cockpit blew off. While he was looking for it, he banked, went into a side-slip, and crashed.

† On display at the National Air and Space Museum in Washington, D.C.

CHAPTER NINE

Losing and Leading

*I*n August of 1929 Amelia was one of nineteen contestants in the first woman's cross-country air derby. She signed up for the race on her birthday, July 24, the same day the Vega became officially hers, but only after a six-week struggle over rules with the committee for the National Air Races. The all-male committee had suggested that the women's event, which would precede the air races at Cleveland, begin at Omaha rather than Santa Monica to spare the women the dangers of crossing the Rocky Mountains. An alternative suggestion from the committee was that of starting in California but with each woman accompanied by a male navigator. Amelia was outraged. She immediately became the self-appointed spokesperson for the perspective contestants.

On June 11 she sent telegrams of protest to both the NAA contest committee and the national races committee along with a statement to the press. It would be ridiculous, she said, to advertise the derby as an important event if the course was the easy route over the middle west from Omaha to Cleveland. As for taking along a male navigator, the proposal was an insult to contestants who were required to have a minimum of one hundred hours of flight time. If she were not allowed to fly solo from California, she said, she would not enter the race. She was joined in her protest by Lady Mary Heath, Elinor Smith, and Louise Thaden.

The NAA committee passed the buck to the manager of the National Air Races, Cliff Henderson, who persuaded the race committee to accept Amelia's terms. The race, they ruled, would extend over a period of eight days, starting August 18 at Santa Monica. The contestants would fly solo in planes to be rated as CW (85 to 115 cubic inch displacement) or DW (150 to 220 cubic inch displacement). Amelia signed up with six other women. Twelve eventually joined them.

Amelia's effort to gain recognition for women as competent pilots was not made any easier by Will Rogers, aviation aficionado and the nation's most famous humorist. In his nationally syndicated newspaper column, the gum-chewing pseudocowboy from Oklahoma called the race the "Powder Puff Derby." Feature writers followed his lead, referring to the women aviators as "Flying Flappers," "Aerial Queens," and "Sweethearts of the Air." To counteract this public perception of the derby as a female flying circus, Amelia said she thought it would be more important for all of the contestants to reach Cleveland safely than for any of them to set new records. Most did not agree. They flew to win and before the derby was over, one would die, and nearly all would narrowly escape serious injury or death.

Once Amelia had possession of the Vega, she had almost no time to fly it. Instead she spent her time publicizing the derby or working for her new employer, TAT. The last real rest she had was on the weekend before the derby, which she spent at Lake Arrowhead with Lindbergh's friends, Jack and Irene Maddux. One of Keyes's partners in TAT, Maddux was very fond of Amelia but saw nothing wrong in using her presence as his houseguest to gain recognition for himself and the new airline. Three days before the race he gave a dinner aboard a Maddux transport plane for Amelia, five other derby fliers, and the mayor of Santa Barbara. All of the women spoke on a national network hookup over the plane's radio. Maddux also arranged for Amelia and Irene Maddux to arrive in a Goodyear blimp at the start of the derby on Sunday, August 18.

Twenty thousand spectators gathered along the edges of the Santa Monica airfield or stood on a nearby hill under a fiery sun to see the derby fliers take off. Their nineteen planes were lined up at two starting lines on the field, six of the light CW class in front and thirteen of the heavier DW class behind. Amelia's light-green Vega was the sixth in the DW class to leave but at the south border of the field she turned back, circling until the last plane had left before landing. Her electric motor switch had shorted out, costing her fourteen minutes of lost flight time while repairs were made.

The first overnight stop, at San Bernardino, was chaotic. There were not enough mechanics or guards for the planes and long after midnight the women were still wrangling with officials over a scheduled stop the next day at Calexico, California, en route to Phoenix. A number of pilots in the DW-class planes who had used the field the week before said it was unsafe for heavy aircraft. One of them, Florence "Pancho" Lowe Barnes, a Pasadena heiress who had acquired her nickname from reputedly crewing on a banana boat running guns to Mexico, settled the matter. The stocky, profane, cigar-smoking Pancho, clad in riding breeches and leather boots, stomped from room to room with a petition stating that the fliers would refuse to continue the derby unless the first checkpoint was changed from Calexico to Yuma. The officials agreed.

By the end of the second day Amelia's hopes for a safe race to prove women were competent pilots had been dashed. She was one of the offenders, crashing at Yuma when her plane struck a pile of sand and nosed over. The accident did cause an unusual reaction from the derby fliers, ordinarily so fiercely competitive. They voted to give Amelia an extra hour and a half of waiting time without penalty for repairs. Later that day she almost cracked up again when she side-slipped and bounced in for a precarious landing at Phoenix.

As usual she refused to accept responsibility for the crash at Yuma. She had been told, she claimed, that the Yuma field was good for its entire length. "Instead I struck sand," she said. "There wasn't anything to do but let it [the plane] go over." Only a week before, the pilots who had objected to Calexico's field had also said Yuma's was not much better with soft, sandy spots—a difficult place to land.

Other competitors were having a worse time than Amelia. Marvel Crosson, a twenty-five-year-old Alaskan bush pilot, had disappeared after leaving Yuma. The slim, pretty Crosson, holder of a women's altitude record, had refused her colleagues' pleas to wait at Yuma for repairs to an engine that had been overheating since the beginning of the race. She did promise to "take it easy" to Phoenix, where a new engine was to be delivered and installed during the overnight stay there. No one had seen her since soon after she left Yuma.

Bobbi Trout, a twenty-three-year-old test pilot and former altitude and endurance record holder, was washed out of the race after drifting over the border into Mexico where she was forced down at Algondones. Her plane flipped over, destroying landing gear and propeller. Trout was not injured, but she had lost her chance to win the derby.

Carburetor trouble forced German flier Thea Rasche down at Holtville, California. Rasche showed reporters an anonymous telegram that read, "Beware of sabotage." Another contestant, Clare Fahy, echoed Rasche's accusations of sabotage at San Bernardino after mechanics discovered both center section wires of her plane had been severed. They attributed the damage to a rough landing but Fahy's husband, Lt. Herbert Fahy, said the wires had been weakened by acid and advised his wife to drop out of the race.

Four other fliers also had trouble. Ruth Elder reported that San Bernardino attendants had mistakenly put gas in her oil tank causing vapor to form on her goggles and a loss of ten minutes flying time while she circled over the desert cleaning them. Opal Kunz, whose husband was vice-president of Tiffany's, lost her way, ran out of gas, and landed in a creek bed four miles from Prescott, Arizona. A far more militant and outspoken feminist than Amelia, Kunz sought and got help from several male residents of the area who carried enough gasoline in tins to get her plane to Phoenix. Mary Haizlip, a professional flier from St. Louis, was also forced down, at Mexicali.

New Zealander Jessie Maude Keith Miller lost her lead in the CW division when she misunderstood the instructions for a fly-over of Calexico—and landed there. Miller, the first woman to fly from London to Australia (with Bill Lancaster, a man for whom she left her husband) shared a room with Amelia in Phoenix. Her roommate had more to say about the night at San Bernardino than Amelia. She told reporters it had been a waking nightmare in which unauthorized persons climbed in and out of the planes while the pilots were at dinner and none of the women slept more than two or three hours. "We're tired," she said.

Amelia was more worried than tired waiting for news of Marvel Crosson. It came the next afternoon at Douglas, Arizona. Crosson was dead, her body discovered near her plane by a search party in the mountains outside Wellton, Arizona. When Louise Thaden and Gladys O'Donnell heard the news they burst into tears.

There were other, less serious misadventures that day. Vera Dawn Walker, a Los Angeles actress, had been lost in New Mexico for more than an hour and Blanche Noyes, a Cleveland woman, also an actress, had flown almost sixty miles inside Mexico where she landed at Cananes to get her bearings but took off immediately when she saw a mob of villagers running toward her plane. Keith-Miller had damaged her Fleet-Kinner during a forced landing at Elfreida, Arizona, but managed to repair it herself, reaching Douglas late that night.

On the next, the fifth day of the derby, four more contestants met with accidents. At Pecos both Gladys O'Donnell, who ran an aviation school with her husband Lloyd at Long Beach, California, and Edith Foltz from Portland, Oregon, damaged their landing gears, although they completed the day's course to Fort Worth. Pancho Barnes was out of it after she overran the field at Pecos and plowed into a parked car, demolishing her aircraft. The fourth, Noyes, had a fire aboard. She landed thirty miles west of Pecos in some mesquite trees, burned her hands pulling smoking equipment from the baggage compartment, then took off again, tearing the bottom of the fuselage and smashing part of her landing gear. Noyes flew back to Pecos, had her hands bandaged, ordered parts for the landing gear sent to Fort Worth, called in the story to a Columbus newspaper, and took off again for Fort Worth. A fifth flier, Margaret Perry of Beverly Hills, was forced to drop out of the race when she was hospitalized at Fort Worth with typhoid fever.

The exhausted survivors were hustled into waiting cars at Fort Worth and taken to the estate of publisher Amon G. Carter where a banquet was given in their honor. Amelia now had an ally in Will Rogers who had followed news of the derby with great sympathy for the women pilots. He wrote in his column that race officials had been unfair in making the contestants stop "in every buffalo wallow that has a chamber of commerce. They even make 'em eat with Amen [sic] Carter," Rogers added.

On the morning of August 25 in East St. Louis ten of the eleven remaining fliers in the race had their picture taken.* All but two wore grease-spattered coveralls or riding breeches and boots. Only Amelia and Blanche Noyes were in blouses and skirts but they looked just as bedraggled as the others. Before they left, the fliers sent off a collective mes-

*Mary Haizlip was not in the picture. The day before she had been forced down at Washington, Missouri, by a broken fuel line. A farm hand helped her repair it but he was afraid to crank the propeller for her. Barely five feet tall and weighing less than one hundred pounds, Haizlip cranked it herself, then jumped back in the plane and took off for St. Louis, her hometown, where she arrived just before sunset.

sage to the local committee at Columbus where they would spend that night. They would, they said, eat anything except fried chicken, which they had eaten every night since leaving Santa Monica.

Amelia criticized more than the food when she arrived at Cleveland. The committee had left no time for the fliers to rest. They were up at four every morning, on the field by five and off at six, she said. The early flight was only two or three hours but the remainder of the morning was spent signing autographs and answering questions while guarding their planes from curiosity seekers. Most of the fields had no place to rest and no more than a wooden table to sit on. After flying two or three more hours in the afternoon they had to wait to see that their planes were secured before rushing into town to a banquet and then back to the field to make certain their planes had been serviced.

She also said there were unruly crowds wherever they went and that trying to taxi along a runway with people running toward one's plane with its whirling propeller was a frightening experience. Her complaints about the crowds were more than justified. At Columbus, the last stop before Cleveland, eighteen thousand fans overwhelmed the police, swarming onto the runway. A number of these boisterous trespassers leaped aboard the planes the minute they came to a stop and walked the length of the wings. Others poked umbrellas and pencils through the fabric-covered aircraft.

Amelia came in third in the derby, one and three-quarters hours after the winner, Louise Thaden. Thaden won $3,600 in prize money; Gladys O'Donnell, $1,950 for second place; and Amelia, $850 for third.

In the closed-course races that followed at Cleveland Amelia entered one of five for women. She asked Blanche Noyes to join her. "There are two Great Lakes airplanes we can get," she told Noyes. "If you fly one of them, I'll fly the other." When Noyes said she had never flown a Great Lakes before, the supposedly safety-conscious Amelia, who had never flown one either, said, "Well, you can learn."

Noyes learned during the race. She came in third but Amelia was disqualified for missing a pylon. It was obvious that she did not know how to turn tightly at these markers. Commenting on her lack of skill, the great closed-course racer Edna Gardner Whyte said that Amelia was never a good enough flyer for this kind of contest nor did she have the necessary competitive spirit. Another great speed flier, Mary Haizlip, agreed.

The day after her attempt at racing, Amelia was the only woman in a glider demonstration staged by the National Glider Association. Frank Hawks, the man who had given her her first plane ride almost a decade before, arranged the event, which he called "The Famous Motored Pilots' Derby." When Amelia attempted a turn without sufficient air speed the glider went into a spin. She pulled out of it a few feet from the ground but slammed the aircraft down in front of the grandstand, damaging the undercarriage. Hawks, who held the transcontinental speed record at the time, said that if she had lost her head she would have had a bad crash but "she kept her wits about her and did exactly the right thing."

The derby and the races that followed gave Amelia her first extended contact with many of the country's best women pilots. She listened more than she spoke and avoided gossip, asking for suggestions, and repeating praise but never criticism of one pilot by another. The best of her competitors thought her no threat to their supremacy as pilots and at the same time admired her for her public stand on behalf of their rights.

In California, before the derby, Amelia and Ruth Nichols had both talked to their colleagues about forming a women pilots' organization. In Cleveland an informal meeting was held in Amelia's hotel suite. In New York another group, some of whom worked for the Curtiss Wright Flying Service, had also discussed organizing. The group included Neva Paris and Opal Kunz, both derby contestants, and Frances Harrell, Margery Brown, Fay Gillis, Betty Huyler, and Clara Trenckman. All except Trenckman were fliers. This group sent out an invitation signed by Paris, Brown, Harrell, and Gillis to meet on November 2 in a hangar at Curtiss Field in Valley Stream, Long Island.

Amelia was one of the twenty-six women from six states who met in the hangar, where they had to shout over the din of airplane motors and drink their tea served from a toolbox wagon. Nancy Hopkins of Boston, who met Amelia for the first time at the meeting, thought she was very shy, even humble, in the company of many of the women who had more flight time than she. "She seemed apologetic over her unearned publicity from the 1928 flight," Hopkins said.

Amelia had very little to say during the meeting until discussion turned to a suitable name for the organization; she suggested it be called for the number of its charter members. Her suggestion was adopted. Between November and February of the next year the name evolved from The 86s to The 97s to The 99s, later changed to The Ninety-Nines, Inc.

Amelia was an avid recruiter. Her methods varied, depending on how well she knew the potential candidate and her interests. One who was drafted was Mary Haizlip, the petite and very competitive young derby flier who lived in St. Louis with her husband, future Bendix Trophy winner James A. "Jimmy" Haizlip, and her widowed mother, Anna Hays. A frequent houseguest of the Haizlips, Amelia sent Mary a note stating that Mary was now a charter member and should reimburse Amelia one dollar for signing her up and paying the membership fee.

In mid-March Amelia was hostess to twenty-eight members for a meeting at the American Women's Club on 57th Street in Manhattan. The organization was still without officers after the acting secretary-treasurer, Neva Paris, was killed in January when her plane crashed in a Georgia swamp. Amelia steered clear of office holding in an organization of so many strong-willed, competitive women who had yet to agree on anything more than a central purpose of finding more jobs in aviation for themselves and other women.

However, a month later she did agree to be chairman of a group of women pilots who met in Detroit to discuss the coming National Air Races in August of 1930. Overtures were made to contest director Maj. R. W. Schroeder, who tentatively offered a special speed race for women pilots comparable to the Thompson Trophy race for men, a "free for all" open to every type of plane. He advised Amelia that if six pilots "of the gentler sex" entered, he would add to the program a similar contest.

Amelia said she was confident that at least six women would enter but what she wanted was a women's derby like the one of 1929, in which planes of any classification could be entered with appropriate handicaps for the more powerful. A week later the events were announced. Forty-two of the forty-six would be restricted to small planes with none of the remaining four open to women. There would be two women's derbies, neither for larger planes. Amelia and four other women—Nichols, Smith, Thaden, and Noyes—refused to compete.

These members of the "gentler sex" did not intend to protest and then simply disappear. They set August 28 (later changed to August 27) as the date for a meeting of the Ninety-Nines in Chicago during the week of the races, which were to be held there instead of Cleveland, "in order to reach some agreement with the race committee" for the 1931 races. There were nineteen women at the meeting, seven of whom were licensed as transport pilots. The acting secretary-treasurer, Louise Thaden, appointed a committee of three in her place—Amelia as chairman, Jean LaRene of Kansas City, and Gladys O'Donnell of Long Beach. The entire group elected a constitutional committee of three—Amelia, Ruth Nichols, and Marjorie Lesser.

The seemingly shy, retiring woman who had said so little at the first meeting in November, the loser who had washed out of the closed circuit race, and who had almost killed herself trying to fly a glider in Cleveland had become the acknowledged leader of a group claiming 175 members out of the national total of 285 licensed women pilots.

CHAPTER TEN

Reaching the Limits

*T*wo days after the first meeting of the Ninety-Nines in November of 1929, Amelia left for California in the Vega she had flown in the derby. While she worked in Los Angeles she intended to trade the plane in for a better one. Accompanied by her newly hired secretary, Norah Alstulund, Amelia stopped first in Allentown, Pennsylvania, where Dorothy Leh, a charter member of the new flying club, put them up for the night. In an interview Amelia gave to a local reporter, she said that she was traveling on business for TAT. She was. Her business was getting free publicity for the airline. He was giving it to her.

Arriving in Los Angeles on November 8, Amelia, with Norah, was again the houseguest of the Madduxes. Her feisty, charming, forty-two-year-old host, an ex-submariner and car salesman, lacked both high school and college diplomas but his wife Irene had both, as well as considerable social poise and business acumen. A pilot herself, she took over her husband's Lincoln dealership when his airline interests demanded even more time than the tireless Maddux had. At the sprawling, comfortable house on Fremont Place, Amelia divided her time between working for TAT and shopping for her next Lockheed plane at the plant in Burbank.

In a logbook Amelia had started on July 20, she wrote that she tried out a new Vega in Burbank on November 9, the day after she arrived in Los Angeles. However, she was no more accurate in keeping a written account of her flight time than she had been as a novice, writing to Bert Kinner for an estimate. At the beginning of the log book she wrote that her total time to date, that is to July 20, 1929, was 559 hours and 46 minutes. It is difficult to see how she arrived at such a precise figure. The woman who was meticulous in financial matters, keeping records and receipts and demanding them from others, was amazingly casual in recording flight time and destinations. She had written in the new book that she flew her first Vega, "the clunk" she bought in New York, to Los Angeles between August 2 and August 8. No mileage, time, or stops were recorded. For her second Vega, which she flew in the derby, she made entries like the following one:

> Sept. 3, 1929 (thru November 5) NC31E [the plane's registration number] Cleveland-Buffalo-Rochester, NY.

In referring to her search for her third Vega she wrote:

Nov. 9	Lockheed	Trying Wasp job	2:00 hrs.
Nov. 10	"	Landings	1:00 hr.
Nov. 18	"	Speed Run, time not caught	
		" " 197 mph on 1 leg	
		Hooray!	

Newspapers kept a better record of what Amelia was doing. On November 21, after she flew a mile course at the Metropolitan Airport with Lt. Carl Harper, chief test pilot for Detroit Aircraft Corporation, in accordance with NAA rules, she announced she would attempt on the following day to break the women's speed record of 156 MPH held by Louise Thaden. She did it pushing a wooden-bodied, Executive SF Lockheed, a demonstrator owned by Detroit Aircraft and registered as 538M, to an average speed of 184.19 MPH over four laps. Her fastest lap was 197.80, according to the NAA's official timer, Joe Nikrent. However, in spite of Nikrent's careful timing with two chronometers sent on to the NAA in Washington for calibration, the NAA refused to acknowledge the record.

When Norah Alstulund wrote for confirmation of Amelia's record the following February, Maj. Luke Christopher, secretary of the NAA Contest Committee replied: "You will please advise Miss Earhart that there is no category in the FAI rules recognizing speed trials over a one mile straightaway course. The shortest course that is recognized by the FAI is three kilometers and this course is only for world maximum speed records."

"Only for world maximum" meant no category for women. Although Christopher referred to her as "my good friend, Amelia Earhart," and attached a list of recognized speed records to his letter, neither his claim of friendship nor Amelia's status as the newest member of the NAA's contest committee helped to affirm her record.

Amelia had no intention of abandoning her pursuit of official recognition for a speed record but let the matter rest while she continued to shop for a new Vega. She looked over everything Lockheed had, including Lindbergh's new Sirius, built with the special modifications requested by him. Lindbergh was not present for its maiden flight made by Carl Harper but on his last flight of the day in it, Harper took Amelia along as a passenger in the rear control seat.

Amelia could not afford a new, custom-built Sirius like Lindbergh's but she learned all she could about Lockheed's planes before she picked the one she could afford. It was another Vega, serial number 22, built before her derby plane in December of 1928, and previously used as a demonstrator on the East Coast. Although it was not registered to her as NC7952 until February 18, 1930, she had taken possession of it by the end of November and made repeated trial flights in it during the two months she was with the Madduxes.

A few days before she left for New York, the Lindberghs arrived at the Madduxes. Anne Lindbergh, who had previously reported to her family that Amelia was "likeable, intelligent, nice and amusing," when they first met the previous July on the inaugural flight of TAT, now wrote to her sister, Constance, that Amelia was "an amazing person—just as tremendous as C. [Charles Lindbergh]." Noting that Lindbergh had not spoken with Amelia at any length, Anne wrote that she thought the two were very alike. "She has a clarity of mind, impersonal eye, coolness of temperament, and balance as a scientist. Aside from that," Anne added, "I like her."

Amelia later wrote that during their stay at the Madduxes Anne told Amelia she had decided to learn to fly even before she met Lindbergh. Amelia thought Anne's dominant characteristic was "a fine courage to meet both physical and spiritual hazards with understanding."

As for Charles Lindbergh, Amelia had unlimited admiration for his aviation expertise but may have liked him less as a person. In writing about her departure for New York with Norah and thirteen pieces of luggage that comprised their winter and summer wardrobes, plus what Amelia called her "itinerant office," she noted that Lindbergh watched with disapproval:

> During our explanation, I sensed he was making a comparison with the impedimenta of a typical Lindbergh journey.
> He turned to his wife with a grin. "Don't you get any foolish ideas from this," he admonished.

Lindbergh, a devoted husband, was also a traditional one. No husband of Amelia's would have been permitted to tell her how much luggage to bring along.

Some of her reservations about Lindbergh may have been the result of his strange practical jokes. On a night when Anne and Amelia were drinking buttermilk at the Madduxes' kitchen table after a movie, Lindbergh, who was standing behind them, began to drip water from his glass onto his wife's silk dress. Anne got up and went to the door where she stood with her back to them, her head resting on her arm. Aghast at the possibility of gentle Anne driven to tears over her ruined dress, Amelia was soon delighted to see Anne wheel around and douse her husband with buttermilk. Lindbergh also thought it very funny.

Not every victim was as able to retaliate. During a later visit of the Lindberghs, nine-year-old Jack Maddux, Jr., who thought Amelia was a nice lady but whose idol was Lindbergh, was approached by the great man. Clad in his pajamas, the boy was saying goodnight to everyone. "How would you like to make a quarter?" Lindy asked. Jack said he would. Lindbergh made a paper cone and put the smaller end of it inside the front of the child's pajama pants. Then he gave him a quarter and said, "See if you can shut your eyes, hold the quarter up high, and drop it down into the cone." When the boy closed his eyes Lindbergh took a pitcher of ice water and poured it down the cone. The surprise was total, the pain excruciating.

On January 9, Amelia left for New York in her new Vega with Norah and the thirteen pieces of luggage. They spent the first night in Albuquerque at the Alvorado Hotel where a reporter telephoned Amelia's room at 8:15 P.M. and asked if he could see her. After muffled sounds of stuttering and laughter he heard her say, "I'm afraid not. I'm in bed, reading." However, she was willing to give him a telephone interview, most of which was about TAT. When he asked her how Lindbergh liked his new plane, she suggested he ask Lindbergh himself "when he comes through Albuquerque before long."

The next day she took off in freezing weather, attempting to reach Las Vegas, but was forced back to Albuquerque by a winter storm that had grounded all air travel east and west. Amelia had to leave her new Vega at Albuquerque and return to New York with Norah on a train. Leaving the new plane behind was a disappointment but she could not afford to wait for the weather to break. There were commitments to fulfill, magazine articles due, personal appearances scheduled, and family problems to be mitigated, if not solved.

Edwin, whom she had seen in California, was gravely ill. Muriel, pregnant with her first child, was also ill and Albert Morrissey was proving as difficult a husband and miserable a provider as Amelia had feared. Amy Earhart, with little of her own money left, lived with the Morrisseys in an uneasy and depressing household. Even before Amelia's return from the Coast, she had written her mother that it would be best to stay with Muriel and try "to keep out of Albert's way. I'm sorry she's [Muriel] having such rotten luck," she added, although she had always thought the marriage was more bad judgment on Muriel's part than bad luck.

In November on the day she broke the speed record Amelia had gone to see Edwin, who was remarried and was living in a cabin on Eagle Rock in the foothills behind Los Angeles. Although his wife, the former Helen McPherson, earned a small salary as a salesperson for a jewelry company and Edwin had made a down payment on the cabin, he was worried about keeping up his mortgage payments. He had closed his office in town and for much of the legal advice he gave to neighbors and friends he was reluctant to send any bills. "I'm long on friends," he told Amelia, "but short on cash."

Amelia paid the mortgage of about two thousand dollars and had a lawyer draw up a life tenancy freehold giving the property to her father and, in the event of his death, to Helen. Amelia retained title to the house. Soon after, she wrote to Muriel that she had made her the ultimate heir. In the same letter she reported, "I'm afraid Dad may not enjoy his cabin too long, Pidge . . . he looks thinner than I have ever seen him and Helen says he has no appetite at all and tires very quickly now."

These were all temporary measures to solve what she considered serious, ongoing problems. A plan for her mother's support took priority, one that would provide income on a regular basis. Amelia had to arrange it at a time when the world was entering the Great Depression. On October 24, 1929, "Black Thursday" to millions of Americans who had bought stock on a 10 percent margin, the market collapsed in the most catastrophic decline in the history of the exchange. The "crash" started with the dumping of over-inflated airplane stocks, threatening Amelia's own financial future, but she was determined to establish a regular source of income for her mother.

Soon after she returned to New York she wrote to Amy explaining the plan: "I am enclosing a check for $100. Hereafter you will receive it right from the Fifth Avenue Bank. I have put all my earnings into stocks and bonds and the yearly income in your name. The list includes the $1,000 bond of yours which you may have . . . at any time."

She also arranged for an accident endowment through the National Air Pilots' Association in Cleveland, naming Amy as beneficiary "in case I pop off," and in the same letter assured her mother she was not being deprived of her own comforts: "I am able to live easily on what I make and you may have the other. . . . I still have a job with Pennsylvania Railroad besides TAT-Maddux. I plan to work very hard this year and do little else but fly."

She repeated these reassurances in another letter on February 25, the day after she returned from her second trip to the coast to pick up the plane she had left in Albuquerque: "Please do not think you are taking my hard-earned money even tho I would give it willingly. What you receive comes from what the cash receives from being put into bonds, etc. . . . extra to what I earn. I am living with Norah and very economically."

However, what she earned was *not* easy to come by. Aviation was a luxury in a depressed economy. Air shows were resorting to sideshow stunts of the previous decade and to the appearances of celebrities in order to attract the public. At a weeklong exposition in St. Louis, attended by one hundred twenty-five thousand spectators: "A Guernsey cow of famous lineage was carried aloft in a tri-motored Ford from the Parks airport and submitted to being milked in the air well above the smoke of St. Louis. The milk in pint containers fastened to small parachutes was dropped over the side. . . . A pint of the milk is being saved for Colonel Lindbergh who is expected here tomorrow [February 19, 1930] from Los Angeles."

Amelia arrived the next day on her way east in her new Vega, in time to fly in an exhibition with Clarence Chamberlin, Frank Hawks, Elinor Smith, "Speed" Holman, and Jimmy Doolittle. In April she was aboard the aircraft carrier *Lexington* off the Virginia coast observing maneuvers along with Hiram Bingham, the assistant secretaries of Navy and Commerce and members of the Senate and House Naval Affairs Appropriation Committees. Appearances like these were needed to retain the celebrity status that assured her income from lectures, articles, and advertising testimonials.

Between April and the last week of June she gave more than a dozen talks in as many towns, often two in the same day to different organizations. On April 8 she was the only woman guest at a banquet attended by twelve hundred members of the Society of Automotive Engineers in Detroit. Between May 12 and 16 she spoke in Kansas City, Indianapolis, Chicago, and Detroit, flying to all of these engagements.

From Detroit she flew to Philadelphia to ferry a delegation from the Philadelphia Club of Advertising Women to a convention in Washington. Elizabeth Townsend, who was one of three passengers on Amelia's plane, had to leave Amelia at the airport in Washington to meet a welcoming committee but her companions told her that they saw Lindbergh in the terminal building and "were astonished at how much they [Amelia and Lindbergh] looked alike."

Never one to abandon any goal she had set, Amelia continued her efforts to persuade the FAI to set up separate classifications for women in altitude, speed, and endurance records. It was a difficult position for her to take. A believer in real equality with no special wages or working conditions for women by law she had to admit that until women had more flying experience they could not compete with men. Women should be allowed special record categories, she claimed, as well as the right to challenge world records.

As soon as the FAI created these special women's classifications Amelia decided to make a try for speed—this time with all necessary documentation. She started by asking George Fritsche of the Detroit Aircraft Corporation, a holding company that had bought Lockheed, to cable the FAI's American representative organization, the NAA, the following: "Please send book of rules showing proper procedure conducting world record flights. Is barograph needed for three and one hundred kilometer flights? Is electric timing necessary for three kilometer flights? . . . How many times must three kilometer and one hundred kilometer flights be run? Where can we procure two certified timing watches?" The NAA contest committee, of which she was still a member, replied there was no copy of FAI rules, but sent her two typewritten, single-spaced pages of rules.

After another week of sending telegrams and awaiting replies Amelia could wait no longer. She flew the trials in a Vega registered as CN974, lent her by Lockheed, between June 24 and July 5. During the next twelve months more than fifty cables and letters were exchanged by her, Cooper, the NAA office in Washington, and the FAI in Paris. As late as ten months after the trials one official wrote another for affidavits signed by the pylon observers, asking him to send them immediately because "Miss Earhart feels quite strongly about this." Miss Earhart did and Miss Earhart prevailed. One year after the trials the FAI entered on its official roster these three records for Amelia Earhart:

> June 25, 1930. Women's world speed record for 100 kilometers at 174.897 mph. (No load.)
>
> June 25, 1930. Women's world speed record with payload of 500 kilograms over a distance of 100 kilometers at 171.438 mph.
>
> July 5, 1930. Women's world speed record over 3 kilometer course of 181.18 mph.

Proud of her new records, Amelia was just as enthusiastic about aviation as a practical means of transportation. Before the summer was over she helped to organize a new airline, the New York, Philadelphia, and Washington Airways, which opened on September 1. As vice-president in charge of public relations she was on the second plane leaving the New York terminus on that first day of operations. The three-city line was commercial aviation's first version of the modern shuttle, its slogan, "On the Hour Every Hour." Paul F. Collins, the general manager, and his assistant, Eugene Vidal, were both former officials of TAT who were fired by Clement Keyes when TAT merged with Maddux.

Amelia first met Collins in St. Louis when both were with TAT. Arriving alone at Lambert Field in her Vega, Amelia mentioned she was on her way to Washington. Collins said he and his assistant, Don Bartlett, were also going there. When she invited them to fly with her, Collins hesitated. He had been one of the first airmail pilots, one of the few who survived, a typically nervous passenger who had never been piloted by a woman.

> Apparently she sensed my reluctance to fly with her principally because I knew that the cockpit in a Vega was completely shut off from the cabin and there could be only one pilot . . . and no way of exchanging seats. She then asked me if I'd like to fly the Vega myself while she and Don sat in the cabin. . . . This was the first insight I'd had into Amelia's kindness, her generosity and her beautiful character.

After a night's layover in Columbus, they left on the second leg of the flight, but a malfunctioning compass and poor visibility caused Collins to lose his way. He was saved from admitting it by sighting a railway and finally, a rooftop sign reading "Fredericksburg." "I never mentioned my predicament to Amelia and neither did she. Whether or not she sensed the situation, I'll never know. If she did, it was just another illustration of her understanding."

Collins's friend and assistant in the new airline, Eugene Vidal, was a handsome West Point graduate, a former Army pilot, ex-Olympic athlete, and son-in-law of Sen. T. P. Gore of Oklahoma. Two years Amelia's senior, he also met her while working for TAT: "She was an interesting person; a tomboy who liked all men's games, enjoyed being with mechanics working on airplanes, and yet was like a little girl. . . . Although often in trousers, she was very feminine and quite romantic in many ways. She wrote poetry for magazines under another name and often showed me the poems before mailing them."

With Collins and Vidal running it, Amelia doing the public relations, and financial backing from Philadelphia financiers Charles and Nicholas Ludington, the line became a successful one, although not without initial difficulties. On one occasion soon after opening the line, three planes landed at the Philadelphia airport at one time, one from Atlantic City, one from Newark, and one from Washington. Some of the passengers were changing planes and others got out to stretch. In trying to get all of them back on the planes the dispatcher put ten of the Washington-bound passengers on the Newark-bound plane, returning them to the airport they had just left.

Lunches consisted of hardboiled eggs and saltines, thought to be the least likely food to induce air sickness. However the smell of exhaust fumes in a cabin with closed windows and no air conditioning brought about frequent use of cardboard cartons, not always successfully. Nevertheless passengers on the new line were airborne for shorter times than on TAT with less devastating effects than those reported by Ben Howard: "When TAT reached only 75 percent air sickness we thought we'd passed a point in aviation history. . . . People were so sick they used rubber matting instead of carpeting on the floor of the plane. . . . They used to say passengers didn't get out of a plane, they slid out—skated down the aisle."

Collins and Vidal were determined to prove an airline could be profitable without revenue from airmail. They cut costs ruthlessly, using tri-motor Stinson monoplanes that cost half as much as Ford transports. They saved fuel by instructing pilots to taxi to the line on one motor, and after taking off on all three with high-test aviation gas, to switch to cheaper automobile gas once airborne.

During the first ten days of operation the line carried 1,557 passengers. Too cautious to give his own name to the airline, Charles Ludington, chairman of the board, said it was too early to say whether passengers were traveling for curiosity or business. At the end of the first year he changed his mind and the corporation became the Ludington Line after the books showed a profit of $8,073, hardly an overwhelming sum but impressive for an airline without mail subsidies during a year of deepening economic depression.

In the report to the press on the first ten days of operation, the vice-president in charge of public relations said that a little less than half of the tickets had been sold to women, adding, "I know one woman who came up from Washington on an early plane, completed her shopping in New York and returned to Washington in time for dinner." She not only knew her, it is likely that Amelia talked her into taking the trip.

Janet Mabie, a *Christian Science Monitor* feature writer whom Amelia invited on one trip, wrote that Amelia rode a portion of the route at least once every two days. "She keeps her hands still and her voice down and economizes her energy," Mabie claimed.

Amelia certainly needed to "economize her energy." Within a week of starting to work in earnest on the new airline in August she wrote to her mother:

> I saw Dad on the coast and he is desperately ill and starving to death. There is a stricture of some kind which prevents his taking much nourishment. His mind is clear and he says he's better . . . ask Pidge to write his

doctor for a summary of the case. Mrs. Earhart is almost breaking under the strain so I said I'd help out in monthly payments so she could rest. . . . I want to have a good doctor see Dad if the report doesn't seem adequate."

She added that she would like to find time to see Amy who was summering at Marblehead but that she was working very hard and was not feeling well.

On September 3 she forwarded to her mother a cable from Edwin's physician, Dr. C. M. Hensley of Eagle Rock. The doctor wanted a guarantee of $175.00 for blood transfusions. Amelia pencilled on it, "of course I guaranteed." She had also received a wire from Helen Earhart reporting that Edwin weighed eighty pounds and was sinking rapidly. Hensley had written Muriel that Edwin had cancer of the stomach and an operation would hasten his death. The transfusions would be done but there was little hope for the patient's recovery.

Two weeks later Amelia wrote again, apologizing to Amy for the delay because she was so busy on the new airline:

> I received a telegram from Dr. Hensley saying I must come soon. Also Mrs. E [Helen Earhart] wired that Dad was perfectly rational and anxious to see me. It is so hard to get away, so expensive, that I am almost staggered with the thot of going west. However, I feel I must grant [his] wish and will probably shove off tomorrow. One thing, he is not suffering. . . . I suppose he is too weak for an operation but it seems as if I'd prefer that risk than starving as he is now.

Edwin's illness was not all that worried Amelia. Muriel was not getting along with Albert Morrissey, and Amy, who was living with them, was embroiled in this miserable domestic situation. Amelia offered to get Amy a room in her hotel in New York, commenting on Muriel: "I do hope Pidge moves out of her hole. I feel as you do it's bad for health and morale. All the middle-classness of the family heritage bursts into bloom. . . . All the fineness—for there is some—is squashed. It would be unless you were around. These are sad times."

Amelia left the next day on TAT, arriving in Los Angeles on September 19 and remained with Edwin for four days before boarding a return flight for New York. At Tucson, eight hours after her departure, she received word that Edwin had died. During her stay with him she had listed his debts and paid some, arranged for his burial and written his obituary. She did not return for the funeral. Instead, within a few hours of arriving in New York from the two-day-and-night trip on TAT she flew her Vega from Newark to Norfolk, Virginia where she had a lecture scheduled for the same day—September 25.

Coming in for a landing at the Naval Air Station she crashed. Edna "Eddie" Whiting, the thirteen-year-old daughter of station commander Capt. Kenneth Whiting, saw the plane from the upstairs window of their house before the crash trucks arrived: "Runways had not been invented. The air station field was reclaimed land pumped up out of the waters of Hampton Roads. . . . As a result the field had a number of potholes and puddles. As Amelia landed she saw a pothole or puddle. She slammed on her brakes in an effort to miss the hazard."

The latch on the door to the cockpit, which was part of the back of the pilot's seat, gave way, throwing her backward. At the same time, Carl Harper, who was in the back of the plane, leaped forward to close the cockpit door, leaving the rear end without his balancing weight and the plane nosed over.

As usual Amelia told the press it was one of those "little things," but she did admit to "over-application of the brakes." Veteran airman Ben Howard, who had not yet met Amelia but read the news report, said her admission was unheard of among pilots of the time and that he thought "that gal must be something."

Harper's only injury was a broken finger. Amelia was treated for a scalp wound by the station flight surgeon, who fashioned a bandage that looked like a white turban. Eddie's mother added a rhinestone pin to it and Amelia kept her speaking engagement with the Norfolk-Portsmouth Traffic Club.

During the four days Amelia stayed with the Whitings, young Eddie observed that she slouched or draped herself in chairs and had "the longest legs I had ever seen." She made a great many long-distance calls, some of them to George Palmer Putnam. Asked to relinquish her room to the unexpected guest, Eddie was not overly impressed with Amelia, especially after she heard what Amelia was reported to have said to her father. When Captain Whiting asked Amelia what she wanted done about the Vega, she said, "It's your problem. You take care of it and ship the plane back to New York."

If the captain interpreted her comment correctly, his houseguest who had been so frequently praised by hosts for her courtesy showed him very little. She did write a thank you note to Mrs. Whiting on September 30 from New York:

You were very kind to take in so cordially a broken down (up) aviatrix. I appreciated your hospitality and think sometime I'll try to land in your front yard. I have been very busy since my return, carrying on of an airline is certainly a time-occupying occupation. . . . I hope your daughter had a swell time at Annapolis. Please thank the Captain, your husband, for sending Carl Harper and me to Anacostia.

Fatigue and sorrow may have caused her lack of courtesy in regard to the plane but the Whitings were told nothing about the death of her father or of the eight days with little or no sleep that preceded the crackup at Norfolk. In a letter to her mother on October 2 Amelia was more honest about her sense of loss but not about the accident in which the Lockheed was so badly damaged it had to be shipped to the Detroit Aircraft Corporation in Detroit to be completely rebuilt. To her mother she wrote:

I have just returned from Dad to have a little crackup due to a mechanical failure. . . . I wasn't hurt much and neither was the Lockheed. About Dad. The diagnosis was correct. . . . He grew thinner and thinner and waited for me to come and change doctors or get him to a sanitarium or change diet because he didn't want to go. I tried and had X-rays to please him and he hoped until he could not move his poor hands. He didn't miss [me] when I left as we gave morphine at the last so he wouldn't worry about [my] leaving.

His big case [a law suit he hoped to win] was lost and we told him he won. He couldn't have stood the disappointment so it was for the best. I wrote up the little history and paid the hundred little debts he always had. . . . He asked about you and Pidge a lot and I faked telegrams for him from you all. He was an aristocrat as he went—all the weaknesses gone with a little boy's brown puzzled eyes.

At the close of this letter Amelia said she would try to get to Philadelphia to see Amy, who was visiting relatives, but that she was "full of anti-tetanus serum so not feeling up to snuff."

There can be no doubt that she was "not up to snuff." No matter what his faults, Amelia had never stopped loving her father. His death was a painful loss, coming at the close of a year of exhausting work in a kind of perpetual motion. She had met all her goals, fulfilled all her contracts, kept all her promises. Spokesperson for her colleagues, airline officer, lecturer, writer, and breadwinner, she was now in the records books of the FAI. She had been named by famed journalist Ida Tarbell as one of the fifty living women who had done the most for the United States, showing ability "to initiate and create, lead and inspire." A commemorative column to her had been unveiled at Burry Port, Wales, in honor of her Atlantic crossing. But the pace was a killing one, so demanding that she might not have been able to maintain it alone.

Help was being offered. George Palmer Putnam, the man who had "discovered" her, managed her, and published her, wanted to marry her.

CHAPTER ELEVEN

A Marriage of Convenience

On December 19, 1929, Dorothy Putnam divorced G. P. Within hours reporters were calling Amelia, asking if she would be the second Mrs. Putnam. They were given a curt denial. Twenty-five days later, when Dorothy Putnam married again, there were more calls and more denials from Amelia. "There is nothing to the rumor," she said. "I am not engaged to anyone. Mr. Putnam is my publisher—that's all."

When she saw Marian Stabler in New York in January she told her, "Everyone thinks G. P. and I are going to be married."

"Are you?"

"No." Amelia replied. "I think the divorce is a shame. . . . A marriage that's lasted eighteen years with two children shouldn't be that easy to break up."

Amelia did not want to marry G. P. or anyone else. To a friend she wrote: "I am still unsold on marriage. I don't want anything all of the time. . . . Do you remember in 'If Winter Comes,' how Mabel was always trying to get her husband a 'den,' how he hated it? He said he wasn't a bear. A den is stuffy. I'd rather live in a tree."

During the next two years G. P. proposed six times but, like Simpkin the cat with whom Amelia compared him—storing up numerous spare mice for other meals—G. P. did not neglect numerous other projects he had planned. One of them was working with Byrd's agent, Hilton Railey, on an upcoming Putnam publication, the explorer's second book, *Little America.* G. P. monitored the script, as he had Amelia's *Twenty Hours Forty Minutes,* to make sure the book would be in the stores while the author's name was still in the headlines. He arranged for Byrd to write much of the book before his return from the Pole and for Railey to meet Byrd at the Panama Canal Zone and bring whatever was finished back to New York.

In July G. P. gave a luncheon at the Barbizon-Plaza, ostensibly for Byrd, at which he announced the forthcoming publication of seven books on the expedition to be published by G. P. Putnam's Sons. Not long after, Putnam's friendship with Byrd ended, as well as his own affiliation with G. P. Putnam's Sons. G. P. said his difference with Byrd arose from his suggestion to the admiral that Byrd offer the contributors to his expedition a rebate from profits he was making on book royalties and lectures. "Dick," Putnam said, "didn't see it. He felt that as he took the risks, he was entitled to the rewards." Putnam's departure from the firm his grandfather had founded followed the death of its president, his uncle, George Haven Putnam. G. P. sold his shares to his cousin, Palmer C. Putnam.

Already an artists' representative with offices in the Seymour Hotel at 2 West 45th Street, G. P. joined publishers Brewer and Warren, which soon became Brewer, Warren and Putnam. He also wrote a biography of Salomon August Andre, pioneer arctic balloonist who was lost in 1887 and whose bones were found in 1929 on a desolate arctic island. The book, dedicated to "a favorite aeronaut," came out on October 27.

Twelve days later a marriage license was issued to George Palmer Putnam and Amelia Earhart. On Saturday, November 8, Amelia was met at the Groton, Connecticut, train station by G. P. and taken to the house of his mother, Frances (Mrs. George Bishop) Putnam, in nearby Noank. The license was issued by Probate Judge Arthur F. Anderson, a friend of G. P.'s who accompanied G. P. and the town clerk, Henry L. Bailey, to Mrs. Putnam's house for Amelia's signature. But when Amelia found out that G. P. had alerted the press she left in a huff early the next morning for New York and flew to Washington later that same day.

On Monday the Associated Press reported that Amelia denied she and G. P. were married. Carl B. Allen, aviation reporter for the *World* (later for the *New York World-Telegram*), who was a friend of Amelia's, called G. P.'s mother. Frances Putnam said she did not know if they were married yet but "newspapers up here published all sorts of garbled reports." G. P. could not be reached at his Sutton Place apartment.

When Allen called Amelia in Washington and asked if a license had been issued, she evaded his question with, "I have not been married." Did she plan on being married immediately, Allen asked. "Well, not immediately," she replied. In New York G. P. would answer only two of Allen's questions. Was he married? "No." When would he be? He didn't know.

Allen wrote that the Putnam-Earhart story would be a trilogy. The first volume, covering Amelia's withdrawal from Noank to Washington, he titled, "Amelia Goes Voyaging." (David Putnam's first book for boys had been *David Goes Voyaging*, written when he was twelve years old, after accompanying an expedition to the Galapagos Islands as the ship's cabin boy.) The second volume Allen called "G. P. in Baffle Land," parodying *David Goes to Baffin Land*. The third, Allen concluded, "may be expected any day now." He was wrong. Rumors that there would be no marriage were soon circulating.

In late December, after a press conference on a proposed flight by Amelia, she telephoned Allen at the *World.* "I need some advice," she told him "and I need it today." She wanted to talk to him and another aviation reporter-friend, Lauren Dwight "Deke" Lyman of the *New York Times.* Could they come to her apartment? They could.

After receiving their promise of confidentiality, she told the two men that although she had "squelched G. P. in denying reports of the marriage," and he "sulked about it a while," he had apologized for alerting the press, "and he still wants to marry me."

Should she, she asked, marry Putnam? Allen and Lyman were stunned. They had never discussed her personal life with her and did not like being forced by competing newspapers to cover the marriage story. After a long, embarrassing silence, Allen answered. "It seems to me, Amelia, that the question you have just asked Mr. Lyman and me really contains its own answer: either you should be able to make up your own mind or you should put off getting married until you yourself can decide."

As they were leaving Amelia extended one hand to each of them in a "firm and prolonged triangular leave-taking," while she told them that just talking it over had helped. In a later recollection of that meeting, Allen wrote that he told Amelia that Putnam loved the reflected public glorification that she received and was certain that he had helped to create it. "It may be," Allen added, "that you need him as much or more than he needs you—and one of the supposedly solider cornerstones of marriage is mutual need and mutual respect."

There was nothing in Allen's assessment of G. P. that Amelia did not know. The charming, erudite editor counted among his friends and acquaintances many who were famous and few who were not. G. P. liked celebrities.* Amelia also knew that G. P. was a hard-bargaining, often penny-pinching, volatile, hot-tempered man who shouted profanities (although not at her) when frustration induced one of his choleric rages. Her cousin, Lucy "Tootie" Challis, who was working as an editor in New York, commented that "keeping an eye on him would apt to make one cross-eyed. Tho I have always been fond of him, he is unpredictable to say the least."

G. P. admitted to being bossy, saying he "deluged Amelia" with instructions about her clothing, her hats, and her speeches. But years later his fourth wife, a beautiful and intelligent woman who never knew Amelia, said, "He could be arrogant, but only with his equals—not with a brick layer or gardener. . . . He was a charming man, a great raconteur, who had marvelous manners and a wonderful sense of humor."

Putnam claimed, "Amelia Earhart knew me better, probably, than anyone else ever can," adding that their tastes were often the same but their temperaments were not. She was calm. He was not. She hated to hurry. He always did. She wanted to do one thing at a time. He wanted to do many. She remained poised under pressure. He stamped and shouted. He had to be busy. She "was subject to seizures of idleness, times when she was determined not to see anyone and to do absolutely nothing but stay by herself and think."

---

*Among those he saw regularly were humorists Will Rogers, Robert Benchley, and Don Marquis, critic Alexander Woollcott, cartoonist Percy Hammond, and novelists Dorothy Canfield Fisher and Louis Bromfield. He had given artist Rockwell Kent financial backing. His cronies at the Explorers Club were Martin Johnson, William Beebe, Roy Chapman Andrews, and Sir Hubert Wilkins. His banker was Edward Streeter, a vice-president of the Fifth Avenue Bank but also author of a bestseller, *Father of the Bride,* later a successful film. G. P. listed as some of the best conversationalists in America, all of whom he knew well, conductor Leopold Stokowski; editors Clifton Fadiman, Frank Crowninshield and Clare Booth (not yet Mrs. Henry Luce) and Helen Rogers Reid, who took over as editor-publisher of the *New York Herald Tribune* after the death of her husband, Ogden; historian Hendrik Willem Van Loon, and Hollywood dress designer Gilbert Adrian.

In January Amelia made up her mind. If G. P. needed to bask in her limelight, she needed him to maintain that limelight. He had other interests that allowed her the freedom she needed. Her absences in pursuit of her career he would understand. As her manager he would arrange for most of them. He would take care of the "grubby" work.

Her decision to marry was opposed by her mother who said G. P. was "twelve years her senior and a divorced man." (Actually he was ten years older.) Amelia ignored Amy's protest and did not tell her when she would be married. Three days before the ceremony she wrote, "I shan't be home over this weekend. . . . I'm due in Washington tonight and have a luncheon at Newark today."*

She married G. P. three days later, on February 7, 1931, at Frances Putnam's house in Noank. Present for the ceremony were G. P.'s mother, his uncle, Charles Faulkner, Judge Anderson who officiated, the judge's son, Robert, who was Mrs. Putnam's lawyer, and twin black cats. Young Anderson, two years out of law school, recalling the day in November when she signed the marriage license, thought that she was "devoted to George" but that she was afraid that changing her name somehow would diminish her stature. He was right. On the eve of the wedding she wrote to G. P.:

> There are some things which should be writ before we are married . . . you must know again my reluctance to marry, my feeling that I shatter thereby chances in work which means most to me. I feel the move just now as foolish as anything I could do.
>
> I know there may be compensations but have no heart to look ahead. On our life together, I want you to understand I shall not hold you to any medieval code of faithfulness to me nor shall I consider myself bound to you similarly. If we can be honest, I think the difficulties which arise may be avoided should you or I become interested deeply or in passing in anyone else.
>
> Please let us not interfere with the other's work or play, nor let the world see our private joys or disappointments. I may have to keep some place where I can go to be by myself now and then, for I cannot guarantee to endure at all times the confinement of even an attractive cage.
>
> I must exact a cruel promise, and that is that you will let me go in a

---

*That night in Washington she received a record-affirming certificate from the NAA stating that she had flown more than 181 miles per hour for a new women's speed record.

year if we find no happiness together. I will try to do my best in every way and give you that part of me you know and seem to want.

A. E.

Before the ceremony young Anderson sat with Amelia on a couch in a small sitting room at the back of the house. He thought her much more attractive than depicted in the press, "quite delicate looking, with beautiful color." She told him about the autogiro, a new type of aircraft she had flown for the first time in December. After her brief exchange of marriage vows with G. P., she returned to the couch and resumed her description to Anderson of the new aircraft!

When Judge Anderson came forward to wish her happiness, calling her "Mrs. Putnam," she told him she would continue to use her maiden name in her work. A month later the *New York Times* used "Mrs. George Palmer Putnam (Amelia Earhart)" for the first and last time. After that she was Amelia Earhart Putnam.

Amelia sent a telegram to Muriel asking her to "break the news gently" to Amy who was in Philadelphia, where her sister, Margaret Balis, was dying of cancer. The bride was childless but not without a dependent family. As early as four months before her marriage Amelia had written to Amy about the monthly checks she sent to her: "I know how easy it is for you to give it [the money] away to Pidge and the Balises. However, I am not working to support either. . . . I don't know when I shall get over to Philadelphia for a visit. I come over fairly often on business." She did not visit her mother or her aunt and when Margaret Balis died in January, Amelia did not go to the funeral, claiming the telegram had not reached her until after the services.

Amelia insisted that Amy use her allowance for herself and to regard Muriel's needs as a separate issue. When Muriel and Albert asked for a loan for the purchase of a house, Amelia wrote to Amy that she might ask her to look at it and give her opinion, but, she added, "If she [Muriel] hasn't mentioned it to you, don't say anything."

Amy redeemed herself momentarily by her public statements regarding Amelia's marriage. Amelia wrote, thanking her for the interview she had given in Philadelphia and invited her to come and stay in the Putnams' new apartment at 42 West 58th Street [the Wyndham Hotel] where she had "two canaries," just as she had always wanted. She also told her mother that she had sent Muriel twenty-five hundred dollars so that she could "move into a decent house," and had asked Muriel to come to New York "before she becomes too tied down."

Muriel was about to be "tied down" by a pregnancy of which Amelia disapproved because Muriel's husband failed to give her an adequate household allowance. Amelia, who had given Muriel a book on birth control, *The Doctor's Manual of Marriage,* when she married Albert had hoped Muriel might make use of it.

In April Amelia was still annoyed with her sister, complaining to Amy that Muriel had not sent her a properly drawn second mortgage: "I am not Scrooge to ask that some acknowledgement of a twenty-five hundred loan be given me. I work hard for my money. Whether or not I shall exact repayment is my business."

While differences over money contributed to a growing gulf between Amelia and her mother and sister, her marriage brought a new and pleasant family relationship as stepmother to seventeen-year-old David Binney Putnam. The woman who had said she had always put off having a child, "for the air races or something else," proved an interested, understanding friend to David. Young Putnam, who visited his father more frequently than his nine-year-old brother did, had known Amelia since the summer of 1928 when she lived in Rye while writing *Twenty Hours Forty Minutes.* Her handsome, tall (six feet, three inches) stepson, an aviation enthusiast, admired Amelia's courage and was fascinated by her boundless curiosity. "She was interested in everything and wanted to know about everything," he said. He also thought her very attractive, "long-legged and graceful," with "a lovely head, like a beautiful choirboy's," yet very feminine. "She looked like a bag of bones in a bathing suit, she was so thin," he said, "but she had beautiful clothes and she knew how to wear them. When she was all dressed up, she didn't look like she had *tried* to be all dressed up."

When Amelia wrote to Amy that she worked hard for her money she did not exaggerate. She was back at her desk the Monday morning after her marriage. G. P. thought skipping a honeymoon might reassure her that marriage would not interfere with her career, and she reported to her mother, "I am much happier than I expected I would ever be in this state. . . . Of course, I go on in the same way as before as far as business is concerned. I haven't changed at all and will only be busier I suppose."

One of her projects, the new Ludington airline, which was launched three months before her marriage as the nation sank into a deepening financial depression, continued to demand time and effort. Bedridden the previous October with a severe throat infection, Amelia was on the road again for the airline by the first of November and at Thanksgiving reported to the newspapers that seats had been sold out for all stops for the two previous days. By January, business was not that good and manager Eugene Vidal, who had appointed her vice-president in charge of traffic, switched her back to public relations, asking her to meet with the publicity staff once a week in Philadelphia and to handle all complaints and general contacts with the public. She did so and whatever else she could to generate free newspaper publicity for the airline. She took an eye test at the top of the Empire State Building and commented on the impracticality of parachutes for airline passengers after Will Rogers suggested it in his newspaper column. With little or nothing coming in from the airline she gave lectures to earn money, continued to write her column for *Cosmopolitan,* and was paid to endorse the Franklin automobile, along with Lindbergh, Frank Hawks, and Donald Douglas.

In April she was elected vice-president of the NAA, the first woman to become a national officer. However, there were by then 453 licensed women pilots, 39 of them with transport licenses, and at least a half dozen better pilots than Amelia. In January, Bobbi Trout and Edna May Cooper set a new women's endurance-refueling record of 122 hours, 50 minutes. Already holder of two previous solo records, Trout had asked Amelia after the 1929 derby if she would like to partner an attempt at an endurance record that fall. Amelia said she would like to but was "just too busy." Trout, who was certain she could fly any plane made, credited Putnam for keeping Amelia busy. "If I had a promoter like Putnam," she declared, "I could have done the things Amelia did."

Amelia had other rivals. Laura Ingalls, a licensed transport pilot and record-holding aerial acrobat, set a transcontinental speed record of 25 hours, 35 minutes in 1930. Twenty-year-old Elinor Smith had set a women's altitude record of 24,418 feet at Valley Stream, Long Island, in March of 1930 and narrowly escaped death (but not headlines) a year later when she tried again, losing consciousness and diving five miles before recovering in time to land.

Amelia's most formidable rival was her friend and neighbor in Rye, handsome socialite Ruth Nichols. After Nichols bettered Smith's altitude record on March 6, 1931, ascending to 28,743 feet, she broke Amelia's speed record a month later in Detroit, flying 210.683 miles per hour. That spring both Nichols and Ingalls were planning solo transatlantic flights. Amelia needed something to keep herself in the news. She found it in an odd new aircraft—the autogiro.

Amelia was eager to fly this new ship, which could take off and land without a runway. Its Spanish inventor, Juan de la Cierva, claimed that if it were mass-produced it would bring flying safely to the suburbanite at a price no higher than that of an average car. When his American partner, Harold F. Pitcairn, needed to create a market for this predecessor of the helicopter, it was G. P. who saw the opportunity for Amelia to demonstrate this spectacular oddity. The autogiro differed from the modern helicopter in that the four rotor blades over the pilot's head were not motor-powered but turned when the aircraft moved forward, powered by a conventional motor-driven propeller at the front of the fuselage.

James G. Ray, Pitcairn's chief test pilot, gave Amelia her first and only lesson at Willow Grove, Pennsylvania, at the company field in December, 1930. He flew her around the field for fifteen or twenty minutes, made two landings, and then climbed out. "Now," he said, "you take it up." She did, but she said later, "I began to feel exactly as I had when I made my first solo in any airplane eleven years ago." She was not certain "whether I flew it or it flew me."

A week after their marriage, G. P. ordered one for her. There was a waiting line of corporate buyers who saw the publicity value of the plane, among them the *Detroit News,* Coca-Cola, four oil companies, and the Beech-Nut Packing Company, producers of tinned foods and chewing gum.

While Amelia waited for her own plane, she flew for a few hours in the fourth aircraft made by the Pitcairn-Cierva Autogiro Company of America, Model PCA-2. By April she was ready to try for an altitude record, which she insisted was only an attempt to "determine the aircraft's ceiling." Nevertheless, she arranged for NAA official Luke Christopher to bring a sealed barograph from Washington and G. P. invited Movietone News, the wire services, and New York newsmen to cover it.

Watched by five hundred spectators on April 8 she ascended to 18,000 feet but she was not satisfied. "I'm going to try again," she said. After most of the crowd had gone home she made a second, three-hour attempt, returning at dusk. The NAA barograph showed 18,415 feet, an autogiro record for men and women. Actually, no one had tried it before. For Pitcairn's benefit she told reporters that the plane was a "standard job," with a regulation three hundred-horsepower Wright Whirlwind engine, an aircraft identical to the one she had ordered.

Soon after, she cancelled her order when Beech-Nut offered her theirs (serial number B-12) for a transcontinental flight. Although she was hospitalized for a tonsillectomy in late April and wrote to Amy that she was "almost inarticulate," with "knees a bit wobbly," she started the flight on May 29 from Newark. She was accompanied by a mechanic, Eddie de Vaught. At the helm of this giant and fragile grasshopper leaping its way across the country, she needed to take off and land as often as ten times a day. Every time she did she reinforced her identity as America's "Lady Lindy" by the best means possible—the personal appearance.

At that time none of the media could match a personal appearance. Radio coverage was still poor and newsreels so primitive that even the president of the United States had to be asked to repeat his lines for retakes. At every stop Amelia acquired more admirers, as she lifted up children to see the cockpit, shook hands with spectators, and gave interviews to local reporters.

When she stopped in Zanesville, Ohio, for fuel the interview was given beside the bright green plane. Sitting on the grass she fashioned a ring from a daisy for a little girl while she answered the questions of a reporter who asked if she had always been so thin. She said she had, that she weighed 119 pounds and was trying to gain after a tonsillectomy. Although her face was raw from sunburn and her nose peeling, she was described as small-boned, delicate, and very feminine. Her voice, the reporter wrote, was musical, her manners, "quiet and refined." About her marriage she said, "I have stopped off once in marriage and I intend to live always with him for I think one husband is enough. I will never leave him."

Since writing her prenuptial views for G. P., she had either tempered them or knew what Zanesville's citizens wanted to hear. When she landed there again on her return flight she reinforced local opinion that she was a genuine American heroine—brave, intelligent, well-mannered, modest, cheerful, and interested in Zanesville. Ralph Lane and his wife and three children who lived near the field offered her and mechanic de Vaught lunch while they waited for a fuel delivery. In a house without a bathroom Amelia washed her hands in a basin and, after the meal, helped with the dirty dishes. She also gave the children a carton of gum.

Not all of the stops were in small towns. On June 3 thousands of admirers jammed the streets of Denver to see her fly over the city. She arrived at eight in the morning from Cheyenne, where she had left de Vaught with tools and luggage, so that the passenger seat would be available for guest rides. Her schedule, arranged by the Women's Aero Association, included a quick breakfast at the Brown Palace Hotel before returning to the airport where she took off and landed four times, "a sandy-haired goddess" whose ship "jumped from the ground like a scared rabbit . . . over the heads of the awe-stricken crowd."

She knew how to "work a crowd." A year later her mother received a letter from Denverite Fannie Kaley who wrote: "One of the happiest moments of my life was when I met your wonderful daughter in Denver and shook hands with her, the time she came in her autogiro."

Amelia crossed the continent in nine days, arriving on June 6 in Oakland, where fans broke through the barriers to see her. She had not set a record. Professional pilot John Miller had been first to cross the country two weeks before her. For a record she would have to make a round trip, which she did, returning by a southern route.

On the way back Amelia had her first accident in the autogiro, at Abilene, Texas, on June 12. When she failed to rise quickly enough on takeoff the plane dropped thirty feet, hitting two cars and damaging its rotor and propeller. "The air just went out from in under me," she said. "Spectators say a whirlwind hit me. I made for the only open space available." Ever mindful of the plane's builder, who dispatched a second giro to her immediately, she added, "With any other type of plane the accident would have been more serious."

That was probably true but the autogiro was neither a safe nor easy-to-fly plane. Amelia's friend, Blanche Noyes, who was hired to fly one for an oil company, scoffed at Pitcairn's claim that "a ten-year-old boy" could fly it. Blanche said that the trial ship was called the *Black Maria* by pilots because almost all of them cracked up in it. "I think ten hours was the longest any pilot flew it without cracking it up," she said.

In Abilene Amelia stayed with Mr. and Mrs. D. H. Oldham, Jr., who received a belated thank you note in which she referred to the accident as "nothing, really," and added, "You might be interested to know that *five or six hours* [her emphasis] after I turned the second giro over to the regular pilot he cracked it on landing." The second giro had been rushed to Oklahoma City where Amelia told members of the Lions Club that the accident was not a "crash." "I came down where I could do as little damage as possible," she said.

The Aeronautics Branch of the Department of Commerce* did not agree with her. It issued a formal reprimand for "carelessness and poor judgment." R. W. Delaney, their inspector at Abilene, made the report. Amelia, who was in Tulsa when the story broke, insisted that she had to land where she did to avoid hitting spectators and claimed the inspector had never flown an autogiro or even seen one in flight.

She did not mention the accident in a magazine article published in mid-July but did admit the trip was tiring. The crowds, she wrote, came to see the plane, not the pilot, but the autogiro could not talk, eat chicken, make radio speeches, or be interviewed. She had flown nineteen days out of twenty-one, was airborne an average of five hours each day, and gave exhibition flights along the way.

She was tired but she needed the money, so when Beech-Nut offered it, G. P. booked her for two more tours, the first of them to begin on August 12. "Here I am," she wrote to a friend, "jumping through hoops just like the little white horse in the circus!"

Young Jim Weissenberger, who was attending a school picnic in Toledo, watched the autogiro descend in a nearby field. He was wide-eyed when Amelia climbed out, her white silk scarf blowing in the wind. Pointing to the interurban tracks she asked, "Young man, do these tracks go to Cleveland?" He assured her they did, then watched the plane until it disappeared over the horizon before he ran back to tell his classmates he had actually seen Amelia Earhart.

The third time she stopped at Zanesville she took reporter Clair Stebbins for a ride. Before they took off, he was asked to sign away his rights to sue in the event of an accident. "If any death warrants are to be signed," Stebbins wrote, "they couldn't be issued under more desireable circumstances."

Amelia cracked up the autogiro a second time at the Michigan State Fair in Detroit on September 12. She was attempting a slow landing near the grandstand when she failed to level off soon enough and dropped twenty feet to the ground, not unlike the slammer she made in a glider at the 1929 air races, also in front of the grandstand. The aircraft went into a

*Renamed, in 1934, the Bureau of Air Commerce.

ground-loop before coming to rest in a cloud of dust. Amelia emerged smiling, but G. P., who had accompanied her on this second tour and who sprinted toward the scene, tripped over a guy wire, crushing his ribs and spraining his ankle. While he was hospitalized in Detroit she went on to another county fair in Saginaw.

Amelia wrote to Amy that the second crash was a freak accident in which the landing gear gave way from a defect: "G. P. fell over a wire running to pick me up and as he limped up I said, 'It was all my fault,' meaning he was hurt. The papers got it that I said the crack was mine which isn't accurate." With the exception of her crash in the Vega at Norfolk Amelia had yet to admit that any crackup was her fault.

On a third tour through the South, in November, she spent two to four days in each of almost a dozen cities. Between these tours Amelia worked on other projects—lectures (from which she derived most of her income), magazine articles, and her job with Ludington which was now only part-time after the airline failed to win an airmail contract. After her re-election as vice-president of the NAA on July 23, she dashed to New York to meet aviation enthusiast King Prajadhipok of Siam (now Thailand) at Yankee Stadium, a typical Putnam arrangement. Back in Washington the next day, she was photographed with President Hoover and NAA president Hiram Bingham, who had pleaded her cause to the Aeronautics Branch of the Department of Commerce after officials threatened to ground her for ninety days for the Abilene crash. He won the lesser penalty, a formal reprimand.

Amelia was never too busy to help her colleagues find work in aviation. In September of 1931 she was elected president of the Ninety-Nines, which continued to lack both structure and enough members. She recruited new members, wrote to old members, started work on a constitution, bargained for optional coverall uniforms and membership pins, and contributed to the newsletter.

Never a joiner, she accepted membership in only two other women's organizations, Zonta International, and the Society of Woman Geographers, an adventurous, learned group whose members were called "my gang" by anthropologist Margaret Mead. Society president Harriet Chalmers Adams, welcoming Amelia in a letter wrote: "Tell Mr. Putnam that the book I was writing . . . was sidetracked when I broke my back in 1926. As soon as I got up, after two and a half years, I went to Arabia and Libia [sic] for the National Geographic; and to Ethiopia last year . . . [A]s soon as I 'get over' being President . . . I hope to get to work on the belated record of my adventures."

In a year during which Amelia succeeded with most of her projects, she still could not resolve Amy and Muriel's financial problems. She strongly disapproved of Muriel's having a second child in a marriage she considered to be miserable. After her advice on birth control was ignored, she referred to Muriel's pregnancy as the "second coming," and hoped, she told Amy, that Muriel would have learned enough about anatomy to prevent "further trials for a while." She wrote to Amy: "Why don't you suggest to her that Albert go to Dr. Rock and get a little information? Surely if Pidge can't manage things it is important for him to do so. . . . I think he should share the mechanics of being a husband."

Amelia was also annoyed with her mother, who continued to give most of her allowance to Muriel. "I am not working to help Albert, nor Pidge, much as I care for her. If they had not had that money [given them by Amy] perhaps they would have found means to economize before." Amelia's solution was to send Amy half of her allowance of one hundred dollars a month (the equivalent of fifteen hundred dollars today). She banked the other half in Amy's name. Amy countered with the suggestion that she pay the Morrisseys for her room and board, but Amelia said this was "unthinkable" when Amy did all the housekeeping.

Amelia was not heartless. Theodore, or "Theo," Amy's brother who was retarded, had been bilked twice—once by his brother, Mark, who had also lost some of Amy's inheritance, and again by Margaret Balis who borrowed Theo's life savings of two thousand dollars and died leaving nothing in her estate to repay him. Amelia was disgusted. "No enemies could have treated him worse than his own family," she wrote. She would send him a check every month until Margaret's son, Mark Ed Balis, "a good boy," sorted out matters.

The grim caretaker of family finances was a different person in the company of colleagues, an uninhibited, often exuberant companion. Early in 1931 she met with two of her closest friends and rivals, Ruth Nichols and Louise Thaden, at Nichols's house in Rye to draw up a constitution for the Ninety-Nines. All three women were in their thirties. Thaden, married to aeronautical designer Herbert von Thaden, was her husband's business partner. Nichols, ex-banker, airplane salesperson, and organizer of the Long Island Aviation Country Club, was already planning a solo transatlantic flight. But when they finished their work on the constitution they had a wrestling match, described by Nichols: "Probably as the result of the strain of our labors, we three had a grand rough house in my room and on the beds to see who was the strongest physically. As I recall, Louise was able to pin both Amelia and myself down. It certainly was a circus."

Sir Harry Brittain, English balloonist and visiting representative of the British Chamber of Commerce on Air Transport, met with Amelia in 1931. She invited him to tea at the Putnam apartment in the Wyndham Hotel, where the telephone rang constantly while she was trying to make the tea. Seeing she had to take the calls in the adjoining room, Sir Harry offered to do it for her:

> She agreed. The bell rang again. Sitting on the bed I picked up the receiver and called out, "Miss Amelia Earhart's secretary speaking. Who is that?"
>
> "Her husband," came the reply.
>
> I need only say that Miss Earhart was roaring with laughter. She was a great lass.

For the "great lass" 1931 had been a good year, the best part of it still a secret. She was planning the most important project of her life—a solo transatlantic flight.

PART THREE

FLYING HIGH

CHAPTER TWELVE

Victory and Vindication

On a January morning in 1932 Amelia Earhart lowered the morning paper she had been reading at the breakfast table and asked G. P., "Would you mind if I flew the Atlantic?" She knew he would not. No one knew better than he that aviation celebrities were as well known as their last record and Amelia's last was her round trip in the autogiro. Soloing the Atlantic had been done by only one person—Lindbergh. Amelia could achieve two "firsts." She could be the first woman to fly it alone and the first person to cross it twice in a heavier-than-air craft.

Even more than records Amelia wanted collegial respect. For four years she had faced repeated insinuations that she was not a competent professional. Eight pilots had crossed since the *Friendship*'s flight, none of them alone. Two who had tried it solo were lost. Four with partners had also died. But, Amelia said, failure and death could be avoided by meticulous planning and total concentration. And the Atlantic solo would silence her critics.

Only four persons knew of the project. G. P. was the first. The next to be told was Bernt Balchen, Arctic flier and transatlantic pilot for Byrd, who agreed to refit and test the Vega for her. Repaired in September 1930 after her accident in Norfolk, the plane was rebuilt a year later into a Vega 5B by the Detroit Aircraft Corporation. The fuselage was scrapped and replaced with one from another Vega, serial number 68, but the original serial number, 22, was retained. Painted a deep red with trim striping in gold and black, the plane was then chartered to Ludington Airlines. It was released by Ludington on March 5, 1932, registered as NR7952 by Amelia and turned over to Balchen. Just as the curious had supposed the *Friendship* was intended for Byrd's Antarctic expedition in 1928, they now assumed that Amelia's Vega was to be used by Balchen in a transarctic flight with Lincoln Ellsworth.

The third person to know Amelia's plan was Balchen's assistant, Edward "Eddie" Gorski, formerly master mechanic for Anthony H. G. Fokker before Fokker moved his plant from Teterboro Airport in New Jersey, six miles from New York on the other side of the Hudson. Stocky, blond, blue-eyed Balchen and the slim, wiry, twenty-six-year old Gorski worked on the Vega in an empty hangar at Teterboro. They strengthened the fuselage to hold a large auxiliary fuel tank and added more tanks to the wings, increasing the fuel capacity to 420 gallons and the flying range to thirty-two hundred miles. They installed a new Pratt & Whitney Wasp engine, Number 3812, and shortened the exhaust stacks. Maj. Edwin Aldrin, father of astronaut "Buzz" Aldrin, was asked to supervise the fuel supply.

To test the Vega, the two men flew it for hours loaded with sandbags to simulate the weight of the fuel. "We couldn't land with all that weight," Gorski said, "so I pushed the sandbags out while Bernt flew back and forth over the Jersey meadowlands. . . . People thought we were dropping bombs."

Additional instruments were added, a drift indicator and three compasses—an aperiodic, a magnetic, and a directional gyro. Amelia spent hours with Balchen learning all she could about flying solely on instruments, for she and Balchen both knew that the weather over the Atlantic, which was always treacherous, might require more "blind flying" than she had ever done.

On an April Sunday when Balchen had come over from his home in Hasbrough Heights to Rye for lunch and a game of croquet, Amelia put down her mallet and asked him, "Am I ready to do it? Is the ship ready?"

Balchen said she was and it was.

That night Amelia told the fourth and last person, her cousin, Lucy Challis, who had come to stay at the house in Rye in January. Lucy was in the kitchen with G. P. and Amelia, stirring cocoa for their Sunday night supper while G. P. and Amelia fixed eggs and toast.

"Can you keep a secret?" Amelia asked her.

"Of course."

Amelia continued to slice bread while she spoke. "I'm—I'm going to fly the Atlantic again. Alone."

Amelia guarded her secret with a hand that proved quicker than the public's eye—or those of her colleagues. She appeared to be as busy as ever, constantly on the move, giving lectures, being interviewed, maintaining a voluminous correspondence even after her secretary, Norah Alstrulund, left for a trip to South America in April. As late as May 6 she wrote to the regional governors of the Ninety-Nines, suggesting that the annual meeting be held on August 30 and listing room rates for three different hotels in Cleveland.

Amelia was busy but waiting, waiting for the go-ahead from Doc Kimball, the New York weatherman regarded by transatlantic fliers as their most reliable adviser. All during April and the first half of May he had nothing but bad news. One veteran pilot, Louis T. Reichers, who ignored Kimball's advice was forced down seventeen miles off the coast of Ireland. He survived, plucked from the stormy sea by Amelia's old friend, Harry Manning from the *Roosevelt*. Reichers's plane was a Lockheed Altair, holding one hundred more gallons of gasoline than Amelia's Vega with an engine rated at fifty more horsepower. One editorial writer commented that if an aviator as experienced as Reichers failed, his experience should impress others. It did not impress Amelia.*

Every day she drove the thirty miles from Rye to Teterboro in the hopes the weather would turn and every night she came back. G. P. told his friend Walter Trumbull that he could no longer sleep nights, but Amelia did. On May 17 she told her neighbor Ruth Nichols, who was also planning a transatlantic flight, that one had to take chances on long-distance flights, "so I don't bother to go into all the possible accidents that might happen. I just don't think about crackups."

The next day Amelia was at Holmes Airport in New York City, christening the new Goodyear dirigible, *Resolute,* while newsreel cam-

*She asked the NAA for a barograph, which did not arrive until May 16. Although Balchen did not receive the official notice that he was to install it, he did anyway, "a few minutes before the actual takeoff."

eramen photographed her and a group of women pilots. Twenty-four hours later, she was on her way.

On May 19, after driving to Teterboro, Amelia called G. P. who was with Doc Kimball in New York. G. P. told her that at 11:30 that morning the weather was good as far as Harbor Grace. She drove home and picked up her flying suit, two scarves, a comb, a toothbrush, a thermos of soup, and a tin of tomato juice. Wearing jodhpurs, a white silk shirt, and a leather jacket, she raced back to Teterboro, arriving at 3:30. G. P. was waiting at the field with his friend, Dr. Lawrence Gould, the Byrd Antarctic explorer whose work he had published, and Mrs. Gould. Gould noticed that when Balchen taxied the plane for takeoff and Amelia waved from the cockpit window, no one at the field seemed to take any notice of her departure.

Balchen flew and Gorski sat beside Amelia behind the auxiliary fuel tank at the rear. She slept most of the way. They arrived at St. John, New Brunswick, at 5:46, too late to go on to Harbor Grace, Newfoundland. News of the flight reached St. John before Amelia. Balchen assured reporters waiting there that "Mrs. Putnam has ninety-nine chances out of a hundred to cross the Atlantic if she gets an even break. She is probably the greatest woman pilot of today."

After a night's sleep at the Admiral Beatty Hotel, the trio rose at 5 A.M. and left for the field at 6:20. They waited there until 8:30 for the fog to clear before leaving for Harbor Grace, where they arrived at 2 P.M. when the fog was again rolling in. Amelia, who seems to have slept about half the time since her departure from Teterboro, went to a small hotel for another nap. Bernt and Eddie worked over the plane until the fog lifted at six that night when Balchen called her at the hotel. In his diary he wrote, "She arrives at the field in jodhpurs and leather flying jacket, her close-cropped blond hair tousled, quiet and unobtrusive as a young Lindbergh. She listens calmly, only biting her lip a little, as I go over with her the course to hold and tell her what weather she can expect."

She told reporters, "I am confident of success. To all my friends, both far and near, let me say that you will hear from me in less than fifteen hours." She seemed less certain when she stood by Balchen where no one could hear her:

> She looks at me with a small, lonely smile and says, "Do you think I can make it?" and I grin back, "You bet!"

She crawls calmly into the cockpit of the big, empty airplane, starts the engine, runs it up, checks the mags and nods her head. We pull the chocks and she's off.

It was 7:12 P.M.

Back in New York G. P. spent the day at the weather bureau with Kimball and that night in his rooms at the Hotel Seymour, which served as a watch station and news release center. Hilton Railey manned the telephone, periodically calling the Associated Press for any word of ships sighting her at sea. There were none. Carl Allen was also there. G. P. told him that although he was confident, he couldn't help but be anxious for some word of her. "I've spent my life being the father of a distinguished son [David, whose birthday it was] and the husband of a famous wife," he told Allen. He was also determined to make her even more famous. Amelia left Harbor Grace on May 20, the fifth anniversary of Lindbergh Day, the day on which he started his historic transatlantic flight. The date had to be more than coincidence. It had to have been set by the creator of the "Lady Lindy" of 1928—George Palmer Putnam.

The date was perfect but the weather was not. Four hours out of Harbor Grace Amelia was fighting for her life. After cruising at twelve thousand feet into a sunset that faded to darkness while the moon rose over low clouds, she encountered a severe storm along with a series of life-threatening mechanical malfunctions. Her altimeter was not working, leaving her to guess in the dark how high or low she was flying. The electrical storm tossed and battered the Vega while she fought to hold it on course for more than an hour. When she climbed to evade the storm, her tachometer picked up ice and began to spin, making it impossible to estimate her speed and, consequently, the distance she had traveled. She no longer knew if she was on course. About the same time the weld on her manifold cracked and exhaust flames from the engine blazed in the night.

There could be no turning back. Landing at the unlighted field at Harbor Grace would be suicidal. Fire from the manifold and a maximum fuel load carried a death warrant. Flying at what she estimated to be twelve thousand feet, the wings began to ice, forcing her to descend. Heavy with ice, the plane went into a spin. She pulled out of it so near to the sea that she could see the waves breaking beneath her. She had to climb again because at that height it was impossible to navigate by instruments. They would not function so near the surface. Climbing again, she saw ice form on the windshield and felt it weighing down the plane. For the next ten hours she fought to stay low enough to prevent icing but high enough to use her instruments. All through the night she felt the vibrations of the flaming manifold, and tried not to look at it while the rudder bar throbbed under her feet. The cabin stank of gas fumes, increasing the stomach contractions she always had on long flights. To retain her strength and stay alert she forced down part of the chicken soup in the thermos and drank the tomato juice from the tins, which she pierced with an icepick. When she reached up to turn on the reserve fuel tank she discovered the gauge was broken. Gasoline was dripping down the back of her neck. She no longer knew how much fuel remained in her tank.

Shortly after dawn she spotted a ship, then a fishing fleet. She knew she was off the coast of Ireland and would have to land. "Paris was out of the question." Because the waves beneath her indicated a northwest wind, she decided she was south of her course and turned north. Actually she was already north of the course to Paris and by flying even farther north she almost missed the northernmost tip of Ireland, beyond which there was nothing but open sea. After sighting the coast, she flew inland, following some railroad tracks while she looked for an airfield. There was none. She landed in a meadow, "frightening all the cows in the neighborhood," and for a brief moment sat in the plane, looking out at the green hills.

Dan McCallion, herder of the frightened cows, approached the plane as she climbed out, her face smeared with grease. "Where am I?" she asked him.

"Sure, you're in Derry, sir."

"In Derry? Oh, Londonderry." She pointed to a farmhouse across the field. "Whose house is that over there?"

"It belongs to the Gallaghers."

"Could I stop there?"

"Yes, sir—I mean, Ma'am. And have you come far?"

"From America."

"Holy Mother of God!" McCallion muttered as she walked toward the house.

At the James Gallaghers she washed her face and drank two cups of tea but insisted she was neither hungry nor tired. A few minutes later she hailed a passing car and rode into Londonderry to telephone G. P. She spoke to him for six minutes, then returned to the Gallaghers to watch her plane until arrangements were made to guard it—a wise procedure, for it might well have disappeared, a piece at a time, in the clutches of souvenir hunters. The plane secured, Amelia returned to Londonderry and placed five three-minute calls to G. P. When she returned a second time to the Gallaghers, she was mobbed by crowds until 10 P.M. when she retired.

Sunday morning she was again besieged by newsmen, photographers, and autograph hunters, although none gave her the mauling she had suffered at Burry Port in 1928. Congratulatory cables were already arriving, among them two which were of particular importance to Amelia. The first was from the Lindberghs who had learned only ten days before that their kidnapped infant son was dead, his body discovered not far from the young parents' home. (The first sentence in Anne Lindbergh's diary of May 21 was "Amelia landed in Ireland!") The second cable was from Nancy, Lady Astor. "Congratulations," it said. "Come to us and I will lend you nightgown and other garments."

Amelia did stay with the Astors but not until she had been received in London and officially lodged for a night with the American ambassador, Andrew W. Mellon. A Paramount News plane took her from Londonderry to Hanworth Air Park near London, a private flying club. Disembarking in a cloudburst to rousing cheers from club members and a fight between a cameraman and a reporter, she learned that another cameraman and a pilot had been killed when their plane crashed while carrying photographs of her taken in Londonderry to their office in London. Two noted British women aviators, Lady Mary Bailey and Peggy Salaman, were also missing after arriving in Londonderry too late to see her there, then starting back to London. They were found safe the next day.

Dashing through the rain to the clubhouse, Amelia was greeted by Mellon and was read a message from Prime Minister James Ramsay MacDonald in which he addressed her as "my friend, Miss Earhart." She was then taken to London in Mellon's car, with his daughter, Mrs. David K. E. Bruce, and her friend, Mrs. David E. Finley. On the way they stopped at the British Broadcasting Company studios for a broadcast to the United States. After dinner Amelia was interviewed again by newsmen in the embassy library.

Another "circus" like that of 1928 had begun, only this time Amelia did not have Hilton Railey in London to help her. G. P. had an agent in town, a Mr. Grubb, who cabled him on May 23 that if the *Evening Standard* telephoned, the price for an exclusive story from Amelia should be twenty-five hundred dollars. Grubb said he had already initiated the bargaining at three thousand dollars and thought the paper would give twenty-five hundred. But Amelia was left to answer the congratulatory messages as best she could, starting with one from President Hoover who said that she had demonstrated "the capacity of women to match the skill of men in carrying through the most difficult feats of high adventure."

Messages poured in, from heads of state—George V of England, Albert, king of the Belgians, and Crown Prince Wilhelm of Germany—as well as from aviation officials, pilots, and friends. There were several hundred telegrams from women's organizations, including Zonta International, the Ninety-Nines, Business and Professional Women, YWCA, Daughters of America, American Association of University Women, university alumnae clubs, church groups, and the Woman's Christian Temperance Union whose members were delighted when, at a luncheon in her honor, she toasted George V in water.

Press notices were largely adulatory, noting her "modesty and good sense" and how her "glory shed luster on all womanhood." One editorial said that her reckless disregard for her own safety might tempt others to emulate her in what another called "a magnificent display of useless courage," but the criticism was tempered with praise. Only *The Aeroplane,* the British magazine that had treated her 1928 flight as useless publicity seeking, attacked her again, calling her vain and foolish.

Amelia stayed in London twelve days, in a perpetual round of appearances that left her bedridden with a cold and sore throat by the tenth day. In all of her speeches and interviews she stressed two themes. One was that she had made the flight "for the fun of it" and it would add nothing to aviation's progress. The other was that she was certain that safe, scheduled transatlantic flights would take place "in our lifetime."

On her third day in London she was received at York House by the world's most eligible bachelor, the future Edward VIII, who would abdicate to marry Wallis Simpson. Amelia met him again on May 31 at a charity ball. Wearing a gown of shimmering green satin, Amelia arrived shortly after the prince and was escorted to his table, where she bobbed her head in greeting, rather than curtsying. (This pleased an American public fascinated by royalty but disapproving of undemocratic manners demanded by protocol.) The prince, who had danced only once until then, led her to the floor where they danced until the orchestra leader asked permission to stop for the midnight supper. Amelia's only comment was that she hoped the prince was amused and that he was, like most aviators, a very good dancer.

While she was in London Amelia made a new friend, England's pilot-heroine Amy Johnson, the twenty-seven-year-old woman who had flown a Moth biplane from London to Australia. With Johnson was her fiancé, James A. Mollison, who had set a record of eight days and nineteen hours flying time from Australia to England. The couple accompanied Amelia to a civil air show along with Gordon Selfridge, Jr., son of the department store magnate. The same day, the senior Selfridge arranged for Amelia's Vega to be shipped from Londonderry to London where it was displayed in the window of his store.* The editor of *The Aeroplane* complimented Selfridge on his contributions to "air-mindedness" with his Aviation Department but renewed his criticism of Amelia: "Whenever something is done by mechanical means to achieve fame, or even merely notoriety, the Great Warm-Hearted Soft-Headed British Public wants to examine the machinery which did it."

In addition to the Selfridge family, Amelia renewed her friendship with Nancy Astor, with whom she stayed. Her hostess, whose drawing room was a salon for celebrities in every field, was determined that Amelia meet as many as possible. On June 2, Amelia's last day in London, she wrote to her mother from the house on St. James Square that she was waiting for Lady Astor to return. "G. B. Shaw is being towed in to meet me or I him." In the same letter Amelia explained she was meeting G. P. in Cherbourg the next morning because "I thought I just couldn't face coming home alone."

G. P. was on his way. Initially he had said he could not join her because of an important business trip to the West Coast on May 25. It was important, because three weeks later he was named chief of the editorial board of Paramount Studios. Nevertheless, he was looking after her interests at home, lining up paid testimonials and arrangements for her postflight appearances in New York, Chicago, and Boston. The one arrangement he had failed to make was authorization for the flight by the Aeronautics Branch of the Department of Commerce. A Branch official wrote complaining that Putnam had pretended that he thought the Vega's

*NR7952 is on display at the National Air and Space Museum in Washington, D.C.

NR license was all that was needed but he knew better. Nothing came of it. G. P. almost always knew someone important enough to silence the complainers.

G. P. met Amelia on June 3 at Cherbourg where she had arrived aboard the yacht *Evadne* the night before and was met that morning by U.S. consul Horatio Moore and Vicomte Jacques de Sibour.* Putnam's ship, the *Olympia,* was late and he was in none too good a mood. When newsreel cameramen asked the couple to embrace, they were refused. Irritated by G. P.'s surly manner, the Fox Movietone man wrote on his dopesheet that Amelia's reception was "lukewarm" and the French would not forgive her for staying in England when "she should have come to Le Bourget like Lindbergh."

He was mistaken. When the boat train pulled into the Gare St. Lazare it was stopped fifty feet short of the platform by the crowd, which pushed past police lines onto the tracks. On the platform Amelia was separated from G. P. when the crowd swept her and Violette de Sibour toward the embassy car outside the station. Thousands of cheering spectators lined the route to the Hotel Lotti where others stood below the balcony of Amelia's first-floor suite and shouted until she came out to wave to them.

Tennis champion Helen Wills Moody, in Paris for a tournament, had agreed to cover Amelia's arrival for an American newspaper but her feet were too swollen from the day's match to put on shoes, "so I telephoned and to my astonishment she answered the telephone herself." Moody got her story.

During the next five days Amelia was presented to the French Senate and awarded the Cross of the Legion of Honor and a medal from the Aero Club of France. In Rome she was received by the Pope and Prime Minister Benito Mussolini. In Brussels King Albert presented her with the Cross of the Order of Leopold. For twenty-three days she had been received by national leaders and showered with honors. Yet the most satisfying day for her was the one on which her Vega rolled to a stop on that green meadow outside Londonderry. She was a first-class flier. The praise she liked best came from colleagues, comments like that of Eddie Gorski, who said that anyone who could cross the Atlantic with a cracked

---

*By then friends of both Putnams, the French war ace and his wife, Violette, had flown around the world in a Gypsy Moth between September 1928 and June 1929.

manifold and neither altimeter nor tachometer functioning was "a real flier."

Vindicated at last, she knew there was a price to be paid. On June 14 she sailed with G. P. on the *Ile de France* for New York and the reception she had told her mother she could not face alone. Her friend Walter Trumble predicted: "Probably never again can Amelia Earhart walk on the streets of any city with the comfort of an ordinary citizen. She will be pushed and tugged and ever surrounded by the maddening throng."

CHAPTER THIRTEEN

The Last of Lady Lindy

*A*melia Earhart's 1932 transatlantic flight was her rite of passage. The twenty-two-year-old amateur pilot who had called flying a "sport" had become a thirty-four-year-old professional obsessed by it. The obsession was rooted in the little girl who "belly-slammed" her sled down icy hills, the student who kept a scrapbook reflecting the unique accomplishments of women, and the young woman who drove a truck to pay for flying lessons. "I flew the Atlantic because I wanted to," she wrote. "To want in one's head to do a thing, for its own sake; to enjoy doing it; to concentrate all of one's energies upon it—that is not only the surest guarantee of its success. It is also being true to oneself."

In the four years since her 1928 flight, the indecisive drifter manipulated by George Palmer Putnam had become, to a large extent, the master of her own fate, setting seemingly impractical goals but reaching them by very practical means. The basic Amelia remained true to herself while the mature Amelia developed new relationships with the public, the press, her colleagues, friends, and family.

To the public, and the press that conveyed her image to that public, Amelia was not completely honest, revealing none of her resentment of prying reporters and her dread of shouting, shoving, anonymous admirers. In an attempt to evade the official reception scheduled for June 20 in New York she wired Mayor James J. Walker, suggesting that the ceremonies be dropped and the money used for the relief of the unemployed.

Her friend, Viola Gentry, a Ninety-Nine member serving on the welcoming committee, said that Amelia's request was refused by Walker who insisted that the reception would "cost nothing." The charming, if somewhat corrupt, "Jimmy" had a keen sense of what his constituents wanted. They needed proof that human courage could triumph over fearful odds. Amelia was a symbol of that courage at a time when ten million of her fellow Americans were out of work in the worst depression of the twentieth century.

The New York homecoming was even more overwhelming than she had expected, matched only by that given to Charles Lindbergh in 1927. Thousands turned out to see her ride down Broadway through a blizzard of tickertape and pages torn from telephone books. Unlike the demonstration for her in 1928 this one was rightfully hers. She was no longer "Lady Lindy," a woman who deprived Stultz and Gordon of the acclaim owed them because she looked like Lindbergh and went along for the ride.

The daylong celebration began when the *Ile de France* loomed out of the fog off Quarantine and dropped anchor with a thundering blast of its siren, soon joined by the shrieking whistles of tugs, ferries, and pleasure craft crowding the harbor. When Amelia crossed the narrow gangplank to board the city's welcoming boat, the *Riverside,* she was unable to shout above the noise. She smiled and reached out to greet David Putnam and as many others as she could, among them Eugene Vidal, Paul Collins, Bernt Balchen, and the backer of her first flight, Amy Phipps Guest. High above the *Riverside* were nine Army planes and flying beneath them three heavy Douglas observation planes, losers in a competition for attention with three Navy Curtiss Fledglings. Only once did Amelia reveal any tension. When the Fledglings swooped so low that daredevils Frank Hawks and Al Williams, who were standing on the deck next to Amelia ducked, she gasped, "Gracious! I wish they wouldn't do that!"

After being escorted to a cabin at the stern of the *Riverside* Amelia faced the press calmly, answering questions with what one reporter described as "a happy faculty for choosing the right phrase." She posed for photographers, urging the women aviators who had come out to meet her to join her for more pictures at the ship's rail. Once ashore and seated in a processional car with Charles L. Lawrance, president of the Aeronautical Chamber of Commerce and the man who had designed the motor of her first airplane, Amelia pulled off her hat, smiling and waving at the cheering crowds. At Wall Street her admirers broke through the police lines, cutting the procession in two until reinforcements restored a semblance of order just before the parade reached City Hall. Inside the hall, Walker presided at one ceremony, followed by a second outdoors on the steps. A third followed at Bryant Park, where two thousand spectators gathered to see Amelia receive the Cross of Honor from the United States Flag Association.

From Bryant Park she went to the Waldorf-Astoria where one thousand members and guests of the New York Advertising Club were waiting in the ballroom for a luncheon in her honor, followed by another ceremony at which three members of the Society of Woman Geographers presented her with a scroll notifying her she was to be awarded the society's first gold medal. After an hour's rest there were more press interviews and just enough time to dress for the dinner given by the Aeronautical Chamber of Commerce.

The next day she left on a Ludington plane for Washington to receive the National Geographic Society's gold medal. She was accompanied by G. P. and David, her cousin Lucy Challis, Paul Collins, and Bernt Balchen. The Society's president, Gilbert H. Grosvenor, met her at the Washington airport and took her to the White House for what is now called a "photo opportunity." Amelia and President Hoover, who was to present the medal that night, did several "takes" for newsreel cameramen in which she spoke her lines nicely but he became flustered, addressing her as "Miss Earhart, ahem, Mrs. Putnam, I mean. . . ."

After lunch at the Society she was taken by Grosvenor to meet the secretaries of state, war, navy, and commerce, then on to the Senate and House. The Senate was recessed while she stood in the well of the chamber, her old friend Senator Bingham presenting her to the members who filed by to shake her hand. Fannie Kaley, who had seen Amelia fly the autogiro in Denver and was in the Senate gallery that day, wrote to Amy Earhart, "Never have I seen such a greeting as your daughter received. Everyone was on their feet immediately and cheered lustily."

Amelia's second trip to the White House that day was for dinner, an occasion G. P. described as formal, "with a kind of Victorian elegance." He meant dull. Always rather somber and reserved, Hoover was not overjoyed to have a man at his dinner table who had just published a book criticizing him and his party during an election year. Amelia, wearing a pale blue crepe gown, looked frail and very tired. Although the greater part of her earnings came from public speaking, she always dreaded it, so much so that on her lecture tours she customarily asked to be left alone for a few minutes before going on stage. On this night, when she was to describe in detail her Atlantic flight to one of the most discerning audiences she had ever faced, she had to spend the preceding ninety minutes at dinner making conversation with strangers.

From dinner the party went to Constitution Hall where Amelia received the Geographic Society's medal from Hoover before the fortunate thirty-eight hundred who had tickets. Ten thousand had applied. She was the fifteenth person and first woman to receive it, since its first presentation to Commodore Robert E. Peary by President Theodore Roosevelt in 1906. In her speech, broadcast over NBC's thirty-eight-station network, Amelia repeated familiar themes. She made the crossing for her own personal satisfaction. It added nothing to the advance of aviation. The reward was out of proportion to the deed. She would be happy if her "small exploit has drawn attention to the fact that women are flying, too."

The wan, frail heroine observed in Washington may have felt the worst was over once she had delivered her speech because she seemed to have recovered the following day. Back in New York, she was honored at three affairs—an Explorers Club luncheon, a Zonta tea, and a dinner at the Astor Hotel given by fifty womens' clubs and attended by one thousand guests. A friend of Muriel's, commenting on how graciously Amelia accepted the praise given her, wrote that she "charmed everybody." Home from the dinner by midnight, she went to a luncheon given by Standard Oil executives the next day before leaving with G. P. and David for Cleveland. The following day they were in Chicago for another parade.

After a single day of rest, the "circus" resumed on June 27 when the towns of Rye and Harrison gave an all-day civic reception. Although Amelia and G. P. used Rye as their address, the house in Westchester was on property that lay in both townships and both claimed her. Amelia tactfully told her audience that she raised her vegetables in Rye and ate them in Harrison.

On June 29 she arrived in Boston, accompanied by Lucy Challis and Hilton Railey. Amy and Muriel were at the airport but all Amelia had time to say was "Hello, Ma! How've you been?" and "Hello, Sis!" before the official party made off with her. The program that followed left only one hour to see her mother at Muriel's place in Medford between a celebration at Braves Field in the afternoon and a dinner that night at the Copley-Plaza.

When she returned from Boston her book, *The Fun of It,* which she had written before the flight with the exception of the last nine pages, was on sale. G. P. released it at the close of her first week of homecoming ceremonies so that in addition to reviews, which were generally complimentary, photographs of the author appeared in the rotogravure sections of newspapers throughout the country. These included pictures taken with Mayor Walker, President Hoover, and the king of Belgium. In each copy of the first edition was a small record of her BBC-CBS speech from London. Exploiting every sales possibility, G. P. made a special offer to members of the New York chapter of Zonta, an autographed copy for all those who ordered through the club.

There was one more banquet, one Amelia actually pleasantly anticipated, to be given July 8 by the Southern California chapter of the National Aeronautic Association in Los Angeles. The guests would include many old friends meeting in a city she had loved from the time she first lived there in 1920. She could now talk with pilots as a colleague of proven ability. The California members of the Ninety-Nines would be there and her former instructor, Monte Montijo, already had his ticket.

Arrangements for the banquet were being made by Pancho Barnes. Pancho was hostess to pilots and film stars at parties reputed to offer drugs, drink, and sex. However, she was also one of the organizers of the Motion Picture Pilots Association, a union that wrested from tight-fisted film producers an acceptable scale of fees for life-threatening stunts. An expert stunt flier herself, she owned a Travel Air Mystery S (for ship) in which she had broken Amelia's speed record in 1930. If teetotaler Amelia disapproved of Pancho's social life, she admired her skills as an aviator and an organizer. Years later, when Pancho was proprietor of the notorious Happy Bottom Riding Club at Edwards Air Force Base and friend to a young Chuck Yeager, Yeager's wife Glennis observed that Pancho liked men but "there were very few women she would speak to." Amelia was one of the few.

Aiming for a transcontinental speed record on her way back from Los Angeles, Amelia left G. P. and David there when she took off for Newark a few days after the banquet. A faulty gas line forced her down at

Columbus, ruining her plans for a nonstop trip and giving her a lapsed time of nineteen hours and fifteen minutes with almost eighteen hours of actual flying time.

It was evident from her press comments that she would not accept this failure, but before trying again she returned to California to receive the Distinguished Flying Cross on July 29 and to attend the summer games of the Tenth Olympiad. Two days before he opened the games, Vice-President Charles Curtis presented her with the DFC. It was awarded by a joint resolution of the 72nd Congress for "displaying heroic courage and skill as a navigator at the risk of her life . . . by which she became the first and only woman to cross the Atlantic ocean in a plane in solo flight." In a magazine article that was on the stands three days later, she wrote that one of the reasons she made the flight was to prove that "women can do most things men can do," not everything, she added, but "jobs requiring intelligence, coordination, speed, coolness and will power."

Amelia, G. P., and David were all sports fans. In a letter to her mother she wrote that the games were wonderful, the weather ideal, and added, "You know what a track fan I have always been." The track fan met two of her heroes, Paavo Nurmi, Finnish gold medalist in 1924, and the great Jesse Owens. The letter to Amy did not mention receiving the DFC nor the celebrities with whom she was photographed, among them Duke Kahanamoku, Hawaiian swimmer and gold medalist in 1912 and 1920, actress Fay Wray, who would long be remembered as the object of King Kong's affections, comedian Harold Lloyd, and Hollywood's most famous couple, Douglas Fairbanks and Mary Pickford. Amelia, G. P., and David were dinner guests at Pickfair during the games, but to Amy Amelia wrote only family news and that she expected to return east "in a week or so." She did not tell Amy she planned to make a second attempt at a nonstop, cross-country record.

She did it, on August 24–25, in nineteen hours and five minutes, the longest continuous time she had ever flown alone. She also set a women's record for distance—2,447 miles. G. P. and David, who had returned to New York earlier in the week, were not there to meet her. Instead, a shouting, pushing crowd of fans threatened to knock her over when she climbed down from the cockpit. Dressed in wrinkled brown jodhpurs and a crumpled orange silk shirt she motioned wearily, pleading, "Don't come near me. If you knew how I feel. . . ."

How she felt may have been more dreadful than her admirers could guess. In addition to fatigue, air sickness from gasoline fumes, and her abhorrence of being touched by strangers, there may have been another reason she wanted to remain at a distance from the crowd. A Newark aviation mechanic confided to an aeronautical designer there that after one of her long-distance flights her plane had reeked of urine. This may have been the flight to which he referred. Relief tubes designed for men were useless to women. In view of her nearly fanatical fastidiousness, to be in such a state would have been an agony for her.

Before the crowd could reach her the police intervened and a few minutes later she had recovered sufficiently to smile for the photographers and talk to reporters. When one asked why her husband was not there to meet her she explained that he regarded her flying as a routine affair. Not everyone did. Charles and Anne Lindbergh wired, "Splendid flight. So pleased at your success." In her brief account of the flight Amelia said, "If I had had the weather I had on my first attempt, I might have broken the men's record." If she had, it would not have been for long. She was referring to Frank Hawks's time of seventeen hours and thirty-five minutes. Four days after her flight Jimmy Haizlip flew from Los Angeles to Floyd Bennett Field in Brooklyn in ten hours and nineteen minutes, little more than half Amelia's time.

Much as she wanted to try again, she could not. After flying for "fun" for the better part of 1932 it was time to go to work. Before she left for Washington to receive the National Geographic medal, she had told reporters that she was ready to capitalize on her Atlantic flight "in any legitimate way that comes to hand. Any woman who wishes to should be able to do so without stigma." She was "willing to lead the way" but "wouldn't do anything false."

Amelia needed money, for her half of the household expenses at Rye, for the maintenance of an airplane, for Amy's support, and for the limited luxuries she had begun to enjoy—a good car, a simple but expensive wardrobe, and an impressive library. On July 20 she went to Detroit to a three-day introductory celebration for a new automobile—the Essex. Produced by the Hudson Motor Car Company, the first Essex off the line was christened by Amelia on July 22 when she broke a bottle of gasoline over its hood, then watched a parade of two thousand new cars pass by, each driven by a Hudson or Essex dealer. Amelia was given an Essex Terraplane, a stylish little coupe.

Amelia was thrifty. She never left a hotel room without taking all

Amelia as a child. (*Source:* The Schlesinger Library, Radcliffe College)

Amelia and Wilmer Stultz, pilot of the *Friendship,* being congratulated by Mr. and Mrs. Harry Moore after the 1928 transatlantic flight. (*Source:* American Heritage Center, University of Wyoming)

Amelia, wearing the wings presented to her in 1928 as an honorary major in the 381st Observation Squadron, U.S. Army Reserve, at Cressey Field, Presidio of San Francisco. (*Source:* Margaret Haviland Lewis)

Conclusion of the first westbound flight of Transcontinental Air Transport, July 9, 1929. Pictured are Amelia *(third from left),* Dorothy Binney Putnam *(fourth from left),* and Charles and Anne Lindbergh *(third and fourth from right).* (*Source:* Trans World Airlines)

Amelia in the cockpit of the Lockheed Vega that she flew in the Women's Air Derby, August 1929. (*Source:* Harvey C. Christen)

Amelia with Joe Nikrent, official timer of the NAA's Los Angeles chapter, after breaking the women's speed record in November 1929. The plane was a borrowed Lockheed Vega with a wooden fuselage. (*Source:* Office of Public Information, Lockheed-California Company)

Amelia with polar flier Bernt Balchen, the man who outfitted her "Little Red Bug" for the Atlantic solo crossing in 1932. (*Source:* W. M. Tegerdine)

Amelia and George Palmer Putnam shortly after their marriage in February 1931. (*Source:* Marcia-Marie Canavello)

Amelia greeting film star Mary Pickford, the honored guest, at a Fourth of July celebration during the 1933 National Air Races in Los Angeles. (*Source:* Trans World Airlines)

The avid amateur airplane mechanic was fascinated by all mechanical devices not just airplanes. (*Source:* Office of Public Information, Lockheed-California Company)

The power, speed, and beauty she loved, in the air or on the ground, are all here in her new, twin-engine Lockheed Electra 10E and elegant 1936 Cord Phaeton. (*Source:* Office of Public Information, Lockheed-California Company)

AMELIA EARHART TO ATTEMPT FIRST 'ROUND-THE-WORLD-FLIGHT APPROXIMATING THE EQUATO[

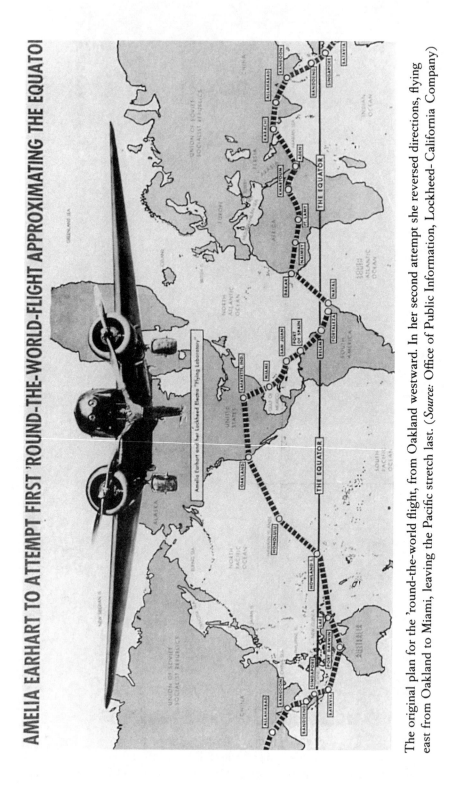

The original plan for the 'round-the-world flight, from Oakland westward. In her second attempt she reversed directions, flying east from Oakland to Miami, leaving the Pacific stretch last. (*Source:* Office of Public Information, Lockheed-California Company)

With Amelia, in one of the last informal photographs taken of her, is Lily
MacIntosh, whose husband W. Bruce MacIntosh took Amelia and navigator
Fred Noonan fishing off the Miami coast. (*Source:* Clinton and Marian
Morrison)

At the Karachi airport with navigator Fred Noonan.
(*Source:* Margaret Haviland Lewis)

Front page of the Chicago *Herald and Examiner,* Monday, July 5, 1937.

the stationery in it. For years she used whatever came to hand, including Bert Kinner's, Dennison Airport's, *Cosmopolitan*'s, and the NAA's. She once wrote to Amy on the back of a Ninety-Nine bulletin and Marian Stabler received a letter on tiny pages from a notepad. In London she used Lady Astor's, and some from the U.S. embassy which caused considerable embarrassment. She had written an endorsement of a Swiss watch used on her flight. When the letter with the embassy's address showing clearly appeared in a trade paper, a jeweler complained to the State Department. A department spokesman said that the use of the ambassador's stationery did not constitute a government endorsement. After that, although she wrote a note to her mother on White House stationery, she was very careful.

Amelia not only needed and wanted work for herself, she looked for jobs and wrote letters of recommendation for her colleagues. Before networking among women began, she was trying to make the Ninety-Nines a central exchange of information on the qualifications of its members and job opportunities. During the National Air Races in August of 1932, when she was re-elected president of the organization, she spent hours in her hotel room writing proposals and letters to enlarge and strengthen it.

She also helped individual members in any way she could. When Nancy Hopkins Tier, who had competed in the 1930 races, had neither a plane nor even a pass to the field in 1932, Amelia gave Tier her pass, remarking with a grin that she thought she could get in without it.

Amelia proposed that the Ninety-Nines have a magazine with Clara Trenckman Studer, a newspaper reporter who had lost her job at Curtiss Wright in a depression cutback, as editor. Amelia would pay her salary until the magazine could raise it through advertisements.

She also found work for Helen Weber, another woman fired by Curtiss Wright, first at Ludington Airlines as her temporary assistant and later as co-author, with G. P., of a boy's book. In 1932, when Weber was recuperating from surgery, she was the Putnams' houseguest and in November of that year Amelia hired her as her secretary.

Amelia certainly needed one. In a letter to Clara Studer on November 11, Weber gave a vivid picture of Amelia's work while she was based at Rye:

> AE left early-early today [Saturday] for Hartford for luncheon, peerade [sic] and lecture tonight, thence by horse car to Williamstown . . . to speak over nation-wide hookup on Sunday night—thence to Keene, New

Hampshire, thence to Waterbury, Connecticut, and I am to have a candle in the window sometime after midnight on Tuesday night. Wednesday is the big SECRET, of course, not more than 6,000 people know about it— don't tell Walter Winchell—but AE is to get the AWA award at a dinner at the Penn Hotel. She will speak on Thursday, the 17th, at McMillan Theater, Columbia University. So I should think she would stay at the Seymour Hotel on Thursday . . . in case you are hankering to see her.

On Friday she was in Portland, Maine, and on Saturday, in Poughkeepsie, New York.

Life was even more hectic when she left Rye for the lecture circuit. She flew when the weather permitted, drove at other times, often alone and at night, and took trains under protest. In the last half of October she was based in Chicago and ranged as far west as Lawrence, Kansas, and Des Moines, Iowa, as far north as Milwaukee, Wisconsin, and Marquette, Michigan. After a week at home she spent most of November and December on the road again, often with two lectures booked for the same day. Along with the lectures, there were autographing sessions in book stores to promote sales of *The Fun of It.*

When she drove she took her favorite car, the big, powerful, black Franklin sedan that G. P. claimed handled like a truck. After taking it to Chicago for a lecture to more than one thousand 4-H Club members, she became so ill with either influenza or food poisoning that she had to leave it in Cleveland a day later. The next day she was flown from Cleveland to Erie, Pennsylvania, where a Ninety-Nine friend, Helen Richey, met her and took her to Williamsburg for her next lecture. A day later she gave two in Detroit before moving on to Cincinnati. Richey again met her and drove her, in the Franklin, to Johnstown, where Amelia had to insist to an eager arrangements committee that she could not join them for coffee but had to have a rest before giving both afternoon and evening lectures. On December 6 she was in Ithaca, on the eighth, in Springfield, Massachusetts, to speak at a luncheon along with Dr. Mary Woolley, president of Mt. Holyoke College. That night she made a network broadcast. On the ninth she was back in Cleveland and on the tenth, in Detroit.

Returning to Cleveland to pick up her car, Amelia drove to Greenville, Pennsylvania, to receive an honorary degree from her father's alma mater, Thiel College. She left early the following day in a blinding sleet storm for Toronto. After returning to Rye for forty-eight hours, on December 17, she gave another National Geographic Society lecture in

Washington. Although she still needed at least fifteen minutes alone before each appearance to prepare for the ordeal, once on stage she spoke with the assurance and grace of a professional actress.

The same assurance was reflected in changing personal relationships. At thirty-five, with no children of her own and no desire to have any, Amelia displayed genuine affection for her nineteen-year-old stepson. She kept open house for his friends and pleaded his cause when he aroused G. P.'s fearsome temper, a fairly frequent occurrence. A handsome, intelligent youth, David was cheerfully impetuous, breaking enough rules to warrant several changes of boarding schools. While he was in California with his father and Amelia, she arranged a job for him with Paul Mantz, stunt man, master pilot, owner of an aviation garage at Burbank, and choreographer of the dog fights in Howard Hughes's great war film, *Hell's Angels*.

Mantz also gave young Putnam flying lessons. After only a few weeks of instruction, David soloed "in a Kinner Fleet, a hot stunt plane in those days." Practical joker Mantz did not make it easy for the young explorer and author. To a crowd waiting to see a Mexican Olympic team arrive at the field, Mantz announced over the public address system, "You will now see a young American make his first flight." Mantz rattled the novice for a moment, but David pulled himself together, took off and soloed successfully, receiving his license not long after.

Amelia gave him his first aeronautical textbook and later, his first automobile, in what she called a "trade." In exchange for the Essex Terraplane she had received in Detroit, she took his raccoon coat, a wardrobe staple for Ivy League students. In spite of her heavy lecture schedule that fall, she found time to accompany G. P. to Providence to see David play on the Brown University freshman football team.

While her relationship with her stepson grew closer, she became increasingly estranged from her mother. Before the solo Atlantic flight there had been disagreement over Amy's expenditure of her allowance on Muriel and other members of the family. In September Amelia suggested that Amy accompany her on at least part of one lecture tour. "It might be just one hotel after another," she warned but if Amy didn't want to tour then she might like to spend a week in Rye that month or the first part of October. She had not yet been to the house in Rye.

This letter was followed by one on September 18 in which Amelia asked her mother to come to Rye for "a day or two" to work out the details for accompanying her on a tour. With the invitation she enclosed only half of Amy's allowance explaining that "if I sent the whole you would spend it on someone else and not have anything left for yourself by the first of the month." The someone else was Muriel.

The invitations to Amy were not renewed. On November 4 Amelia wrote that she had finished her first tour and that G. P. would go with her on the next to New England. When Amy suggested she come along, Amelia replied, "I don't know what to say about your coming. . . . You said maybe it was just as well that you didn't go so there would be no chance of your disgracing me or words to that effect."

She followed this with a halfhearted promise to try to work something out if Amy really did want to come along "for a few days" but nothing came of it. On Christmas Eve Amelia wrote Amy a long letter describing her visit to Thiel College on December 11. If Amy were jealous of Amelia's affection for Edwin the letter would have done nothing to placate her. The devoted daughter who had never stopped loving her father wrote:

> I met several people who were in Dad's class and others who knew him. I found his record for scholarship, ie., age of graduation has never been equaled. He was fourteen when he entered college and only eighteen when he got his degree. . . .
> Everyone remembered Dad as so handsome and bright. . . .

She could not extend to Amy the childlike love she felt for Edwin. As a youngster she had expected and received affection and guidance from her mother. As as adolescent she had followed Amy's example in withdrawing from an alcoholic Edwin and turned to her mother for the money for college fees and her first airplane. But from the time she became a self-supporting adult she romanticized her father while assuming a caretaker's role toward her mother.

Neither Amelia's gratitude for past support nor her voluntary assumption of financial responsibility for Amy could overcome other differences—in personality, values, and generational perceptions. The mother whom the child Amelia had thought intelligent and determined seemed to have become opinionated and stubborn. Amelia disagreed with Amy's focus on the extended family as the center of life. To the older woman, anyone within the family, no matter how inept or even dishonest, deserved her consideration and, often, assistance. After a miserable adolescence caused by a father she refused to condemn, Amelia was a confirmed loner, no longer tied to the family, reserved even with friends.

On the surface, the conflict between mother and daughter centered on money. Amelia had had so little until after she was thirty that she spent it carefully and invested wisely. Never stingy, she enjoyed giving it to her mother as well as to a number of friends in need but, having given it, she was angered by Amy's use of it. Her mother lived in an ill-kept, often cold house with Muriel and the husband Amelia despised. Amy was co-housekeeper, cooking, sewing, cleaning, and baby-tending. When she was not giving her money and labor to the Morrisseys, she went to Philadelphia to tend her dying sister, Margaret Balis, a woman who had borrowed and spent the life savings of their retarded brother without a hope of repaying him.

In addition to withholding half of Amy's allowance and banking it for her, Amelia bought her clothing and asked that doctor bills be sent directly to her, because either Amy did not have the money to pay them or, worse, would not see a physician when she really needed one. If Amelia's letters seemed domineering and insensitive they were in response to a determined and evasive mother who pretended acquiescence and then did as she pleased. Nevertheless, Amelia wrote frequently, more than to any other person, remaining a concerned, dutiful, and frequently exasperated daughter.

Amelia's relationship with G. P. also changed. He remained her publisher and agent as well as her husband, but she was no longer his student or prodigy. He himself affirmed this when he first heard she had landed in Ireland, telling a reporter, "This is her stunt. She's doing it under her own name, Amelia Earhart. That's the name she made for herself."

If he slipped back into his previously domineering role, she did not hesitate to correct him. During a press conference aboard the *Riverside* a reporter noted that when G. P. continually interrupted her she turned to him and said, quietly but firmly, "Just a minute, dear," then continued to give her account of the Atlantic crossing. Later, when G. P. again interrupted to say, "Tell them about your lunch with the king and queen of Belgium," she ignored him, describing instead how admirably the British press had treated her. She was confident but not angry with him. Two hours later, speaking to the Flag Association, she said that much of the credit for her flight belonged to her husband. "It was much harder for him to stay than it was for me to go," she said.

She repeated this praise in a magazine article, written with G. P., entitled "My Wife—My Husband," reminding the reader that her husband was a publisher, writer, and explorer, who was not accustomed to stand on the sidelines while others played the game. Yet he had cancelled an important business engagement when she called and asked him to come to England and help her with appointments and correspondence. For his part, G. P. wrote that they had from their "bargain of partnership" mutual independence of action. When she told him the chances of getting across the Atlantic were one in ten, he was not happy about it but it was her show, he said, and if the engine held out she would.

They could hardly be critical of one another in a magazine article but their claims of compatibility were confirmed by friends. Amelia's confidante of college days, Marian Stabler, was not so sure at first. She disliked G. P. intensely, calling him a "lion hunter" who discouraged Amelia's friendship with anyone except the famous. Marian had also heard a story about them soon after their marriage, told her by a friend who worked in an automobile agency. The friend said that Amelia had come to the salesroom before G. P. and accepted a demonstration ride. While she was gone, he arrived and "fussed and fumed, walking up and down like a caged lion." When Amelia returned, "he took her to task in a very humiliating way in front of the two salespeople . . . for not waiting for him."

Marian was certain that G. P. was responsible for the infrequency with which she saw her old friend. On one of the rare occasions she dined with them, Marian said that Amelia's warm cordiality was not enough to compensate for her host's rude, patronizing manner. Yet in spite of her dislike of him, Marian said, "That night I was there, after dinner they settled down together and I could see that she cared for him and he cared for her. I'm quite sure they were in love."

If G. P. was as rude to Amelia as the car story indicated, her calm manner and growing assertiveness put a stop to such scenes soon after. In commenting on G. P.'s unrestrained profanity during one of his frequent temper tantrums, Bradford Washburn, a young author who was sitting in the office one day during a typical outburst, later remarked, "Putnam would never speak like that in front of Amelia."

Whether she was in love or not, the marriage Amelia had told Marian was one of "convenience and necessity" proved very convenient and not nearly as confining as she had anticipated. Much of their limited time together was spent at the house in Rye where they shared an avid interest in gardening. Helen Weber looked out the window one day when she was working as Amelia's secretary and saw G. P. giving Amelia a ride in the wheelbarrow, racing up and down, tipping and tilting the vehicle while his passenger alternately squealed in delight and roared with laughter.

Another shared interest, a new one to Amelia, was entertaining. Cousin Lucy Challis, who resented news stories that she thought "masculinized" Amelia, said that Amelia managed the Rye house perfectly and liked entertaining. Although she was reluctant to "make conversation," she found no need to do so when entertaining with G. P. The guests, friends of G. P.'s as well as some she had met on her own, all had careers or professions that interested her.

At the close of 1932, on the night before New Year's Eve, Amelia and G. P. entertained at a gathering that G. P.'s columnist friend Walter Trumbull called "one of those famous parties given by George Palmer Putnam and Amelia Earhart." The fifty or more guests included Roy Chapman Andrews, the naturalist just back from an expedition to Central Asia, Arctic explorers Vilhjalmur Stefansson and Sir Hubert Wilkins, African adventurers Martin and Osa Johnson, novelist Fannie Hurst, aviators Hilton Railey, Eugene Vidal, and Paul Collins, and the Elliott Roosevelts, Bernard Gimbels, and Ogden Reids.

Their hostess was as famous as any of her guests. In a single year she had been awarded the Distinguished Flying Cross, crosses of the Belgian Order of Leopold and French Legion of Honor, the Rumanian Order of Virtutea Aviation Medal, National Geographic medal and medals from the Comite France-Amerique, Le Lyceum Societé des Femmes de France at New York, the Columbia Broadcasting System, the Commonwealth of Massachusetts, and the cities of Chicago, New York, and Philadelphia. She also received awards from the Aero Club of France and the Aero Club Royal de Belgique.

An article in *U.S. Air Services* magazine claimed that her solo crossing of the Atlantic had carried "Amelia Earhart Putnam . . . into the PLAN to RAYM volume of the next and all succeeding editions of the *Encyclopedia*

Britannica." As predicted, she was in succeeding editions of the Britannica, but not under "P" with the three Putnams—G. P., his grandfather George Palmer Putnam, and his uncle George Haven Putnam. Amelia was listed under "E" for "Earhart, Amelia, U.S. aviation pioneer," a title she would both justify and exploit in the coming year.

CHAPTER FOURTEEN

Queen of the Air

*I*t's a routine now, Bert. I make a record and then I lecture on it. That's where the money comes from. Until it's time to make another record." Pilot Winfield Kinner, Jr., stood near the runway at Burbank, listening to Amelia and his father, Bert, on a February day in 1933. The two men had just left a plane to be inspected and licensed when Amelia saw them and stopped to talk. Twelve years before that day, back at Kinner Field, schoolboy "Win" Kinner had marveled at Amelia's skill as a contortionist but thought she "was inclined to make sloppy landings." The last time he had seen her was in 1929 when his mother cooked pork chops for her the night before she flew back east in the little Avro Avian she bought from Lady Heath.

The "Queen of the Air" was reminiscing with Bert as if she were still twenty-three years old instead of thirty-five. Her grin was the same but her blue-grey eyes were older and the fair, smooth complexion Win recalled was tanned and marked with fine lines from sun and wind. Amelia wasn't really complaining to Bert as much as explaining. In 1921, the rules of the game had been "No work, no pay. No pay, no fly." The game was bigger now but the rules were the same.

Amelia told Bert she had just sold her Vega and bought another. She was at Burbank to talk about the overhaul of her purchase made in January.* To buy the Vega she had to sell her "little red bug." Except for the motor installed by Balchen and Gorski for the Atlantic flight, the plane was worth very little, unless it were bought as memorabilia, like Lindbergh's *Spirit of St. Louis* which the Smithsonian Institution had acquired. Amelia's Philadelphia friend, Dorothy Leh, suggested the Franklin Institute's museum might buy it. Amelia's former employers, the Ludington brothers, had given one hundred thousand dollars to the Institute for a Hall of Aviation in 1930.

Amelia followed Leh's advice. "After some bickering," she wrote Leh, "the Franklin Institute finally bought my plane. . . . Do I owe you a commission? I'm serious about this." "No, darling," Leh answered, "no commission," adding her thanks for a free ride Amelia had given her to Cleveland.

However, seventy-five hundred dollars was not enough to pay for and update the Vega from 5B to the newer, faster 5C that Amelia needed if she were to break any records. While Lockheed worked on the plane, she would have to return to lecturing and cultivating the publicity that brought more bookings and bigger audiences.

There were no holidays for Amelia. Even before she left for the West Coast and a lecture tour on January 27 she was working eighteen-hour days. In the first two weeks of 1933 she bought the new plane, received four medals (two in a single day) all requiring acceptance speeches, and wrote two dozen or more letters on behalf of the Ninety-Nines. She also gave a long interview to the Sarah Lawrence College newspaper and attended the opening of the new Roxy Theater in the Radio City complex. There she sat for Edward Steichen who photographed her in the women's lounge before an engraved glass mural depicting her Atlantic flight. *Vogue* ran it with the caption, "The First Lady of the Sky."

On January 16 she went to Washington to testify before the Senate on the development of a Washington municipal airport. Three days before she had received a medal from the Rumanians, along with Charles Lindbergh. In her diary Anne Lindbergh wrote, "Amelia Earhart, a shaft

*The Vega Model B, serial number 171, was built in August of 1931 for John Henry Mears as a "high-speed special." When he refused delivery on it, Elinor Smith bought it for a projected Atlantic flight she never made. After Smith, the most severe critic of Amelia's flying skills, cracked it up in an accident in Garden City, she transferred ownership to her husband, Patrick H. Sullivan, who sold it to William W. Hart, Jr., of New York City. Hart sold it to Amelia, the bill of sale dated January 7, 1933.

of white coming out of a blue room." About G. P. she added, "Amelia Earhart's husband hovering." G. P. hovered with a purpose. He was planning a dinner in honor of Auguste Piccard, the Belgian who had ascended in a balloon to a record height in the stratosphere. Before leaving Belgium for the United States, Piccard, an acknowledged authority on cosmic rays and radiation and currently studying stratospheric rocketry, told reporters that Earhart and Lindbergh were his American heroes. G. P. intended inviting a dozen or more aeronautical celebrities, including Lindbergh. Lindbergh refused the invitation. G. P. then suggested a small, private dinner at the house in Rye and Lindbergh accepted.

There were only nine present—Amelia, G. P., the Lindberghs, David Putnam, explorer-naturalist Roy Chapman Andrews, William Beebe (designer of an undersea vehicle, the bathysphere, in which he had descended to a record depth in the sea), Piccard, and his business manager, Sylvestre Dorian. The next day the *New York Times* had a complete account of the conversation at dinner and a description of Piccard putting down knife and fork to take an enormous slide-rule from his waistcoat pocket to convert kilometers into miles for Amelia and Lindbergh. For the remainder of the dinner, the report said, Piccard used the rule as frequently as his knife and fork. Portions of Lindbergh's conversation with the scientist were quoted directly, and twelve days later, the dinner was again described in an article in the *New Yorker* magazine. G. P. apologized to an angry Lindbergh, insisting that he was not the tale bearer, but that Dorian was and had done it for forty dollars offered by a reporter.

Guilty or not, G. P. continued to take an active part in promoting Piccard's visit. The Putnam touch is evident in plans to celebrate the Belgian's birthday the following Saturday. Arrangements included a dirigible descending to the roof of the St. Moritz to take the professor and other guests for a flight over Manhattan. Amelia, who disliked these stunts as much as Lindbergh did, escaped this one, leaving the previous day on the Twentieth-Century Limited for Chicago. From there she flew as a guest of Northwest Airways to Minneapolis–St. Paul, then on to the West Coast.

Her speaker's agency, the Emerson Bureau, had booked a lecture tour, starting in Portland on February 1, but G. P. arranged the free flight with Northwest on a survey trip for a proposed northern route to Seattle. Amelia got a free ride and the airline good publicity because of her. There was a reception for her in Bismarck, North Dakota, on January 28, and at

Helena, Montana, one thousand admirers came out to the airport for her arrival. She stayed in Helena overnight, and made a five-minute address the next day to a joint session of the Montana state legislature. Everywhere reporters clamored for interviews, quoting her at length and describing her in great detail.

When her flight was cut short at Spokane by a winter storm, one wrote that she "didn't look like an aviatrix," however they were supposed to look. He gushed:

> She was merely a lovely feminine-looking young woman who graciously accepted the greetings of the curious who approached her in the lobby [of the hotel]. . . . There were no air trappings, no wings, no helmets. She stood there with her tousled hair, which had become her trademark, set off against the soft collar of her handsome coat [a full-length sable], a tall young woman . . . carrying a bouquet of pink sweet peas.

At the next stop in Portland, a reporter overheard a woman who saw Amelia at the train station say, "Why—she's quite a beautiful person!" and another newsman wrote that her pictures, which suggested a "masculine nature," were misleading. He also claimed, "She likes to keep long hours, she likes to meet people and she isn't a tomboy." Flying was just a hobby for her, he wrote, her real job was making a home for her husband. Amelia's interviewer was so impressed by her femininity he could not hear the feminist speaking to him.

The sum of her statements in Portland is a familiar one today: 1) modern science has cut back on household drudgery; 2) a woman could run a home and have a career; and 3) if she did, her husband should share household and child-raising duties. As for women doing the same work as men, perhaps they could. If they were made equal under the law and given the opportunity they would soon find out. There were still no women pilots on scheduled airlines, partly because of prejudice but also because they lacked experience, she said. Army and Navy training was not open to them; they had to pay for their instruction and flight time. They could not afford the hours of experience needed by the airlines to assure the safety of passengers.*

---

*Almost fifty years later U.S. Air Force pilot Maj. Nancy B. Samuelson repeated Amelia's complaint, claiming that women were all but totally eliminated from training programs paid for by taxpayers. "This is particularly true of flight training programs and especially true of military flight training programs," she wrote.

At her next stop, in Seattle, Amelia added a new proposal to her program for the emancipation of women. "Draft women!" she declared, a strange proposition to be made by an avowed pacifist and one that is still controversial a half century later. "If women were drafted," she claimed, "I think it would be an effective means of ending war. They would learn how horrible it is."

In Vancouver the next day she expounded on this theme. Individual aptitude, rather than sex, should determine the possibility of women becoming wartime flyers. In the event of casualties, "So far as sex is concerned, women are no more valuable than men."

Amelia gave these opinions in interviews but her lectures were limited to a description of her Atlantic crossing, the advantages of commercial aviation, and twenty-five hundred feet of newsreel film. For each lecture she was paid three hundred dollars, half the price of a new Buick. Between February 1 and 7 she gave a total of eight, in Portland, Seattle, Vancouver, San Francisco, and Los Angeles, earning twenty-four hundred dollars in a single week. G. P., who was Paramount Pictures' New York chief story advisor, met her in Los Angeles and took her to lunch at Paramount Studios. The next day Hollywood columnist Louella Parsons published the "rumor" that Miss Earhart might act as adviser on a coming Paramount aviation film.

The June edition of *Screenland* magazine carried a story on Amelia; she was photographed with Gary Cooper, allegedly going over reels from his latest film in which he played the role of a flight officer. It is doubtful Amelia did any advising. But G. P. saw to it that she was also pictured with Gene Raymond, Tallulah Bankhead, and Marlene Dietrich, and that the Putnams were described as "the world's only regular airplane commuters between New York and Hollywood." Soon after, Helen Weber, who was still helping Amelia with her correspondence, wrote to a mutual friend that Amelia "is getting a bit fed up, I think, of the constant travel, particularly when it must perforce be by train in this winter weather." Amelia herself described the tour as "much more intense than I had planned, because the management [G. P.] kept trying to squeeze in more, and in these times, I thought I might as well do as much and get as much as I could." She did.

Amelia had already begun to proclaim in no uncertain terms the causes of feminism, pacifism, and the use of commercial aviation that she advocated on the lecture tour soon after her Atlantic flight. Three months after President Hoover presented her the National Geographic's gold medal in June of 1932 she was back at the White House—this time with a petition for an equal rights amendment to the constitution. "I join with the National Women's Party," she told Hoover, "in hoping for the speedy passage of the Lucretia Mott Amendment which would write into the highest law of our land that men and women shall have equal rights throughout the United States."

In addition to the equal rights amendment, Amelia suggested that the federal government take the lead in eliminating discrimination. As an example she cited the Department of Commerce's recognition of legal equality for men and women in licensing pilots. If the actual treatment of women aviators was less than fair, the licensing was at least a starting point for further improvement.

When Amelia called for equality she meant just that; she did not want affirmative action. Equal rights legislation would put a stop, she said, "to sentimental attitudes about protective legislation for women. . . . Wages should be based on work itself, not on sex." Although she had joined the National Women's Party, she regarded a separate political party for women as a necessary evil to be abandoned as soon as discriminatory legislation was eliminated.

In a letter to the editor of the New York *Sun* she complimented the paper on its editorial disapproval of a special minimum wage law for women. "It is true that in all too many instances conditions and wages [for women] are deplorable," she wrote. "However, civilization's duty is to men as well as women and any sincere welfare program must see them safeguarded also. The right to earn a living belongs to all persons."

On her first lecture tour of 1933 Amelia had said whatever she pleased, but she went wherever G. P. sent her. If she expected a rest after her return to Rye on February 7 she was disappointed. A few days later she flew to Chicago for a wedding in which G. P. was best man. He must have insisted because she resented having to go. "I loathe the formal kind [of wedding]," she wrote to her mother, "and have never attended any since Pidge got me inside a church for hers. (I don't mean only church weddings are awful, of course.)" What she seemed to mean was that all weddings were "awful," and that she remained as critical of marriage as she had been before her own. Whether she told G. P. this or he sensed it, he treated her to a brief vacation as soon as they returned to Rye, a drive south with David. On the way they stopped overnight at Aberdeen, North Carolina, where she played golf the next morning.

The vacation was for three days, ending on February 24 when she was back in New York for a nationwide broadcast, "The Inside Story," which combined a dramatization of her life with an interview conducted by Edwin C. Hill, the most popular radio commentator of the time. Amelia repeated her feminist views—she did not believe a woman should be a prisoner of her home; her husband "would no more interfere with my work than I would with his"; and her reason for flying the Atlantic solo was to demonstrate that "women like to do such things, and can."

On March 4, 1933, Amelia and G. P. went to Washington for the inauguration of Franklin Delano Roosevelt at the invitation of Eleanor. Eleanor and Amelia were already friends. Just two weeks after Roosevelt was elected the previous November Eleanor gave the introductory remarks for one of Amelia's lectures, at Poughkeepsie, New York. Before the lecture Amelia and G. P. were guests at an informal dinner at Hyde Park for the Roosevelts' houseguest, Lady Nancy Astor. The only other guests were Mrs. Henry Morganthau and her son Henry, Jr. Lady Astor also spoke at Amelia's lecture, prompting the local newspaper to exclaim that "three of the world's outstanding women" were all on stage at the local high school—the first woman to fly the Atlantic, the first American woman elected to Parliament, and the next First Lady of the United States. Amelia did not hesitate to petition the new president in her role as pacifist. She signed a request from the Women's League for Peace and Freedom to cut military and naval expenditures and to use the money for unemployment relief. She signed a second from the American Women's committee for the Recognition of Soviet Russia.

A week after the inauguration Amelia had lunch at the White House and a month later she returned with G. P. for dinner and an overnight stay before her lecture to the Daughters of the American Revolution on April 21. On that first night Amelia took Eleanor, who was an enthusiastic booster of commercial aviation, for an airplane ride, a stunt arranged by G. P. After dinner Amelia and Eleanor, still in formal dress and long white gloves, were taken to the airport to board one of Eastern Air Transport's new two-motored Curtiss Condors, flown by two of the airline's regular pilots. A half-dozen women reporters were invited but men were banned except for one male photographer, Eleanor's brother Hall, G. P., and Eugene Vidal. On the round trip to Baltimore Amelia took the controls long enough to be photographed at them wearing long, white evening gloves, before G. P. suggested that Eleanor take a turn in the cockpit while the captain demonstrated the controls to her. "It was like being on top of the world," she told one of the reporters aboard. When another asked if she felt safe, "knowing a girl may be flying this ship," Eleanor said she did and added, "I'd give anything to do it myself!" She meant it. Three months earlier she had discussed learning to fly with Amelia. Amelia sent her to her physician for the physical examination needed by student pilots. Eleanor passed it but when she asked Franklin for his approval he told her he thought it would be a waste of time because she could not afford a plane. Eleanor sent the student pilot's permit she had obtained to Amelia.

The next night Amelia made front-page copy on her own when she threw down the gauntlet of pacifism to the Daughters of the American Revolution. Before a full house at Constitution Hall she declared that no organization should advocate armaments unless its members were willing to bear arms themselves. Calling it "a point on which this organization and I don't see eye to eye," she repeated her claim that equality of opportunity with men was essential in everything, including the draft in the event of war.

Although her stand on equal rights had previously aroused remarkably little criticism, her proposal to draft women did and not just from the D.A.R. In November, on the eve of Armistice Day, she gave an interview to *Yale Daily News* reporter Whitelaw Reid, whose parents owned the *Herald Tribune*. This time she added that women not only should be drafted, they should "be made to do the dirty work, and real fighting instead of dressing up and parading down the streets." The oldest people should be drafted first, she said: "They are the ones who start war and if they knew that their verdict to fight meant their getting out in the line of fire themselves, they would be a great deal slower in rushing into an armed conflict."

The Yale interview was picked up by the Associated Press and ran in newspapers from coast to coast. In a letter to the *New York Times,* one of Amelia's critics, a woman, claimed that American women had served in the First World War both overseas and at home, and they paraded in the streets to sell Liberty Bonds, not to show off. "A woman with Miss Earhart's fine courage and high order of intelligence should have a better knowledge of her own sex than her flippant remarks would indicate," she wrote. Perhaps Amelia was too young to know what her country-women had done from 1914 to 1920!

The feminist-pacifist also defied her old friend Hiram Bingham of the NAA, resigning on May 6 from her posts as vice-president and contest committee member. She objected to Bingham's insistence that membership be expanded and the control of the monthly magazine be given to "a promoter who will operate it for his own gain," or so she claimed. Amelia had already waged a two-year campaign to abandon the magazine, winning approval of the executive and contest committees but the dictatorial Bingham ignored their action. "Wholesale resignations" had been predicted but Amelia's was the only one.

In her letter to Bingham she said their viewpoints were "too dissimilar" but she had only the friendliest personal feelings toward him. He was not as charitable, claiming that she apparently wanted the NAA to do nothing except sanction air meets, but he urged her to keep her honorary membership.

However, she did side with Bingham when he threatened to suspend all NAA-FAI license holders for one to three years if they took part in "unsanctioned" (by the NAA) air meets. His threat was aimed at the *Chicago Tribune*–sponsored American Air Races, scheduled for July 1 through 4, the same dates as the NAA-sanctioned National Air Races to be held in Los Angeles. Pilots protested that Bingham's ukase banning them from participation in the Chicago races would cause them to lose potential prize money but Amelia supported Bingham's efforts to sustain what she thought the most basic function of the NAA, the sanctioning of air meets. The day before she resigned as vice-president she protested the use of her name as a member of the Chicago meet's pilots' committee, saying she had no connection with the meet because it was scheduled in direct opposition to the National Air Races.

Back from Washington after her resignation, Amelia stayed home for most of May and June. In May her mother came for her first visit in the house in Rye since Amelia's marriage more than two years before. The mother-daughter relationship reflected in their letters had evolved into one in which Amelia, Amy's primary source of support, sounded like the parent, and Amy, the child. Amelia sent checks, advice, and packages, including a bottle of "tooth wash," a "scientific solvent," recommended by her dentist. Amelia's customary admonishments regarding money and

Muriel continued. "Enclosed is a check. Please don't give it all away if the giving means fostering dependence and lack of responsibility." When Muriel asked Amelia for a second mortgage on the Morrisseys' house, Amelia tried to find out from Amy how much help Amy was giving the couple from her allowance. Amelia doubted the Morrisseys could hold on to the house under any circumstances, but she sent the necessary documents to Muriel.

Amy's visit to Rye in May was followed by a series of letters concerning where and with whom Amy would spend the month of August. Amy suggested Maine. Amelia countered with Stonington, Connecticut, where her friend from college days, Elise von R. Owen, and her mother had converted their pre-depression home into a guest house. Amy then changed to Marblehead and wanted to take both her grandchildren with her. Amelia said she could have one, part of the time, but not both. "I will not permit it under any circumstances," she wrote, threatening to withhold Amy's monthly check if she took them. In the end Amy went to Marblehead where Amelia urged her to stay through autumn. There was no mention of how many grandchildren went with her in subsequent letters.

That summer Amelia, as president of the Ninety-Nines, stepped up her efforts on behalf of her colleagues, a strong-willed and unconventional lot, sometimes contentious and always competitive. Determined to increase the membership, she opposed Gladys O'Donnell's suggestion that there be a special women's committee for the National Air Races, affiliated with but separate from the Ninety-Nines. Amelia warned O'Donnell that there were already complaints that the organization was run by and for professionals who comprised only a small number of the six hundred women licensees in the United States.

Amelia also used her own fame to gain publicity for the Ninety-Nines. She made arrangements to model an inexpensive flying suit for *Vogue* magazine—one she thought might make an optional Ninety-Nines uniform—but she could not get an agreement from the regional directors in time to meet the magazine's deadline and the picture was used without mention of the organization. To publicize an all-woman air race staged by Annette Gipson, a beautiful young aviatrix, at Roosevelt Field on June 4, Amelia took all the participants to lunch before the race, then waved the starting flag while thirty thousand spectators watched, many standing on the roofs of their parked cars.

In a letter to Margaret Cooper, the woman she wanted to succeed her as president, Amelia revealed managerial talent and political acumen. Bylaws were needed; so was new stationery, but the old should be sold to "patriotic" members, she said following the Earhart rule of putting style first, with frugality close on its heels. She also warned Cooper that she should consider the hazards of a lawsuit before attempting to eject an undesirable member.

Amelia wrote to Cooper because she was not certain she would arrive in time for the annual meeting and election of officers in Los Angeles on July 3. She had just entered the Bendix, the transcontinental race sponsored by Vincent Bendix, with Ruth Nichols. "Racing," Amelia wrote to Cooper, "is not the most reliable way to travel. . . . The schedule calls for our leaving July 1, but it's along [sic] way from here to there."

It *was* a long way. The two women were given only two weeks notice that women would be eligible, with a special prize of twenty-five hundred dollars for the winner. Nichols, who had cracked up her Vega at Newfoundland while attempting an Atlantic crossing a year before, had borrowed a Lockheed Orion that her friend Clarence Chamberlin was trying to overhaul in a few days. Amelia's sole "test flight" for her rebuilt Vega was to Chicago for a three-day visit to the World's Fair with G. P., his twelve-year-old son, George, Jr., and a Rye neighbor, Betty Chester. If she had known she would be flying in the Bendix she might have put it through more rigorous testing.

Amelia and Nichols were scheduled to take off a little after midnight on July 1 from Floyd Bennett Field, six hours before the men, who had faster ships. The crowd of two thousand that gathered at the airport to see them leave dwindled to two hundred after Nichols's plane developed motor trouble and the fog rolled in from the sea, followed by a severe thunderstorm. Amelia found a bed in one of the airport offices and slept for three hours while mechanics worked on Nichols's plane and G. P. studied weather reports from the west. At 3:30 A.M. it was obvious that Nichols's Orion needed more work. Amelia took off twenty minutes later after telling reporters she would insist that her rival not be penalized for the delay in starting.

The delay was only the first in a series of mishaps that plagued both women. After refueling at St. Louis, Amelia almost lost consciousness from gas fumes in the cockpit before landing at Wichita. Shortly after she left there the hatch cover of her Vega blew open, "blanketing" the tail and threatening her control of the aircraft. She spent an hour and a half at Winslow, Arizona, while mechanics made repairs. Soon after she left Winslow, motor trouble forced her to return to Wichita where she stayed overnight. On July 2 she reached her destination, the Los Angeles Municipal Airport, but was forced by ground rules to circle over the field for more than a half hour until the fifty-mile free-for-all race was over. Amelia was the last of the three remaining contestants out of six to finish the Bendix. Russell Boardman, who crashed at takeoff from Indianapolis, died on July 3. Harry Thaw dropped out after his plane was badly damaged on takeoff, also at Indianapolis, and Ruth Nichols withdrew at Wichita.

Last in the Bendix and entering no other event, yet mobbed by admirers at the grandstand, Amelia stayed on through the last day, July 4. For the grand finale, manager Cliff Henderson had arranged for Mary Pickford to arrive on a trimotored Fokker, escorted by six Boeing pursuit planes. Amid the blare of trumpets, Amelia greeted her, along with Col. H. H. "Hap" Arnold, who would become one of the great air commanders of World War II. Pickford, who had announced the breakup of her marriage to Douglas Fairbanks two days earlier, smiled bravely for the photographers when Amelia shook her hand. The syndicated photographs of "America's Sweetheart" and the "Queen of the Air" appeared in hundreds of newspapers across the country.

In spite of her poor showing in the Bendix Amelia had lost nothing by entering. Along with the national news coverage G. P. wanted for her she had given the reconditioned Vega a shakedown it needed for another try at breaking her own transcontinental speed record for women.

Late on the night of July 7 she taxied the heavily laden plane, its red and silver paint glistening in the moonlight, down the runway of the Los Angeles Municipal Airport and took off for Newark. Three hours later the lock on the hatch cover broke again. The first time the rigid sheet of metal had blown off, narrowly missing the rudder. This time it fluttered in the propeller's wake, again threatening to shear the rudder. With one hand on the controls, Amelia reached up and caught the edge of the cover, then held it for the next seventy-five miles as she headed toward Amarillo. She knew she would have to use both hands to land. Arm bruised and numb, she released the hatch, pulled back the throttle to slow the ship and grasped the wheel for a landing. The latch held.

After a two and a half hour delay while the lock was repaired, she left Amarillo but was soon involved in a new battle for survival when carbon monoxide gas again drifted into the cockpit. Nauseated and faint, she held out until Columbus where she had to land for fuel. While waiting there she walked up and down the field to restore her circulation. Her knees kept buckling, but the fresh air revived her. From Columbus she fought a heavy rain squall over the Pennsylvania mountains before approaching Newark at 8:19 P.M. on Saturday, July 8. The field was still lit by a summer sunset as she came to a halt on the runway. She had beaten her old record by almost two hours; the new time, seventeen hours, seven minutes, and thirty seconds.

A crowd of three hundred fans, most of them women, rushed the plane as soon as she pushed back the hatch cover and looked out, grinning and running her hand through wind-matted hair. G. P. was waiting for her when she jumped down from the plane, her grimy overalls spattered with oil and grease. "Well," she said to him, "I'm back and nice and dirty as usual." After seventeen hours of constant tension and nausea she took G. P.'s arm, walked with him to the car, got in on the driver's side, and drove off toward Rye. The "Queen of the Air" had reasserted her right to the throne. The record was won, the routine had gone full circle. It was time to make some money again.

CHAPTER FIFTEEN

The Queen and the
Minister of Finance

*A*melia Earhart's recordbreaking transcontinental flight in July of 1933 was her last until January of 1935. For the next eighteen months she was grounded, back in the center ring of the circus she dreaded, jumping through the hoops held by G. P. At times she rebelled, but not often and not for long. Fellow aviator and publicist Harry Bruno overstated the case when he observed: "She loved flying; wanted to fly all the time. she was not after money at all. But George Palmer Putnam was a businessman and he wanted to cash in on it."

Amelia wanted to make money, but she wanted to make it in aviation. G. P. aimed for the greater profits to be made from maintaining and exploiting her fame. While he was always just a friend of the famous, Amelia was one of them, a natural. Her friendship with Eleanor Roosevelt was invaluable to him, leading to one of his finest publicity coups, one involving the president, Eleanor, and the newest conquerors of the Atlantic, Capt. James "Jimmy" Mollison and his wife, Amy Johnson Mollison.*

---

*Amelia had met the Mollisons in London a year earlier, just before Jimmy made a solo Atlantic flight, east to west, August 18–21, 1932. Amy set a record of her own in 1931 when she took a patched-up DeHavilland Moth biplane from London to Australia. Twenty-six years old, with less than one hundred hours of flight time, she flew eleven thousand five hundred miles in twenty days, landing in Darwin on May 24.

On July 23 the Mollisons reached the American east coast from London. Weary and heading into darkness, Jimmy Mollison turned back just twenty miles short of New York where ten thousand people were waiting to see the couple land at Roosevelt Field. When he attempted to put down at Bridgeport, Connecticut, he overshot the field and crashed in a swamp bordering the field. Amelia was with G. P. and Helen and Ogden Reid beside the Reids' swimming pool in Purchase, New York, when she heard the news on the radio. She called the hospital in Bridgeport where both fliers were taken, suffering from bruises and shock. The next morning she drove there, bringing clothing for Amy. The couple were moved the same day to the Hotel Plaza in New York City where they rested until the following Friday when Amelia drove them to the house in Rye.

That weekend the Roosevelts were vacationing at Hyde Park. After announcing on Friday that he would not receive anyone over the weekend, the president changed his mind on Sunday morning and asked the Mollisons, Amelia, and G. P. to lunch. They were the only guests. Franklin's mother, Sara Delano Roosevelt, who still ruled the family roost at Hyde Park, was the official hostess. Photographs were taken of the Roosevelts, the Mollisons, and Amelia. The English public was delighted, the Mollisons got some of the publicity they needed if they were to secure backing for a new plane, and Amelia shared in all the press notices.

Never one to leave anything to chance, G. P. had already been at work before the president's unexpected invitation. He and Amelia brought the couple to their swimming club at Manuring Island where they were photographed on the beach. More pictures were taken at the house in Rye, pictures that appeared in rotogravure sections of newspapers across the country. The day after their official Broadway parade in New York, and while they were still front-page news, the Mollisons were given a second official reception by Atlantic City, New Jersey. G. P. arranged this one with Amelia as official hostess.* He also arranged for guests to be flown there in planes provided by Eastern Air Transport's president, Thomas B. Doe, the same man who had helped him set up the April flight for Mrs. Roosevelt.

*The guests included artist Howard Chandler Christy, woman explorer Blair Niles, set designer Norman Bel Geddes, boxer Gene Tunney, novelist Fannie Hurst, fliers Eugene Vidal, Eddie Rickenbacker, and Clarence Chamberlin, and journalists Lauren Dwight "Deke" Lyman, Margaret Bourke-White, Carl B. Allen, and Ralph Ingersoll.

The success of G. P.'s celebrity-wooing, along with Amelia's considerable charm, was reflected in news comments like this one: "No public luncheon or dinner, no private party, is complete without Miss Earhart. She is the one essential, apparently, for a successful entertainment."

In addition to the interviews he scheduled for her and the articles he arranged for her to write, G. P. also wrote some of his own. In Paris on a business trip, he gave an article to the Paris edition of the *Herald Tribune,* on the "49.5 Club," an invention of his allegedly composed of the husbands of Ninety-Nines. In another of his articles he claimed that it was not so bad being known as "Amelia Earhart's husband," and that he was not the only man with a wife more famous than himself. Describing the filming of celebrities Mary Pickford and Douglas Fairbanks with Amelia for a charity fund drive, G. P. wrote:

> Mary and Amelia had some shots taken on the lawn. Then Douglas and I barged in.
>
> "I," said Doug, introducing himself to Miss Earhart, "am Mister Pickford."
>
> "And I am Mister Earhart," I said to Mary.

There were times when he crossed the line into territory rightfully Amelia's. In January of 1933 when he arranged the free ride she took on Northwest Airlines he said she was to "assess the desirability of flying the route in mid-winter," and report her findings to the postmaster general. The assignment was ridiculous. She may have been less prejudiced but she was certainly not as qualified as the airline's regular pilots to make such a report. However, Northwest officials had more in mind than Amelia's opinion and so did G. P. They wanted a government appropriation for airfield improvements along the fifteen-hundred-mile air route, about $1.2 million worth. G. P. wanted a piece of the action.

Two weeks after FDR's inauguration, Col. Lewis H. Brittin, vice-president of Northwest and its representative in Washington, wrote to company president Croyl Hunter: "Amelia Earhart had lunch last week at the White House and I think it is quite possible a meeting can be arranged where we would have an opportunity to lay our problem . . . directly before the new Administration. . . . Apparently Eugene Vidal is slated for the Department of Commerce job, [director of the Bureau of Air Commerce] although it has not yet been officially confirmed."

G. P. wrote to Hunter in June, looking for a "mutually advantageous" deal. He told Hunter it was time to push for the new route and to work toward recapturing "some of the airline's stock." He also implied that he and Amelia were responsible for the appointment of Vidal, by then a certainty although not official.

Vidal's son Gore later claimed that Amelia and Eleanor Roosevelt did some "backstage maneuvering" for the appointment. Certainly Amelia thought Vidal ideal for the job. Soon after it was confirmed in September she sent him a photograph of herself inscribed, "To Eugene Vidal whose greatest fault in aviation is thinking too far ahead of the industry." Gore thought Amelia was in love with his father who shared her belief in the boundless future of commercial aviation. Always a romantic, Amelia could have loved him for that shared faith but there is no evidence that she shared his bed, then or later.

In 1932 Amelia, Vidal, and Paul Collins, their friend and fellow employee in Ludington Airlines, had invested in a salt-water swimming pool at the Washington-Hoover Airport. It was a losing proposition when Amelia met Washington real estate man Sam Solomon who offered to bail them out. A handsome ex-Army officer and amateur basketball star, Solomon sold their lease to a New York man, taking his first airplane ride to close the deal. Sam liked the ride and he liked all three aviators. Amelia, Vidal, and Collins then asked him to find them another investment.

In the summer of 1933 when they met at Amelia's house in Rye, she said, "Let's start an airline."* Vidal and Collins agreed immediately, but Solomon said he didn't know anything about airlines. Collins, who had already been approached by officials of the Boston and Maine Railroad about starting an air service operation, said Solomon's financial skills were what they needed. He knew operations and Vidal was both salesman and administrator. Amelia could handle public relations.

Solomon was convinced. "Count me in," he said, "and I want to be a vice-president." Each of the partners contributed twenty-five hundred dollars for a total capitalization of ten thousand dollars, enough for two used airplanes and a few month's operating expenses. They named their new company National Airways.

When Boston and Maine officials asked Collins how he knew the line would cover all the proposed stops with safety, he said he didn't know yet, but he and Amelia would find out. If they were given a car and

---

*The failure of Ludington Airlines to gain a government airmail contract had forced its sale to Eastern Air Transport.

driver at Portland, Maine, they would have an answer at a meeting in Boston by two o'clock the next afternoon. The designated stops were at Portland, Rockland, Bangor, and either Waterville or Augusta. Collins said, "We met the driver and car as planned at the Portland station, drove to Rockland where we walked over the field in darkness, studying the length, width, approaches and surface. There was not a runway or aid to navigation as we know them now north of Boston." Working all night Collins and Amelia stopped at all five fields, inspecting each before driving back to Portland where they caught the train to Boston and met the railroad officials promptly at 2 P.M.

They got their contract, signed on August 6, an agreement to start five days later with at least two round trips a day for which the railroad would pay National Airways forty cents a mile. Tickets would be sold by the railroad at its stations and by the airline at the airports. To the public the airline would be known as the Boston and Maine Airways, with a railroad official, Phillip F. Payson, as president.

G. P. deserted Northwest for the Boston and Maine, announcing to the press that Collins and Amelia would operate the new line. To Putnam's statement one newspaper added that Mr. Putnam "was said to be one of the principal stockholders." It is possible that Amelia's twenty-five hundred dollars was actually G. P.'s.

In three days Collins hired his staff and bought two Stinson ten-seater airplanes from Eastern Air Transport—the same planes he had flown for Ludington, now secondhand and cheaper. On August 9, Amelia joined him in Boston as a passenger on one of the planes, which was moved to Portland's airport at Scarboro. Along with all hands on both planes, she helped to unload equipment for the home office, a tiny room in the hangar, headquarters of what may have been the world's most underfinanced airline. The next day they took off from Portland for Rockford where a crowd of one thousand had been waiting for more than two hours to see Amelia. The pilot circled the field several times, a move he soon regretted as eager admirers overran it, forcing him to land at the very edge. This time Amelia, who ordinarily disliked these mass demonstrations, was delighted. "You will see me often," she told the crowd, "for I shall be down here to sell tickets to all of you."

She meant it. When she believed in any cause she was inexhaustible, possessed by the same exuberant energy manifested in the fragile young Columbia student who sat up all night translating French poetry and then rose, as if from the dead, after a twenty-minute nap. This energy fascinated Helen Weber's eight-year-old daughter, Marcia-Marie. One day while the child played in the living room at Rye and Amelia paced up and down, explaining to Helen her hopes and plans for the new airline, Marcia-Marie saw Amelia leap up on the sofa, laughing, her head thrown back and arms extended, still talking to Helen. "I thought she wanted to be high in the sky," Marcia-Marie told her mother.

Amelia sought help for the new airline wherever she could find it. When Jimmy Mollison sailed to England with the remnants of his aircraft Amelia asked Amy, staying on at Rye as a houseguest, to lend a hand. The two women flew and drove through New England, giving talks on the women's club and tea circuit. Amelia also cabled her stepson, David, who was a member of a team exploring British Guiana and Northern Brazil, to come home. She had a job for him as dispatcher at the Augusta airport.

On August 21, the day after David returned, Amelia called a press conference, combining David's latest adventure with a boost for the airline. The tall, moustached explorer, not yet twenty-one years old, exhibited a dead tarantula, which he placed on Amelia's hand for photographers, then told a few stories of odd behavior in animals facing death. Amelia added a story of her own. It concerned a Ludington Airline pilot who encountered a flock of pigeons during flight and, after landing, found one of the birds alive, sitting between cylinder heads. It had passed through the propeller blades moving at fifteen hundred revolutions per minute, she said. When reporters hooted, she said, "Now you tell me one." After everyone did, they elected her president of the Monday afternoon Exaggerated Narrative Club. For a cause she espoused, Amelia could run rings around G. P. gaining press coverage.

After an impressive start, the operation of the infant airline became a nightmare. During a cold fall and subzero winter, snow often blocked the roads into airports for an entire day before it could be cleared. Mechanics worked in unheated hangars. With only limited use of city snow plows, Collins had to put snow chains on the airplanes' tires to get sufficient traction for landings made in cross winds. To raise enough money for operating costs and salaries, he completed flights from Boston to Portland and back on which there were no passengers at all, so that he could collect the subsidy paid by the railroad for each completed flight.

Amelia, who received a check for one dollar, marked "salary," from

National Airways, Inc., on December 30, helped whenever she could. Between one lecture tour for six weeks, starting in October, and a second one in the southwest in December, she traveled the line, selling tickets, talking with passengers, and posing for photographs with them, wrapped in her sable coat, a hat pulled over her ears to prevent frostbite. On the lecture circuit she never failed to mention her affiliation with the airline.

After Vidal left the line in September to become chief of the Bureau of Air Commerce, Amelia represented it in Washington. At congressional hearings on the National Recovery Act's code for pilots she protested a section of the code stating that "members of the code agree not to initiate service between cities already served by another member over an identical route." She claimed the rule would create monopolies and prevent establishment of new airlines.

If Harry Bruno was wrong about Amelia's total lack of interest in money, he was not about G. P.'s efforts to "cash in" on her name. Since 1928 G. P. had arranged for the most direct method—product endorsement—with Amelia testifying to the excellence of a certain spark plug, airplane engine, automobile, gasoline, or oil. In April of 1933 she did the text for a two-page magazine advertisement extolling Kodak cameras and film, entitled "Part of the Fun of It." It was a clever pitch merging Kodak's products with her latest book in the disguise of an illustrated magazine article.

However, her principal source of income was from lectures, which both enhanced her fame and made it pay. Within a year of her Atlantic flight the word "aviatrix" brought an automatic response of "Earhart" from the average American. On the road again in October, she had a schedule of thirty-nine lectures, extending into the first week of the new year. With winter weather too uncertain to fly she drove her twelve-cylinder Franklin, often leaving at midnight for the next town on her schedule. Checking into a hotel at dawn, she frequently gave newsmen an interview while she ate breakfast, then caught a few hours of sleep before the next lecture.

On the October tour Amelia brought Amy as far as Chicago where she left her with friends. From there Amelia made seven stops in the Midwest before spending a weekend in Atchison with Lucy Challis's parents, Jim and Rilla. In a letter to Amy, who was still in Chicago, Amelia wrote, "Everyone is very cordial and it seems 'Millie' [Amelia] hasn't changed at all—heaven help her."

In many respects she had not. She found time in her tight schedule to visit her Uncle Theo, Amy's brother, and Mary Brashay, the woman who had looked after him (and Amelia, when she was a child) for thirty years. Theo hauled freight with a horse and wagon. Later, when the horse died, Amelia bought him another, and she sent a monthly check regularly as part of his support after relatives had lost what little capital he possessed.

While Amelia was with the Challises, Rilla also wrote to Amy: "I tried to forget she was a celebrity and treat her as just Millie Earhart, for she looked a bit tired and I know she needed relaxation. She seems to stand up under her strenuous program, but I really wanted to put her to bed for a day."

Tired or not, Amelia kept to her schedule, drawing record crowds—fourteen hundred in Mason City, Iowa, and two thousand in Kansas City. After working her way back through the Middle West to Toledo, Lansing, and Detroit, she had a day of rest at home, then left for Wheeling and Huntington, West Virginia. She drove back from Huntington to Rye. stopped there for two days, and left again by car with G. P. for lectures in Watertown, New York, and Ottawa. She traveled more than seven thousand miles by car, much of it alone, in six weeks, giving at least one newspaper interview as well as a lecture at each stop.

In Alton, Illinois, a reporter who couldn't find her after the lecture waited in the hotel lobby until he saw her return, then called her room. "All right," she sighed. "If you can stand it, I can." In Toledo the duration of the press conference was "one omelet, six pieces of toast, a canteloupe and a pot of hot chocolate" in a hotel suite after an all-night drive from South Bend. She spoke at eleven o'clock that morning, then left for an evening lecture in Lansing, Michigan.

At the end of the tour she was near the breaking point when Huntington reporter Mary Yvonne Scales walked into her dressing room and saw her sitting in a chair, her hand over her eyes. No one had told Scales that Amelia always asked for five minutes alone before going on stage. However, Scales was forgiven and told to wait in the dressing room until after the lecture. After her talk Amelia was mobbed by men, women, and children who rushed the stage, some crowding behind the curtain to stare at her. "Oh," one woman shouted, "I got a good look at her that time!" as if Amelia were an exotic animal. Fighting her way back to the dressing room, Amelia saw Scales waiting there. "Oh, yes," she said. "There's still you." But Scales got her story before Amelia left at midnight for Pittsburgh.

She left again in early December for the Southwest. In Fort Worth she borrowed a car from a friend and drove to Amarillo, Wichita Falls, then Lubbock. On December 8 while she was in Lubbock a magazine of that date published an article on "Mrs. and 'Mr.' Earhart" in which G. P. was described as: "a fellow who will get an idea at the dinner table, drop his fork and begin calling San Francisco, Chicago, Denver and all points. . . . The whole project may fizzle out before the coffee is cold, or it may net him a hundred thousand dollars in a week."

G. P.'s newest project for Amelia would not net one hundred thousand dollars in a week. Amelia was to be a fashion designer. He may have had the idea for a year, ever since they entertained Elsa Schiaparelli, world-renowned designer, at a Sunday lunch the previous February. Already known as one of the best-dressed women in America, Amelia talked with Elsa about functional clothing for what she defined as "active living."

This newest project was pursued by G. P. with his customary vigor. Three days after the article on "Mr. Earhart" appeared Macy's department store announced the presentation of a new line of women's clothing designed by Amelia Earhart and to be sold exclusively by Macy's in the New York area. Amelia, the announcement stated, was lecturing in Texas but she had already completed fifty outfits for outdoor, sports, travel, and spectator wear. The clothing would be sold under franchise by only one store in each metropolitan area, with thirty stores already under contract. Manufacturing rights were sold by G. P. to four New York firms, with hats to be made by a fifth.*

This first announcement opened a country-wide sales blitz. With Amelia on tour much of the winter G. P. had already closed the house in Rye and moved into their suite at the Hotel Seymour on 45th Street. Between lectures Amelia worked on the clothing in the living room where one corner was occupied by a fitting dummy and a seamstress who worked at a sewing machine. G. P. issued an open invitation to the press to drop in and interview Amelia about her new career.

*The firms were J. J. Rueben-Rachael Holsten Company, David Crystal, Inc., M. Cowen and Son Apparel Corporation, and Schnaiman Sportswear Company. Hats were by John B. Stetson Company.

Associated Press feature writer Sigrid Arne was one of several who wrote just what G. P. wanted. The neophyte designer "uncurled from an armchair" to greet Arne, fastening the needle she held in the collar of her tailored lounging pajamas. The other chairs in the room were draped with dresses and the sewing machine hummed in the corner. Her desk was piled high with swatches of silk and fan letters. Why, asked Arne, this new career? "I just don't like shopping very much," Amelia told her. The sewing machine, she added, was hers at Ogontz where she made most of her clothing. (There was never any mention of this in her letters to her mother.) Of course, she added, she would like to fly again. Her plane was parked only an hour's drive from the hotel room but "some other girl should be breaking my records," she added wistfully. "I don't have the equipment and planes don't grow on bushes."

If bushes wouldn't produce airplanes Amelia was willing to cultivate other sources created by G. P. During the first four months of 1934 articles with photographs of Amelia modeling clothing she had designed received nationwide news coverage. Her concept of style for function was emphasized, the clothing made of wrinkle-proof, washable materials with simple lines, broad shoulders, ample sleeves, and natural waistlines. Several of her ideas were revolutionary for 1934. One was making matching "separates" in which sizes could be "scrambled" so that a woman could buy a size 12 blouse and a size 14 skirt or slacks. Another was a coat of Harris Tweed with a zip-in, washable lining.

G. P.'s clothing sales campaign got off to a good start by mid-December when a United Press dispatch affirmed Amelia's title as "Queen of the Air" for another year. Four days later, on the thirtieth anniversary of the Wright brothers' Kitty Hawk flight, she gave the dedication speech at the opening of the new aviation hall at the Franklin Institute Museum in Philadelphia. The red Vega she had sold, without its motor, to the Institute was also unveiled.*

A perfect example of the publicity G. P. sought appeared in a Boston newspaper announcing she would be the principal speaker at a Rotary Club luncheon January 24. The picture was of Amelia modeling one of her suits, the caption stating she had designed a whole new line of clothing. The story said she was a vice-president of the Boston and

*The plane went to the Smithsonian Institution in 1966 in a sale engineered by Ralph Barnaby, curator of the Franklin Institute.

Maine's National Airways and that her talk on modern aviation would be broadcast by NBC. Here he had a combination of Amelia's interests as leading aviator, airline official, lecturer, and clothing designer.

Nevertheless, Amelia was not willing to do everything G. P. asked. On a day she lunched at the Biltmore with him and Hilton Railey, he displayed a hat he had ordered, a cheap article with a silk band bearing a facsimile of her signature. She took it from him and examined it, eyes narrowing in disapproval. It would not do, she said. They were already being made up, he told her. "Tell them to *unmake* them. Now," she said, pointing to a telephone at the table. He held out until she threatened to sue him.

The phenomenal endurance she displayed in pursuit of a flight record or a cause she believed in gave out selling clothing. By the end of January she was bedridden with laryngitis and forced to postpone a lecture tour. Her mother claimed that designing and promoting the clothing was "one of the hardest strains she ever went through, because she was doing so much at the time."

Amy was probably right, but after a few days in bed Amelia was off again, driving alone to Atlanta. Arriving on a Saturday, she gave a long interview to the press, flew a Bellanca monoplane for its owner and his guests, and met four members of the Ninety-Nines' Georgia chapter at Candler Field so that they could get their picture in the papers along with a description of the organization. On Sunday she gave her lecture. From Atlanta she drove to Rome to visit a school for handicapped children, then to Tuscaloosa and Birmingham for more lectures before returning home via Chattanooga and Washington. She did it all in one week.

In March H. Gordon Selfridge, Jr., amateur pilot and manager of Selfridge's Provincial Stores, Ltd., of England, met her in Boston where he interviewed her.* She talked about what really interested her—the value of the National Recovery Act in forcing businessmen to discuss and solve problems affecting the whole community; the need to abolish discrimination against women in transportation; and the need for a secretary of transportation with cabinet rank. Asked what powers the secretary

---

*Amelia wore a watch given her by the senior Selfridge when she was in England after her Atlantic flight in 1932. The watch had been given DeHane Seagrave, champion outboard motorboat racer. When he was killed his widow gave it back to Selfridge. Amelia was wearing it when she disappeared in 1937.

should have, Amelia said that *he* (even she could not imagine a woman as secretary) should control all commercial transportation to eliminate confusion and loss of efficiency. She denied this would lead to government ownership, insisting the government could supervise without ownership.

She was not always a proponent of sweet reason and graceful tact. Her obsessive commitment to public acceptance of commercial aviation made her intolerant of inefficiency. The day after she talked to Selfridge she gave a cold, insensitive assessment of the Army's brief and tragic attempt to fly the mails in which a dozen pilots had already been killed or injured.* Although the Army was not fit to fly mail at present, she said, no doubt its pilots would receive instruction in the future in instrument flying. "As a result," she said, "the next war—and I hope there will be no next war—will not be called off on account of rain as far as the Air Service is concerned."

Four days later she was in Washington where she testified before a Congressional Post Office committee, asserting that the airmail subsidy system was outmoded. "Airlines," she claimed, "should stand on their own two feet," and payment to them for carrying mail should be only slightly more than the actual postage. She again recommended the establishment of a department of transportation, opposing Lindbergh and Rickenbacker, both of whom wanted an independent agency to control air travel, divorced from any supervision over rail or other means of transport.

In July, after she had worked continuously through the spring and early summer, G. P. took her to Carl Dundrud's Double Dee ranch, sixty-eight miles south of Cody, Wyoming, for a two-week vacation, their longest together since their marriage three and a half years earlier. Dundrud was an old friend of G. P.'s. They had met on a packing trail in 1916 and ten years later G. P. asked Dundrud to accompany him on his expedition to Baffin Island. A man of few words—all of them blunt—Dundrud's few on Amelia were surprisingly complimentary: "She was just one of the gang in camp and for a woman, let me tell you she's a great mechanic. If you want to know about things she does you have to ask her. Then she

---

*On February 9, 1934, all airmail contracts had been cancelled by Postmaster General James A. Farley who charged the commercial airline contractors with collusion to bilk the government of $47 million. When the Army Air Service took over, five pilots were killed and six critically injured during the first week. By March 30, the total killed reached twelve. On April 20, Farley announced he would accept bids again for airmail contracts.

answers what you want to know. She doesn't try to cut you off or make a long story of it."

Accompanied by Dundrud, Amelia and G. P. went fly-fishing in mountain streams, rode along steep trails, their gear on pack horses, slept in tents, and cooked over campfires. Over one campfire Amelia anticipated environmentalists' concerns by forty years, challenging Carl and G. P. to justify the killing of wildlife for sport: "I held out, as always, against killing for killing's sake. To acquire food, to protect property or livestock, or to provide museums with specimens for scientific purposes seem to me to be the only possible justification for slaughter. Even those . . . should be controlled . . . lest animals face extinction."

While they were at the ranch G. P. and Amelia made plans to build a cabin near the deserted town of Kerwin, seventy miles from a railroad. "We'll have to pack in the last nine miles," she told reporters in Cheyenne on her way back, adding with a wide smile, "We'll even be safe from reporters." Even there she was not safe from G. P.'s compelling need to use their experiences for profit. She wrote a magazine article on the vacation, published with pictures of her, including one of Dundrud cutting her hair. G. P. took the pictures.

As soon as she returned to New York Amelia resumed her work for the Boston and Maine, more recently the Boston, Maine, and Central Vermont air service. The week the airline celebrated its first anniversary she was the main attraction in a "Woman's Day" promotion, backed by local chambers of commerce and women's clubs in the cities of Bangor, Waterville, and Augusta. During three days she accompanied 659 women on sample flights, nine to each flight on one of the company's ten-passenger Stinsons. She walked the aisle, answered questions, and gave autographs.

She arrived in Bangor on Saturday, August 11, with chief pilot Milton Anderson, railroad publicist Herbert Baldwin, and Sam and Mrs. Solomon, just in time for "Amelia Earhart Night" at the Lucerne-in-Maine, a seaside resort hotel. The next morning state and local police were out in force to control the crowd of ten thousand gathered at Godfrey Airport for a glimpse of Amelia. Two hundred women held free tickets for twenty-seven flights over the city that day. Amelia went on twenty-five of them.

On the sixth flight when she asked passenger Sally Miller what she enjoyed most about the flight, "Sally," who was the local amateur entertainer Ralph Mills, leaped up, pulled off "her" hat and a wig, and shouted,

"You cannot keep men away from such attractive women!" During the explosion of laughter from the passengers, Amelia leaned over and kissed him on the cheek. That night she drove to the Lakeside Theater in Skowhegan where Groucho Marx shared the stage with her between the first and second acts of a comedy in which he was the lead. They brought down the house. For two more days she was "a gracious hostess who talks to each and every one" who bought an airline ticket, until she took a train to Washington "to get some sleep" before an airline conference the next day.

On August 4 her friend Frances Harrell Marsalis was killed in an accident at the Women's National Air Races in Dayton.* Amelia was not there nor was she at the National Air Races in Cleveland a month later, her boycott part of her struggle for the right of women to compete on an equal basis with men. Even after she gained the approval of the NAA contest committee, Cliff Henderson barred women from NAA-sanctioned races in New Orleans early in 1934. Henderson said women pilots failed to enter any except women's events. The one exception, Florence Klingensmith, was killed in the 1933 races at Chicago. Her death influenced his decision, he admitted. He also eliminated even the women's events from the National Air Races of 1934. When he asked Amelia to pilot Mary Pickford from Chicago to Cleveland for the opening ceremonies, she refused.

Amelia's views were aired at length by her old friend Carl Allen in a series of articles he wrote about aviation's "most dependable reoccurring feud—the row over women participating in air meets." Allen was by then aviation editor of the *Herald Tribune,* a job Amelia got for him. When Helen Reid asked Amelia what she thought of the paper's aviation coverage, Amelia told her that the best aviation reporter in New York was the *World-Telegram*'s man Carl Allen. Amelia then went to Allen and told him to ask Reid for the position. Early in 1934 he did, and got it.

Amelia continued her defense of women in aviation at the *Herald Tribune*'s annual two-day forum in September. Reid's friend, Eleanor Roosevelt, opened the forum and FDR closed it with a broadcast from Washington to the three thousand ticket holders at the Waldorf-Astoria

---

*Marsalis was killed when the wingtip of her plane struck the ground after she dived to avoid a collision. A year before, when Marsalis, who divorced her husband William, reported to Amelia that she was "broke," Amelia sent her a box of clothing. "Honey," she wrote to Amelia, "the suit fits. I'll put many hours in it."

Hotel. Amelia spoke on the lack of opportunities for women in aviation. She said New York University's School of Aeronautics would not admit qualified women and that in the industry itself women, who were paid less than men for the same work, were outnumbered forty to one. Dr. Edwin C. Elliott, president of Purdue University, in West Lafayette, Indiana, who had preceded her as a speaker, was impressed. He invited her and G. P. to lunch with him the next day and asked her to come to Purdue to counsel the five hundred women students there on possible careers. Amelia accepted, rearranging her October lecture tour to include a stop at Purdue.

The prospect of working at Purdue was interesting but the rest of the fall tour was not. Amelia was tired—of lecture tours, of designing clothing, of the politics of feminism, of G. P.'s promotional schemes and, most of all—of being grounded. She wanted to fly. In October when she started west she kept right on going, all the way to the Coast and Burbank, where her Vega had been moved. Telling the press she was on vacation, she rented a house for the winter, a modest place but in a fashionable area of North Hollywood, near Toluca Lake.

At four o'clock in the morning of November 27, two days before Thanksgiving, fire broke out at the house in Rye. G. P. had gone to the city on Sunday night. Although he had designed the house himself back in 1925, without Amelia there he no longer liked staying in it, retreating to his suite at the Hotel Seymour or staying with his mother in Connecticut. The houseman, who had been left in charge, forgot to turn off the heater under an empty boiler. In less than an hour one wing of the sixteen-room, six-bath Spanish mission–style structure had been destroyed. The dining room was a shell, the stairway and banister of imported wood blackened, the blue tiling brought back from China by G. P.'s explorer friend Andrews for the front hall cracked and buckling.

Although Amelia disliked the East Coast—Boston with its dark, cold winters and its staid conservatism, and New York with its frantic adulation for money and fame—she loved the house at Rye. She liked the full book shelves in every room, the half-dozen bedrooms for houseguests, the living room where she often stood gazing out the round view window at one end or curled up on a long, low bench at the other, reading poetry in front of the open hearth with its blazing logs. She liked the garden where she dug and weeded, often helped by G. P., away from the din of New York and her desk piled high with drafts of unfinished magazine articles and unanswered fan letters. After her 1932 flight she had written to a friend that her life had resumed some sense of the normalcy she needed, offering as an example, "I dug in the garden yesterday and uncovered crocuses."

Damage was estimated at thirty thousand dollars in addition to irreplaceable articles including early paintings by Norman Rockwell and Amelia's aeronautical memorabilia. Saved was a case filled with her awards and medals that G. P. had seen her open only once, for a fourteen-year-old boy who asked to see them. "The old lady shows her medals!" she hooted.

For Amelia the greatest loss was her papers and a small wooden box in which she kept a score of poems written over her lifetime. When G. P. called to tell her, she took a plane for New York the next day, but missed her connection in Chicago because of the winter's first snowstorm. With four lectures scheduled for Friday and Saturday in Minneapolis, she could not get back to Rye. On Sunday she took another plane to Los Angeles, to the refurbished Vega and her preparations for a new venture, a gamble for even higher stakes than she had ever played before. The house at Rye would be restored and Amelia would return to it now and then but neither was the same again.

CHAPTER SIXTEEN

Across the Pacific

She lived on the west coast and he lived on the east. He couldn't manage her so he married her and then he couldn't manage her." When Amelia Earhart rented a house in California in the fall of 1934 this comment by a colleague was not entirely off the mark. The move indicated the end of one phase in Amelia's partnership with George Palmer Putnam. The young woman G. P. had both managed and manipulated back in 1928—with her knowledge and consent—had needed him more than he needed her. During the six years that followed, more than three of which she was married to him, Amelia had changed. The Boston social worker Putnam made a celebrity was now more skillful than he in handling the press and certainly more popular. Reporters were frequently irritated by him, a manager who seemed to promote himself as much as his client. They called him "the lens louse," because he wanted to be in every photograph taken of Amelia. But they seldom found fault with her.

Nevertheless, G. P. remained her manager and she continued, for the most part, to follow the agenda he set for her, signing the contracts and making the appearances he wanted, working at the frenzied pace he set. She refused only those propositions and schemes she considered too impractical, tawdry, or insulting to the public and press.

On October 3, 1934, while she was still living at Rye, two conflicting reports of her plans for another long-distance flight appeared in the press. The first claimed she would attempt a solo flight across the South Atlantic from Natal, Brazil to the African coast. The second said she would fly from San Francisco to Honolulu for a prize of ten thousand dollars offered by a group of Hawaiian business men. She denied both stories after a ten-day cross-country drive alone. When she arrived in Los Angeles on November 6, she told reporters her plane had been sent on ahead but when they asked which flight she would attempt she said, "Neither." She was "on vacation" for a month.

In one sense she was. She was back in the place she loved, the land of hot sun and blue skies that had first enchanted her as a determined, impetuous, and often foolhardy twenty-four-year-old student pilot. At thirty-six, she checked her fuel gauge before a flight and resisted the impulse to fly between high voltage wires just to shorten a landing. But, if less impetuous, she was even more determined to make a flight no person had ever made before—not a woman's record but a world record. Her denial to the press of either plan was truthful. She intended to reverse one of the predicted courses, flying from Honolulu to San Francisco, because, she told G. P., it was "easier to hit a continent than an island."

The plan suited them both. He could make commitments for advertising endorsements, lectures, and articles and be certain of an initial ten thousand dollars to finance the flight. She could attempt to become the first person, man or woman, to fly alone over the twenty-four hundred miles of open water in a single-engine plane. The night she arrived in Los Angeles she went to a dinner given for Sir Charles Kingsford-Smith, who had crossed the Pacific in 1928 while she was waiting at Trepassey for the flight of the *Friendship* to London, and who had just flown from Sydney to Los Angeles. She would be repeating the Honolulu leg of his flight but he had been accompanied by a navigator and she would make it alone. She told no one at the dinner of her plans.

The next day she was at Burbank, ready to work with Paul Mantz, the man she had chosen to overhaul her Vega at United Airport in Burbank, now the Glendale-Pasadena-Burbank Airport. Stunt pilot, engineer, businessman, speed-record contender, and president of the Motion Picture Pilots' Association, Mantz was six years younger and no taller than Amelia, a dapper, well-built, compact man with a pencil-line moustache and hair slicked back from a high forehead. Assertive and articulate, he enjoyed telling stories about the motion picture celebrities he flew on his charter service, United Services, Ltd. Mantz owned six planes, two of them Lockheeds, and was a pioneer in filming combat scenes in the air. On one occasion he cut a hole in the side of a plane and mounted a camera there to photograph simulated combat from close range. He was as meticulous as he was imaginative in his preparations. "I am not a stunt pilot," he told a business partner. "I am a precision flier."

In spite of the business-like image he cherished, the thirty-one-year old flier was not as staid as he claimed. He was cashiered from the Army's Air Service the day before graduation for "buzzing" a train. A month before he started work on Amelia's Vega he was cited by the Bureau of Air Commerce for diving within a few feet of the rooftops of Redwood City, in a salute to his bedridden mother. Soon after, while testflying Amelia's Vega, Mantz buzzed the ranch of Western screen star William S. Hart. He "damned near shook the bricks out of the chimney," Hart complained. The Department of Commerce traced the plane to Amelia, who went with Mantz to apologize.

Nevertheless, Mantz could be a perfectionist and a hard taskmaster. One associate said, "He wanted someone to back him up, not second-guess him. Too many pilots . . . assert their ideas, telling other pilots how to fly. You didn't do that with Paul."* Amelia didn't. She was an eager, attentive pupil. Although six years Mantz's senior, she had not learned to fly until she was twenty-three. All of her training was haphazard, taken between jobs and, later, between public appearances. Mantz, who learned at sixteen, had flown for fifteen years. Amelia gave him the respect he demanded.

For the flight, Mantz stripped the Vega of its ten seats and installed fuel tanks, increasing fuel capacity to 470 gallons of gasoline and 56 gallons of oil. In the cockpit he installed and checked magnetic and aperiodic compasses, a directional bank and turn indicator, an ice-warning thermometer, fuel and temperature gauges, a tachometer, and a supercharger pressure gauge. The engine, the same Pratt & Whitney S1D1 Amelia had used to cross the Atlantic, was overhauled by Mantz's chief mechanic, Ernest Tissot.

With the plane in good hands, Amelia juggled a half-dozen other preflight tasks. While she looked for a house to rent, she stayed with Jack

---

*Mantz died in a crash, on July 8, 1965, flying a makeshift stuntplane as a double for actor James Stewart.

Maddux, most of her time there spent in a one-room building behind the main house, poring over maps with Maddux and Clarence Williams, a retired Navy lieutenant commander who was charting her course for her. On November 21, a permit for a radio was issued her in Washington, one that could be used "only for communication with ships and coastal stations when in flight over the sea." In New York, G. P. denied to reporters that she was planning an overseas trip, saying she wanted it for experimental radio work. A month later Amelia was licensed as a third-class operator of a radio telephone, hardly the degree of expertise warranting experimental radio work.

After Amelia moved into the house she had rented at 10515 Valley Spring Road in the Toluca Lake district of Hollywood, she sent for her mother to come and stay with her. G. P. joined them in mid-December. Amelia spent most of her time at United Airport in or near Mantz's shop, watching him work on the Vega and listening to his detailed instructions, but was relaxed enough to enjoy the company of other pilots at the field, among them Bobbi Trout. Trout introduced Amelia to the joys of motorcycle riding, and they raced up and down the airstrip on two Indian Pony bikes.

In early December Amelia was in Oakland, where she had her picture taken with Flight Lt. Charles T. P. Ulm, who intended to fly from Oakland to Australia.* He took off for Honolulu on December 3 but didn't make it. Forty-eight hours later an extensive search near the Hawaiian Islands began for Ulm and his two companions. They were never found. The news did not change Amelia's plans, which were still supposed to be very secret.

It was a strangely kept secret. On December 22 Amelia boarded the Matson Line's luxury liner, *Lurline*, for Honolulu.† With her were G. P., Paul Mantz and his wife, Myrtle, mechanic Ernest Tissot, and the Lockheed Vega, NR965Y, lashed to the aft tennis deck.

On the day after Christmas Amelia wrote a long letter to her mother.

---

*Ulm, one of Kingsford-Smith's crew in the 1928 Pacific flight, had also accompanied three other men in 1933 on a flight from England to Australia.

†On December 20 Amelia was named one of the ten best-dressed women in America by the Fashion Designers of America. Others were First Lady Eleanor Roosevelt, film star Kay Frances, society matron Mrs. Robert H. McAdoo, hostess Elsa Maxwell, stage actress Ina Claire, sportswoman Mrs. John Hay Whitney, singer Gladys Swarthout, artist Georgia O'Keeffe, and author Fannie Hurst.

It began with an apology for the formula Christmas greeting cabled her, one sent to a long list of people and signed "Amelia and George." Amy was number seventeen on the list. Amelia also apologized for what was obviously a miserable evening for everyone the night before her departure. "My indisposition of the night before leaving wrecked everything the last hours." Before every long flight Amelia was always tense in the company of close friends or family members, yet among strangers able to sleep. She had slept in a hotel room in Boston before the 1928 flight but with Amy in the house this time she could not. So deaf that she could not take part in a normal conversation and shunned by many, Amy was querulous and stubborn, an unhappy, frustrated woman with a younger daughter who needed her too much and an older one who didn't need her at all. In her letter Amelia told her, "Please try to have a good time. You have had so many squashed years, I know its hard to throw them off. But it can be done. I'd like you to take this trip and I am going to plan to that end." G. P., Amelia wrote, "said you were an awfully good sport to stay alone in the little house. I said I had known that a long time."

For the first time Amelia also gave Amy details of her plans. She wrote that she had used the radio on the plane, picking up airway stations, one as far away as Kingman, Arizona. If all went well, the Mantzes would be back in Hollywood in ten days. (The Mantzes were neighbors who would help Amy if she needed it.) Amelia would have G. P. cable when she actually started, but Amy might not see her on her return if she decided to fly on to Washington. Amelia also included her customary instructions to Amy on how to deal with reporters. "Reporters may call you. If so, be pleasant, admit you're my mother if you care to, and simply say you're not discussing plans. If they ask you what you think of my doing such things, say what you think." This is followed by Amelia's saying what Amy ought to think: "It is better to do what want [sic]—etc."

When the *Lurline* docked in Honolulu on December 27, Amelia gave reporters even less. She brought the Vega along, she said, in case she wanted to use it. "Maybe we'll use my plane to fly to every one of the islands." Then again they might take advantage of "the kind invitation of Stanley Kennedy and fly on Inter-Island planes." *If* she decided to make a transoceanic flight, she said, she would not take Mantz. She would not "take a cat along." She insisted she was on a vacation with her husband. Paul Mantz was a family friend. She and G. P. would stay at the Waikiki Beach house of millionaire Chris Holmes, Paul's friend.

189

The press notices that first day were filled with conjecture about her plans but warmly welcomed her to the islands. Twenty-four hours later they turned harshly critical. In an era without airmail service the latest issue of *Editor and Publisher* had arrived along with Amelia on the *Lurline*. In it was an article claiming that Amelia's projected flight from Hawaii to California was a stunt to provide publicity for the territory,* sponsored by the Pan Pacific Press Bureau. The story stated that a confidential memo had been inadvertently sent to *Editor and Publisher* by Pan Pacific, an organ of an advertising and publicity firm working for sugar interests. The memo said, "Before the time of the flight we will put into circulation rumors that it is to take place and at the same time deny the rumors. This will create a situation of immediate suspense of very high news value."

Although G. P. had denied more than once that Amelia was planning a long flight, now he denied designing the campaign of rumors and denials. Amelia insisted that she had come to the islands on a vacation. While it was true, she added, that she was equipped for a long-distance flight she did not know if conditions for it would be favorable and to announce flight plans in advance would be foolish. It had been a toss-up, she said, as to whether she and G. P. would fly from New York to Mexico City or visit Hawaii.

A few days later the *San Francisco News* added to the charges leveled by *Editor and Publisher*. Pan Pacific's campaign, the paper said, was part of the fight by Hawaiian sugar interests against quotas on sugar exported from Hawaii to the mainland. G. P. had accepted a payment of ten thousand dollars in exchange for the use of Amelia's name and her complimentary remarks about the islands. Releases on the flight by Pan Pacific would emphasize the theme of the territory of Hawaii being an integral part of the United States. If so, a quota or tariff on its products would be unfair. Pan Pacific had already released a story stating Amelia was interested in the inauguration of an airmail express service between Hawaii and the mainland because it offered "an opportunity to emphasize . . . that Hawaii is an integral part of the United States, ready for statehood." Amelia repeated the theme before boarding the *Lurline* when she said, "Anything I can do, to help close the time gap between Hawaii as an integral part of the United States, will be work into which I can throw myself heartily." She had expressed different sentiments to her mother. "I

*Hawaii did not become a state until 1959.

suppose," she wrote, " . . . tomorrow we shall slip on grass skirts and never leave the island paradise. (Chamber of Commerce, travel agencies, press are worse than the California species.)"

There was worse to come. John Williams, the reporter for the *Honolulu Star-Bulletin* who had written the story on the accusations made by *Editor and Publisher,* followed it with one claiming that "if Amelia Earhart intends to fly solo from Hawaii to the mainland, responsible authorities should stop her." A single-engine plane was very poor equipment for a transoceanic flight that would prove nothing not already known, he wrote. If she failed, "the ghastly Ulm search would be repeated." Williams also claimed that Army airmen were uneasy about the flight. He was right. On December 30 Lt. Leroy Hudson cabled the Bureau of Air Commerce in Washington, asking if there were restrictions regarding equipment on transoceanic flights by licensed U.S. pilots. There was, Lieutenant Hudson added, "a rumor of a flight by Amelia Earhart to the West Coast." The answer was that the bureau had no authority or control over the proposed flight. The *Star-Bulletin* followed up with an editorial asserting that, although no laws forbad the flight, the concern for Amelia was really a tribute to her and a wish for her to avoid needless risk.

Williams kept up the pressure. Why, he asked, did the Army let her use Wheeler Field? Why was the plane completely overhauled by Army aviation mechanics? Army radio experts were making radical changes in her radio, work which neither she nor Mantz could direct because they didn't know enough about it, Williams charged. The Army had installed a sending unit adaptable to telegraph work but Amelia did not know how to send. Quoting "Army experts," Williams wrote that the plane would have to take off with 450 gallons of fuel over a very rough field, too risky a feat with only one engine. If Amelia were forced down at sea the search could cost a million dollars in taxpayers' money.

Williams was not the only critic. Others recalled the Dole race of 1927 when only half the eight starters from California reached the islands and two were lost at sea, one of them a woman. On January 6 Capt. Frank A. Flynn, an NAA member, sponsored an open letter to Amelia, asking her to abandon the flight in memory of the ten aviators who had already lost their lives in attempts to fly from California to Hawaii.

Under pressure like this, the businessmen who had put up ten thousand dollars for the flight asked Amelia to reconsider. She would not. At a private meeting she accused them of listening to unsubstantiated rumors regarding political influence that she did not have. Flying, she said, was her business. She had already spent half of the ten thousand on preparations. She would fly to California with or without their support.

While her backers worried and reporters criticized, the University of Hawaii's students gave her an overwhelming vote of confidence when she gave a lecture at Farrington Hall. Those who could not get a seat in the packed hall listened to the broadcast of the speech on their car radios. Parked outside the hall, they hoped to get a glimpse of her when she left. Aside from this one lecture and a day's air tour of the islands, she avoided public appearances and refused the invitations of islanders eager to entertain her. While she waited for takeoff, which depended on favorable weather and the delivery of needed fuel, she spent part of each day at Wheeler Field where Mantz worked and G. P. hovered.

G. P. was angry about a delay by Standard Oil in delivering the promised fuel. If the weather cleared Amelia would need to leave within hours, before it closed down again. G. P. held Mantz responsible for this because Mantz had advised using Standard, both for its "fine service" and possible endorsement fees after the flight. As perfectionistic, impatient, and egotistical as G. P., Mantz was annoyed with both Standard and Putnam.

Amelia spent hours walking on the beach near Holmes's place or stretching out on a beach chair, basking in the hot, tropical sunshine. She no longer worried about the damage already done by sun and wind to her delicate skin. Although her youthful figure belied her age, seen close up, the fine lines at the corners of her eyes and the freckles over her nose and cheeks made her look all of her thirty-six years. Waiting, she thought about death as she always did before each of her long flights. She had already written to her mother, telling her to take possession of the contents of a zipper compartment in her briefcase. "Put it away until I turn up and if I don't, burn it," she wrote. "It consists of fragments that mean nothing to anybody but me."

On January 8 she wrote to G. P., "As you know the barrage of belittlement has made harder the preparations in many ways. I make the attempt to fly from Honolulu to the mainland of my own free will. I am familiar with the hazards. . . . If I do not do a good job it will not be because the plane and motor are not excellent nor because women cannot fly. Though I have taken off with excessive loads a number of times there is many a slip—well, anyway, here's hoping and cheerio."

Preceded by the consignment of very personal papers to her mother, it was a curiously impersonal letter to G. P. and may have reflected her annoyance with his apparently bungled efforts to capitalize on the flight.

Along with G. P.'s letter she left a note to be delivered to a Major Clark at Wheeler Field, only if she did not survive. "If the 'test take-off' proves satisfactory," she wrote, "I plan to try for the mainland. . . . It is clearly understood that in assisting me the Army is in no way chargeable with any responsibility connected with the flight. . . . You did for me only what you would do for any other responsible pilot . . . properly pointing out the risks involved. . . . The entire responsibility for the flight I assume."

The "test take-off" was on Friday, January 11. That morning she rested at the Holmes house until noon, when G. P. took her to the house of Lt. and Mrs. George Sparhawk at Wheeler Field. The Army's radio expert at Wheeler, Sparhawk had invited Mantz and Navy Lt. E. W. Stephens to join them at lunch. A heavy rain, which had started at eleven o'clock, did not let up. Amelia retired for a nap and Stephens, a Navy aerologist, continued to check the weather for her.* G. P. rushed back to the field with Mantz to check on the Standard Oil employees. Having finally brought the gasoline, they left the field for lunch in the midst of filling the tanks. Mantz rounded them up but, when the tanks were nearly full, discovered they were short by two drums. Two more were finally produced but G. P. was frantic. Amelia needed a Friday departure and Saturday arrival to make the Sunday papers. She would need the break because the trial of Bruno Hauptmann for the kidnapping of the Lindberghs' child was claiming the front page of every newspaper in the country.

At 4:30 Amelia arrived from the Sparhawks. She had obviously said her goodbyes to G. P. earlier, for she scarcely looked at him while she slipped into a fur-lined flying suit and walked to the plane. Mantz had it warmed up for her. She climbed the ladder, slid into the cockpit, listened to the motor, gunned it, and looked at the instrument panel. There were no more than one hundred people there to see her off, most of them

---

*Stephens was to regret it later, writing to Mantz that the U.S. Weather Bureau in San Francisco "raised hell" about his forecast, claiming the Navy was meddling. He wanted a letter from Amelia to Admiral Yarnell citing the forecast as satisfactory.

Army men and their wives. She did not look down at G. P. who paced below, but grinned at the crowd, then waved at the ground crew to remove the blocks under the wheels. The plane rolled slowly toward the end of the field followed by two cars, G. P. in one and a group of Army officers in the other.

In her own account of the takeoff, she said that while she taxied to the runway she looked out the cockpit window and saw Ernie Tissot running alongside. Mud came up over the tops of his shoes and he looked gloomy, a cigarette hanging from the corner of his mouth, his face "as white as his coveralls." She also saw three fire engines and one ambulance lined up in front of the hangars, "and all the Army men seemed to be holding fire extinguishers while their wives had handkerchiefs out, obviously ready for an emergency."

At the end of the rough, sodden field she lined up the cumbersome plane and began her takeoff, the Vega swaying from side to side, its wheels sinking several inches into the mud, the propeller flinging a stream of mud over the fuselage. Three thousand feet down the field, the plane rose, seemed to stall momentarily in midair, then ascended into the grey, cloud-laden sky. She had taken off in half the distance needed by Kingsford-Smith two months earlier.

The flight pushed her to the limits of her courage and endurance. There was almost continuous fog. Banks of clouds rolled in under or over her. A ventilation cover blew off, admitting a continuous, stinging stream of air that blew into her eye. Without equipment for blind flying, and unable to execute celestial navigation, she had nothing but dead reckoning to go on and could not check her course. She was four years older than when she made her last transoceanic flight, she tired more rapidly, and was troubled by what she called a "mental hazard"—the criticism of her reasons for making the flight and of her Vega as inadequate for it.

Two and a half hours out she spoke on her radio to G. P. in Honolulu, reporting that the skies were overcast and she was flying at five thousand feet. She wanted to climb to eight thousand to save fuel but four and a half hours later she was at three thousand in a fog. Seven hours later she radioed she should be halfway. She was actually short of the mark by more than an hour's flying time.

Her sporadic reports that "everything is O.K." left Clarence Williams exasperated because she did not give her location. She couldn't.

She could only guess. And everything was not O.K. After eleven hours up she said, "I'm becoming quite tired."* An hour and a half later she again reported she was "O.K." and had descended from six thousand feet to seven hundred, a move guaranteed to make her forget her fatigue. Wiping the stream of tears from her swollen eye, she throttled down to conserve fuel.

After sixteen hours out she was certain she must be off course. Williams had marked the standard radio beams for guiding aircraft on her chart but she could not home in on any of them. She leaned to the left to peer out the window and saw a small, perfect circle in a solid cloud bank. In the exact center of the circle of blue water was a ship. She flew down and alongside the ship. It was the S.S. *Pierce* of the Dollar Line, out of San Francisco. She radioed a request that the ship contact a shore station and ask it to broadcast her location. When the shore station came in she knew for the first time in ten hours her exact position.† Her course verified, the last two and a half hours were easy.

It was 1:31 in the afternoon when she landed at Oakland, two hours behind schedule because she had throttled down to save gas. The crowd at the field had grown to ten thousand, many in it waiting for hours. She surprised her admirers, coming straight in without circling the field for a perfect landing two hundred feet from its center. A roar swept over the rain-sodden field, a mix of cheers, shouts, whistles, and automobile horns, as the crowd broke through police lines and reached the Vega just as the propeller stopped turning. One unfortunate eighteen-year-old freshman from the University of California at Berkeley was knocked down and trampled, suffering a broken elbow and a broken leg. As police succeeded in pushing the crowd back, the isinglass cockpit cover opened and Amelia pushed herself up where the crowd could see her. She smiled and waved, leaning down to take a huge bouquet of roses before airport attendants, fearing she would be manhandled and the aircraft damaged, pushed the Vega backward into a hangar. Inside the hangar her first words were, "I'm tired," but when someone offered her

---

*Later she insisted she had been misunderstood; she had actually said "I am getting tired of the fog."

†After she told her friend Eugene Vidal the story he said, "I knew she felt it unbelievable that a hole should open in the clouds directly over a ship just when she was becoming anxious."

a chair, she said, "I don't want to sit down. I've been sitting down a long time."

"Are you going on to Chicago or Washington?" a reporter asked. She shrugged. "I'll have to check the weather," she replied. A few moments later when a mechanic asked her about refueling, she said, "No, not yet," and moved toward the exit where a police escort waited to accompany her to a hotel. There she again refused to sit down while she answered reporters' questions. She was swaying with fatigue. At the airport she had said she was so dirty that, given a choice between a bath or sleep, she would take the bath. But as the reporters were leaving she said, "I want to sleep more than anything."

There remained one more task, to write her own account of the trip for the North American Newspaper Alliance.* A doctor who arrived to examine her declared she was exhausted and her eyeball was bruised but her general physical condition was excellent. Always airsick from gasoline fumes, she had eaten only one hardboiled egg during the previous twenty-four hours. In her room she had a bowl of chicken broth, muffins, and a glass of buttermilk, wrote the NANA story, and went to bed.

By ten o'clock the next day she was at the field checking the weather. She was out of luck. Storms covered the Midwest. Still determined to prove that a flight from Honolulu to Washington could be made with only a one-night stop, she decided to fly to Los Angeles and check weather conditions over Arizona and New Mexico. When she tried to take off from Oakland the wheels of the Vega bogged down in mud over the hubcaps and a tractor had to be used to haul it to another runway. She made it to Los Angeles but there was a blizzard raging over Arizona. Still hoping to make the flight, she gave instructions to mechanics to tune up the motor and fill the tanks, then left the field. Reporters assumed she would go to the house on Valley Spring Road where Amy was waiting but she did not, not at least for the next few hours. No one knew where she went. Amy may have been deeply hurt, although it is possible she realized Amelia was trying to conserve her energy for the next flight and reporters were besieging the house. There was no onward flight. Storms continued all across the country and by the next morning she was home with Amy telling newsmen that it would be foolish of her to continue the

*Her complete account appeared in *National Geographic* 67, no. 5 (May 1935).

flight because the stopover had already been too long to demonstrate "how easy and little fatiguing such a trip would be . . . to link the Hawaiian capital with the national capital."

The national capital was waiting for her. Eleanor Roosevelt cabled the day after the flight that she was "so relieved to have you back safely." A second cable invited Amelia, and G. P. if he were with her, to stay at the White House when she arrived in Washington. The First Lady's interest filtered down. Rex Martin, acting director of the Bureau of Air Commerce, asked her to advise him if she did decide to come to Washington so that official arrangements could be made for her reception. The bureau's man at Los Angeles was instructed to send word when she took off and to report her bearings all during the flight. Delayed in California, Amelia was feted a week after her flight at a dinner in Oakland. At the speakers' table were former president Herbert Hoover and Mrs. Hoover, California governor Frank Merriman and Stanford University president Lyman Wilbur. After dinner, a letter from FDR was read, lauding Amelia for proving that "aviation is a science which cannot be limited to men only." He called her a trailblazer like those pioneers who opened the West, women who "marched step in step with men."

Praise like FDR's was not universal. When Kingsford-Smith was asked for a comment he said it was "wonderful" but followed immediately with, "at the same time a man is a fool to fly an ocean in a single engine plane." Presumably a woman would be, too. He said he had done it the preceding November because he was broke and trying to sell his Lockheed Altair, the *Lady Southern Cross*. It was the only way he could get to the States and find a buyer, but he took a navigator along.*

A week after the flight *Newsweek* magazine commented, "Every so often Miss Earhart, like other prominent flyers, pulls a spectacular stunt to hit the front pages. This enhances a flyer's value as a cigarette endorser, helps finance new planes, sometimes publicizes a book."

The Nation magazine proved the fiercest critic, expanding on previous accusations of Amelia's working for Hawaiian sugar interests. An article entitled "Flier in Sugar," written by a "well-known author" under the pseudonym, Leslie Ford, claimed a campaign against a sugar tariff

---

*Two months later Kingsford-Smith attempted to fly from England to Australia after he failed to sell the Altair. Accompanied by a navigator, he was lost somewhere between the Burma and Australian coasts.

was being waged by a public relations firm, Bowman, Deute, Cummings, Inc., which in turn created the Pan Pacific Press Bureau. Its clients included the Hawaiian Sugar Planters Association, the Matson Line, the Hawaii Tourist Bureau, and the Hawaiian Pineapple Company. "A transoceanic flight," Ford wrote, "especially by our foremost woman aviator, is front-page news. From it flow publicity releases, personal interviews, signed stories, lectures, radio broadcasts—and in this case a possible motion picture featuring Miss Earhart and built around her flight by her husband, George Palmer Putnam of Paramount."

Although all these were legitimate byproducts of the flight, the propaganda for the sugar interests that ran through them was not. Ford wrote that although Amelia was unquestionably more interested in aviation than in sugar, she mentioned more than once the leit-motif of "Hawaii as an integral part of the U.S." and in her NANA story on the flight she called Hawaii "the alluring southwest corner of the United States."

Ford claimed that the reason the *Honolulu Star-Bulletin* and the *San Francisco News* had urged her to abandon the trip was because they knew it was a publicity stunt. The most nervous persons during the eighteen-hour flight, he wrote, had to be publicist Bowman and husband Putnam who made the arrangements for it. "Luck," Ford said, "was with them. The newspapers, knowing the truth, had been kind enough not to mention it in their stories on the flight."

How much of Ford's criticism was warranted and by whom is impossible to assess. Amelia certainly did not think of the trip as a stunt but she had to know that G. P. was not getting all those flattering press releases put out by Pan Pacific without giving something in return. And she did refer to Hawaii as part of the U.S. on several occasions.

The British weekly, *The Aeroplane,* which had bitterly criticized her two Atlantic flights, called this one "A Useless Adventure." "She is thirty-six years old and ought to know better," the writer claimed. Why didn't she? Certainly not because she was an unattractive woman seeking fame or notoriety, he wrote. She was attractive and had already proven her courage and ability. The answer, he claimed, lay in "boredom—a dangerous feature of modern life."

In a sense he was right. Amelia revealed in her poem "Courage" her fear of a life squandered on "little things," lived in "dull, grey ugliness." Loving life intensely, she was willing to risk it in order to enhance it. In her pursuit of that state of ecstasy she called "peace," the romantic poet of the previous decade had imagined paying for it with "vivid loneliness" and "bitter joy." These she experienced, but they were not enough. The ultimate price was as mundane as the world she tried to escape—the need for money.

By January of 1935 she had become the first person to fly solo between Honolulu and California, in either direction. She was also the first person to cross the Atlantic twice in an airplane, the first woman to fly it solo, and the first woman to fly an autogiro, the first to make a solo crossing of the continent, the first to cross it nonstop. To reach out for the unknown again she needed cash. She was in hot pursuit of it within days of her Pacific flight, on a course laid out by that master of promotion, George Palmer Putnam.

CHAPTER SEVENTEEN

The Flying Preacher

A month after her Pacific flight in January of 1935 Amelia Earhart sent her husband a telegram she had received at a Chicago hotel: "WELCOMING GRAND LADY OF THE AIR CROWNING GLORY OF EARTH'S WOMANHOOD. . . ." Across the bottom she had penciled, "For G. P., so he may appreciate me."

He did. Amelia set the records and charmed the public. G. P. wrote the scenario for each flight, publicizing preflight preparations, arranging for services and fuel, choreographing postflight celebrations. He also found sponsors and advertisers, supervised her lecture schedules and radio broadcasts, and contracted for her magazine and newspaper articles.

In a letter to Paul Mantz he wrote, "After all, record flying is terribly expensive and we have to accept legitimate returns where we can get them." To get them Amelia lectured. To fill the lecture halls G. P. wrested free advertising through newspaper stories in which Amelia did something unusual.

During the two weeks before a lecture tour starting February 11 she went to Washington for breakfast at the White House, gave a lunch for the Ninety-Nines in New York, and attended a party given by G. P.'s plane designer friend, Paul Hammond. Six days later she was in Neenah, Wisconsin, for her first lecture of the tour.

While she was away, G. P. took care of the mail and called her almost daily. He sent Amy, who was still in the house in Hollywood, a check for the rent and another for expenses but told her to withhold a monthly payment of fifteen dollars for the board and lodging of the house owner's dog. The dog, he said, must be sent back to its owner. G. P. must have called Amelia the same day because she sent a wire to Amy from Neenah telling her to ignore Putnam's instructions regarding the dog. Amelia was thrifty but not stingy and she was not certain about the dog agreement.

She finished the Midwestern tour on February 24, arriving in Washington the following Friday for a speech to the National Geographic Society.*

Again a guest at the White House, Amelia was pressed by Eleanor Roosevelt to stay until the following Tuesday so that she could accompany Eleanor and the president's mother, Sara Delano Roosevelt, to the Woman's National Press Club dinner at the Willard Hotel. The next day the wire services ran pictures of Eleanor, her stern old mother-in-law, and Amelia whom the old lady liked.

Amelia sat beside Eleanor during her morning press conferences and on one occasion persuaded her hostess to ride in the Dymaxion auto, a three-wheeled speedster designed by futurist Buckminster Fuller.[†] Fuller drove them down Executive Avenue, then onto the drive under the White House portico where he spun the car around on its third wheel while photographers recorded the event. In her next weekly radio broadcast the president's wife called Amelia one of the friends she considered sources of inspiration.[‡] Not even G. P. could have arranged better publicity.

While she was a guest at the White House Amelia telephoned Sam Solomon late one morning and asked him to take her to lunch. Sam, who took a taxi but forgot to ask the driver to wait, walked her in the pouring

*In twelve days she had lectured one or more times in Neenah, Battle Creek (Michigan), South Bend and Indianapolis (Indiana), Chicago, Kansas City, Omaha, Rockford (Illinois), and Detroit.

[†] Amelia was fascinated by the Dymaxion, which could go more than one hundred miles an hour. She had already driven it from Rye to Ophir Farm to demonstrate it to Helen and Ogden Reid.

[‡] Amelia was in distinguished company with Nobel Prize winner Jane Addams, feminist Carrie Chapman Catt, Secretary of Labor Frances Perkins, and novelist Dorothy Canfield Fisher.

rain to a nearby restaurant where the thoroughly drenched couple ate an enormous lunch. She thought this so funny that she told a friend. The day after she left the White House a Boston newspaper quoted her as saying she was hungry all the time she was there.

Eleanor sent her a telegram asking, "Amelia, why didn't you raid the icebox? I do." The Victorian-raised, Ogontz-educated Amelia was very upset. She wired back that she had *never* said any such thing, only that she hadn't been able to eat any meal except breakfast at the White House because of previous engagements, probably a white lie because Eleanor herself later recalled that she "fed everyone for a time on the same menus that had been worked out for people on relief during the depression."

On the road again, Amelia did a second lecture tour, in New England. After her speech to the Vermont legislature a woman who heard her wrote to Amy, "We all thought Lindbergh was a marvel but our 'Amelia' has shown the world what a woman can do." The writer, like most American women at the time, could identify with a woman who combined the stuff of dreams with the demands of reality. The comely, daring adventurer was also a married woman and "a perfect lady."

Never one to let Amelia rest on previous laurels, G. P. was already making arrangements for another long-distance flight. This time Amelia would fly nonstop from Mexico City to Newark. A week after the plans were announced (on a Saturday for the Sunday newspapers), William Lear, the inventor of a radio homing compass, announced (also on a Saturday) that Amelia would test his compass on her Mexican flight. In return for "testing" the device, Amelia was hired as one of FDR's "dollar-a-year experts" by her old friend, Air Commerce director Gene Vidal.

To raise money for the flight Putnam persuaded Mexican president Lazaro Cardenas to approve the overprinting in Spanish on a Mexican twenty-cent airmail stamp the message, "Amelia Earhart Good-Will Flight Mexico, 1935."* Of the 780 overprinted, 480 would go to the Universal Postal Union. Amelia, G. P. said, would carry fifty autographed covers, cancelled first in Los Angeles, then again in Mexico City. At Mexico City she would take on thirty-five more, also autographed, and at Newark all eighty-five would be cancelled.

---

*"Amelia Earhart Vuelo de Buena Voluntad Mexico 1935."

Amelia had carried cacheted mail before. In 1929 when she was copilot of the first amphibian passenger-service flight from Detroit to Cleveland, the mail was cacheted in Cleveland with "Amelia Earhart Special Pilot." On both her Atlantic and Pacific solo flights she had carried fifty covers, autographed and numbered.

In Los Angeles, where the Vega was fitted with extra fuel tanks, Clarence Williams charted a course for Amelia, using Rand McNally maps of the United States and Mexico for an overview and transferring intermediate positions to state maps of both countries. Amelia was supposed to calculate her position along the way from compass readings and time elapsed with the aid of tables Williams made, showing distances covered at various speeds. She also had a two-way radio-telephone but frequently complained about the inconvenience of the trailing antenna, which she had to let out after takeoff from a reel under the pilot's seat and rewind again before landing. It was her principal aid to navigation because she did not know how to use a telegraph-radio, nor how to take sightings for celestial navigation. The Lear homing compass worked only within the borders of the United States, so for much of the way she would have to depend on the radio-telephone or dead-reckoning with Williams's charts, the least reliable of all means of navigation.

She took off from Burbank on April 19, a Friday night, at 9:55. G. P.'s plan was for her to reach Mexico City on a Saturday afternoon in time for a story in the Easter Sunday papers. He had already done this for three of Amelia's previous long-distance flights, all of which began on Friday and appeared in Sunday papers—the 1932 Atlantic flight, her 1933 transcontinental crossing, and her 1935 Honolulu-Oakland flight.

Amelia discarded Williams's flight plan just before takeoff when adverse weather conditions were reported on the route. Instead she decided to fly south along the coast until she was parallel to Mexico City, then turn east to her destination. It was almost noon of the following day before she turned inland and she knew at once that she was off-course. "I suddenly realized there was a railroad beneath me," she wrote, "which had no business being where it was if I were where I ought to be."

She was already using a hand pump to restore failing gasoline pressure when "an insect, or probably some infinitesimal speck of dirt, lodged" in her eye. Forced to land, she brought the Vega down on an empty lake bed outside Nopala, sixty miles from Mexico City and one hundred miles off her course. Villagers, "and at least fifty cowboys" who gathered around the plane knew who she was and pointed her in the right direction. A half hour later she took off again, arriving in Mexico City where G. P. was waiting at the field with the foreign minister, Portes Gil, and a dozen other notables.

Her arrival was like that in Oakland with ten thousand spectators breaking through a cordon of soldiers and rushing toward the plane, but she managed to cut the engine before anyone was injured. The tumultuous welcome was followed by eight days of nonstop festivities in her honor while she tried to prepare for the flight to Newark.

The first and most threatening problem would be raising her fuel-heavy Vega off the ground at an altitude of seven thousand feet. G. P. persuaded the chief of the Mexican air force, Roberto Fierro, to have a three-mile-long runway built for her on the bed of Lake Texcoco.* Mexican soldiers with picks and shovels did the work while Putnam returned to New York to telephone weather reports back to Amelia and arrange for her arrival at Newark.

Delayed by bad weather, Amelia did not leave until the morning of May 8, when she sent word to fill the tanks of the Vega, which had been moved from the Pan American hangar to the improvised runway. Fears and doubts never kept her awake. She went back to sleep for two hours, ate breakfast at the hotel, and drove to the runway.

Dawn was just breaking when she closed the cockpit cover and waved for takeoff. The three-ton plane was loaded with 472 gallons of high octane fuel, a potential Molotov cocktail if she were to deviate from the course marked by white flags on the runway or fail to gain enough airspeed before the end of it. She did neither. Engines wide open, the Vega roared down the narrow path marked by the white flags and rose slowly up and over the snowcapped mountains enclosing the makeshift field.

The route Amelia chose was as dangerous as the takeoff. To reach New Orleans she could either fly around the Gulf of Mexico or over it. Before she left Los Angeles she told Wiley Post she could save an hour by crossing the Gulf. When Post said, "Don't do it, it's too dangerous," he had made the choice for her. If the great Wiley Post thought it too

*Fierro and his mechanic, Arnulfo Cortes, had flown from New York City to Mexico City in 1930, in 16 hours and 33 minutes.

dangerous, then she would have to prove she could do it. She did, maintaining an altitude of ten thousand feet for most of the twenty-one hundred miles over water, then headed north for the last thousand to Newark.

Gene Vidal was waiting for her at Hoover Airport in Washington.* When she flew over he radioed, "You've done a splendid job, so come down." She answered, "Thanks for the invitation. I'm going through."

That night at Newark a crowd of three thousand swarmed past police onto the floodlit field as the Vega rolled to a stop. Police cars, sirens blaring, inched through the throng while other officers formed a cordon around the bare-headed, smiling woman emerging from the cockpit. One of two policemen attempting to escort her to safety took her right arm and the second, her left leg, and, she said, "the arm holder started to go one way while he who clasped my leg set out in the opposite direction." Dragged along by this animated "torture rack" Amelia was met halfway by G. P., who had already lost his temper, shouting that compared to this crowd "the lowliest peons of Mexico were more civilized." Amelia, who had always loathed the touch of strangers, kept right on smiling.

Eight hours later the "legitimate returns" G. P. sought for Amelia began to pour in. Publicity came first. Photographers were taking her picture while she was still eating breakfast. By midday she had been interviewed by reporters, attended an informal reception at City Hall, and eaten lunch with her friends and fellow directors of National Airways, Paul Collins and Sam Solomon. At the Newark airport where the Vega was parked in a Standard Oil hangar, one thousand persons came to see it before the end of that day.

Vidal sent her an official message praising her "complete knowledge of aircraft operation and cross-country navigation." He exaggerated. Her courage was far greater than either her knowledge of aircraft or of navigation. Two other friends, Helen and Ogden Reid, sent a personal telegram and ran an editorial in the *Herald Tribune* stating that Amelia had demonstrated "how closely dignity stems from modesty and courtesy from a warm heart. The country could not have a better ambassador-at-large."

Amelia was back at the Newark Airport five days later to christen the new Douglas Dolphin amphibian plane (and dowse herself with

---

*She reached Washington in thirteen hours and six minutes, besting Lindbergh's 1932 record in the slower *Spirit of St. Louis* by fourteen hours.

champagne while the newsreel cameras rolled and Frank Hawks doubled up with laughter). Twenty-four hours later she was in Chicago to receive a medal from the Italian government during a conference of two thousand women's club presidents and program chairmen—two thousand potential subscribers to an Earhart lecture.

Preaching her gospel of air travel, she made a convert of Helen Reid after both women received honorary degrees at Oglethorpe University in Atlanta. Until then Reid had been a frightened passenger who also worried about her amateur-pilot son, Whitelaw. On the way back from Atlanta she sat with Amelia, then wired Whitelaw, a junior at Yale, "Skies fine between Atlanta and New York. . . . Perfectly competent to do blind flying. Love. Mother."

While Amelia was almost universally admired, G. P. was not. To describe him his critics used adjectives like overbearing, snobbish, fast-talking, scheming, and acquisitive. The press homed in on the stamp deal that paid for the flight. Of the 300 stamps remaining after 480 went to the Universal Postal Union, G. P. was said to have purchased 240. Some were on covers. The Gimbels' department store claimed, "by dint of great effort," it had secured three of the 35 autographed covers brought from Mexico, priced at $175 each when Byrd's covers from the South Pole sold for 90 cents. The three covers were sold by Putnam to Jacques Minkus of Gimbel Brothers. Irate stamp collectors wanted to know why Putnam was permitted to control most of the 300. *Newsweek* magazine claimed that 24 went to six Mexican philatelic associations, 35 to the Mexico City post office, one to President Roosevelt, and the rest were G. P.'s.*

G. P. insisted there was nothing wrong with the stamp deal. *Newsweek* countered by calling three other of his financing schemes greedy, verging on dishonest: the autogiro tours for Beech-Nut, the rumored financing of the Hawaiian flight in exchange for publicity against sugar quotas, and a radio campaign by the Mexican government to promote tourism that coincided with Amelia's flight. The magazine claimed that while G. P. was in Mexico he proposed an even more ambitious tourism campaign for a price at which one Mexican official gasped, "There isn't that much money in Mexico!"

*Walter Curley, librarian at the Cardinal Spellman Philatelic Museum, Regis College, in Weston, Massachusetts, wrote that Putnam kept 250, not 240, 83.3 percent of the 300.

Undaunted by his critics Putnam scheduled a ten-day round of personal appearances for Amelia, starting on May 30 when she became the first woman referee at the Memorial Day race in Indianapolis—the twenty-third "Indy 500." He also booked her for a lecture in Indianapolis the night before the race and another in Muncie the night after. The next day President Elliott of Purdue announced that Amelia had accepted an appointment at the university as a consultant on careers for women and that same day, June 1, *Forum* magazine was on the stands with an article by G. P. entitled, "A Flyer's Husband."

Forty-eight hours later Amelia made her first parachute jump—off a 115-foot training tower in Propertown, New Jersey. In a note to Gene Vidal, who also jumped, G. P. reported: "In case you missed the *Tribune*, it was on the front page and first page of the second section. All the papers are correspondingly good. All four newsreels, I think, will carry a yarn. . . . Publicitywise [sic] it was just about 10 percent success—far better than I dared expect." In most of the photographs Amelia looks faintly embarrassed.

To conclude the publicity blitz Amelia went to Atchison, Kansas, on June 7, the guest of honor at the Kansas Editorial Association's convention. The hometown heroine rode in a mile-long parade on a flower-decked airplane float and that night spoke at Memorial Hall where she was introduced by Gov. Alfred M. "Alf" Landon. (Landon was the Republican candidate for president the following year, losing to FDR by a landslide.)

Mary Brashay, who looked after Uncle Theo, reported to Amy that there were twenty-five thousand people watching the parade and hundreds were turned away from the hall after every seat had been taken. She wrote: "Theodore was sure proud of the turnout. I dress [sic] him up and he looked real nice. Amelia came up on Saturday afternoon . . . to see Theodore. He was so tickled to see her."

Amelia seemed a veritable goddess to many of her young Atchison admirers. Twelve-year-old Louise Bode, who brought roses for her to the Challises' home where Amelia was staying, wrote to Amy that "Miss Earhart was so gracious as to shake hands with me." Luanna Hartsock was too shy to introduce herself but told Amy, "I think she is the most famous, most greatest, most pleasantest, most beautiful woman I have ever seen."

Late Saturday afternoon a family friend, Balie Waggener, took

Amelia and G. P. to the Kansas City Airport to catch a plane for St. Louis where she had left the Vega. Although they sat at a table in the back of the airport restaurant, "the kids found her there," Waggener said. "She treated the children wonderfully and was just as sweet about giving each of them her autograph." If G. P. was at the table he had learned to be more patient with young fans than Amelia's friend, Marian Stabler, remembered him at a New Jersey school. There he had shooed them away, saying, "Now, come on children, if you want Miss Earhart's signature, write to her office."*

From the West Coast Amelia wrote to Amy that they had rented a house in Hollywood for one year and she would stay there but did not know when G. P. would return from New York where book and picture negotiations were keeping him. "We are still hoping," she wrote, "to get to Wyoming for July and August."

They did not. Exhausted by three long-distance flights and three lecture tours in six months Amelia was hospitalized with a severe sinus infection. On June 25, the day after her last lecture, she entered Cedars of Lebanon Hospital for surgery. She told her mother she was "tired of being beaten up with washings out" (in which a syringe was used to pump a solution into the atrium to flush out the debris of suppurating tissue which then drained from the patient's mouth. The alternative was surgery to enlarge or correct blocked nasal passages for normal drainage).

From the hospital she went to the Oceanside ranch of G. P.'s friends, the Louis Lightons, to recuperate. She was bedridden there when a backache she assumed was caused by a strained muscle was actually pleurisy. When G. P. arrived on the Fourth of July she was still in bed with her ribs strapped, but her nose was healing.

Illness did not prevent her from giving more advice than her mother wanted about where Amy should spend her vacation. Amelia had already sent $250 for a three-week stay at a resort—"not a cheap hotel," and Amy was not to go any place where she had to do housework. Amy went where she pleased, to an inexpensive place in Rockport, Massachusetts, taking Muriel and the children with her. Amelia gave up and sent more money for another week after Amy said they planned to leave on July 15.

While they were at the Lightons, G. P. persuaded the editor of the

*Putnam's children and grandchildren said he was a wonderful companion who liked all small children. He may have been trying to meet a tight schedule that night in New Jersey.

Oceanside paper to print extra copies with an article he had written on the front page:

> Mrs. George Palmer Putnam (nee Amelia Earhart) . . . has announced her retirement from cross-country riding. "I used to think parachutes were hard to sit on," was her only comment. The horse had nothing to say.
>
> Among the guests are Mr. Putnam who lately has often (about every six months) been seen with Miss Earhart; Dorothy Parker and Alan Campbell and Paul Mantz who is taking flying lessons from Mr. Putnam and Mrs. Mantz who is taking lessons from Mr. Mantz.

G. P. was in high spirits. Amelia was on the mend and he had just received news of the birth of his first grandchild on July 6, a daughter born to his son David and wife Nilla. However Putnam's announcement to the press said more about Amelia than it did about Baby Binney, starting with "Amelia Earhart is now a grandmother." He noted that the twenty-one-year-old father was a dispatcher for the Boston and Maine Airways of which Amelia was a vice-president, and that Amelia would soon begin work on her third book.

Three weeks after her operation, Amelia was photographed with three other Lockheed owners at the Lockheed plant. Her Vega was being remodeled nearby at the Union Air Terminal into a pleasure craft by Paul Mantz.* A reporter who saw her go to a corner of the hangar between photo sessions took a picture of her "sitting on a pile of rags . . . permitting her tired eyes a few minutes rest."

She looked terrible but nothing could keep her away from the Union Air Terminal after she decided to lease the Vega to Mantz. She would receive 50 percent of the profits from it until the first two thousand dollars for its repairs was paid. After that, revenue from it would go into a corporation that would include Mantz's maintenance and movie stunt services, his fleet of planes for charter and a new Earhart-Mantz Flying

---

*The others were Laura Ingalls, Roscoe Turner, and Amelia's old friend, Wiley Post. Ingalls had broken the women's cross-continental speed record the week before. Turner, holder of the Distinguished Flying Cross and winner of both the Harmon and Thompson trophies, wore a natty pseudomilitary uniform and flew accompanied by a four-hundred-pound lion named Gilmore. Gilmore had once chased a terrified Lockheed employee up several flights of stairs but Amelia was not afraid of him. Post, who had flown around the world twice—once solo in 1933—disliked stunts and the publicity required to earn a living as a pilot. The one-eyed oil field roustabout claimed that the only aviator who ever made any "real money" was Lindbergh.

School. They also wanted to stage an air circus in September. The restless Putnam was soon drawn into their plans and bought a house in the Lake Toluca district on July 28, minutes before he boarded a plane for New York.* There he prepared news releases and advertising copy for the most recent Earhart franchise, Amelia Earhart luggage.†

G. P. also sent a contract to Mantz for the incorporation of United Air Services, Ltd., which gave Mantz a controlling interest of 51 percent of the stock to be issued, but made Amelia the other principal shareholder and a member of the board of directors. Along with a payment of ninety-five hundred dollars Amelia's chief contribution was the use of her name. The agreement required that both Amelia and Mantz put part of their stock in escrow along with written instructions so that in case either died the deposited stock would go to the survivor or survivor's heirs.

The assumption that a partner might die was not unusual for pilots at the time. A few days later in Washington where Amelia was in the Capitol building with Sam Solomon they heard that Wiley Post and Will Rogers had just been killed in a crash at Point Barrow, Alaska.‡ Amelia was visibly shaken. "There was something in her reaction," Solomon said, "that made me feel she had a premonition of her own end."

Just eleven days before his death Rogers had written a column for his 40 million readers in which he said, "This Amelia, she would be great in any business. . . . The thing I like about her is that she always has a fine word to say about all other aviators."§

*Amelia updated her will so that the house, which was in her name, would go to G. P. in trust for Amy Earhart during the latter's lifetime with any income from it going to her.

†Amelia Earhart luggage is still being sold. She helped to design the first line of lightweight, waterproofed, canvas-covered plywood. The original franchise was held by the Real Aeroplane Luggage Company, a division of the Orenstein Trunk Corporation of Newark.

‡Post did not want to make the flight but he had to, he told his friend, Harry Bruno, because he was broke. The crash occurred moments after takeoff when the plane stalled at three hundred feet. Bruno claimed Post turned downwind trying to reach deeper water, a choice most pilots avoided. Lockheed aeronautical engineer Clarence "Kelly" Johnson thought the plane was nose-heavy with an engine too large for the mixed construction of Orion body, Sirius wings, and floats instead of wheels.

§Rogers was an enthusiastic booster of commercial air travel who had flown 300,000 miles even though he was airsick much of the time. Gene Vidal said that by the end of 1934 Rogers was using only one airsickness bag for every five hundred miles, compared to one for every fifty miles ten years earlier.

Amelia liked Rogers but her feelings for Post were much deeper. Although she had always avoided discussing the death of colleagues in accidents, she wrote an obituary for Post in the *Forum and Century* that was both sensitive and sentimental. In it she said:

> I met him first when he was a test pilot for Lockheed in 1929. . . . Six years is a long time for pilots doing the kind of flying Wiley did for us to know each other. . . .
>
> Lost to the world are his ability, his humor, his conquering spirit. Lost to his friends are his tales of adventure, told while he denied he had had any.

Back in California by the end of August Amelia decided to fly the Bendix air race before her nine-month lecture tour. She wired G. P. in New York, "Paul and I in Bendix entered for fun since ship only stock model."

Mantz thought she could place fifth in her aging plane for a prize of five hundred dollars, which would pay expenses. Amelia flew most of the way while mechanic Al Menasco and Mantz sat in the back playing gin rummy and sharing a pint of whiskey. "Amelia couldn't smell it back there," said Mantz. They came in fifth, as Mantz had predicted. The next day police had to be summoned to protect her from autograph hunters who stormed the grandstand where she sat.

On the return trip G. P. joined her, Mantz, and Menasco. While Paul flew the Vega, Amelia noted in her private log that men liked to have a male confederate fly. "It is my ship, . . ." she wrote, "but when principal is not at stake, I let them have their way."

The fall lecture tour began a month later. In 1935 Amelia was on stage 135 times, before audiences totaling more than eighty thousand. At three hundred dollars a performance, the lectures not only provided her principal income but also gave her the chance to air her convictions about commercial aviation, equal rights for women, and pacifism. On stage she entertained with stories of her own flights, then closed with a pitch for commercial air travel.

Her insistence that it was safe and convenient was justified. But air travel was far from comfortable. Planes flew at less than two hundred miles an hour in altitudes under ten thousand feet, their closed cabins occupied by passengers who were frequently airsick. However, Amelia predicted a great future for aviation, with stratospheric flights "bringing nations to the physical status of neighbors." At one time she criticized the lack of coordination of transportation in the United States, saying that

Russia—"the new, young Russia—is already ahead of us in some ways as far as aviation is concerned." But Amelia changed her tune at Senate hearings in August on a bill putting airlines under the control of the Interstate Commerce Commission, giving the ICC power to require certificates of convenience and necessity for scheduled airlines. This was going too far. She recommended competition, "and let the best survive." The admirer of "the new Russia" was not ready for state control.

Offstage, through newspaper and magazine interviews she aired her other views. She continued to advocate the military draft for women, combining pacifism with feminism as she declared, "To kill, to suffer, to be maimed, wasted, paralyzed, impoverished . . . to die 'gloriously.' There is no logic in disqualifying women from such privileges." If women were strong enough to scrub offices, stand at washtubs, and work fields, she said, then they were strong enough to fight. *She* planned to go to jail along with traitors, cowards, and other conscientious objectors.

At Chatauqua she told an audience of five thousand that a woman was flying a regular airmail schedule. The pilot was her friend, Helen Richey, who flew for Central Airlines, the only woman of 72 with transport licenses piloting for a scheduled airline carrying mail. That was in August. Three months later Richey resigned. Although she said she left in "a very friendly spirit," Amelia claimed otherwise, accusing the all-male airline pilots' union of ignoring Richey's application for membership, which she needed to keep her job. The Department of Commerce did not permit a nonunion member to fly passengers in bad weather. Richey confirmed Amelia's statements.

Amelia once said that she never took a man along on a recordbreaking flight because even if he slept all the way, when he crawled out of the plane he would be credited for the flight. But she soon reverted to less militant speech regarding Richey. In thanking Clarence Chamberlin for defending Richey, she said that her initial statement was "premature" and she had intended to wait for a ruling from the Air Line Pilots Association as to admission of woman pilots before commenting. Convinced that the carrot was more effective than the stick, she advised Mabel Britton, president of the Ninety-Nines, to include stories in the newsletter about individuals and companies giving opportunities to women. There was no need to be "terribly feministic," only to "show a little character."

As a career counselor at Purdue, Amelia distributed a questionnaire that anticipated present-day problems of career women. If the woman student intended to work and her husband agreed to become the home-maker, would she consider his work the financial equivalent of hers? Amelia favored shared housework for working couples but had doubts about careers for mothers of young children. When she told Muriel "there was never enough time" to have a child, she did not mean the pregnancy itself but the need of the child for full-time mothering. With this exception she assured her students they could be physicians instead of nurses, business executives instead of secretaries. At the same time she warned them that they would have to face discrimination, legal and traditional.

She also warned them that sexual attraction was often mistaken for love and was not enough to preserve an incompatible marriage. "Surely we must have something more to contribute to marriage than our bodies," she said. "We must earn true respect and equal rights from men by accepting responsibility."

At Purdue she lived in a women's dormitory, where she often sat after dinner, elbows on the table, chin resting in cupped hands, listening intently to the students. When they began to imitate her, the dean of women, Dorothy C. Stratton, told them to sit up and get their elbows off the table. "If Miss Earhart can do it," one asked, "why can't we?"

"You can," Stratton answered, "as soon as you fly the Atlantic."

The townspeople of Lafayette were not as impressed as students with this woman who was the first to wear slacks "downtown."* Her defenders replied that she was glamorous, chic, and very feminine.

One of the students, nineteen-year-old Frances Merrit, said she was afraid of the tall, slim women in impeccably tailored slacks and mink coat until Amelia spoke to her. "She talks right into your eyes and you forget who she is," Merrit said, " . . . and when she goes by in that car of hers and waves I feel like somebody."

Another student, Marian Frazier, whose room was next to Amelia's, thought their mentor did not get enough sleep. "I hear her typewriter clear up to midnight." Frazier was right. By April of 1936 Amelia had worked and traveled at a frantic pace for eighteen months. Amy, who was living in the new Hollywood house, said that after each lecture and

---

*Earhart and film stars Katharine Hepburn and Marlene Dietrich were primarily responsible for the acceptance of women's slacks as suitable streetwear by the close of the 1940s.

question-and-answer period "thoughtless" people would hold a reception for her. "She came home dead tired, saying to me, 'No talkee, Mother. My cocoa and good night' . . . One look at her face was enough."

Amy understood Amelia's need for rest and privacy but Muriel did not. She wanted to give a dinner in a restaurant for friends in Boston while Amelia was in the area. Amelia wrote that she and G. P. would be glad to eat at Muriel's house "with *just the family*," and if Muriel would let her pay, to hire a maid to help. G. P. told Amy that "for self-protection she simply has to be hard-boiled about getting away . . . this is a problem repeated two and three times every day for the last few months."

Amelia seldom showed her fatigue to the public or press. After a lecture in Zanesville where the high school auditorium was so noisy she had to shout until the audience settled down, she was uncharacteristically short with a reporter who asked a question when she had left the stage. "Why didn't you ask me that during the lecture?" Amelia snapped. When the reporter reminded her of her promise to give an interview, Amelia apologized and talked with her interviewer until after midnight, then left at four o'clock to drive to Buffalo for a lecture there that night.

At private parties Amelia showed no interest in purely social conversation. One hostess who thought her a disappointing guest was Dorothy Fleet, whose husband, Reuben, was the founder of Consolidated Aircraft. Mrs. Fleet described Amelia as "a tall, thin-faced woman whose obsession for aviation dominated the conversation. . . . she spoke of engines and fuel mixtures and flight patterns until I knew I was under no obligation to lighten the dinner-table chatter with any feminine observations."

Amelia may have been a disappointing guest but she was a loyal, generous friend. At a dinner party given by the Lotus Club of New York the night before she left for a Florida vacation, she was forced to listen to the principal speaker, New York socialite Mrs. Preston Davis, assail the Roosevelt administration as "neither honest nor honorable." In Florida the next day Amelia said she was unaware politics were to be discussed and was embarrassed by the attack on the administration that she thought had done far more than any of its predecessors to recognize the rights of women. She agreed with Mrs. Davis's contention that women should take an active part in politics but added, "with nearly everything else she said, I disagree."

She had defended Helen Richey as much out of friendship as feminist convictions. When Frances Marsalis was divorced and penniless,

Amelia wrote to her frequently and sent her clothing. She hired Helen Weber when Weber was ill and unemployed. She backed Clara Trenckman Studer as editor of *Airwoman* because Clara needed the job. She wrote the foreword to a children's book by Estonian pilot Elzy Kalep and lent her money to set up a business.

Soon after Blanche Noyes's husband, Dewey, was killed in a plane crash in December of 1935, Amelia asked Blanche to join her and G. P. on a trip to the West Coast. Amelia still had eight more lectures to give along the way but she and G. P. stopped frequently so that Blanche could sightsee or have dinner in a good restaurant. They also stopped, Blanche said, whenever Amelia saw an injured animal beside the road. "She'd either take the animal to the next town or find someone to take care of it."

A few months later Amelia asked Gene Vidal if there might be a job for Blanche in the Air Commerce department. If there were, she wrote, she would pay Blanche's fare to Washington for an interview (although he was not to tell Blanche). Vidal gave Blanche a job marking air routes.

Although no close friend ever betrayed Amelia, Paul Mantz's wife, Myrtle, named Amelia a co-respondent in a bitter divorce suit she brought against her husband. Myrtle told a crowded courtroom that when she left on a trip to Texas Paul had promised to ask Amelia, who was staying in their house, to leave. But he did not. A witness testified that Myrtle was angry when Mantz flew to Cleveland with Amelia for the Bendix.

In New York, G. P. said that both he and his wife had stayed with the Mantzes in Hollywood on several occasions and the Mantzes had been the Putnams' guests in Rye as well as on the trip to Honolulu a year ago. It was *his* idea, G. P. claimed, for Miss Earhart to bring Mantz and Menasco along on the Bendix race. G. P. did not mention that Amelia wired him first, but he obviously had no doubts about her conduct.

Mantz told the court Amelia stayed at his place while waiting to move into a new house and said he was never alone with her, "not even for a meal." Several of the Mantzes' friends testified that the red-haired, freckle-faced Myrtle was insanely jealous and emotionally unstable. On one occasion she had stood outside a bedroom window and pointed a gun at her husband who was reading in bed. After she fired, but missed, Mantz said, "I ran outside . . . took the gun away and slapped her face."

Although the divorce trial generated rumors of a love affair between Amelia and Mantz and predictions of divorce for the Putnams, Amelia made light of the whole affair. To Amy she wrote, "Poor old Myrtle

Mantz had to get nasty at the trial. . . . I cannot but feel she will eventually do something so disgraceful the whole world will know what she is. . . . I really have been fortunate, for anyone who has a name in the paper is a target for all sorts of things."

At that time Amelia wrote frequently to Amy who was back in Medford with Muriel. She confided in her that she had paid three thousand in back taxes on Edwin Earhart's house, along with a purchase of half lots nearby, and that she would try to help Muriel and Albert financially after they lost their house in Medford. She also reported that she and G. P. had finished renovation plans for their new Hollywood house. But like most daughters writing to their mothers, Amelia skipped the bad news. In February she was in an automobile accident in Los Angeles; a driver "reading a newspaper" crossed her path at the intersection of Hollywood Way and Burbank Boulevard. Her car overturned but she was not injured. Soon after she wrote to Amy from Dallas that she had come by air, "leaving my ship and auto and husband in L.A." She did not mention why she left the car there.

Amelia also told Amy that if she heard a rumor about her making a world flight in June, it was just "applesauce." She was going to have a new "airyplane" to play with by then but, "it would take months to prepare such a trip—maybe a year."

It would take eleven months. The "airyplane" had been ordered from Lockheed on March 20, 1936, a powerful, two-motored monoplane, the Electra 10E. Winner of a second Harmon trophy for her Honolulu-Oakland flight in 1935, Amelia was ready to try for another record. She would fly around the world at its equator. No woman—or man—had ever tried it.

PART FOUR

POINT OF
NO RETURN

CHAPTER EIGHTEEN

A Threatened Partnership

*T*he world flight was Amelia's idea, one that met with George Palmer Putnam's enthusiastic approval. He immediately proposed arranging everything for her—a new plane, the permits and licenses, the landing fields, the refueling depots, the publicity, and the profits. Critics who saw G. P. as Pygmalion to Amelia's Galatea claimed that without him she would have been just another woman aviator hustling for a living in a male-dominated world. After all, wasn't her 1928 flight a Putnam scenario, the leading lady selected for her looks and her manner rather than her piloting? Didn't Putnam arrange for her to write a book *before* her 1932 flight across the Atlantic on the fifth anniversary of Lindbergh's crossing, a book that needed only a final chapter after the flight before it was rushed to the bookstores while the feat was still news? Didn't he find the Hawaiian sugar money and get the invitation from the Mexican government, as well as that government's special stamp issue? She could never have made her flights without G. P., they said.

It is possible Amelia might not have become the world's best-known woman pilot without G. P., but he needed her as much as she needed him. No other woman pilot had the necessary combination of courage, intelligence, looks, and charm. No other was so obsessed with showing the world that women were the equals of men. Certainly no other woman aviator had the patience and self-esteem required to be G. P.'s wife and business partner. It was Amelia who described their marriage as "a reasonable partnership . . . conducted under a satisfactory system of dual control."

It was not always clear that the control was dual, nor who was in charge, particularly in their relations with the press. The dynamic G. P. seized every opportunity to publicize Amelia and when no opportunity existed, he invented one. However, most journalists accused him of interrupting and disrupting their interviews with Amelia and photographers claimed he pushed his way into their pictures of Amelia. Without him Amelia charmed her interviewers, providing them with enough material for a good story while artfully steering them away from questions she did not want to answer. So far dual control had worked for G. P. and Amelia. This flight would test the arrangement to its limits.

Early in the fall of 1935 Amelia told a reporter in St. Paul that she couldn't break any more records because her Vega was too old. "I'd like to find a tree on which new airplanes grow," she said. "I'd certainly shake myself down a good one."

A month later G. P. did it for her. The tree was Purdue and he knew how to shake it. Accompanying Amelia to Purdue for her first stint as a student counselor, G. P. persuaded President Elliott and a group of alumni to contribute fifty thousand dollars for a new airplane for Amelia. The money was to be placed in a fund managed by the Purdue Research Foundation but actually Amelia would have complete ownership and control of the aircraft. This done, G. P. began shopping for the plane, using Paul Mantz as his agent on the West Coast.

The impatient G. P. wired Mantz during the Christmas holidays, asking the price of a new Lockheed model. When Mantz failed to answer immediately, G. P. sent a second telegram on January 4 and wrote a letter the same day. He wanted data on a small Lockheed Electra, a cheaper version of the new Electra 10 which was a twin-engined, ten-passenger aircraft already in use by commercial airlines. He thought the junior Electra would be about thirty thousand dollars without engines, propellers, or instruments. Mantz, who was bogged down in the divorce proceedings instigated by his wife, was slow to answer. G. P. could not wait. If Mantz couldn't cope, *he* would go to Lockheed.

Three days later G. P. wrote again, two letters—one for Mantz's eyes only and a second for him to show at Lockheed—a typical Putnam scam to suggest that Mantz was revealing confidential information from G. P. In the letter Mantz was to show at Lockheed, G. P. included a copy of Mantz's telegram suggesting that a Sikorsky S-43, a seaplane, would be ideal for Amelia's flight, a suggestion he would certainly investigate. He also asserted that Lockheed's price of thirty thousand dollars to put pontoons on the plane in place of wheels was ridiculous. A New York man had offered to provide and install pontoons for only ten thousand.

G. P. followed his threats with enticements. The money was there and he wanted to buy immediately. Pratt & Whitney had already agreed to supply the engines, and the flight would be sponsored by Purdue University and, perhaps, the National Geographic Society. He was certain, he wrote, that Lockheed would not attempt to make money out of A. E., not when an Electra on floats making the first round-the-world flight at the equator would be such a "uniquely valuable exploitation bull's eye" for its makers. After all, he insisted, Amelia was recognized by commercial airlines as "the most important single agency in America today popularizing air travel." In a reversal of the carrot and stick, he added in a postscript that he had been to see the Sikorsky people. Their plane was probably the safest, he thought, but Amelia would not want to use a Sikorsky after the world flight. She would want an Electra.

G. P. settled for the larger Electra but with wheels instead of the more expensive pontoons. When Lockheed agreed to turn over a partially built Electra in March, Paul Mantz sent G. P. a list of the equipment he thought Amelia should have. It included a Sperry Robot pilot, a special rear hatch for the navigator's celestial sightings, and Western Electric radio equipment that would receive all wave bands and transmit in both voice and code. Mantz also asked Clarence Belinn, chief engineer of National Airways, to design a cross-feed system for ten gasoline tanks to be placed in the wings and fuselage with one master valve in the floor of the cockpit. The tanks would give Amelia's ship a range of twenty-five hundred to three thousand miles. Belinn did the work, although he thought Amelia was already living on borrowed time. The four wing attachment brackets on her old Vega, which he examined right after her Atlantic flight, had all cracked to the yield point. She was lucky to be alive, he told Mantz, without tempting fate again.

Mantz was beginning to wonder if Belinn might be right. He was shocked at G. P.'s attempts to cut costs in bargaining, which suggested to Mantz an indifference to Amelia's safety. G. P. insisted there was only so much money to be spent and at best Purdue would cover no more than two-thirds of the plane's total cost. Mantz countered with a request that G. P. acknowledge his written list of equipment and that Amelia send him a list of what *she* wanted. He also asked for her itinerary so that he could write or telephone her, as if he suspected G. P. might not give her his messages.

Once Mantz went to work on the plane, G. P. turned to his next objective, planning the flight itself so that it would be perceived by the public as unique—another record for Amelia. This was not easy. The Australian, Sir Charles Kingsford-Smith, had flown from California to Australia, then on around the world by way of England back to California, crossing the equator twice. Wiley Post flew around the world twice, once with Harold Gatty in 1931 and once alone in 1933. But Kingsford-Smith took a crew of three, while Amelia would take only a navigator and drop him as soon as she had crossed the Pacific to Australia. Post's solo route was much shorter than the one proposed by Amelia. Although the French and the Germans flew the mail across the South Atlantic and Pan American's clippers would soon reach Hong Kong, none of them crossed both oceans. No one had flown all the way around the world as close to the equator as Amelia would.

Once her goal was defined Amelia left the specific arrangements to G. P. He started at the top, with a letter to Amelia's friend, Eleanor Roosevelt, asking her help with flight permits. On previous flights Amelia had ignored the regulations of the departments of State and Commerce for flights over or into foreign territory. In 1932 she had no permit from Commerce nor any visa for Ireland. In 1935 she reentered the United States from Mexico illegally, making her subject to a five-hundred dollar fine. Mrs. Roosevelt assured G. P. she would be glad to help. Within days Richard Southgate, chief of protocol at the State Department, was assigned to handle the matter.

G. P. then wrote to the Department of Commerce asking permission for the flight and that the department send on its approval to the Department of State. Setting a tentative route and a starting date for the flight of late February or early March of 1937, he promised that there would be no firearms or motion-picture cameras aboard and gave as the primary purpose of the flight "a thorough field test of a two-motored plane . . . part of the program [at Purdue] of aeronautical activities conducted by Miss Earhart." He was told that his letter would be forwarded to the State Department but that Amelia's transport license had expired and it would have to be renewed. She would also need to obtain an instrument flying rating for such a long overwater flight.

G. P. also asked Gene Vidal, whose Bureau of Air Commerce handled his request, to act as a go-between with the Navy. The Navy reluctantly provided Pacific weather data a month later, but sent it to Vidal's office with the admonition that it was not for general distribution and had to be returned by Mrs. Putnam. Undaunted, G. P. wrote to the secretary of the Navy asking that a flying boat be assigned to execute a midair refueling of Amelia's plane over the Navy base at Midway Island. This would permit her to take off from Honolulu without the danger of a full load of fuel and she could receive enough at Midway to take her either to Tokyo or Manila via Guam, he claimed. He seemed unaware of the danger to Amelia of a flight of more than four thousand miles over water without sleep.

When the Navy failed to respond, G. P. wrote to Marie Mattingly Meloney, the editor of the *Herald Tribune*'s Sunday magazine and a close friend of Eleanor Roosevelt's. He told "Missy" Meloney that Adm. W. H. Standley, the Chief of Naval Operations, had his proposal for refueling Amelia's ship but had not approved it because of "precedent and policy." Would Meloney see that Standley has word from the "TOP?" Her secretary answered with a note that Meloney would take the matter up with Mrs. Roosevelt. Two months later Meloney wrote, apologizing for the delay. She had been ill, but when she did speak to Mrs. Roosevelt about Amelia's flight, Eleanor assured her that she loved Amelia and that she would be "delighted to personally take up any problems with Naval Operations or any other government group." G. P. or Amelia should tell her, she said, exactly how she could help.

The message came in January, too late for the impatient G. P. The day after Meloney first promised to speak to the president's wife, G. P. had Amelia write to FDR. He may have drafted the letter himself, one in which Amelia asked Roosevelt to approve her request to practice refueling operations with Navy planes at their San Diego base. On the margin of her letter, the president scrawled, "Do what we can and contact Mr. Putnam." That brought an instant response from the Navy to the president's secretary, Missy LeHand. Everything possible would be done for Miss Earhart. By the time G. P. wrote a thank you note to LeHand, Amelia had heard directly from Standley. The Navy would cooperate.

By then, G. P. had another plan up his sleeve. Amelia could land on a tiny atoll in the Pacific—Howland Island. Howland, with two other islands, Jarvis and Baker, had been placed under the jurisdiction of the Department of Interior in May of 1936. G. P. undoubtedly heard about it from Vidal when the Bureau of Air Commerce was asked to assess the islands as sites for emergency landing fields for commercial aircraft; at least that was the stated purpose of a government anxiously watching Japanese military expansion in the Pacific.

After considerable interdepartmental squabbling, it was agreed that there would be three landing strips on Howland. The project was approved in late December of 1936 and budgeted for $9,881.* This time the government's aid was not entirely gratis. G. P. would pay the wages of four workers, the federal government the other eight. He was required to open a joint bank account with Richard B. Black from the Department of the Interior, in charge of the project along with the Air Commerce man, Robert A. Campbell. Except for his cable assenting to the joint account, G. P. was promised that his name would not appear on any further communications concerning Howland. Black said later that he was told confidentially that the scratch-grade runway was to be used by Amelia but there is no firm evidence that the project was initiated especially for her.

Neither the arrangements for the flight nor his contract with independent producer Emmanuel Cohen of Major Pictures to publicize eight pictures that year prevented G. P. from sending frequent directives on the Electra to Mantz.† When Mantz suggested that the rudder, stabilizer, and wing border be painted red or orange to facilitate locating it if it were forced down, G. P. refused. The colors, he said, would have to be those of Purdue University. He also refused Mantz an opportunity to use the ship in a film. It would remain at Purdue for "political reasons," G. P. wrote. He needed another ten thousand dollars in addition to money he was trying to raise by selling Amelia's Vega. He had also made a number of other commitments for the plane, he wrote to Mantz, one with an ad agency and another for the installation of the Bendix radio compass. In Novem-

---

*Air Commerce would supervise construction; the Works Progress Administration would provide the laborers from relief rolls; the Department of Interior, the food for all personnel; the Army and Navy, the equipment; and the Coast Guard, the transport.

†One of the films he publicized was *Go West Young Man,* starring former burlesque queen Mae West. The reviews were bad but the film was a hit where it counted—at the box office.

ber it would have to be taken to Hadley Field in New Jersey for a check on the radio by Bell Laboratories and Western Electric. In other letters G. P. complained to Mantz about material not reaching Bo McKneely, who was supposed to work on the Electra at Purdue. When the plane did get back to Burbank, he said, they would have to lay out a definite program for repairs and overhauling. Mantz, described by one of his charter passengers to Las Vegas as "a small man with a large ego," was being told how to run his business.

Publicizing the flight was yet another task assumed by G. P., one that required all of his huckster's skills. Amelia was thirty-nine years old with a lot of records behind her. The years of postwar escapism were ending and public interest focused less on sports and film stars, explorers and aviators, gangsters and "G-Men," and more on serious issues—the lingering economic depression, a presidential election, and the nation-wide struggle between management and new and powerful labor unions. Abroad, Franco's rebel troops had taken Madrid, Hitler and Mussolini were rattling sabres in Europe, and Japan was determined to control all of Asia. Timing of any release on Amelia's flight would be crucial. The story could fizzle out if it peaked too soon.

When Dr. Elliott announced the purchase of the Electra, he said nothing about a world flight. Taking his cue from G. P., Elliott told reporters the Electra was to be a "flying laboratory," a term G. P. borrowed from another great public relations man, Jack Maddux, who first used it to describe Lindbergh's new plane back in 1930. When reporters asked Amelia if she intended to fly around the world, she said she did not. She continued to deny it for the remainder of the year. In April she wrote to Amy that the rumors of the flight were "all applesauce." She denied it again a month later when Lockheed officials announced it and Mantz confirmed their announcement, and yet again in September when a Department of Commerce official let the persistently reappearing cat out of the bag. G. P. had scheduled the official announcement for February of 1937, a month before her departure. Until then, holding off speculation suited Amelia, who dreaded preflight hype for fear something would go wrong.

Not since 1928 had G. P. been so totally in control of flight arrangements. Soon after the *Friendship* flight Amelia had begun to make many of her own decisions—for her cross-country tour in the Avro Avian, the women's derby, the Detroit speed trials, the autogiro trips, and her second Atlantic flight in 1932. However, after each flight, she had more commitments for lectures, magazine articles, public appearances at special events and, now, counseling at Purdue. She had a house being remodeled and a mother, and by then, a seriously ill mother-in-law to look after. She also wanted to campaign for the Democrats in an election year and somehow, she would have to put in more flight time in the Electra before she took it on the most dangerous flight of her life.

In the spring of 1936 she decided that her mother needed a rest from what Amelia thought was a life of endless drudgery in the Morrissey household. She booked passage for her on a Red Star ship sailing June 15 for a seven-week tour of England, Scotland, and France. Amy would be accompanied by a young relative, Nancy Balis. To discuss the details, Amelia left the White House where she was again an overnight guest on May 13 to see her mother in Medford. Either the meeting was too brief or Amy was too deaf for Amelia to be certain she understood the arrangements, because two weeks later Amelia wrote an incredibly detailed set of instructions and admonishments to her mother.

Amy was not to criticize the Roosevelts (like many Republicans she called FDR "that man in the White House"). She was to be careful of reporters if they discovered who she was and to "smile for photographs" because "the serious face in real life looks sour in print, the grinning face, moderately pleasant." When mentioning things that impressed her to the press, Amy should talk about English things in England and French things in France but not Westminster in Paris, Amelia advised.

There was also an "order of dressiness" list with instructions on what to pack. She was to keep her kid gloves out of the rain and to wear cloth ones instead and not to pull "from the top" the new hose Amelia had sent her. As for her young escort, Nancy Balis, Amy should not be "reactionary" with her. "Let her be radical," Amelia wrote. "Youth which isn't is pretty poor and all her family are sticks."

Although Amelia loved Amy, she may not have liked her. Certainly more separated them than the normal generational gap and lack of mutual interests afflicting many mother-daughter relationships. Amy often felt the world had dealt with her cruelly. Amy could be cranky. Amy was deaf. Amy was also stubborn and proud. For nine years, from the moment Amelia began to earn a decent income, she had sent money and gifts to Amy only to see a major portion of both passed on to others. The penniless, young amateur flier with the yellow sports car and unpaid medical bills had become financially responsible, but neither her mother, the wealthy judge's favorite daughter, nor her sister, the Smith College graduate, had followed her lead. Refusing to admit the reality of her near poverty, Amy gave money to Muriel and to relatives or friends she thought were in need while ignoring needs of her own. Muriel, whose husband failed to give her an adequate household allowance and who often feared that her gas, electric, or telephone services might be cut off, also had unpaid bills from S. S. Pierce's very elegant and expensive food market.

If Amelia preached and scolded, she also accepted her family responsibilities. These extended to G. P.'s mother as well. While Amy was in Europe, Frances Putnam was living with Amelia in North Hollywood. She moved there in September of 1935. G. P. remained in New York most of the time and a household staff looked after the ailing Mrs. Putnam when her daughter-in-law was on the road. On June 30, when Frances Putnam died, Amelia was with her but G. P. was still in New York. Reporting the death to her own mother, Amelia wrote, "All the while poor Fannie was getting weaker but not alarmingly so until the last few days. I wired G. P. to stand by, but the end came before he could get here. He arrives tomorrow morning from New York."

Three weeks after Mrs. Putnam's death, the Electra was ready. Amelia took it up for the first time with test pilot Elmer McLeod who did most of the flying. She was delighted with the plane. It was worth the price of eighty-thousand dollars, thirty thousand more than Purdue had given her.* It was worth the senseless statements G. P. asked her to make to the press about her "flying laboratory" and the "exhaustive study of human reactions to flying" she was supposed to be planning. Three days after that first flight with McLeod, Amelia took delivery of the Electra in Salt Lake City on her thirty-ninth birthday.

For the next five weeks she learned as much as she could about the Electra from McLeod and Mantz. McLeod took her on one practice run with landings and takeoffs at Mills Field, Alameda Air Base, and Burbank in a single day. Mantz took her on more but not enough to satisfy him that she knew the aircraft as well as she should. When he continued to

*At present-day prices the Electra would cost approximately $1.5 million. The bill of sale, signed by McLeod, described the plane as "one Electra monoplane complete, being manufacturer's serial number 1055, Department of Commerce Number NR-16020." The Commerce license number was applied for by Lockheed on July 19, but not officially approved until August 21, 1936.

press her for more flight time, she decided to enter it in the 1936 Bendix race. The flight from Los Angeles to Floyd Bennett Field in New York for the start of the race would give the plane a "shakedown cruise" and Amelia some practice before crossing the country again in the race back to the West Coast on September 4. Fortunately, Mantz and McKneely went along because the two 550-horsepower engines leaked oil all the way to Kansas City.

Before leaving California, Amelia told reporters she would fly the race solo, probably to prevent rumors that she could not handle the plane without a man to help her. Once in New York she asked Helen Richey, her friend whose forced resignation Amelia had protested so vigorously a year before, to accompany her. In a race that was disastrous to many of the contestants, Amelia had her share of trouble. Moments after she took off at 2:47 in the morning the navigator's hatch blew open and almost pulled her and Richey out of the cabin. They managed to close it and tie it down with a rag. It was secured when they refueled in Kansas City but soon after leaving there Amelia had trouble with the fuel system. Either it was faulty or she didn't know enough about it. They came in fifth and last, one and a half hours after the winners, Louise Thaden and Blanche Noyes.*

Amelia stayed in Los Angeles for the remainder of the National Air Races, which her reporter friend Carl Allen of the *Herald Tribune* thought were a fleecing of the public. Allen cited "too much Hollywood ballyhoo," primitive sanitary facilities, no food except hot dogs and water at five dollars a glass. When Amelia returned to Burbank, Mantz needed more time to work on the Electra and she needed more flight experience in it, but G. P. had already promised it would be based at Purdue. Amelia flew it there in late September, taking G. P. and McKneely with her.

For the remainder of the year, while Mantz waited in California for the return of Amelia and the Electra, and while G. P. worked on flight

---

*Amelia was lucky to bring home the Electra intact. Some of the country's best fliers had ruined their ships. Before the race Roscoe Turner crashed on his way to New York and Jacqueline Cochran, newest star on the women's circuit, cracked up on a test flight. During the race Joe Jacobson's Northrop Gamma exploded over Stafford, Kansas, blasting him into the sky. Jacobson managed to open his parachute in time. The favorites, Ben Howard and his copilot wife, Maxine, crashed at a lonely spot in New Mexico where they lay pinned in the wreckage for four hours before help reached them. Both of Maxine Howard's legs were fractured and Ben's heel was severed, necessitating the amputation of his foot.

arrangements, Amelia shuttled ceaselessly by car or train from Purdue to the Midwest and the East Coast. In addition to her lectures, her other commitments included campaigning for the Roosevelt administration. A few days after she arrived at Purdue she drove to upstate New York, joining a woman's "caravan" of speakers in cars that stopped in small towns to rally Democratic voters. Without a microphone Amelia's vocal cords began to fail, but when she realized her audience in Mechanicsville could not hear her from an open window of a ground-floor office, she asked for a desk to be brought out onto the sidewalk. She gave her speech standing on top of the desk, a performance that gained her and the campaign nationwide news coverage.

Two days later she drove to Syracuse for the state Democratic convention to second the nomination of her friend and neighbor in Rye, Caroline O'Day, the incumbent congresswoman-at-large and the only woman candidate. When Amelia made her seconding speech the cheers that followed O'Day's nomination swelled to a roar of approval. Back on a lecture tour of the Midwest, she followed up with an endorsement of the Roosevelt administration at all twenty-eight of her appearances in October.

No matter how busy she was, Amelia found time to express her beliefs. Both principled and practical, she endorsed Roosevelt because she thought he had done more for women than any other president. At the same time she continued to support the National Women's Party, sending a contribution and a message to their national convention in New York: "I am deeply interested in women's obtaining full equality under the law. . . . Today women still stand victims of restrictive class legislation and conflicting interpretations of statutes . . . their rights must be made theirs by definition, that is by Constitutional guarantee."

The militant feminist also remained an uncompromising pacifist. The first woman to lecture at the U.S. Naval Academy in 1935, she returned in 1936, a few days before Armistice Day, when she told the midshipmen that traditional speeches and parades were "uncivilized," and what was really needed was "education for peace." It was an odd place for such a message but she never forgot the wounded in that Toronto hospital.

G. P. was with her for that weekend when both were the guests of the academy's superintendent, Adm. David Sellers. He was also with her on the Democrats' "caravan" campaign and for another weekend in South Bend, Indiana, as a guest of Vincent Bendix, president of Bendix

Aviation Corporation and donor of the Bendix prize. G. P. cultivated all their hosts. Amelia was present, but she did not enjoy these weekends as much as he. In much of the gossip about a pending divorce for the Putnams there were always rumors of another man. If Amelia had left G. P., it would not have been for another man, but to live alone. She was tired of G. P.—of his endless schemes, his demanding schedules, his hot temper, his pursuit of the powerful, and his apparent need to share the public attention she found increasingly distasteful.

One of the first persons to know this was her old friend, Gene Vidal. Although Vidal maintained friendly relations with G. P., the help he gave to him on the world flight was really for Amelia's sake. Vidal made a point of seeing her whenever they were in the same city. He was with her at the National Air Races in Los Angeles and he met her when she arrived at Purdue in September. On November 28, a week after she flew the Electra from Purdue to New York for inspection of its radio system, Vidal took her to the Army-Navy football game in Philadelphia. He had refused an invitation from the West Point Society of Philadelphia so that he could escort her and his ten-year-old son, Gore, to the game.

The boy was fascinated by Amelia. He thought her voice was beautiful and her "white" eyelashes very unusual. She wrote poetry and encouraged him to write. He was sure Amelia was in love with his father, who had been divorced for a year, but was even more certain his father's affection for Amelia was platonic. He was probably right. Among Vidal's papers at the University of Wyoming is a leather wallet with three passport pictures in it. One is of a motherly looking, white-haired woman, a Mrs. Scovill, manager of a Santa Monica hotel where Vidal lived while working for TAT in 1929 and whose advice he sought later in finding a good summer camp for Gore. A second picture is of Gore, and the third, Amelia. The collection is that of a family man, not a lover.

On the train returning to New York, while curious fans peeked in the window of their compartment, Amelia talked with Vidal and his son about the world flight. When the boy asked her what worried her the most, she told him she feared being forced down in an African jungle. He said he thought the Pacific Ocean looked more dangerous. She replied that there were islands in the Pacific and that she would love to live on a desert island. Gene Vidal was not as enthusiastic as Amelia about life on a desert island but he was willing to discuss methods of extracting salt from sea water. He knew Amelia loved to discuss problems of that sort.

Later, Gene told his son that Amelia disliked her husband and that she was tired of the constant attention resulting from his publicizing of her career. By 1936 she had made up her mind to find a figurative, if not a literal, desert island on which to live.

That same November Amelia met a woman who became a second, intimate friend in whom she could confide, perhaps even more than she did in Gene Vidal. Jacqueline Cochran Odlum was also an aviator, confident, daring and eager to show the world what a woman pilot could do. Other than that, there was little the two women had in common. Cochran was eight years Amelia's junior, the founder-owner of a cosmetics company who had recently married one of the country's wealthiest financiers, Floyd Odlum. A tiny, shapely blonde who ordinarily preferred the company of men, she was intelligent but uneducated, a compulsive talker exuding a nervous, pent-up energy.

Growing up in Atchison, eight-year-old Amelia had played at trapping the neighbors' chickens; six-year-old Cochran trapped them for food in the camp for itinerant workers where she lived. At eight, this unwanted foster child of ignorant, often cruel guardians went to work in a cotton mill in Columbus, Georgia, on the twelve-hour night shift for six cents an hour. Cochran fled the schoolroom on her third day there, after the teacher hit her and she struck back. Although her formal education was infrequent and intermittent, it did not prevent her from speaking her mind. An oft-repeated, if apocryphal, story about Cochran claimed that when she was shown the relief tube in a military plane just before she took it up for a test flight, she said, "I never pee when I fly."

This small, uneducated, and, some said, ruthless woman and tall, well-read, gentle Amelia liked each other from their first meeting. A few days later Amelia invited Cochran to accompany her in the Electra when she took it to the West Coast.

The trip took a week. Held up by weather in St. Louis and Amarillo, the new friends talked. They discussed everything that interested either or both of them—politics, business, science, religion, aviation, and, surprisingly for Amelia, their own lives. The ebullient Cochran proved a sensitive listener. Although she flew for the love of it, she realized that her new friend was seeking in flight an elusive peace, one she had failed to find in college, nursing, social work, or any of her other earlier pursuits.

During the trip Cochran told Amelia she had psychic powers. These were tested the first night in Indio, California, where Amelia was a guest at the Odlum ranch. After they heard that a Western Air Express plane was missing on a flight from Los Angeles to Salt Lake City, Amelia, who had always been a respecter of scientific verification, asked Cochran to locate the plane. Cochran gave Amelia a number of clues. Amelia called Paul Mantz in Los Angeles, who found the locality Cochran had indicated on his aerial maps. Amelia drove half the night to Los Angeles, where she took off with Mantz in the Electra on a search for the missing aircraft. They didn't find it, but when the snows melted the following spring, Cochran claimed it was where she said it would be. On December 27 a United Airlines plane was lost outside of Burbank. Cochran again claimed she told Amelia where to look and Amelia found the plane but in their column on February 16, 1937, it was Amelia whom Drew Pearson and Robert Allen credited with psychic gifts in locating the wreckage as well as that of a second plane lost on January 12. Cochran, who would have been furious at anyone else upstaging her, made no protest.

Cochran had invited Amelia to visit her at the Cochran-Odlum ranch, Indian Palms, as soon as they arrived in California. Before her marriage to Odlum, Cochran had built a small house on twenty acres in Indio. Odlum, a former utilities magnate who was president of Atlas Corporation and later took over Paramount Pictures, purchased another eight hundred adjacent acres and expanded the accommodations to a main house, six guest cottages, a golf course, stables, and a swimming pool. Amelia loved the place. Delighted, Cochran described her guest as "streaking across the desert on horseback with the joy of living mirrored in her face," or "stretched out full length on the floor before the fireplace, studying maps, talking or . . . just watching the shooting flames."

Amelia spent the last few days of 1936 at Indian Palms. This time G. P. and Floyd Odlum were both there, along with Floyd's thirteen-year-old son by a previous marriage. Amelia, who was fascinated by anything mechanical, charmed young Bruce Odlum by her interest in a twelve-dollar used car he had managed to put in running condition. She was obviously fond of both Cochran and Odlum who returned her affection. Odlum was cordial to G. P., but Cochran did not like him from the moment she met him after her solo flight in 1932. Always watchful of any woman who might challenge Amelia's standing as the leader of the pack, G. P. had asked Cochran, "Well, little girl, what is your ambition in flying?" Cochran snapped back, "To put your wife in the shade."

Years later, she told a friend that Amelia might have been in love with Putnam early in their marriage but she had become suspicious of his motives and thought he was using her name to further his own ambitions. Both Vidal and Cochran were convinced that Amelia no longer thought that her "reasonable partnership" with G. P. gave her the kind of support she wanted for the most ambitious and dangerous flight of her career. With just ten more weeks left to prepare for it, the Putnams' duality of control was beginning to falter.

CHAPTER NINETEEN

Crackup

*B*y the beginning of 1937 Amelia's fate was locked into the world flight. Her old friend, Hilton Railey, described her as being "caught up in the 'hero stream' of fliers, compelled to strive for bigger and braver feats necessary to the maintenance of her position as the foremost woman pilot in the world." She was going to make this most dangerous flight of her life in her first two-engine plane, a powerful, complicated aircraft loaded with special equipment, in which she had had very little flight experience. Yet in the ten weeks remaining she spent most of her time earthbound.

Her lack of flight time worried Paul Mantz. When he suggested she make a quick trip with him to New York and back in the Electra, she refused. Instead she made a series of short trips out of Burbank with Mantz demonstrating procedures to her, but he was not the best of teachers for an emancipated woman. Mantz used expressions like "Listen to Papa," and he once called Amelia a good pilot but "a woman's pilot," who tended, like many old-timer women pilots, to "jockey the throttles."

In late February she had a second instructor, Clarence "Kelly" Johnson, the Electra's designer. While Mantz tended to patronize her, Johnson taught her as he would any new Electra pilot. He accompanied her as flight engineer rather than copilot while they flew the big plane at various weights, altitudes, and engine power settings. He also taught her how to use the Cambridge analyzer, setting the fuel mixture control for maximum mileage. Johnson thought she was a good pilot—sensible, studious, and attentive.

However, Amelia was a part-time student distracted by too many extracurricular activities, some obligatory, many voluntary. There were details for the flight route that G. P. could not clean up. When he told her that work on the runway at Howland Island had not begun because the Bureau of the Budget would not authorize funds for it, Amelia wired Franklin Roosevelt for help. Three days after this second request for FDR's assistance, she was notified by his aide, Marvin McIntyre, that the money had been allocated to the WPA by order of the president.

There was the new house in Hollywood. With G. P. in New York Amelia was left to supervise work on it. Built on two lots alongside the Toluca Lake golf course, it incorporated the original small bungalow and a new, larger addition with a double study, master bedroom, guest room, and staff quarters.

Amelia hired a staff for it, including a houseman and gardener, Fred Tomas, a housekeeper, Mrs. DeCarie, and a secretary, DeCarie's daughter, Margot. Young and inexperienced when Amelia hired her, Margot DeCarie worshipped her employer. "I was spoiled working for A. E.," she said. "She . . . thought I could conquer the world and I felt I could too." Amelia was her hero-saint, a woman who spoke often and freely about anyone she liked but said nothing at all about those she did not. At first G. P. was approved of by DeCarie simply because Amelia, who never made a mistake, married him. Later DeCarie changed her mind, calling him "egotistical and selfish," a publicity-seeker with no regard for others.

The house at Toluca Lake was where Amelia intended to live on her return. If she gave an interview in February about another—the one in Rye—to *Better Homes and Gardens,* it was for G. P.'s sake, perhaps to help him find a renter when they needed money so desperately. The California house was also where she intended her mother to live, in a special room designed to accommodate Amy's favorite pieces of furniture, a place in which she would be neither underfoot nor isolated.

When the new wing neared completion in late February, Amelia told her mother to find a temporary room in Boston and send on all but her necessary belongings. She was *not*, Amelia said, to keep Muriel's children with her. This admonition resulted from Muriel's decision to divorce Albert Morrissey, a move that received Amelia's wholehearted support.

In a long letter dated January 31, Amelia gave Muriel specific advice. She was to transfer one thousand dollars in stock, given her by Amy and held by G. P. but in Albert's name, to G. P. She was to ask Albert for the five hundred dollars Muriel had given him in a separate transaction. A week later Amelia wired her mother that she was leaving for New York on February 8 and would see Muriel while she was there. Fearing a crisis in which Muriel would not have the address of the lawyer she had recommended, Amelia said to get it from G. P. A legal separation would be necessary, she thought, to insure an income for the children, and Muriel might have to remain in Boston until it was arranged. Under no circumstances, Amelia told Amy, was Muriel to leave the house before Albert.*

The apparently happily married woman who knew so much about divorce proceedings had already missed celebrating her sixth wedding anniversary on February 7. She was further delayed by mechanical difficulties with the Electra but arrived in New York on February 11, in time for the press reception G. P. had arranged at the Barclay Hotel to publicize the world flight. G. P. did not get the news coverage he wanted. Reporters were tired of G. P.'s promotional schemes. Typical of the stories appearing the next day was one in the *New York Times,* less than a half column on page 25.

Never discouraged for long, G. P. followed up five days later when New York's feisty mayor, Fiorello La Guardia, appeared with Amelia on the steps of City Hall to wish her bon voyage. In his speech La Guardia insisted her flight would be "in no sense a stunt," a declaration G. P. might well have written for him. When he accompanied Amelia on her flight back to the coast, G. P. staged one more incident that did receive national coverage by the wire services. Amelia had landed the Electra at Blackwell, Oklahoma, after a propeller went out of synchronization. While it was being repaired she borrowed a car from a local dealer and drove G. P., McKneely, and Harry Manning, who had taken leave to be

*Muriel Earhart Morrissey, who taught English to students in Medford and Belmont schools for almost forty years, remained married to Albert Morrissey until his death in 1979. Amelia, she said, "exaggerated" their marital differences. "[Albert] was a wonderful person."

her navigator on the world flight, to Ponca City for lunch. Before they left, G. P. contrived to have her arrested by a local policeman who did so when she drove back through Blackwell. In court Amelia pleaded guilty, telling the judge that she hadn't seen any signs but supposed she might have been going too fast. The judge, who knew nothing about the joke, regarded her with suspicion. She was from New York but said she was driving a borrowed car. "All the way from New York?" he asked. "No," she said, "I came in an airplane." He ruled a fine of $1.00 and $2.50 in costs before the mayor arrived, embarrassed because a famous aviator had been treated so badly in Blackwell. After G. P.'s prank was explained to Amelia, the judge, and the mayor, a banquet was arranged for that evening when a ten-foot key to the city was given to Amelia. In the afternoon three thousand fans turned up at her hotel, where she signed autograph books in the lobby for more than an hour before retreating to her room with the promise that if the remaining books were left at the desk she would sign as many as she could before leaving at five o'clock the next morning.

G. P. added even more commitments to Amelia's schedule. Faced with a paucity of preflight coverage and a growing need for cash, he reneged on his original promise to Lockheed that news of the flight would be free and available to all. Instead, he made a deal with the *New York Herald Tribune*. Amelia would write her own account of the trip, sending a dispatch from each major stop along the way, stories that G. P. could later compile for a book to be published after her return. The *Herald Tribune*'s syndicated feature service could sell Amelia's stories to any client newspaper and Amelia's friend, Carl Allen, would do extensive preflight features as part of the series.

If G. P. thought Amelia's friendship with Helen Reid would permit him any advantage in the agreement he was wrong. Amelia was told by a *Herald Tribune* editor to "forget God ever gave her a tongue" until each of her stories was written and dispatched. She was not to carry any photographs for any agency nor to help any organization except the *Herald Tribune* and its representatives, and only after they proved their identity. Reid herself added that only *Tribune* representatives should be granted interviews. G. P. replied that if Amelia refused to talk to newsmen she would look ridiculous. *Where possible,* he wrote, she would not answer questions until she had dispatched her own story, but he could not stop the Navy and Coast Guard from permitting reporters aboard the three ships assisting in the Pacific flight. The *Herald Tribune* settled for G. P.'s terms.

Putnam also bartered Amelia's name for goods and services. In a single feature written by Allen for the *Herald Tribune,* benefactors mentioned included Bausch and Lomb (nine pairs of sunglasses and a light meter), Vincent Bendix (a radio direction-finder), Standard Oil (fuel depots and services of their representative, Vicomte Jacques de Sibour), Pan American (for flight plan assistance), and Amelia's franchised luggage (she would carry one Amelia Earhart overnight case on the flight).

In addition, G. P. tested the Hollywood waters for a feature film, although Amelia said she would not act in it; he would have to find someone else for the starring role. Lectures and guest appearances were already scheduled for her return. Gimbels had assumed promotion of the six-thousand five hundred cacheted covers Amelia would carry, to be sold at $5.00 each if autographed and $2.50, if not. Even the kitchen of the Toluca Lake bungalow was paid for with Amelia's name. When she showed the room to Allen she explained that G. P. had arranged for a mailorder house to outfit it. In the exchange, Allen observed, "the firm had permission to tell America's housewives all about its 'Amelia Earhart kitchen.'" Amelia, Allen claimed, would never have had the gall to look for the deals G. P. found or created.

The first week of March, while Amelia was still in Hollywood, the Bureau of Air Commerce's coordinator for the flight, William T. Miller, arrived in Oakland. Superintendent of airways for the bureau, Miller was the man who had assessed Jarvis, Baker, and Howland islands for possible emergency landing fields in the summer of 1935 on an expedition for which he was cited for bravery and "putting the mission before personal interests." A pilot and lieutenant commander in the Naval Reserve, he had already worked on Amelia's flight arrangements in Washington. Miller was a master of government paperwork and protocol, a man who thought of everything.

He suggested that G. P. write to the secretary of war for permission to use Wheeler Field in Hawaii. He secured orders for a naval aerological officer and two mechanics to be sent to Howland to assist Amelia there, then advised Capt. Kenneth Whiting, commanding officer of the Fleet Air Base at Pearl Harbor, that a run-in cylinder assembly and a full set of spark plugs for the Electra would be sent along with the three men. He sent strip maps of the Caribbean landing fields and advice on what radio bands Navy and Coast Guard ships transmitted as well as received. He arranged for thirty drums of oil to be shipped by the Coast Guard to Howland and sent a dozen cans of tomato juice to Honolulu with instructions to keep six for Amelia's flight to Howland and to send on the remainder for the flight from Howland to her next destination, Lae, New Guinea.

As soon as he arrived at Oakland, Miller set up an office at the airport and hired a local woman, Vivian Maatta, to be Amelia's secretary. Although the twenty-seven-year-old Oakland woman worked most of the time for Miller or G. P., who paid her salary, she soon knew all of the flight team members. Maatta thought Amelia was "quiet but nice," much prettier than her pictures, and very energetic. In a new, informal division of labor—a fortunate one for Amelia—Miller had taken over the flight arrangements while G. P. worked on finances. She spent most of her time with Miller, poring over maps and charts at his desk.

Just before Amelia brought the Electra from Burbank to Oakland in early March, she met her old friend Gene Vidal in Los Angeles, where G. P. arranged to have them photographed for the newspapers examining an emergency signal kite that Jackie Cochran had given Amelia. It was rumored that Vidal, who was on a vacation after resigning as head of the Bureau of Air Commerce, would join Amelia and G. P. in a business venture. Although he would neither confirm nor deny the rumor, he had really stopped in Los Angeles to see Amelia and to talk about the flight because he knew it would please her. His visit gained more publicity for her and on his return to Washington soon after he discussed the flight with reporters. Amelia was capable of making it, he told them, but added with a smile that he doubted she would contribute much to research on "the human element" because, he said, "what is easy for Amelia might be awfully difficult for the rest of us."

At Oakland Amelia moved into the airport hotel, where she became the center of attention from a group of students of the Boeing School of Aeronautics who were living at the hotel. Amelia chatted with them every morning at breakfast in the coffee shop and she permitted one of them, Harkness Davenport from Clyde, Ohio, to take pictures of the interior of the Electra with his new 35mm camera. The morning conversations with Amelia ended abruptly for Davenport and his fellow students when G. P. arrived from Hollywood. "He'd go screaming through the lobby—the great George Putnam—" Davenport complained, "and it was 'out of the way, boys.'"

On the day Amelia flew to Oakland there was a message from Air Commerce reminding her that her license would expire on April 15. Two days later she qualified for her instrument rating. Young Davenport, who had taken his the year before and barely passed, said the inspector who gave it remarked that he hadn't given it to anyone else so inept since Amelia Earhart, who also barely passed. There is no evidence as to whether she had improved since that previous rating. She didn't take her written and radio tests until March 14, a day after she had originally planned to take off. Delayed by bad weather, she took and passed both and the Electra was also certified by Air Commerce for the flight.

When Carl Allen arrived to do his preflight features for the *Herald Tribune,* he met Amelia and G. P. for breakfast in the hotel coffee shop. After they were seated Allen saw Amelia reach for her orange juice and G. P. push it away, replacing it with a stack of cacheted covers and a pen. "Don't forget our agreement, darling," he said. The agreement, Amelia explained to Allen, was for ten autographs before her orange juice, fifteen more before her bacon and eggs, and twenty-five each night before retiring.

Amelia was willing to do whatever G. P. said was necessary to promote and pay for the flight, but she was upset when he meddled in technical matters. When she was alone with Allen for the first time she told him that she was leaving for a long weekend at the Cochran-Odlum ranch. "I've just got to get away for a couple of days by myself," she said, "before it drives me crazy." G. P. was trying to do everything he could to help, she explained, but he was "trying too hard," especially with Mantz.

G. P. and Mantz had never been friends. Putnam tended to treat Mantz as an employee rather than a colleague, putting pressure on him and demanding instant solutions to complicated problems. G. P. and Mantz were too much alike, egotistical, shrewd self-promoters, skilled at their work, with their sights fixed on private profit and public recognition. G. P. claimed that Amelia no longer trusted Mantz and intended to terminate their partnership as soon as she returned.

If Amelia had misgivings about Mantz, Jackie Cochran certainly reinforced them. Cochran did not have Amelia's patience with Amelia's chauvinist mentor nor did Mantz like Cochran. When Cochran's plane broke down and she withdrew from the 1936 Bendix race, Mantz told

Amelia he was not surprised. "She never won a race or finished a flight in her life," he insisted years later, after she had done both.

In addition to the growing tension between G. P. and Mantz, Amelia was also worried about her choice of Harry Manning for navigator. She liked Manning, who had taught her the principles of navigation in 1928 while he was captain of the liner that brought her back from the *Friendship* flight. But she had doubts about his skills as an aerial navigator, doubts shared by Cochran who thought he was a nice fellow but "not up to high speed navigation in a plane." Cochran suggested that Amelia take him out to sea on a clear night and see if he could find his way back. "She did," Cochran observed, "and he couldn't."

For once Mantz agreed with Cochran. Weeks before Manning arrived at Oakland with Amelia, Mantz wrote to G. P. that he had enjoyed meeting Manning but that ocean navigation differed drastically from aerial navigation and he would like to see Manning "intercept a ship two or three hundred miles out to sea."

Not until March 13, four days before she left for Honolulu, did Amelia consent to a backup for Manning, a man G. P. wanted to hire. He was Fred Noonan, a slim, good-looking man with a long, weatherbeaten face and engaging grin. Noonan had made eighteen trips across the Pacific as navigator of Pan American clipper ships as well as taught other navigators for the airline before he was fired for alcoholism. Once again Amelia was threatened by the disease that had caused her father to abandon her and Bill Stultz to risk her life on the *Friendship*. Noonan assured Amelia he had conquered it, but even Vivian Maatta, who was hardly a confidante of Amelia's, noticed that she "had her doubts." James Bassett, the *Los Angeles Times* man covering the story, thought that G. P. wanted Amelia to take Noonan because another navigator *was* needed and the reputed alcoholic would work for very little money.

Reluctant to hurt Manning, Amelia announced she would take "two hitchhikers," Mantz and Noonan. Mantz would relieve her at the controls as far as Honolulu, where he planned to meet his fiancée, Terry Minor. Noonan would relieve Manning as navigator as far as Howland, so that Manning could spend more time on the radio. From Howland, she and Manning would continue to Darwin, where he would leave her to finish the flight alone.

On March 17, after lunch and a nap in the offices of a naval hangar, Amelia was bustled into a naval car and rushed to the waiting plane. The six thousand five hundred cachets she was taking were already on board, handed to Amelia earlier in the day by Oakland Postmaster Nellie G. Donohue, with news photographers recording the event, material to boost Gimbels' stamp sales.*

Once aboard and the hatch down, Amelia changed places with Mantz, who took over the throttles from the lefthand seat while Amelia handled the flight controls in the copilot's seat. Although she had taken the Electra up more than two dozen times by then, Mantz wanted to demonstrate the process once more. "Never jockey the throttle," he told her. "Use the rudder and don't raise the tail too quick."

A few minutes later the Electra roared down the field, plowing through one sheet of muddy water after another and rising slowly into the slate-grey sky at 4:37. Bill Miller sent a telegram to the White House immediately, following it with other more detailed reports to the Bureau and Richard Black aboard the *Shoshone* at Howland Island. Miller said she had taken off in twenty-five seconds in a fourteen-mile-an-hour wind using 1,897 feet of runway, "an excellent takeoff on a muddy runway." The takeoff was really Mantz's.

After they leveled off at eight thousand feet Mantz again changed places with Amelia, who insisted on flying fifty minutes out of each hour for the next fifteen hours. She held to the magnetic compass headings, compensating accurately when she was off a degree or two, but Mantz thought she seemed tired and unusually upset by Manning's repeated appearances in the cockpit to shoot a string of star sights through the upper hatch or to reach over her head for the radio controls.

Just before dawn on March 18 Mantz took a reading on the direction finder, locating them off Makapu Point on Oahu. "Do you want to land it?" he asked.

"No, you land it," she answered.

"When we got to Wheeler Field I wrapped it around and took a look at the wind direction," Mantz said later, "and Amelia yelled, 'Don't! Don't!'"

"What's wrong?" Mantz asked.

"Some people get exhausted after a long flight," she murmured.

"What do you want me to do," he asked, "drag the runway area and make the regular approach?"

*Two thousand less than originally promised by G. P.

"Would you?" Amelia sighed.

"*That,*" Mantz said, "was pilot fatigue."

Several hundred people were waiting in the predawn light—some of them still in evening clothes—when the Electra, which had broken a record, rolled to a stop at Wheeler Field.* Amelia immediately told reporters that Mantz had landed the plane, and added, "I'm terribly tired," before leaving the field with base commander Lt. Col. John McConnell.

Her original plan was to leave for Howland that night after sleeping a few hours at McConnell's house. Fortunately, adverse weather conditions forced another postponement and she went with Mantz to the Waikiki Beach house of his friends, Chris and Nona Holmes. The Holmeses had arranged a party for Amelia and Mantz's fiancée, Terry Minor. Minor thought Amelia was "awfully nice but not very social," an observation borne out by Amelia's refusal to attend the party. Instead she remained in her room until morning.

Early the next day, Amelia went to Wheeler Field with Mantz to move the Electra to the larger and better surfaced Luke Field, which was shared by the Army Air Corps and Naval Fleet Air Base. At Luke, Mantz discovered that the gasoline trucked from Wheeler was contaminated. He had to get permission from the military to buy 590 gallons of aviation gas. There were other problems. The weather reports continued to be less than promising and the Honolulu representative of Pratt and Whitney, Wilbur Thomas, discovered the propeller bearings of the Electra were almost dry. They had been improperly lubricated at Oakland, Thomas claimed, and might have forced the Electra down at sea if Miss Earhart had taken off for Howland immediately as she had planned. Amelia might have wondered just how good Mantz's maintenance of the plane was, but to her a more immediate cause for worry was her new navigator, Noonan. That same day in a confidential talk with Jim Bassett, who had gone to Honolulu for the story, Amelia said that Noonan had been drunk the night before in his hotel room and she did not want him on the flight.

Almost superstitiously wary of preflight revelations, Amelia wrote in her first story for the *Herald Tribune* before the flight, "So many things can happen . . . to change plans." She was right. Before dawn on March 20 she cracked up the by then one-hundred-thousand-dollar Electra.

*The flight was the fastest westward from the mainland to Honolulu, fifteen hours and fifty-one and a half minutes.

In the early morning darkness seventy-five civilians and Navy and Army men who came to watch her take off saw the plane begin to sway as it sped down the runway. Seconds later the left wing dropped, the right wheel was ripped off, and the landing gear collapsed. For a moment spectators froze while a single flame that shot into the air was reflected in the fuel-soaked runway, but there was no explosion. Amelia had cut the switches before the plane came to a halt. Neither she nor her two companions were injured, but when she pushed back the hatch cover and emerged from the cockpit her face was white, her hair wet with perspiration, and her voice shrill. "Something went wrong," she wailed to the first of the spectators to reach her. "It seems as if I hit a wet spot. The ship began to go off course and I couldn't stop it."

A few hours later she changed her mind, claiming that the left tire blew out and she reduced power on the opposite engine, swinging the plane from right to left but the load was too heavy, the momentum continued, and there was nothing she could do but let the plane ground-loop.

There were other versions of what went wrong. The Associated Press man agreed with Amelia that the left tire blew out but the *New York Times* said it was the right tire. There were spectators who said the plane was overloaded and others who claimed the opposite—that with only nine hundred gallons of fuel in tanks which could hold more than eleven hundred, the gasoline had sloshed around, increasing the momentum of the swerve.

Air Corps Brig. Gen. Barton K. Yount said Amelia's first comment about a "wet spot" was incorrect. The field was in perfect condition and, while it could have been a blowout, her tires had been checked just ten minutes before takeoff. Referring to her prompt cutting of all switches, the general said he had never seen anyone with "cooler nerves." Yount's conclusions were both gallant and self-serving. Miss Earhart was very brave and the Air Corps was in no way responsible for the accident.

Two of her severest critics were her mentor, Paul Mantz, and the young Army Air Corps officer-of-the-day, Lt. William C. Capp. Mantz was certain she had done just what he had told her not to do—"jockeyed," or overcompensated on the throttles. Capp said she was an inept pilot who would not take the advice of experts. He did not cite whose advice she had failed to take or in what way she was inept except as a navigator. She had, he said, been lost on her Hawaii-Oakland flight in 1935, so lost that the captain of the liner *Lurline* had to turn his ship around to point her in the right direction.

Capp did allow for several possibilities that might have made the takeoff more difficult. There could have been a cross wind or unusual wind currents, or a sloppily loaded plane. There was also a peculiar arrangement of buildings at the end of the runway, he said, which created a threatening illusion similar to that of sailing under a bridge. But basically Capp thought Amelia was not a good pilot.

His disapproval was reinforced by what he considered her discourtesy to the naval base commander, Capt. Kenneth Whiting, who had been at the airfield by 4 A.M. to see her off. Whiting was the same man who was commandant of the air base at Norfolk in 1933 when Amelia overturned her Vega. On that occasion Whiting said she had arrogantly assumed that he would crate and ship her damaged plane for her. This time, as she walked off the field with him, Capp heard her say, "Every time I see you I get into trouble." Her attempt at humor was perceived by both men as undeserved sarcasm.

Amelia also failed to report the accident, an offense subject to a five-hundred-dollar fine, which the Bureau inspector at Honolulu, Emil Williams, chose not to levy. Both her remark to Whiting and her violation of a basic rule of aviation indicate that she was still in shock, induced more by the sight of the shattered Electra than by her narrow escape from a fiery death.

Two hours later Amelia had recovered enough to write her account of the crackup for the *Herald Tribune* in an automobile returning to the Holmeses'. From there she made reservations to return to California on the Matson liner, *Malolo,* sailing the same day at noon. She also called G. P., who had already received the first damage estimate from Mantz. Although Bill Miller requested a second one from an Air Corps officer at Wheeler, it was soon obvious that the Electra would have to be shipped back to Lockheed for repairs.

While Miller worked through channels, G. P. did not. He sent a telegram to Col. J. M. Johnson, newly appointed Bureau of Air Commerce chief, stating the aircraft was being disassembled by the Army at Luke Field. (It was not.) The plane, he said, could be shipped on a Matson liner on the following Saturday, March 26, if the military would move it to the docks. He assured Johnson that local authorities had told Amelia they would be glad to handle it but they needed authorization. Johnson answered that he could not give it. G. P. would have to ask the War Department.

On March 25, after five hours of telephone calls and cables, Miller got authorization for the Hawaiian Air Depot at Luke Field to dismantle and pack up the Electra. G. P. did not get the free ride he wanted for it to the Matson docks but thirty-six hours later it was moved to the docks on a commercial barge.

On the day the Electra was being dismantled at Pearl Harbor, Amelia arrived in San Pedro on the *Malolo*. After five days of rest, she looked a very different woman from the one who had boarded on March 20 still wearing oil-stained brown slacks and a leather jacket, her hair limp from a drizzling rain and dark circles under her eyes. That day she had refused to talk to reporters as she ran up the gangplank clinging to Paul Mantz's arm. At the San Pedro docks she laughed when one newsman remarked that this was her sixth crackup. Crackups were always possible in her kind of flying, she told him. This one, she promised, would not stop her from trying again—about the first of May if the plane was ready.

Amelia did not tell him the choice was no longer hers.

CHAPTER TWENTY

The Vortex

*F*rom the moment the Electra lay crumpled on the runway at Honolulu, Amelia was caught in the vortex of two converging currents—pride and money. Her reputation for honesty, commitment, and courage was at stake. So was her livelihood. With almost all of her capital invested and her future earnings pegged to a successful flight, she had to circumnavigate the globe.

Within twenty-four hours of her return she went to Indian Palms to see Jackie Cochran. For the first time in her life she needed to talk about a crackup. At the ranch she found a sympathetic audience of three—Cochran and two guests, Ben and Maxine Howard, who were still recuperating from the serious injuries they had suffered seven months before in the 1936 Bendix race. Amelia had visited them soon after, in a Chicago hospital, where she offered Ben the Electra "to practice on," he said, "until I could learn to fly with a wooden foot."

That night Amelia sat on the floor in front of the fireplace, her thin, pale face lit by the firelight as she reviewed every detail of the accident. Finished, she looked up to her three friends, waiting for their comments but there were none. "What!" she said, "Aren't you going to ask me 'Are you going to try again?'" Only Cochran answered. "I hope you don't," she said.

Cochran spoke out of concern for a friend but Amelia was bitterly criticized by Marine Maj. Al Williams, test pilot and naval racer, in a syndicated newspaper article. He said that the worst exploitation of aviation for fame and fortune was that of individual transoceanic flying, presented under the banner of "scientific progress." Claiming Amelia's "flying laboratory" was the latest useless stunt staged for a trusting public, Williams said her proposed Pacific flights were already being done by Pan American and, although she had made the one to Hawaii faster than the two Pan American planes, they were still operating while hers was being shipped home in a box.

Williams wanted to know why in all the publicity stories nothing was said about Amelia's profits from lecture contracts, magazine and book rights, and stamp cachets. Instead, he wrote, the public got a garbled account of the crackup and a false story of heroism in which Amelia cut the switches and saved her crew. Actually, Williams wrote, she had lost control of the ship. He hoped that the Bureau of Air Commerce would refuse permission for her second attempt and put an end to aviation's biggest racket, this "purely scientific" ballyhoo.

Williams's first story was published by the Scripps Howard syndicate on April 30. G. P. waited until it was repeated a week later in the Cleveland *Press* before denying that Amelia had made any claim to "purely scientific" flight. When the trip was announced back in February, she said that the research program had been postponed until after the world flight, G. P. insisted, and her stated reason for going was "because I want to." At the same time, G. P. pointed out, she had explained that the only revenue aside from her own writing would be the cacheted covers. Amelia's only comment on the Williams story was "I'm glad a woman didn't write it."

Williams' criticism was the least of Amelia's troubles. Assuming that the BAC would grant another flight permit to her she needed fifty thousand dollars—twenty-five thousand for repairs to the Electra and twenty-five thousand for another set of flight arrangements, this time in the opposite direction, from west to east because of changing weather conditions. In an appeal to her friend, aviation promoter Harry Bruno, she employed more than a little of the feminine guile that she ordinarily scorned.

"She came into the office," Bruno said, "and she was pretty, well—

she was an unhappy girl. She said, 'I don't know how it happened, but I guess I'm all washed up.'"

Bruno asked her how much she needed. "I don't know," she told him. "Let's call George." G. P. said he thought thirty thousand dollars in addition to what he himself could raise would be enough. Bruno called Vincent Bendix, who said, "For Amelia, with pleasure," and offered twenty thousand dollars. Floyd Odlum gave another ten thousand. Master financier and friend of FDR, Bernard Baruch, gave twenty-five hundred dollars and Richard Byrd, in spite of his falling out with G. P., gave fifteen hundred. He was returning, he said, the gift that Amelia had once made to his South Pole expedition, her fee for the cigarette endorsement that had aroused so much criticism of the nation's newest heroine back in 1928.

Paul Mantz could not help. He still owed her fifty-five hundred dollars from their partnership deal in United Air Service and he had just lost a damage action for four thousand dollars compensation for a United plane wrecked by renters, a suit in which Amelia testified as an expert witness.

In addition to money from friends, Amelia earned whatever she could. She agreed to an appearance on a popular radio network program, the Kraft Music Hour, with Bing Crosby, actor John Barrymore, G. P., and Mantz. In mid-April she signed a contract with Harcourt, Brace and Company to write a book on the flight. New arrangements for cacheted mail were made with Gimbels. The first lot of sixty-five hundred, retrieved from the Electra and sent back to Oakland, were restamped, "Held over in Honolulu following takeoff accident of March 20, 1937." On April 24 she appeared in the store's eleventh floor restaurant to boost the sale of an additional one thousand covers.

Not all of Amelia's attention centered on the flight. She took time to make the best arrangements she could for her sister and her mother. There was very little she could do for Muriel, who had changed her mind about divorcing Albert. Muriel needed money and Amelia did not have any to give. For a fee Muriel had given a national network radio interview three days after the Honolulu crackup, one in which she had said that Amelia looked much younger than she because, "taking care of a house and two children is more care, it would seem, than flying solo across the Atlantic," and "there were times when even the best behaved children tire you." Muriel also claimed that she knew how to fly but her duties as a housewife and mother did not allow her time to get a pilot's license. Amelia said nothing about the interview, although it must have annoyed her. Instead she sent Muriel clothing and shoes and used, but expensive, curtains and blankets.

It was both more imperative and easier to provide for her mother. By mid-April Amelia had moved her from the Morrisseys' in Medford to the new house at Toluca Lake. She intended it to be Amy's permanent home.

On May 2 Amelia returned to California from her last trip to New York. The day before, her picture had appeared on the cover of *McCall's* magazine with the accolade, "America's Great Women: Amelia Earhart, Who Spanned an Ocean and Won a World." She had generated a flurry of publicity for the world flight, signed a book contract, and completed her sales pitch for the covers sold by Gimbels. Her will was made, her mother settled in California.

Amelia's personal affairs were in far better order than the flight arrangements. Harry Manning, whose leave from the U.S. Lines would expire before the Electra could be repaired, was dropped from the flight. Manning was no great loss but the BAC's William Miller was. He was sent on an assignment to New Zealand and Australia.

The only man with the same gifts as Miller—pilot and master of detail and government regulations—who was still with the flight was Jacques de Sibour. He had already sent along information on weather conditions in the eastern hemisphere and west coast of Africa and a complete set of aerodrome maps for all points plus emergency landing grounds along the Arabian coast. He had even asked the Cairo office to prepare a letter in Arabic stating that Amelia was on an important mission on behalf of King George VI and was not to be harmed, just in case she made a forced landing in Arabian territory.

But Vicomte de Sibour was in London and control of the flight was in the hands of two men who did not like or trust each other—George Palmer Putnam and Paul Mantz. G. P. was neither as patient nor as prompt as Miller with paperwork. Not until eleven days before Amelia was to take off on her second world flight attempt did he write to the BAC chief, Colonel Johnson, that weather conditions had required changing her flight direction. He had, he said, notified the Navy, Coast Guard, and departments of Interior and State that Amelia would be flying from west to east this time, but the State Department wanted a new letter of authorization from Johnson. Johnson gave it and the State Department concurred just three days before the flight began.

In spite of the tension between G. P. and Mantz, they did agree on hiring Fred Noonan as navigator. Mantz thought he was good and Putnam knew he was cheap. Amelia did not want him. Albert Bresnik, hired by G. P. to do all of Amelia's publicity photographs for the world flight, was sure of this. Already well-known for his portraits of film stars, the seventeen-year-old Bresnik had fallen in love with this "genius in a farm woman's body whose radiance made her beautiful." He watched her every move, listened to everything she said. He was certain she did not trust Noonan.

Noonan had done nothing to reassure Amelia. Divorced from his first wife in Mexico a few days before he left with Amelia on the flight to Honolulu, Noonan married again two weeks after they returned to California. A week later, he was one of the drivers in a two-car collision in which his wife was seriously injured. The other driver was a thirty-seven-year-old woman with an infant passenger. No official charges were made against Noonan but Amelia could not be sure that he was keeping his promises of sobriety.

Amelia told her secretary, Margot DeCarie, that she really wanted to go alone, that too many people were involved in the flight. When DeCarie asked her why she didn't do what she wanted, Amelia said, "We cannot always do as we wish." DeCarie thought she seemed "discontented" and far from as resigned as she claimed.

G. P. and Mantz both wanted her to take Noonan as navigator. Amelia knew that if she refused, Noonan's reputation as an alcoholic would make it almost impossible for him to find other work. Her friend Cochran thought she was too poor a navigator to go without expert help. Noonan was good, Cochran said, but good navigation might not be enough. He could probably bring the plane to within two or three miles of Howland but she still didn't see how Amelia, "without dumb luck . . . was going to hit that island." Howland, Cochran insisted, was no bigger than the Cleveland airport.

Amelia spent most of the last three weeks she was on the West Coast at Indian Palms. Cochran had hoped that riding, swimming, and enough sleep would improve Amelia's health, but feared that her friend was still too tired and frail for such a demanding flight. Although Amelia insisted she was doing it because she wanted to, Cochran thought her decision was not so much self-willed as determined by "some inner compulsion beyond her control." Once Amelia had made up her mind, Cochran did whatever she could to help her prepare for the flight.

Gene Vidal was also concerned about Amelia. Suspecting she might be going through an early menopause, Vidal was certain that she was tired of G. P. and of the constant exposure to the public that he asked of her. Vidal was in Washington but kept in touch by mail and telephone. A few days before Amelia left Oakland she sent him a thank you note for his "sweet giftie . . . as attractive and useful as can be," but made no mention of what it was. It might have been underdrawers. His son Gore said that although G. P. thought Amelia wore his boxer shorts when she was flying, in fact, she wore Vidal's jockey shorts. In a second note Amelia thanked Vidal for calling her and told him she expected to take off on May 21.

The Electra was ready on May 19, completed by a Lockheed crew that worked overtime, time they donated to Amelia. On May 21 she flew it from Burbank to Oakland, where the stamped covers were secretly put aboard. G. P., Noonan, and McKneely were with her. Mantz was not. He was in St. Louis, flying competitive aerobatics at an air meet, when he heard on the radio that she was in Oakland. He was very concerned.

Mantz thought she needed more time, time in which he could give her power settings for fuel consumption on each leg of the journey. He also was dissatisfied with the five-hundred-kilocycle band on her radio, which could provide a second, backup system to the Bendix homing device that was relatively unfamiliar to Coast Guard radiomen. They would want the five-hundred-kilocycle frequency in use for emergency SOS calls at sea and the Electra's telephone-radio did not have enough power on the five-hundred band for direction finders on the ground or on ships at sea to get a "fix" on the plane. When Mantz asked Western Electric experts for advice, he was told a trailing wire at least 250 feet long should be used. In St. Louis he remembered how Amelia had complained about the nuisance of reeling out the long wire every time she was airborne and he worried. G. P., with his moneymaking schemes, had won the battle for Amelia's time and attention. She was leaving without the guarantees Mantz thought essential for the flight's success.

At Oakland on May 21 Amelia told reporters that she was on a leisurely shakedown cruise to Miami to test the Electra's equipment, explaining her lack of candor later by repeating her career-long insistence that announced flight plans brought accusations of publicity-seeking and of cowardice if the flight was cancelled.

That same afternoon she flew to Tucson, where backfire after landing touched off a blaze in one of the engines. It was extinguished immediately, but while Mantz worried about the radio and fuel charts, Amelia was more concerned about the aircraft itself. She asked for a full, overnight checkup. Although the Electra's record as a ten-passenger commercial aircraft was good, her plane had had more than its share of malfunctions. Before the 1936 Bendix race, the oil seals leaked and during the race the hatch blew off. In January one engine, then the other, had ignited while mechanics were warming them for takeoff at San Francisco. In February Mantz reported that the Lockheed crew was working day and night on "unavoidable difficulties," and that the Sperry people would have to fix the horizon, which was causing a five-degree turn every ten or fifteen minutes. Before the crackup in Hawaii, the Pratt and Whitney man claimed the propeller bearings were dry.

From Tucson Amelia flew to New Orleans, where she was met by Ninety-Niner and ex-Navy nurse Edna Gardner. Probably the best and certainly the most competitive woman pilot in closed-circuit racing, Gardner disliked G. P. She was certain he manipulated Amelia for his own benefit and that after making a fortune publicizing Lindbergh he found another hero-figure to exploit in Amelia. "When he asked her to promote a plane or a project," she said, "she would do it. With not enough experience, not enough [flying] hours, she had the courage to do it."

It was almost six o'clock on a Saturday night when the Electra landed at Shushan (now Lakefront) Airport in New Orleans. After Amelia and G. P. checked into the airport hotel, they had dinner with Gardner, Noonan, and the airport manager. "He [G. P.] was so domineering and so pushy," Gardner said. "We were at dinner and Amelia was saying something about her radio and he said, 'You had a chance to change. It's too late now.'"

When Gardner saw Amelia, who looked very tired and pale, lower her head and stare at her plate, she heard G. P. say, "Stop your sniveling." "She wasn't sniveling," Gardner said, "she just sat there and he was just as cruel as he could be, right in front of all of us."

At Miami the next morning Amelia brought the Electra in for a near crash landing. A reporter who was there wrote that the "creak of metal could be heard all over the field as the big ship landed with a thud." Emerging from the cockpit, her sunburned forehead wrinkled in mock astonishment, Amelia said, "I certainly smacked it down hard that time."

When reporters asked her about her plans she lied again, telling them she had none and would stay several days in Miami while two technicians sent by Pan American district superintendent W. O. Snyder worked on the plane, particularly on the radio. After that, she said, she would return to Oakland and start on her world flight from there about the end of the month.

Amelia learned a few hours later that the bad landing was caused by shock absorbers that were improperly packed and leaked fluid all the way from New Orleans. Her troubles with the Electra were not over. She telegraphed to Mantz the next day that the fuel-flow gauge had a broken wire on the engine armature and the oil lines were still leaking. These were being repaired with a product used by Eastern Air, she told him.

At that time Carl Allen of the *Herald Tribune* was the only reporter informed of her plans to start the world flight from Miami. He met her there, bringing his Oakland notes for updating the story. Going over a checklist with her Allen noticed that the marine frequency radio operating on five hundred kilocycles with a Morse key was missing. "Oh," she told him, "that was left off—when Manning had to drop out of the flight." She explained to Allen that neither she nor Noonan could operate a Morse code key fast enough to justify carrying the extra weight. That left, as Mantz already knew, the only means of sending or receiving a "fix" on her location the five-hundred-kilocycle band on the Western Electric telephone-radio that required the 250-foot-long trailing antenna. Before the week was up, Amelia had done just what Mantz feared. She dropped the trailing wire. He did not learn about it until after she had left Miami, when a letter from G. P. informed him that the radio that gave them "unending trouble" was finally fixed by technicians in Miami, who decided the aerials were all too long and shortened them.

On May 29 Amelia announced her revised plans to the press. She would leave from Miami, flying east to west on Pan American's regular route through the West Indies and along the east coast of South America. She would not, she said, use the code wireless set (she did not admit she had dumped it) but would depend entirely on voice broadcasts of her position on a daytime frequency of 6210 kilocycles and a nighttime one of 3105. Her only cargo was the six thousand five hundred original flight covers and two thousand more, stamped for the second attempt.

Amelia spent most of her time at the airport until Sunday, when Noonan persuaded her to go fishing for pompano. He had already charmed a Miami business man, W. Bruce MacIntosh, into offering him an office, and when he told MacIntosh that Amelia liked pompano, the Miami man and his wife, Lily, invited Noonan and Amelia to spend the day fishing on their boat. MacIntosh noticed that Amelia was too distracted to do much fishing but she seemed to enjoy the outing, so much so that when he asked her about her departure time she told him she couldn't say but suggested that he come to the airfield early Tuesday morning. He did, later claiming he was the last man to shake her hand before she left the country.

Other than this one Sunday, G. P. took over any time Amelia was not at the municipal airport. There were numerous interviews and news photography sessions, including one in which David and Nilla Putnam, who had come from Fort Pierce to say goodbye, were pictured. On May 31, Amelia's last full day in Miami, G. P. escorted her to the Pan American operations base at Dinner Key to thank the mechanics and officials for their "splendid assistance." They met Noonan there visiting his former colleagues after picking up two pairs of eyeglasses. He had broken his only pair, he said. He sat on them while driving to the airport.

Amelia and G. P. left Dinner Key without Noonan, for lunch with Harvey Firestone at his Miami Beach House. After lunch Amelia was supposed to spend the afternoon napping in her hotel room but she spent at least part of it at a dentist's office where her upper right third molar was extracted "to cure headaches."

A better cure for her headaches might have included a navigator with a reputation for sobriety, a single supervisor responsible for all aspects of the flight, more practice flying in the Electra, and a husband less eager to cash in on the flight. She had always insisted that anticipated dangers were seldom realized. This time she was not so sure. She had given Cochran a small, silk American flag, one she had carried on all her long-distance flights. When Cochran asked her to take it with her and autograph it when she returned, Amelia said, "No, you'd better take it now."

When she asked Carl Allen what her chances were, he said he thought about fifty-fifty. Amelia told him that she thought she might never complete the flight. "It's not a premonition," she said, "just a feel-ing." Except for Noonan's sake, this didn't worry her, she said to Allen. "As far as I know, I've got only one obsession—a small and probably feminine horror of growing old—so I won't feel completely cheated if I fail to come back."

CHAPTER TWENTY-ONE

Just One More Flight

*A*t 5:56 on the morning of June 1 Amelia's friend Carl Allen watched the silver Electra lift off the runway at Miami Airport. This was to be her last "stunt" flight. "I have a feeling there is just one more flight in my system," she told him. " . . . this trip around the world is it." After that she was going to settle down "for keeps," to fly only for lecture tours, for research at Purdue, and "for fun."

Amelia had left the hotel at 3:15 with G. P. in the first car of an entourage. David and Nilla Putnam were in the second, and Noonan in the third, driven by a woman friend. Five hundred of Amelia's admirers also came to see her off, the light from their cars piercing the darkness on every road leading to the airport. When the Electra was rolled out onto the ramp and the gates of the field opened for the spectators they rushed forward, pushing back a line of policemen for a glimpse of their idol.

Amelia could still attract five hundred people willing to get up in the middle of the night just to see her take off. Newspaper editorials praised her for her courage and "careful planning" even as they claimed the risk outweighed the value of the flight. But banner headlines on June 2 went to a battle between striking steel workers and police in South Chicago in which five died and one hundred were injured, on June 3, to the marriage of Wallis Warfield Simpson of Baltimore to Edward of England. That week Germany and Italy abandoned any pretense of neutrality in the

Spanish civil war and Franklin Roosevelt continued his efforts to "pack" the Supreme Court with three additional justices. Amelia's flight was relegated to short stories on inside pages of most newspapers.

For six days she flew along the eastern coast of Central and South America, stopping at San Juan, Puerto Rico, Caripito, Venezuela, Paramaibo, Dutch Guiana [Surinam],* and Fortazela and Natal in Brazil. She was up most mornings by three or four, averaging five hours of sleep a night. On the longest flight, from Paramaibo to Fortazela, she crossed 1,628 miles of jungle and ocean in ten hours.

At Natal, her last stop before crossing the South Atlantic, she wrote in her log, "Gas fumes in the plane from fueling made me sick again this morning. . . . Stomach getting weak, I guess." The plane was noisy, the cabin cramped, and her chief means of communication with Noonan was by notes fastened to a line with a clothespin and passed back on a fishpole that hung along the top of the bulkhead at her right. The alternative was for one or the other of them to climb over the auxiliary fuel tanks that blocked the area from cockpit to the table at which Noonan worked at the rear.

The flight across the Atlantic was the first real test of the Electra and her crew. The plane passed with honors. So did Fred Noonan, whose navigation was very accurate. Amelia did not do as well. When they were near the African coast, she chose to ignore Noonan's advice to turn south for their destination of Dakar, French West Africa [Senegal]. Instead she turned north flying for 50 miles along the African coast until she sighted St. Louis, 163 miles north of Dakar, then sent a note to Noonan asking "What put us north?" She did. She admitted the error soon after, writing "The fault was entirely mine."

Navigating by instinct was not her worst mistake. She had already made that in Miami when she dropped the trailing antenna for her DF and the CW (telegraph code key) transmitter. Over the Atlantic she passed two Air France mail planes during the night but could not communicate with either because they were equipped with CW only, a far more dependable system than her MCW (microphone voice transmission).†

---

*For countries whose names have changed since 1937, current country names are designated in brackets.

†Anne Lindbergh thought the CW transmission and reception so important that by 1931 she had a license and could send and receive an acceptable seventeen words per minute.

Amelia's neglect of so vital an element as telegraph-radio originated in her own nature and past experiences. In spite of her denials she was a romantic about flight. It was a near-transcendent experience for her and she instinctively avoided the communication that broke her isolation from the earthbound and mundane. As a student she was intelligent but impatient, reluctant to record the steps by which she arrived at an answer. Learning telegraphic code was dull, time-consuming work—the kind she avoided whenever possible. She also lacked the time. Joseph Gurr, the radio expert who worked on the Electra's system before and after the aborted March flight, said, "I finally got her into the airplane on the ramp at Paul Mantz's. . . . We had barely covered the preliminaries when Amelia had to leave. She was hard to pin down because she was obviously in demand in other places." On her 1935 flight from Hawaii to Oakland, she had used the radio to listen to music from the West Coast, to talk with G. P. and to report the weather, but not to give her position. Without a position report the crews of four Coast Guard cutters one hundred miles out from San Francisco to escort her home could not find her and had to return to port without making contact.

Amelia reached St. Louis on the African coast on June 7, after thirteen hours and twenty-two minutes fighting off recurrent nausea while bucking rainstorms and headwinds, and nursing the Electra's two engines, which she was reluctant to "open up" for fear of damaging them. She spent that night at the airfield in a barracks-like room where she discovered "a couple of bugs" in her bed and kept the light on all night "thinking the creatures might not venture out under the glare." The toilet facilities she described as "execrable."

Nevertheless that first week was a good one. She had flown more than forty hours for four thousand miles. Added to the official start from Oakland, she had completed one fourth of her journey. Although the story of her flight was relegated to the back pages of most newspapers, on June 8 she was the subject of Eleanor Roosevelt's widely read syndicated column, "My Day." The president's wife wrote that she was relieved to hear that her friend Amelia Earhart was safe in Africa. "All day I have been thinking about Amelia Earhart somewhere over the Atlantic," she wrote, adding that she would be glad when the entire trip was over because she was much more interested in Amelia as a person than as a recordbreaking pilot.

After a short flight the next day to Dakar, Amelia was held up for two days by bad weather. Too impatient to wait any longer, on June 10 she changed her next destination from Fort Niamey to Gao in French West Africa [Mali]. She would try to "squeeze between" a tornado to the south and sandstorms to the north. She succeeded, flying eleven hundred forty miles in under eight hours. The next day she flew almost one thousand miles, from Gao over the Sahara to Fort Lamy, now N'Djamena in French Equatorial Africa [Chad], where it was so hot the plane could not be refueled until after sunset for fear of gasoline igniting on hot metal. She left early the following morning for El Fasher in Anglo-Egyptian Sudan [Sudan] and "pressed on" the day after, June 14, to Assab, present-day Aseb, Ethiopia on the shores of the Red Sea. It was a twelve-hundred-mile flight, a "long day" in which she had lunch and wrote a dispatch at Khartoum in the Sudan and had tea at Massawa, Eritrea [Mits'iwa, Ethiopia]. In two weeks she had flown fifteen thousand miles from Miami and was more than halfway to her goal.

On June 15 she crossed the Red Sea and the Arabian Sea to Karachi, Pakistan (then part of British India), almost two thousand miles in thirteen hours and twenty minutes. The trip was without incident except for a broken fuel analyzer. Jacques de Sibour met her at Karachi and G. P. called that night from the *Herald Tribune* office in New York where their conversation was recorded for a story. He was already pressing her to give him a possible ETA for Howland Island, but she put him off with a promise to give him one at her next stop, Calcutta.

During the call G. P. asked her if she was the first person to fly from the Red Sea across Arabia to Karachi. She hadn't thought about it, she said, but she would try to let him know. He didn't wait. He secured a statement from the air attaché at the British Embassy in Washington who said it was probably the first time the route across the Arabian sea had been negotiated—"a pretty long and difficult one." This feat did not boost news coverage of the flight. The *New York Times* ran three sentences on her arrival at Karachi on page 25 with most newspapers following suit.*

She stayed in Karachi for two days with little or no rest in the blistering subcontinental heat. She went to the post office to choose the stamps and supervise the cancellation of the seventy-five hundred covers

---

*That same day Amelia's name appeared in a story *she* would have liked. *Equal Rights* magazine's lead editorial called her an "ardent feminist" who had set off to make aviation history circling the globe and who deserved credit for her well-articulated views on women's rights.

she was now carrying. She also took two camel rides, which added interest to her daily travelogue for the *Herald Tribune,* before leaving on June 17 for Calcutta. During the first part of the flight across the subcontinent, she found no escape from the heat, not even at fifty-five hundred feet where the temperature was still 90° Fahrenheit. Later there were rainstorms and air currents, which pushed her plane up and down as much as one thousand feet in seconds. At Calcutta there was a telegram from G. P. assuring her that the Dutch airlines KLM which also used the type of fuel analyzer she did would repair hers there or replace it in Singapore. He also asked her to call in her next story to the *Herald Tribune.*

Amelia's old friend from Boston and Maine days, Paul Collins, said there was a second telephone call from India that he and Eugene Vidal overheard G. P. take at his Hotel Seymour suite. Collins heard Amelia say, "I'm starting to have personnel trouble." When G. P. told her to stop the flight immediately, she said there was "only one bad hop left and I'm pretty sure I can handle the situation." G. P. did not explain what Amelia meant by "personnel trouble," but Collins and Vidal assumed that Noonan was drinking.

On June 18 Amelia took off from a water-logged runway at Calcutta's Dum Dum Airport; the Electra barely cleared the trees at the end of the runway. The monsoon rains "beat patches of paint off the edges of the plane's wings" while she crossed the Bay of Bengal and headed for Rangoon, Burma, and she had to put down at Akyab [Sittwe] on the west coast. She tried to reach Rangoon once more that day but failed, an effort Noonan described as "two hours and six minutes of going nowhere." On June 19 they reached Rangoon and the following day went on to Singapore, where Amelia collected twenty-five dollars for winning a race with a KLM plane from Rangoon. In Singapore she was told that KLM mechanics would overhaul her plane at Bandoeng, Java, in the Netherlands East Indies [Bandung, Indonesia]. She reached it on the last day of her third week out of Miami, but not without alarming observers who watched her circle the field for fifteen minutes on a clear day, "apparently unable to see the airdrome markers." She may have panicked the way Mantz claimed she had at Honolulu the previous March, when she shouted at him to pull up and circle the field once more in a frenzy he diagnosed as "extreme pilot fatigue."

She had flown twenty thousand miles by then in 135 hours. For twenty-one nights she had slept in strange, often primitive accommodations, without air-conditioning in a tropical climate. She was always awake by three or four o'clock in the morning, ate very little, and suffered from nausea and diarrhea. She may have realized how near the edge she had pushed herself because she announced that she would remain at Bandoeng for three days for repairs to the Electra but stayed without too much protest for six except for one abortive start that ended 350 miles later in Soerabaya [Surabaya]. Malfunctioning navigational instruments forced her to return to the KLM base for more repairs. At sundown on June 27, three days after G. P. had hoped she would already be at Howland, she landed at Koepang [Kupan] on Timor Island, unable to reach Port Darwin [Darwin] Australia before nightfall.

At Koepang, high on a cliff where the grass-covered field was bordered by a stone wall "to keep out the pigs," Amelia and Noonan, with some help from villagers, turned the Electra around and staked it down for the night. "I will rise at 4 A.M.," she wrote, "and would like to reach Lae but fear headwinds will make it imperative to stop at Port Darwin." It was imperative. She did not reach Port Darwin until ten o'clock on Monday morning, still Sunday night, June 27, in New York. That same day the *Herald Tribune* used G. P.'s announcement that she would make three radio broadcasts, the first as soon as she arrived in Honolulu, the second from San Francisco, and the third on WABC's "Radio Theater" on the first Monday after her arrival at Oakland.

From the time she arrived in Darwin it was evident that the flight was the most mismanaged she had ever made, and the most difficult part lay ahead—from Lae, New Guinea to Howland Island. This time there was no Bill Miller to take over. Instead management, such as it was, had become a triumvirate: Putnam, Richard Black of the Department of Interior who was G. P.'s representative aboard the Coast Guard cutter *Itasca*, and Cmdr. W. K. Thompson, captain of the *Itasca*. These three, often working at odds with one another, could not provide the help Amelia needed. G. P. worked first through Washington, while he was still in New York, and after June 24, through the Coast Guard's division command in San Francisco. Black did everything he could to oblige Putnam but with an eye on the interests of his own department, which administered Howland Island. Commander Thompson set up a network of weather information stations for Amelia and tried to confirm radio arrangements but he had no control over her decisions and clearly thought the *Itasca* deserved more significant duties than looking after a "stunt" flyer.

G. P. sent his messages from the Coast Guard's radio station in San Francisco to Black on the *Itasca* to be forwarded to Amelia wherever she might be. Even before she reached Darwin he asked Black to make certain that she brought negatives and motion pictures if any were taken of her arrivals and departures at Lae and Howland. Black was also to remind her to file her story directly from Howland to the *Herald Tribune* in Oakland and to get some aerial pictures of Howland.

G. P. wanted her home by the Fourth of July, a Sunday. His first message to her was followed by another Black was asked to forward to Lae:

FLIGHT CONTINGENCIES PERMITTING IS ARRIVAL SATURDAY LATELY [sic] SUNDAY EITHER PERFECT STOP CONFIDENTIAL WANT YOU TO KNOW VERY IMPORTANT RADIO COMMIT-MENT MONDAY NIGHT NOTHING ELSE WHATSOEVER.

The last three words were both promise and apology.

He repeated this query the next day, asking again if there was any likelihood she might arrive in Oakland by Monday morning. There was also a request from his Honolulu representative, William Cogswell, to Black for word on whether she would arrive at Luke or Wheeler Field in Honolulu. Cogswell needed to know because G. P. had arranged for her to broadcast immediately after her arrival.

While G. P. pressed Amelia for an early arrival, he also gave errone-ous information on her radio equipment to the Department of Interior to pass on to Black on the *Itasca*. Assuming that her five-hundred-kilocycle radio range had been made operative by Pan American in Miami, G. P. said Amelia would broadcast on radio telephone at a quarter to and a quarter after the hour on 6210 daytime and 3105 at night and would also "try 500 close in" (when she was close to her destination). On June 25 he again informed Black that Amelia would broadcast on 500 (no "close in" this time) as well as 3105 and 6210. He added that her DF (direction finder) covered a range of 200 to 1400 kilocycles.

G. P.'s messages were not the only ones handled by the second man in the triumvirate, Black. He also sent and received information from the Coast Guard in San Francisco, the Navy and Army Air Corps in Honolulu, and the Department of Interior in Washington. In doing so Black proved a constant irritant to the *Itasca*'s captain Commander Thompson.

A by-the-book, seagoing regular Coast Guard officer, Thompson had been ordered to take his ship to Honolulu ahead of its scheduled departure from San Pedro and, once there, to leave immediately for Howland Island "to act as plane guard and furnish weather" to Amelia Earhart. He had also been required to take along four passengers, two reporters, James Carey of Associated Press and H. N. Hanzlick of United Press, an Army Air Corps observer, Lt. Daniel Cooper, and Black. Without consulting Thompson, Black and Cooper borrowed an experimental DF from the Navy to set up on Howland. Thompson let them bring it along but logged an official opinion that the equipment was inadequate and that the Coast Guard did not request and would not receipt it. When Black recruited several additional radiomen from the Navy, Thompson flatly refused to accept them. Eventually he did add one extra radioman second class from the Coast Guard to the ship's company.

As soon as the *Itasca* left Honolulu, Thompson began to organize a chain of weather reporting and relay stations reaching across the Pacific from the west coast to Australia and New Guinea, employing stations at Honolulu, American Samoa, Christmas and Fanning islands, and two other Coast Guard cutters, the *Ontario* and the *Swan*, also on plane guard for Amelia. Added to this heavy radio traffic were the messages from and to Black, Putnam, the Department of Interior, and the San Francisco Coast Guard. By June 26, before Amelia left Bandoeng, Thompson could endure no more. He demanded that division headquarters give him complete control of communications. He would do his best for Mr. Black, he said, but Coast Guard–Navy procedures would be used with no interference from San Francisco.

Thompson had done what he could to provide Amelia with weather reports although transmission was so slow that the data was never current. For the other part of his mission, to act as plane guard, he needed to know when and how Earhart intended to communicate with the *Itasca* once she left Lae. He had the information G. P. had forwarded and Black's assurances that Amelia would send her requirements to the *Itasca*, the *Ontario* stationed between Lae and Howland, and the *Swan* midway between Howland and Honolulu. He had also seen the message Black sent to Amelia at Darwin, giving her the *Ontario*'s range as 195 to 600 kilocycles (too low for her without the aerial) and the *Swan*'s (too far away to matter until after she reached Howland).

Suspecting there were too many amateurs providing information, Thompson wanted to hear directly from Amelia. On June 23, the day the *Itasca* reached Howland, he sent her a message requesting she advise him at least twelve hours before she left Lae of her preferred frequencies and communications schedule. He would conform to any frequencies she wanted, he said, and pass the information on to the *Ontario* and *Swan*.

Two days later he received two contradictory messages, the first from San Francisco and the second from Amelia. San Francisco quoted Amelia as saying her DF range was from 200 to 1500 and 2400 to 4800 kilocycles. However the San Francisco command suggested Thompson should try a low range, 333 or 545, because high frequencies for DF were unreliable. The second message from Amelia directly to Thompson stated that she could not give him a definite broadcasting schedule as yet but would probably give a long call by voice on 3105 at a quarter after the hour and "possibly a quarter to." She asked that the *Ontario* transmit on 400 kilocycles the letter "N" for five minutes with its call letters repeated twice at the end of every minute and that the *Itasca* follow the same procedure using the letter "A" on the half hour at 7500 kilocycles.

What was Thompson to do? With the exception of the *Ontario*, Amelia was asking for high frequencies up to 7500 from *Itasca*. San Francisco requested he use 333 or 545 for her DF and gave her highest range as 4800, yet she asked for 7500. Thompson opted for the message directly from Amelia. She was the pilot. Hers would be the *key message* for him, the one on which he would base his future communications with her. Thompson did not know she had left both her CW or key transmitter and her antennae for receiving 500 kilocycles and below in Miami when he radioed to her that the *Itasca*'s transmitters were calibrated for 7500, 6210, 500 and 425 on CW (of no use to her without the key) and for 3105, 500 and 425 on voice. The last two were out of her range without the antenna, leaving one—3105—on which she could send and receive, not a reliable range at dawn just before the change from nighttime to daytime frequencies. Thompson also informed her that the ship's DF worked only from 550 down to 270, again too low for her to receive.

While Thompson worried about radio communication and Putnam worried about publicity, Amelia was more concerned about the weather.

She sent daily queries to the *Itasca* and informed the ship that adverse reports kept her from leaving Lae. Impatient to be off, she was delayed from Wednesday, June 30 to Friday, July 2 (Howland time). The weather was not her only worry. In her report to the *Herald Tribune,* she said Noonan was unable to set his chronometers because of radio difficulties, but in a private message to G. P. she warned that "radio misunderstanding and personnel unfitness probably will hold one day." "Personnel" had to be Noonan.

In notes she made for her book on the flight she crossed out one line that read, "I think will have recovered tomorrow," and left, "perhaps was well did not try to fly today." Paul Collins said that Amelia called in her report from Lae on June 30 to G. P. at the *Herald Tribune* office. Gene Vidal was with him and told Collins about the call later. Amelia said she was still having "personnel trouble" but she thought the situation had improved and expected to leave the next day.

On their first night in Lae, Amelia had dined with a local couple, the Eric Chaters, and Fred spent the evening at the hotel with J. A. Collopy, the District Superintendent of Civil Aviation for the Territory of New Guinea. Collopy said he and Noonan "forgot to eat" and were up rather late, long after Amelia retired. When Noonan was escorted to his room by Collopy he failed to see the mosquito netting tucked under the mattress and threw himself onto the bed causing "a very loud noise which awakened the whole place including Amelia." However, Collopy said, on the night before takeoff, both Noonan and Amelia, who had spent most of her time at the hangar or in her room resting, went to bed early. Noonan told Collopy that he had had some differences with Amelia during the trip but the district superintendent thought none seemed of any consequence and neither Noonan nor Earhart appeared unduly worried about the flight to Howland. They should have been. Although Amelia told Carl Allen that Howland was so small "every aid to locating it must be available," every aid was not.

Even if Noonan was not drinking he faced a formidable task in locating a sand bar in the mid-Pacific that was two miles long and three-quarters of a mile wide, with a maximum elevation of twenty-five feet. His chronometers had given him trouble both in Indonesia and again at Lae. His gyroscope, like most at that time, did not always hold a true course when subject to vibration. He would need star sights for celestial navigation but the latest meteorological reports cited headwinds of twenty to thirty knots with rain squalls and overcast skies for most of the way. The government charts on which Clarence Williams relied for Amelia's course were inaccurate, placing Howland seven miles northwest of its actual location.

Amelia must have been far more worried than Collopy thought. She invited Harry Balfour, the New Guinea Airways radio operator at Lae, to accompany her and Noonan to Howland either because she wanted someone to watch Noonan or because she realized how inadequate her radio skills were and how desperately they might be needed. She was in a hurry. The weather reports were far from promising but G. P. was pressing for her return and she was eager to put this most difficult leg of the entire journey behind her. The Electra would require a full load of fuel, more than one thousand gallons, for the 2,556-mile flight but she had to take off from a one-thousand-foot-long dirt runway. Once airborne, she needed to calculate her fuel consumption with great accuracy but the Cambridge fuel analyzer had already malfunctioned in India and again in Indonesia. Taking precedence over all these problems was her own exhaustion. Since Miami she had flown on twenty-one of thirty days, on three of those days for more than thirteen hours, and on another seven of them, for more than seven hours. Her previous long-distance flights had been a matter of hours, not weeks. She was never physically strong, only determined. This time her once slim body was emaciated, skin over bones. But if pride and willpower could not get her to Howland, they could not permit her to turn back.

At 10:22 on the morning of July 2 at Lae, the heavily laden Electra lumbered down the crude runway for a "hair-raising" takeoff, earthbound until the last fifty yards. The propellers were so close to the ground their turbulence raised clouds of red dust. For a moment the silver plane was lost to view, disappearing behind the dropoff at the end of the runway. When it reappeared, it was no more than five or six feet above the water of the bay, rising slowly to one hundred feet before it vanished into the morning mist.

For the next seven hours, Lae radioman Harry Balfour was in touch with Amelia. She was on course and 750 miles out when he advised her to maintain the same radio frequency because he was still receiving her clearly. Whether she did or not, he lost her soon after. No one heard from her again until after midnight on Howland. She should have passed over the *Ontario* where three men kept visual watch and the radio operator stood by but they neither saw nor heard her. The weather had been good in that area until nightfall but after midnight there was a severe squall, lasting until dawn. It might have slowed Amelia down considerably or required a dangerous amount of fuel to outmaneuver.

Not until the early hours of July 2 in the United States did others who waited for news hear that she had left Lae. G. P. was at the Coast Guard radio in San Francisco. Amy was at the North Hollywood house with Amelia's secretary, Margot DeCarie. Muriel was in Medford, where she had mailed a letter to her mother the day before saying she hoped to "get some broadcasting" fees for radio interviews about her sister, money to be paid on an overdue S.S. Pierce bill. Amelia's friend Eleanor Roosevelt, who had already declared how relieved she would be when the flight was over, was at Hyde Park for the long July Fourth weekend after the marriage of Franklin, Jr., and Ethel DuPont on June 30. They all waited but there was no more news.

Aboard the *Itasca* Commander Thompson was worried. He did not even know when she left Lae until San Francisco radioed him two reports, the first of which gave the wrong time. She had not acknowledged any of the weather reports the *Itasca* sent on the hour and half hour starting at midnight. At 2:45 A.M. chief radioman Leo G. Bellarts heard her, along with the two wire-service reporters, Carey and Hanzlick, who recognized her voice.

At 3:45 they heard her again. This time so did Black and Lt. Cooper, standing with Hanzlick and Carey in the doorway of the radio shack, which was off-limits to unauthorized personnel. Her voice was muffled, the delivery abrupt but they heard "Earhart. Overcast. Will listen on 3105 kilocycle on hour and half hour."

On schedule at 4 A.M., the *Itasca* called her on 3105 asking, "What is your position? When do you expect to arrive Howland? Please acknowledge this message on your next schedule."

She did not.

At 4:53 A.M., while the *Itasca* was sending her the weather in code and voice on 3015, Amelia broke in, off her schedule, with a garbled message at a volume of S-1, the lowest grade of five, too faint to discern anything except, "partly cloudy," before she was drowned out by static.

Thirty minutes later, Lt. Cooper and radioman Frank Cipriani went ashore to Howland to man the high-frequency radio borrowed from the Navy and powered by gun batteries from the ship.

At 6:14 A.M. Amelia came in again on schedule, fifteen minutes before she was due at Howland, according to Noonan's ETA. The volume had increased to S-3. "Want bearing on 3105 kilocycles on hour," Amelia said. "Will whistle in microphone." Her whistle was difficult to distinguish from the whining sounds of Pacific radio reception at dawn. Cipriani could not get a "fix" on her.

At 6:45, fifteen minutes past Noonan's ETA, Amelia came in at S-4. "Please take bearing on us and report in a half hour. I will make noise in microphone. About one hundred miles out." Her voice was clear but the message too brief to take a bearing on her.

Answering her request for a bearing in a half hour the *Itasca* broke its own schedule and broadcast to her by voice on 3105 at 7:18, "Cannot take bearing on 3105 very good. Please send on 500 or do you wish to take bearing on us?"

There was no answer.

At 7:42 she came in at S-5, her delivery much as Paul Mantz once described it, "a quick drawl like from a rain barrel."

"We must be on you but cannot see you but gas is running low. Been unable reach you by radio. We are flying at altitude one thousand feet." A second radioman's log, claiming she said "Only one-half hour gas left," was verified by other witnesses.

The *Itasca*'s operators immediately began transmitting on both 3105 and 500 assuring her that they heard her and asking her to acknowledge. A minute later she came in again, "Earhart calling *Itasca*. We are circling but cannot hear you. Go ahead on 7500 either now or on the schedule time on half hour." Her voice registered a loud S-5.

At eight o'clock Amelia acknowledged the *Itasca* for the first time, again at S-5 volume. "KHAQQ calling Itasca. We received your signals but unable to get a minimum [a bearing]. Please take bearing on us and answer on 3105 with voice."

The *Itasca*'s answer was that it could not take a bearing on 3105 because its DF worked only up to 500 kilocycles. The operator on Howland heard her on the Navy high frequency DF at 3105 but again, her transmission was too brief to get a bearing. From 8:07 to 8:41 the ship's operators transmitted and listened on all wavelengths including 7500 because it was the only one on which she had acknowledged having heard the *Itasca,* just before eight o'clock.

Apprehensive about the flight from the beginning, Commander

Thompson now knew he faced a real emergency. Not once in her messages had Amelia given him her position, her course, her speed, or her ETA. She was past the ETA Noonan had sent from Lae, and the half-hour of gas she mentioned at 7:42 would have been exhausted. On Howland, Cipriani could not get a bearing on her because her messages were too brief and by this time he had exhausted the gun batteries on which he operated the high frequency DF.

At 8:44 Amelia's voice—shrill and breathless, her words tumbling over one another—came in at S-5 on 3105 kilocycles. "We are on the line of position 156–137. Will repeat message. We will repeat this message on 6210 kilocycles. Wait. Listening on 6210 kilocycles. We are running north and south."

The *Itasca* responded immediately, continuing to transmit by voice and key and to listen on every frequency she might use. There was no answer. Twenty-three days before her fortieth birthday Amelia Earhart's last flight was finished. The death that she called part of her "high risk" profession must have come as she wished. "When I go," she said, "I would like to go in my plane. Quickly."

Over the nine years spanning her first and last transoceanic flights, Amelia Earhart became one of the most famous women in the world. The private Amelia disliked that fame intensely. But the public Amelia played on it relentlessly as a platform on which to fight for her ideals of equality for women, international peace, and a world where flying would be a commonplace, acceptable and accessible to all. She lived—and died—in dogged pursuit of her vision, and by so doing brought it ever closer to reality.

EPILOGUE

Amelia Earhart was the object of the most extensive mass rescue attempt ever made for a single lost plane. Four thousand men manning ten ships and sixty-five airplanes combed two hundred fifty thousand square miles of the Pacific—an area as large as Texas—in a sixteen-day search. The *Itasca* and *Swan* were joined by the battleship *Colorado,* the aircraft carrier *Lexington,* three destroyers, a British freighter, and two Japanese naval vessels. They found no trace of the Electra and on July 19 naval authorities declared the search for Amelia Earhart was over. They were wrong. It had only begun. Nothing she might have said or done, no scheme George Palmer Putnam might have designed, could so enhance Earhart's renown as the mystery of her disappearance. She had been famous. By vanishing she became legendary.

The mythologizing process began in 1943 with a Hollywood film, *Flight to Freedom.* Anti-Japanese wartime propaganda, the movie starred Rosalind Russell as a famous pilot who volunteers for a secret mission in which she becomes deliberately "lost" on a Pacific flight. By this self-sacrifice the heroine provides a reason for a search in which the U.S. Navy can scrutinize Japanese-mandated islands for suspected fortifications in violation of their League of Nations mandate. The story was fiction but the doomed heroine was clearly meant to be Earhart. After the film was seen by thousands of American servicemen stationed in the Pacific area, rumors began to spread that Earhart really had been on a secret mission.

No one has been able to prove beyond doubt how, why, where, and when Amelia Earhart disappeared. Records have been examined again and again, expeditions made, and theories expounded in magazine articles, books, and lectures. In general, the explanations—none with conclusive evidence—have made claims that Earhart was on a U2-type mission, aided by her friend, Franklin Roosevelt, that she overflew the Caroline Islands as agreed but became lost in bad weather, ran out of fuel, and landed or crashed in the area of the Marshall Islands. A less imaginative version omits the spy mission. With minor variations both assert that she was captured by the Japanese and a) was executed, b) died of dysentery, or c) was imprisoned in Tokyo until her rescue by Allied forces in 1945 when she was shipped home incognito by an embarrassed government, which provided her with a new identity and residence in New Jersey.

Among those who knew her best, none believed she was on a mission of espionage, although Amy Earhart later consoled herself with a vague theory that Amelia must have been serving her government in some fashion or other.

Eleanor and Franklin Roosevelt both denied Amelia had any such mission and historian Arthur Schlesinger, Jr., authority on the Roosevelt administration, said, "I know of no evidence connecting Roosevelt and Earhart in espionage." In a letter to Paul Mantz written ten months after Earhart disappeared, Eleanor Roosevelt said that she and FDR were satisfied that everything possible had been done in the search for Amelia.

For a brief time Mantz thought she might have reached Saipan after a generator like one he had installed in the Electra was fished from the harbor, but it proved to be Japanese-made. Eventually he was convinced that she went down near Howland.

Jackie Cochran, Earhart's closest confidante during the last year of her life, knew of no secret mission. Cochran felt the loss of Earhart so deeply that it was difficult for her to talk about it forty years later. If there had been a grain of truth in the espionage story Cochran would have been the first to make certain the public knew that her friend was a bona fide heroine who sacrificed her life for her country. After repeatedly warning Amelia that Howland would be difficult, if not impossible, to find, Cochran was not surprised to hear Earhart had disappeared. She credited her psychic powers with a picture of the Electra landing at sea and floating for two days before it sank but she was practical enough to double-check this scenario. She wrote to Eleanor Roosevelt and Paul Mantz for affirmation from more prosaic sources.

Eugene Vidal was certain Amelia was not a spy but hoped at first that she might have landed on a Pacific atoll. Her plan, he said, was to hunt for Howland until she had four hours of fuel left, and then, if she had not located it, to turn back to the Gilbert Islands and land on a beach. He eventually abandoned that hope.

Paul Collins said she might have almost reached Howland but any experienced flyer could realize how easy it was to miss it looking into the morning sun under the stress caused by dwindling fuel and the fatigue of an all-night flight.

Kelly Johnson was convinced that she ran out of gas, attempted to bring the plane down on the ocean and failed. She had been airborne for twenty-three hours, he said, "and, so help me, that's all the time they had fuel for." As for spying, Johnson added, "the only camera she had was a Brownie." Carl Allen agreed with Collins and Johnson.

Capt. Irving Johnson, who was at the War Plans office of the Navy at Pearl Harbor and had access to a file on Earhart, said there were no intercepted Japanese messages on her disappearance or capture.

The Japanese also denied any contact with Earhart. Inouye Shige-yoshi, in charge of the Japanese Naval Affairs Bureau in 1937, said he had never seen any evidence of such involvement.

Japanese historian Masataka Chihaya, a graduate of the naval academy in 1930 and later contributor to the *U.S. Naval Institute Proceedings* magazine, said that stories of the Japanese finding Earhart and Noonan were false. Claims that they were captured and transferred to a naval seaplane had to be erroneous, he said, because the largest Japanese naval seaplane in 1937 was the Type 91 Hiro H4H1, with only three seats. Other reports that they were transported as prisoners on the naval vessel *Kamoi* were also wrong, he said. The ship was not in the area at the time.

What *really* happened to Amelia Earhart? The so-called solutions to an alleged mystery are pure conjecture, ideal material for Sunday supplement writers. Her family, friends, colleagues, and reputable historians all offer the same simple answer. She lost her way on a flight from Lae, New Guinea to Howland Island and died somewhere in the Pacific.

BIBLIOGRAPHY

Adams, Mildred. "Woman Makes Good Her Claim for a Place in the Skies." *New York Times Magazine,* June 7, 1931.

Aircraft Year Book. New York: Aeronautical Chamber of Commerce of America, 1929, 1931, 1932.

Allen, Carl B. Papers, A&M 2252, Box 8. West Virginia and Regional History Collection, West Virginia University Library, Morgantown.

Allen, Frederick Lewis. *Only Yesterday.* New York: Harper and Row, 1964.

Allen, Richard Sanders. *"Friendship:* Fable of a Fokker." *Air-Britain Digest* 34, no. 1 (Jan.–Feb. 1985).

Arne, Sigrid. "She Breaks Precedents: Amelia Earhart," *Knickerbocker Press,* Midstream with Modern Women, No. 3. May 16, 1934.

Balchen, Bernt. *Come North with Me.* New York: E. P. Dutton, 1958.

Bell, Dana. "History of the Hawaiian Air Depot," Air Force Museum, Bolling, W.V.

Boykin, Elizabeth McRae. "Amelia Earhart at Home." *Better Homes and Gardens* (February 1, 1937): 46–47.

Cochran Papers. Dwight D. Eisenhower Library, National Archives and Records Service, General Services.

Collins, Paul F. *Tales of an Old Air-Faring Man: A Half-Century of Incidents, Accidents, and Providence.* The Reminiscences of Paul F. Collins. Ed. with an introduction and afterword by William L. M. H. Clark. University of Wisconsin-Stevens Point Foundation Press, 1983.

Curley, Walter. "Amelia Earhart: The Aviation Record of America's Most Famous Woman Pilot." Weston, Mass.: Cardinal Spellman Philatelic Museum, Regis College, 1966.

Davis, Burke. *Amelia Earhart.* New York: G. P. Putnam, 1972.

Dolphin, Marie. *Fifty Years of Rye.* Rye, N.Y.: The City of Rye, 1955.

Dwiggins, Don. *Hollywood Pilot: The Biography of Paul Mantz.* Garden City, N.Y.: Doubleday, 1967.

Earhart, Amelia. "Flying and Fly-Fishing." *Outdoor Life* (December 1934).

————. "Flying the Atlantic." *American Magazine* (August 1932).

————. "A Friendly Flight Across the Country," *NYT Magazine,* July 19, 1931.

————. *The Fun of It.* New York: Harcourt, Brace, and Company, 1932.

————. *Last Flight.* New York: Harcourt, Brace, Jovanovich, 1968.

————. "My Flight from Hawaii." *National Geographic* 65, no. 5 (1935).

————. *Twenty Hours Forty Minutes: Our Flight in the "Friendship."* New York: Arno, 1979.

————. "Wiley Post." *Forum and Century* (October 1935).

————. "Women's Status in Aviation." *Sportsman Pilot* (March 1929).

Fédération Aeronautique Internationale (FAI), Paris. Records Feminine, Miss Amelia Earhart (Etats Unis).

Fleet, Dorothy. *Our Flight to Destiny.* New York: Vantage Press, 1964.

Gentry, Viola. *Hangar Flying: Stories of Early Fliers in America.* Chelmsford, Mass.: V. Gentry, 1975.

Gilroy, Shirley Dobson. *Amelia: Pilot in Pearls.* McLean, Va.: Link Press, 1985.

Goerner, Frederick Allen. *The Search for Amelia Earhart.* Garden City, N.Y.: Doubleday, 1966.

Greenwood, Maxine, and Tim Greenwood. *Stunt Flying in the Movies.* Blue Ridge Summit, Pa.: TAB Books, 1982.

Haggerty, James J. *Aviation's Mr. Sam.* Fallbrooke, Calif.: Aero Publishers, 1974.

Hatfield, D. D. *Los Angeles Aeronautics, 1920–1929.* Hatfield History of Aeronautics, Northrop Technical Institute, 1973.

Hawks, Frank. *Speed.* New York: Brewer, Warren and Putnam, 1931.

History of the Ninety-Nines, Inc. Oklahoma City: Ninety-Nines, Inc., International Organization of Women Pilots, 1979.

Johnson, Clarence "Kelly," with Maggie Smith. *More Than My Share of It All.* Washington, D.C.: Smithsonian Institution Press, 1985.

Lash, Joseph P. *Eleanor and Franklin.* New York: W. W. Norton, 1971.

Lindbergh, Anne Morrow. *Hour of Gold, Hour of Lead: Diaries of Anne Morrow Lindbergh, 1929–1932.* New York: New American Libraries, 1974.

————. *Locked Rooms and Open Doors: Diaries and Letters, 1933–1935.* New York: Harcourt, Brace, Jovanovich, 1974.

McDonough, Kenneth. *Atlantic Wings.* Hemel Hempstead, England: Model Aeronautical Press, 1966.

Mills, Ralph W. "Dad's Flight with Amelia Earhart." *Down East: The Magazine of Maine* (April 1983): 72.

Moolman, Valerie, and the Editors of Time-Life, Inc. *Women Aloft.* Epic of Flight Series. Alexandria, Va.: Time-Life Books, Inc., 1981.

Morrissey, Muriel Earhart. *Courage Is the Price: The Biography of Amelia Earhart.* Wichita, Kan.: McCormick-Armstrong, 1963.

————. "The Reminiscences of Muriel Earhart Morrissey" (1960). Oral History Collection of Columbia University, New York.

Mudge, Robert W. *Adventures of a Yellowbird: The Biography of an Airline.* Boston: Branden Press, 1969.

Nichols, Ruth. *Wings for Life.* Philadelphia: J. B. Lippincott Co., 1957.

Oral History Collection, Columbia University, New York.

Putnam, George Palmer. *Wide Margins: A Publisher's Autobiography.* New York: Harcourt, Brace and Company, 1942.

———. *Soaring Wings: A Biography of Amelia Earhart.* New York: Harcourt, Brace and Company, 1939.

Samuelson, Maj. Nancy B., USAF. "Equality in the Cockpit: A Brief History of Women in Aviation." Unpublished paper for Armed Forces Staff College, Norfolk, Virginia, 9 May 1977. National Air and Space Museum Archival Support Center, Suitland, Maryland: Margaret Merrick Scheffelin/Dacowits Collection.

Smith, Elinor. *Aviatrix.* New York and London: Harcourt, Brace, Jovanovich, 1981.

Smith, Frank Kingston. *Legacy of Wings: The Story of Harold F. Pitcairn.* New York: J. Aronson, 1981.

Smith, Henry Ladd. *Airways: The History of Commercial Aviation in the United States.* New York: Alfred A. Knopf, 1942.

Southern, Neta Snook. *I Taught Amelia to Fly.* New York: Vantage Press, 1974.

University of South Carolina, News Films Libraries. Earhart, Amelia, File 14-849.

Vidal, Eugene. Vidal Collection 6013, American Heritage Center, University of Wyoming, Laramie, Wyoming.

Vidal, Gore. "Love of Flying." *New York Review of Books* 31, nos. 21 and 22 (January 17, 1985).

Williams, Clarence. "Charting A.E.'s Course to Mexico." *Airwoman* 3, no. 5 (May 1936).

Zonta International. Manual, Amelia Earhart Fellowship Awards, 1938–1984 (1984).

REFERENCE NOTES

Notes are identified by page number.

Abbreviations

AYB   *Aviation Year Book*
CG Log   Log of the Coast Guard cutter *Itasca* at sea, Pacific Ocean, July 19, 1937. Trea-
              sury Department, United States Coast Guard, File 65-601.
COHC   Oral History Collection, Columbia University
DDEL   Dwight D. Eisenhower Library
LAT   *Los Angeles Times*
NASM   National Air and Space Museum
PSC   Purdue University, Special Collections
SB   *Star Bulletin* (Honolulu)
SLRC   Schlesinger Library, Radcliffe College
NYHT   *New York Herald Tribune*
NYWT   *New York World-Telegram*
NYT   *New York Times*
PEB   *Philadelphia Evening Bulletin*

Chapter 1. A Double Life

3–4   Tomboy behavior: Earhart, *Fun of It,* 11–12.
4   Amelia's name: Ninety-Nines Archives.
5   Photograph and house description: *Globe* (Atchison, Kan.), July 21, 1963.
6   Holidays and behavior at school: Morrissey, *Courage Is the Price,* 67.
           Hunting: Muriel Earhart Morrissey, interview, April 19, 1983.
7   Private railroad car: *Globe,* July 21, 1963.

7 Childhood games: Morrissey, interview, April 19, 1983.
   "I must recount": SLRC, A-129 F. 7, May 12, 1903.
8 "like a big game hunter": Earhart, *Fun of It*, 4.
   "just like flying": Morrissey, interview, April 19, 1983.
9 "It was a thing of rusty wire": Earhart, *Fun of It*, 4.
   Promotion: Morrissey, *Courage Is the Price*, 86.
10 Twelfth Night dance: Morrissey, interview, April 19, 1983.
11 "Of course I'm going to B.M.": SLRC, 83 M-69 F. 4, March 1914.
   Chicago: Morrissey, interview, May 20, 1983.
   Schools for Amelia and Muriel: Morrissey, interview, April 20, 1983.

Chapter 2. Arrow without a Target

13 Abby Sutherland: Ellen Masters, letter, June 14, 1984.
14 Description of Abby Sutherland: SLRC, 83 M-69 F. 7, October 25, 1916.
   Treatment of faculty members: Masters, letter.
   "We treated her like a queen": Myra Thomas, *Times Chronicle* (Jenkintown, Pa.), p. 20.
15 Letters to Amy: SLRC, M-69 F. 7, October 25, 1916.
16 Time at Camp Grey: ibid., August 1, 8, and 15, 1917.
   "Honor is the foundation": ibid.
   Cruel and discourteous: Masters, letter.
17 "I nearly had my head taken off" and "lost all my friends": SLRC, M-69 F. 7, November 1917.
   Oscar Wilde: Masters, letter.
   "Good girl, Helen!": SLRC, A-129 F. 2.
18 St. Regis Hotel: SLRC, M-69 F. 7, February 21, 1918.
   Watching soldiers: Morrissey, "Reminiscences," COHC, 4.
   "I'm not going back": Manual, Zonta Amelia Earhart Fellowship Awards, 1938–84 (1984), p. 20.
   "Ailments of the chest": Susan Dexter, interview and correspondence, January 13, 1984.
   Face of a mature woman: Marian Stabler, interview, June 16, 1984.
   Description of college: Dexter, interview.
   "on duty from seven": Earhart, *Fun of It*, 12.
19 RCAF pilots: Morrissey, "Reminiscences," COHC.
   "mingled fear and pleasure": Moolman et al., *Women Aloft*, 61.
   "I have Sunday morning off": SLRC, A-129 F. 7.
   "Don't think for an instant": SLRC, 83 M-69 F. 7.
   "I think of God": Putnam, *Soaring Wings*, 48.
20 "a serious word of thanksgiving" Earhart, *Fun of It*, 21.
   "the incongruity": Morrissey, *Courage Is the Price*, 106.
   Lake George: Morrissey, "Reminiscences," COHC, 4.
   Description of Amelia: Stabler, interview.
22 "One of the worst things": Morrissey, interview, April 19, 1983.

Looking after Amy: SLRC, M-69 F. 6, April 24, 1920.

Boarders: Morrissey, *Courage Is the Price*, 116.

23   Dating Sam Chapman: Morrissey, interview, April 20, 1983.

Military personnel: Hatfield, *Los Angeles Aeronautics*, 27.

Inquiries about flying and first flight: Earhart, *Fun of It*, 24–25.

Chapter 3. Linen Wings and a Leather Coat

25   Barnstormers: Collins, *Tales of an Old Air-Faring Man*.

26   Cecil B. De Mille: Hatfield, *Los Angeles Aeronautics*, 12.

First airplane ride: ibid., 15.

27   "I want to fly": Southern, *I Taught Amelia to Fly*, 101–3.

Cora Kinner: Cora Kinner, interview with Donna Kinner Hunter, January 24, 1980.

"visionary and not too practical": Morrissey, interview, April 19, 1983.

28   "the kid who could fix anything": Cora Kinner, interview.

regarded it with approval: Southern, *I Taught Amelia to Fly*, 104.

Its top speed: Collins, *Tales of an Old Air-Faring Man*, 34.

Teaching Amelia to fly: Southern, *I Taught Amelia to Fly*, 122.

29   "He'd come out there": Cora Kinner, interview.

30   "I think he has the mating instinct": Southern, *I Taught Amelia to Fly*, 111.

31   Scrapbook quotes: SLRC, A-129 F.3.

"Amelia was usually dressed": Waldo D. Waterman, letter to Clara Studer, April 19, 1962.

32   Chronic abscess: Winfield B. Kinner, Jr., interview, October 27, 1985.

Oil-stained jacket: Southern, *I Taught Amelia to Fly*, 143.

"regarded by many people": Morrissey, "Reminiscences," COHC, 4.

"We shellacked the canvas wings": Zonta Awards, p. 20.

"life was incomplete": Earhart, *Twenty Hours*, 61.

Kinner plane: Winfield B. Kinner, Jr., interview.

33   "give up that truck": Cora Kinner, interview.

Three-cylinder engine: Southern, *I Taught Amelia to Fly*, 121–22.

"all over again": ibid., 125.

"Amelia set her little Kinner": *Bellingham Herald* (Washington), November 10, 1968.

Accident and soloing: Southern, *I Taught Amelia to Fly*, 125.

"scared . . . to death": Earhart, *Twenty Hours*, 54.

NAA license: National Aviation Association Records, NASM Library.

34   "a thoroughly rotten landing": Earhart, *Twenty Hours*, 56.

"Pacific Coast Ladies Derby": Hatfield, *Los Angeles Aeronautics*, 80.

"Luckily I was over the field" and "the moment I flew up": Davis, *Amelia Earhart*, 55.

"After flying my Kinner Airster": Hatfield, *Los Angeles Aeronautics*, 57.

35   Vassar College: PSC, Scrapbook #1.

"She handled the ship": Jim Montijo, letter, July 5, 1984.

36   First flying record: Earhart, *Fun of It,* 77–78.
            Sixteenth woman in FAI: Patrick Welsh, letter from National Aeronautic Asso-
                ciation to Federation Aeronautique Internationale, March 31, 1926.

Chapter 4. Ceiling Zero but Lifting

37   "no pay, no fly": Earhart, *Fun of It,* 26.
            "I think that Dad imagines": Bobbi Trout, interview, January 4, 1984.
38   "There is no way": Morrissey, *Courage Is the Price,* 119–27.
            "The kid must have frozen": Donna Kinner Hunter, interview, January 6,
                1984.
39   Photography class notebook: SLRC, A-129 F. 3.
40   Crossing Canada: PSC, misc. documents.
            Medford, Mass.: Earhart, *Fun of It,* 50–51.
            Yellow Peril: Morrissey, interview, April 19, 1983.
            "I need the money": Ninety-Nines Archives.
            "As long as I have that motor": Hunter, interview.
            "This time she lived poorly": Stabler, interview.
41   Classical music: Elise von R. Owen, interview, June 16, 1984.
            "I want a figure": Stabler, interview.
            "No, I did not get into MIT": ibid.
42   On not marrying: ibid.
            Amelia and Sam: Morrissey, interview, April 19, 1983.
            Scrapbook: Morrissey, *Courage Is the Price,* 134–35.
            Children of Denison House: SLRC, A-129 F. 3.
43   "tenderness for children": Stabler, interview.
            "a sound education": Davis, *Amelia Earhart,* 64.
            Dennison Airport: Morrissey, interview, April 19, 1983.
            Denison House: PSC, Scrapbook #1: *Herald* (Boston), July 3, 1927, p. 2.
44   "Though I haven't a real job": Stabler, interview.
            "May I report": Hunter, interview.
            Ruth Nichols: Adams, "Woman Makes Good Her Claim," 6.
            Letter to Ruth Nichols: Nichols, *Wings for Life,* 93–94.
45   Letters to Bert Kinner: Hunter, interview.
            Interview with Railey: Morrissey, *Courage Is the Price,* 140.
            Charles Lindbergh: Allen, *Only Yesterday,* 181, 183.
46   Amy Phipps Guest: Putnam, *Wide Margins,* 292–93.
            Finding a woman to fly the Atlantic: Railey, *PEB,* September 10, 1938.
            "A thoroughly fine person": Reginald K. Belknap, *Sunday Star* (Washington,
                D.C.), May 22, 1932, sec. A, p. 5.
            "Her resemblance to Colonel Lindbergh": Railey, *PEB.*
47   "You may grant me pardon": Stabler, interview.
            George Palmer Putnam: Margaret H. Lewis, interview and material provided
                subsequently, October 24, 1985.
            Interview: Morrissey, *Courage Is the Price,* 141.

"Was I willing to fly the Atlantic?": Earhart, *Fun of It*, 60–61.

48　"I found myself in a curious situation": Morrissey, *Courage Is the Price*, 141.
Boarding the train: Morrissey, interview, April 20, 1983.
Money from royalties or advertising: Earhart, *Twenty Hours*, 110.
"Courage": Zonta Awards, p. 9.

49　Will and letters to parents: Morrissey, *Courage Is the Price*, 146.

50　To Hilton Railey: Railey, *PEB*.

Chapter 5. Across the Atlantic

53　Description of Richard Byrd: Emory Land, COHC, vol. 1, pt. 3.

54　Stultz's agreement with Boll: *NYT*, June 3, 1928, p. 2.
Stultz as alcoholic: C. L. Zakhartchenko, interview, February 10, 1985.
Friendship crew: *NYT*, June 3, 1928, p. 2.

55　Purchase of *Friendship*: Allen, "*Friendship*," 16–17.
Alleged promise: *NYT*, June 3, 1928, p. 3.
Thea Rasche: *NYT*, May 6, 1928, p. 22; May 16, 1928, p. 2.
Other crossings: *AYB*, 1929, 156.
First prize: *NYT*, May 14, 1928, p. 9.
"I did not dare": Earhart, *Fun of It*, 62–63.
Women's flying organization: Nichols, *Wings for Life*, 44–45.

56　"The mob should be thought of": Earhart, correspondence, Earhart Collection, NASM Library.
"the first woman chosen": NAA, Boston chapter, press release, May 29, 1928, p. 1.
Weather reports: *NYT*, June 8, 1928, p. 6.
Letter to Muriel: *NYT*, June 5, 1928, p. 3.

57　*Friendship* takeoff: ibid., p. 1; Earhart, *Twenty Hours*, 115–17.
Descriptions of Amelia: *NYT*, June 4, 1928, p. 2.

58　Accuracy of description: Morrissey, interview, April 19, 1983.
Amelia's hair: Bernard Wiesman, interview, December 10, 1985.
Stenographer's notebook: Earhart, *Twenty Hours*, 119–20.

59　Halifax: ibid.
"Boston Girl Starts Atlantic Hop": *NYT*, June 4, 1928, p. 1.
Longest nonstop flight: *NYT*, June 5, 1928, p. 1.
Pumping gas: *NYT*, June 5, 1928, p. 3.
"Miss Earhart's slightness": ibid.
"Good trip from Halifax": ibid., p. 1.

60　"No laundry": Putnam, *Wide Margins*, 288.
Attempts at takeoff: *NYT*, June 7, 1928, p. 1; June 8, 1928, p. 4.
Beaching the plane: Earhart, *Twenty Hours*, 160–61.
Invitation from Mabel Boll: *NYT*, June 14, 1928, p. 16.
Stultz drinking: Morrissey, *Courage Is the Price*, 151–52.
Amelia taking command: PSC, 1928 Atlantic Flight, Preflight Correspondence.

61　Gordon leaving: Morrissey, *Courage Is the Price*, 152–53.

Weather conditions: ibid.
Sobering Stultz: ibid.
Cable to Putnam: *NYT,* June 18, 1928, p. 2.
Taking off: *NYT,* June 18, 1928, p. 2.
Stultz's bottle: Morrissey, interview, April 19, 1983.
62   Gordon takes over flying: Earhart, *Twenty Hours,* 170–99.
Last part of flight: ibid., 182, 192.
Flight over: Morrissey, *Courage Is the Price,* 156.

Chapter 6. The Circus

63   Burry Port: Morrissey, *Courage Is the Price,* 156–57.
64   "men, women, and children": *NYT,* June 19, 1928, pp. 1–2.
"The accident of sex": Earhart, *Twenty Hours,* 201.
"Excited?": Railey, *PEB.*
Never touched controls: *NYT,* June 19, 1928, p. 1.
Day in Southampton: ibid., 1–2.
65   "Amelia Earhart Flies Atlantic": *NYT,* June 19, 1928, p. 1.
"unquenchable determination": *The Times* (London), June 19, 1928.
"to render service": *NYT,* June 19, 1928, p. 3.
"a feat none of her sex": *Daily Express* (London), June 19, 1928.
"to bring home to everyone": *Daily Telegraph* (London), June 19, 1928.
"The voyage itself": Earhart, *Twenty Hours,* 291–92.
"the palpitating interest": *Liberté* (Paris), June 19, 1928.
66   "from first to last": Morrissey, interview, April 19, 1983.
Welsh marriage proposal: *NYT,* June 21, 1928, p. 1.
Ride through London: ibid.
Telegram from Henry Ford: PSC, 1928 Atlantic Flight, Miscellaneous.
Lady Mary Heath: *AYB* 1929, p. 158.
Purchase of Avro Avian: *NYT,* June 27, 1928, p. 14; Richard S. Allen, letter, January 20, 1986.
Selfridge and the de Sibours: *NYT,* June 22, 1928, p. 1.
Lady Nancy Astor: *NYT Magazine,* June 3, 1928, p. 1.
67   "tousled golden curls": *NYT,* June 26, 1928, p. 26.
"Everyone I have talked to": *NYT,* June 28, 1928, p. 16.
Sailing for New York: ibid.
Foreign vessels: *NYT,* June 21, 1928, p. 1.
Prince of Wales: *NYT,* June 27, 1928, p. 26.
68   "It's bad enough in London": Morrissey, *Courage Is the Price,* 162–63.
Stultz's death: *NYT,* July 2, 1929, p. 1.
Boarding the *Macon: NYT,* July 7, 1928, pp. 1–2.
Ruth Nichols: Nichols, *Wings for Life,* 95–96.
New York greeting: *NYT,* July 7, 1928, p. 2.
69   Auction: PSC, 1928 Atlantic Flight, Miscellaneous.

Amy's feelings: SLRC, 83 M-69 F. 3.

"rigidly erect of carriage": *NYT,* June 19, 1928, p. 2.

70   Public affection: Unidentified newspaper clipping, Earhart Collection, NASM Library.

"She was just the same": Wiesman, interview.

Quitting social work: Morrissey, *Courage Is the Price,* 166.

"a secret tryst": *Herald and Examiner* (Chicago), July 10, 1928, p. 5.

71   "daunted by the sea of faces": *Pittsburgh Press,* July 24, 1928, p. 1.

Chapter 7. The Hustler's Apprentice

72   "It was a beautiful car": Charles LeBoutillier, interview, May 10, 1986.

73   "For occupation might write skeleton": PSC, 1928 Atlantic Flight, Preflight Correspondence.

Dedication: Earhart, *Twenty Hours,* 7.

The house in Rye: Dolphin, *Fifty Years of Rye,* 57–60.

Dorothy Putnam's interests: Sally Putnam Chapman, interview, September 21, 1985.

"an educated and cultivated person": *NYT,* July 18, 1928, p. 3.

Paying for Avro Avian: R. S. Allen, letter.

74   Leaving Rye: Letter to Stabler, August 16, 1928.

Plans for flying west: SLRC, 83 M-69 F. 8.

Crackup: *NYT,* August 31, 1928, p. 1.

"All they had to do": *Daily Phoenix* (Muskogee, Okla.), September 5, 1928, p. 1.

Country club dance: *Post Dispatch* (St. Louis), September 4, 1928, p. 3.

75   "to some man, too" and "She was really sort of homely": *Daily Phoenix,* September 5, 1928, p. 1.

Leaving for Glendale: *LAT,* September 14, 1928, pt. 2, p. 7.

National Air Exhibition: ibid., September 15, 1928, p. 1.

"a glimpse": *Examiner* (San Francisco), September 17, 1928, p. 5.

76   "I didn't want to bother with her": Hunter, interview.

Silver pilot's wings: *Herald* (Boston), November 12, 1928, p. 16.

Visit to Utah: *Tribune* (Salt Lake City), October 4, 1928, p. 1.

Complexion: *World-Herald* (Omaha), October 11, 1928, p. 1.

"Why they even cut pieces": *World-Herald,* October 12, 1928, p. 6.

77   "scandalizing progress": Earhart, *Twenty Hours,* 286–87.

Chrysler roadster: *NYT,* July 11, 1928, p. 9.

Flying suit: *NYT,* July 23, 1928, p. 5.

Tobacco endorsement: Morrissey, interview, April 20, 1983.

78   "a symbol of new womanhood": *Cosmopolitan,* November 1928, p. 21.

Ella May Frazer: Ella May Frazer, letter, February 26, 1983.

Public appearance: Putnam, *Soaring Wings,* 77–79.

79   Smiling: Morrissey, interview, April 20, 1983.

Yale University: *NYT,* October 21, 1928, sec. 2, p. 1.

Detroit Adcraft: *Free Press* (Detroit), October 27, 1928.

"I was considered important enough": SLRC, 83 M-69 F. 8.

Kill Devil Hill: *Evening Star* (Washington, D.C.), December 18, 1928, p. 2.

80   Air tour of New York: *NYT,* December 26, 1928.

Chapter 8. The Vega

81   Visit to Le Roy, N.Y.: *Democrat Chronicle* (Rochester), January 25, 1929.

82   "a slender figure in grey chiffon": Jane Dow Bromberg, letter, December 19, 1984.

"Not that I am advocating": *Free Press,* April 12, 1929.

Ohio Federation of Women's Clubs: Letters of March 4 and 7, 1929, Earhart Collection, NASM Library.

"the Lindbergh line": *NYT,* July 2, 1929, p. 2.

83   TAT's first flight west: *NYT,* July 8, 1929, p. 1.

TAT itinerary: *NYT,* July 9, 1929, p. 3.

"very likeable": Lindbergh, *Hour of Gold,* 52.

"a matter of a weekend": *LAT,* July 9, 1929, sec. 2, p. 1.

Free publicity: *LAT,* July 13, 1929, sec. 2, p. 5.

84   "the mind of a woman": *Sportsman Pilot,* August 1929, p. 48.

"the sex line washed out": *Free Press,* April 12, 1929.

Colonial Transport: *NYT,* February 6, 1929, p. 15.

"she took a few flights": *Express* (San Antonio), March 10, 1929, p. 22.

Aviation Bureau: National Archives, RG 237 805, Washington, D.C.

Fourth woman to hold transport license: *NYT,* March 29, 1929, p. 16.

New York to Washington: *Washington Post,* March 20, 1929, p. 22.

85   Violent thunderstorm: *News* (Buffalo), March 29, 1929, p. 18.

Consolidated Aircraft: ibid., March 27, 1929, p. 18.

Flying with Leigh Wade: Maj. Gen. Leigh Wade (ret.), interview, January 14, 1985.

Flying with Elinor Smith: Smith, *Aviatrix,* 93–94.

86   Smith's opinions of Putnam and the Vega: ibid., 69–74, 93–94.

Flying with Ralph DeVore: *Plain Dealer* (Cleveland), May 14, 1929, p. 1.

Muriel's marriage: *Herald* (Boston), June 30, 1929, p. 47.

87   Purchasing the Vega: Herbert Bowen, interview, January 14, 1984, sales records, Lockheed Corporation, Burbank, California; R. S. Allen, letter, May 27, 1985; Harvey C. Christen, interview, October 26, 1985.

Flying to Chatauqua: *Chatauqua Daily,* July 22, 1929, p. 1.

Flying the Vega for the first time: Ben O. Howard, COHC, vol. 2, pt. 2, p. 66.

88   Broadcast to Byrd: *Post Dispatch,* August 3, 1929, p. 5.

Leaving for Los Angeles, *LAT,* August 8, 1929, pt. 2, p. 10.

Stephens's crash: *Republican* (Phoenix), August 12, 1929, p. 4.

Trading the Vega: Christen, interview.

Chapter 9. Losing and Leading

89   Protest: *NYT,* June 12, 1929, p. 28.
90   Signing up for derby: *NYT,* July 25, 1929, p. 16.
    Powder Puff Derby: *LAT,* August 19, 1929, pt. 2, p. 1.
    Setting records: *LAT,* August 15, 1929, pt. 2, p. 2.
    National network hookup: SLRC, 83 M-69 F. 8.
    Start of the derby: *LAT,* August 16, 1929, p. 8.
    Starting lineup: *LAT,* August 19, 1929, pt. 2, p. 1.
91   From Calexico to Yuma: *NYT,* August 20, 1929, pt. 2, p. 1.
    Landing at Phoenix: *LAT,* August 20, 1929, pt. 2, p. 2.
    "Instead I struck sand": *Arizona Republic,* August 20, 1929, p. 1.
    Crosson, Trout, Rasche, Fahy: *LAT,* August 20, 1929, pt. 2, p. 1.
92   Cleaning goggles: *LAT,* August 21, 1929.
    Kunz, Haizlip, Keith-Miller: *LAT,* August 20, 1929, pt. 2, p. 1.
    Crosson, Walker, Noyes, Keith-Miller: *LAT,* August 21, 1929, p. 1.
93   Barnes, Noyes: *NYT,* August 23, 1929, p. 3.
    Perry: *LAT,* August 24, 1929, p. 1.
    Banquet: ibid.
    Haizlip: *NYT,* August 25, 1929, p. 1.
94   Fried chicken: *Plain Dealer,* August 26, 1929, p. 1.
    Servicing planes: *Woman's Journal,* October 1929, pp. 10–11, 18, 26.
    Fabric-covered aircraft: *Plain Dealer,* August 26, 1929, p. 1.
    Prize money: *Plain Dealer,* August 27, 1929, p. 1.
    "There are two Great Lakes airplanes": Noyes, COHC, vol. 1, pt. 3, p. 13.
    Turning at markers: *NYT,* August 28, 1929, p. 1.
    Competitive spirit: Edna Gardner Whyte, interview, January 24, 1984.
    Haizlip: Mary Haizlip, interview, January 13, 1984.
95   "she kept her wits about her": Hawks, *Speed,* 260–86.
    Amelia's hotel suite: Smith, *Aviatrix,* 141.
    Women pilots' organization: Nichols, *Wings for Life,* 96–97.
    "She seemed apologetic": Nancy Hopkins Tier, interview, September 24, 1984.
    Charter member: Gentry, *Hangar Flying.*
    The Ninety-Nines: *History of the Ninety-Nines.*
96   Haizlip: Haizlip, interview.
    American Women's Club: Cochran Papers, DDEL, Ninety-Nines Series, Box 6.
    Neva Paris: *NYT,* January 10, 1930, p. 1.
    National Air Races: Ninety-Nines Archives.
    "the gentler sex": *Pittsburgh Press,* June 29, 1930, automotive sec., p. 8.
    Refuses to compete: *NYT,* August 6, 1930, p. 14.
    "in order to reach some agreement": ibid.
97   Constitutional committee: Newsletter, September 1930, Ninety-Nines Archives.
    Licensed women pilots: *Herald and Examiner,* August 24, 1930, p. 5.

Chapter 10. Reaching the Limits

98   Traveling on business: *Chronicle and News* (Allentown, Pa.), November 5, 1929.
       Madduxes: John L. Maddux, interview, June 4, 1985.

99   Total time to date: R. S. Allen, letter.
       Flight records: ibid.
       Women's speed record: *LAT,* November 21, 1929, pt. 2, p. 1.
       Breaking women's speed record: R. S. Allen, letter.
       Fastest lap: *LAT,* November 25, 1929, pt. 2, p. 2.
       "You will please advise": Letter, March 1, 1930, Earhart Collection, NASM
         Library.

100   Lindbergh's Sirius: *LAT,* November 20, 1929, pt. 2, p. 1.
       Trial flights: R. S. Allen, letter.
       "an amazing person": Lindbergh, *Hour of Gold,* 102.
       "a fine courage": Earhart, *Fun of It,* 174–75.

101   "During our explanation": ibid.
       Lindbergh's jokes: Putnam, *Soaring Wings,* 183–84.
       Maddux: Maddux, interview.

102   "when he comes through": *Journal* (Albuquerque), January 11, 1930, p. 14.
       Return to New York: *LAT,* January 11, 1930, p. 5.
       "to keep out of Albert's way": SLRC, 83 M-69 F. 8.
       "I'm long on friends": Morrissey, *Courage Is the Price,* 175.
       "I'm afraid Dad may not enjoy": SLRC, 83 M-69 F. 8.

103   Stock market crash: *NYT,* October 25, 1929, p. 1.
       Letter to Amy: SLRC, 83 M-69 F. 8.
       "A Guernsey cow": *NYT,* February, 19, 1930, p. 19.

104   Exhibition: *Post Dispatch,* February 23, 1930, p. K6.
       Aboard the *Lexington: NYT,* April 26, 1930, p. 28.
       Society of Automotive Engineers: *Free Press,* April 9, 1930, p. 11.
       Speaking engagements: *Star* (Kansas City), May 12, 1930, p. 2; *News* (India-
         napolis), May 14, 1930, p. 10, and May 15, 1930, p. 1; *Tribune* (Chicago),
         May 15, 1930, p. 9; *Herald and Examiner,* May 16, 1930, p. 3.
       "were astonished": Elizabeth Townsend Trump, interview, June 16, 1984.
       Challenge world records: Earhart, "Women's Status in Aviation," 9.
       Rules: Earhart Collection, June 9 and 11, 1930, NASM Library.

105   "Miss Earhart feels quite strongly": ibid., April 24, 1931.
       Three records: FAI.
       TAT merge with Maddux: *PEB,* September 1, 1930, pp. 1–2.
       Collins flying with Amelia: Collins, *Tales of an Old Air-Faring Man,* 103–4.

106   "She was an interesting person": Vidal Collection, Box 19, p. 94.
       Changing planes: Vidal, "Love of Flying," 17.
       Air sickness: ibid.

107   "When TAT reached": Howard, COHC, vol. 2, pt. 2, pp. 64–67.
       Fuel: Smith, *Airways,* 216–17.
       Profit: ibid.
       "I know one woman": *NYT,* September 15, 1930, p. 27.

"She keeps her hands still": PSC, Scrapbook #10: *Christian Science Monitor,* September 1930.

108   "I do hope Pidge moves": SLRC, 83 M-69 F.8.

Edwin's death: *LAT,* September 24, 1930, pt. 2, p. 9.

109   "Runways had not been invented": Edna Whiting Nisewaner, interview and letter, June 30, 1984.

"little things": *World* (New York), September 26, 1930, p. 11.

"That gal must be something": Howard, COHC, vol. 2, pt. 2, pp. 64–67.

Speaking engagement: *World,* September 26, 1930, p. 11.

Staying with the Whitings: Nisewaner, interview and letter.

110   "I have just returned from Dad": SLRC, 83 M-69 F. 8.

"to initiate and create": PSC, Scrapbook #10: *World,* September 13, 1930.

111   Commemorative column: *NYT,* August 9, 1930, p. 6.

Chapter 11. A Marriage of Convenience

112   First denial: *LAT,* December 21, 1929.

Subsequent denials: *NYT,* February 8, 1931, p. 1.

"Everyone thinks G. P. and I": Stabler, interview.

"I am still unsold": Moolman et al., *Women Aloft,* 64.

113   Byrd: *World,* May 4, 1930, p. 4.

Luncheon: *NYT,* July 8, 1930, p. 2.

"Dick didn't see it": Putnam, *Wide Margins,* 221.

Flew to Washington: *World,* November 10, 1930, p. 1.

Associated Press: *NYT,* November 10, 1930, p. 7.

114   Marriage rumors: *World,* November 10, 1930, p. 1.

Meeting with Allen and Lyman: Carl B. Allen, unpublished manuscript, Earhart Collection, NASM Library.

115   Celebrities: Putnam, *Wide Margins,* 224.

"keeping an eye on him": SLRC, 83 M-69 F. 45.

"deluged Amelia": Putnam, *Wide Margins,* 224.

"He could be arrogant": Margaret Haviland Lewis, interview, October 24, 1985.

"was subject to seizures of idleness": Putnam, *Wide Margins,* 282.

116   "twelve years her senior": Morrissey, *Courage Is the Price,* 176.

"I shan't be home": SLRC, 83 M-69 F. 9.

New speed record: *NYT,* February 5, 1931.

Wedding ceremony: *NYT,* February 8, 1931, p. 1.

Changing her name: Jeff Mill, "Residents Recall Earhart Wedding," *The News* (Groton, Conn.), November 12, 1976, p. 1.

Letter to G. P.: Memorabilia booklet, 1976, Dawson Historical Center, Harrison, New York.

117   Amelia Earhart Putnam: *NYT,* March 7, 1931, p. 6.

"break the news gently": Morrissey, *Courage Is the Price,* 176.

"I know how easy it is": SLRC, 83 M-69 F. 8.

Relationship with Amy and Muriel: ibid., F. 9 and 32.

118   "for the air races": Morrissey, "Reminiscences," COHC, p. 18.

"She looked like a bag of bones": David Binney Putnam, interview, November 11, 1985.

Interfere with career: Putnam, *Soaring Wings*, 80.

"I am much happier": SLRC, 83 M-69 F. 9.

119   Seats sold out: *World*, November 27, 1930, p. 12.

Vice-president: Vidal Collection, Box 22, November 28, 1930.

Empire State Building: PSC, Scrapbook #4: unidentified clipping, March 16, 1931.

Parachutes: *NYT*, April 14, 1931, p. 28.

Franklin automobile: *Wall Street Journal*, May 5, 1931.

NAA officer: *NYT*, April 26, 1931.

Transport licenses: Adams, "Woman Makes Good Her Claim," 6.

Endurance-refueling record: *NYT*, January 10, 1931, p. 1.

"If I had a promoter": Trout, interview.

Laura Ingalls: *AYB* 1931, p. 459.

Elinor Smith: *NYT*, January 28, 1931, p. 1.

New altitude and speed records: *AYB* 1932, p. 485.

120   Solo transatlantic flights: *NYT*, May 7, 1931, p. 16.

Price and description of autogiro: *NYT*, September 1, 1929, sec. 10, p. 11.

"I began to feel exactly": Earhart, *Fun of It*, 132–33.

Corporate buyers: Smith, *Legacy of Wings*, 182.

Sealed barograph: *NYT*, April 9, 1931, p. 1.

Altitude record: Univ. of South Carolina.

121   Engine: R. S. Allen, letter.

Transcontinental flight: Smith, *Legacy of Wings*, 182–83.

"knees a bit wobbly": SLRC, 83 M-69 F. 9.

Radio coverage: Univ. of South Carolina.

122   "a sandy-haired goddess": *Post* (Denver), June 3, 1931, p. 1.

"One of the happiest moments": SLRC, 83 M-69 F. 98.

Oakland: *Chronicle* (San Francisco), June 7, 1931, p. 1.

John Miller: Smith, *Legacy of Wings*, 183.

Accident: *Times* (Oklahoma City), June 13, 1931, p. 1.

"I think ten hours": Blanche Noyes, COHC, vol. 1, pt. 3, p. 17.

"You might be interested": Letter from Eric N. Harris, April 22, 1983, Earhart Collection, NASM Library.

123   "I came down": *News* (Enid, Okla.), June 16, 1931.

Reprimand: *NYT*, June 20, 1931, p. 3.

Amelia's response: *NYWT*, June 26, 1931.

Crowds: Earhart, "A Friendly Flight," 7.

"Here I am": Putnam, *Soaring Wings*, 209.

Jim Weissenberger: *Blade* (Toledo), September 22, 1985.

"If any death warrants": *Sunday Signal-Times*, August 23, 1931, p. 1.

124   G. P. in hospital: *NYT*, September 13, 1931, p. 16.

"G. P. fell over a wire": SLRC, 83 M-69 F. 9.

Third tour of South: PSC, Scrapbook #3: *News Observer* (Raleigh), November 5, 1931, p. 1; *News* (Charlotte), November 10, 1931, p. 1 and November 11, 1931, p. 1; *Herald* (Augusta), November 20, 1931; *Chronicle* (Augusta), November 23, 1931; *Telegraph* (Macon), November 23, 1931; *Inquirer-Sun* (Columbus), November 26, 1931; *Constitution* (Atlanta), November 26, 1931.

King Prajadhipok: *NYT,* July 24, 1931.

Penalty: *NYHT,* July 25, 1931.

"Tell Mr. Putnam": Society of Woman Geographers, Archives, Washington, D.C.

125 Family matters: SLRC, 83 M-69 F. 9.

"Probably as the result": Cochran Papers, Ninety-Nines Series, Box 8, History (1).

126 "She agreed": Sir Harry Brittain, COHC, vol. 6, pt. 1, pp. 26–27.

Chapter 12. Victory and Vindication

129 "Would you mind": Putnam, *Soaring Wings,* 99.

Competent: C. B. Allen, unpublished manuscript, Earhart Collection, NASM Library.

Concentration: Earhart, "Flying the Atlantic," 17.

Balchen: Balchen, *Come North with Me,* 196.

130 Exhaust stacks: R. S. Allen, letter.

Fuel supply: Earhart, *Fun of It,* 211.

"We couldn't land": Pat H. V. Reilly, letter, October 22, 1984, New Jersey Aviation Hall of Fame.

"blind flying": Earhart, *Fun of It,* 211–12.

Lucy Challis: Putnam, *Soaring Wings,* 99–100.

131 Annual meeting: Cochran Papers, DDEL, Ninety-Nines Series, Box 11, Official Correspondence, 1932 (1).

Weather: *NYT,* June 28, 1931, sec. 9, p. 8.

Louis Reichers: *NYT,* May 14, 1932, p. 1; May 16, 1932, p. 3.

Barography: William F. Enyart, letter, May 16, 1932, Earhart Collection, NASM Library.

Every day: *Globe,* July 21, 1963.

Amelia slept: PSC, Scrapbook #7: *Times-Herald* (Dallas), May 29, 1932.

"so I don't bother": Nichols, *Wings for Life,* 209.

Dirigible: *NYT,* June 8, 1932.

132 Packing: Putnam, *Soaring Wings,* 105.

Departure, PSC, Scrapbook #7: *Dallas Times-Herald,* May 29, 1932.

"Mrs. Putnam has": *NYT,* May 20, 1932, p. 1.

Working on plane: ibid.

"She arrives at the field": Balchen, *Come North with Me,* 196–97.

"I am confident": *NYHT,* May 20, 1932.

"She looks at me": Balchen, *Come North with Me,* 196–97.

133   "I've spent my life": *NYWT,* May 21, 1932.

Cracked manifold: Earhart, *Fun of It,* 214–18.

134   Stomach contractions: Nichols, COHC, p. 21.

Eating: Earhart, *Fun of It,* 214–18.

"Paris was out of the question": *NYT,* May 22, 1932, p. 1.

"frightened all the cows": Earhart, *Fun of It,* 217–18.

Dan McCallion: PSC: *Daily Record* (Glasgow), May 23, 1932; Edwin C. Hill, broadcast, February 24, 1933.

135   Mobbed by crowds: *NYT,* May 22, 1932, p. 1.

Lindbergh kidnapping: *NYT,* May 13, 1932, p. 1.

Diary: Lindbergh, *Hour of Gold,* 257.

"Congratulations": PSC, 1932 Atlantic Flight, Postflight Correspondence.

Lady Mary Bailey and Peggy Salaman: *NYT,* May 22, 1932, p. 1.

136   Exclusive story: PSC, 1932 Atlantic Flight, Postflight Correspondence.

"the capacity of women": *NYT,* May 22, 1932, p. 1.

WCTU: PSC, 1932 Atlantic Flight, Postflight Correspondence.

"modesty and good sense": *London Sunday Express,* May 22, 1932, p. 1.

Reckless disregard: *Chronicle* (San Francisco), May 23, 1932.

"a magnificent display": *NYWT,* May 25, 1932.

Vain and foolish: *The Aeroplane,* May 25, 1932, p. 922.

Illness: *NYT,* May 30, 1932, p. 13.

Transatlantic flight: *NYT,* May 24, 1932, p. 13.

Edward VIII: *NYT,* May 25, 1932, p. 21.

Midnight supper: *New York Daily News,* June 1, 1932.

137   Dancing with the prince: *Evening Star,* June 20, 1932, p. 1.

Gordon Selfridge: *NYT,* May 29, 1932, p. 3.

"Whenever something is done": *The Aeroplane,* June 8, 1932, p. 1053.

G. B. Shaw: SLRC, 83 M-69 F. 9.

"I thought I just couldn't": ibid.

Flight authorization: National Archives, RG 237 835, Amelia Earhart Flights.

138   The de Sibours: *NYHT,* May 10, 1930, p. 8.

"she should have come": Univ. of South Carolina.

Hotel Lotti: *Excelsior* (Paris), June 4, 1932, p. 1; *Paris Herald Tribune,* June 4, 1932, p. 1; *NYT,* June 4, 1932, p. 3.

"so I telephoned": SLRC, 83 M-69 F. 96.

139   "Probably never again": PSC, Scrapbook #7: *Dallas Times Herald,* May 29, 1932.

Chapter 13. The Last of Lady Lindy

140   "I flew the Atlantic": Earhart, "Flying the Atlantic," 15–17, 72.

141   New York reception: Gentry, *Hangar Flying,* 156.

Tickertape parade and planes: *NYT,* June 21, 1932, p. 1.

"a happy faculty": *NYWT,* June 21, 1932, p. 3.

142   Honors: *NYT,* June 21, 1932, p. 1.

President Hoover and Senator Bingham: PSC, Scrapbook #7: *Washington Herald,* June 22, 1932.

"never have I seen such a greeting": SLRC, 83 M-69 F. 96.

White House dinner: PSC, Scrapbook #7: *Evening Star,* September 21, 1937.

143   Frail and tired: PSC, Scrapbook #7: *Washington Daily News,* June 22, 1932.

National Geographic Society: *NYT,* June 22, 1932, p. 3.

New York affairs: Gentry, *Hangar Flying,* 156.

"charmed everybody": SLRC, 83 M-69 F. 44.

Chicago: *NYT,* June 24, 1932, p. 14.

Rye and Harrison: *Rye Chronicle,* July 2, 1932, p. 1.

Boston: *NYT,* June 30, 1932, p. 2.

144   Pictures: *NYT,* June 26, 1932, rotogravure section.

Zonta club: *The Zontian,* September 1932.

Aeronautical Society: PSC, Scrapbook #6: unidentified clipping.

John Montijo: Jim Montijo, interview, October 19, 1985.

Pancho Barnes: Greenwood and Greenwood, *Stunt Flying in the Movies,* 70–71.

"there were very few women": *LAT,* November 17, 1985, pt. 4, pp. 15–19.

Transcontinental speed record: *LAT,* August 26, 1932, p. 1; *AYB* 1933, p. 382.

145   "displaying heroic courage": PSC, 1932 Atlantic Flight, Postflight Correspondence.

"women can do most things": Earhart, "Flying the Atlantic," 17.

Track fan: SLRC, 83 M-69 F. 9.

Celebrities: PSC, Scrapbook #6: unidentified clipping.

Pickfair: David Putnam, interview, November 11, 1985.

"in a week or so": SLRC, 83 M-69 F. 9.

Distance record: *AYB* 1933, p. 383.

"Don't come near me": *LAT,* August 26, 1932, p. 1.

146   Long-distance flights: C. L. Zakhartchenko, interview, February 10, 1985.

Flying a routine affair: *New York American,* August 26, 1932, p. 1.

"Splendid flight": PSC, 1932 Miscellaneous Correspondence.

"If I had had the weather": *LAT,* August 26, 1932, p. 1.

Jimmy Haizlip: *AYB* 1933, p. 383.

"in any legitimate way": PSC, Scrapbook #7: unidentified clipping, June 22, 1932.

Stationery: National Archives, RG 59. 124.023/33, Box 740.

Essex Terraplane: *Detroit Times,* July 20, 1932, p. 1.

147   Ninety-Nines: Cochran Papers, DDEL, Ninety-Nines Series, Box 11, Official Correspondence, 1932 (1).

Nancy Hopkins Tier: Tier, interview.

Ninety-Nines magazine: Cochran Papers, DDEL, Ninety-Nines series, Box 12, Clare Studer (3).

Helen Weber: Mrs. Robert C. Canavello, Correspondence, January 20, 1985.

248 *(sic)*

Portland and Poughkeepsie: PSC, Scrapbook #9: unidentified Poughkeepsie newspaper clipping, November 20, 1932.

148 Lectures during fall: PSC, Scrapbook #9: *Mining Journal* (Marquette), October 24, 1932; *Sentinel* (Milwaukee), October 20, 1932; *Times* (Erie), November 30, 1932; *Sun-Telegram* (Williamsburg), December 3, 1932; *Detroit News,* December 3, 1932; *Tribune* (Johnstown), December 5, 1932; *Union* (Springfield, Mass.), November 30, 1932; Detroit Women's City Club Bulletin; *Chatauqua Weekly,* December 15, 1932, p. 2; unidentified and undated newspaper clipping.

149 Paul Mantz: David Putnam, interview, November 11, 1985.
Invitations to Amy: SLRC, 83 M-69 F. 9.

151 "This is her stunt": *NYWT,* May 21, 1932, p. 3.
"Tell them about your lunch": *NYHT,* June 21, 1932, p. 2.

152 "It was much harder": *NYT,* June 21, 1932, p. 1.
Chances of crossing Atlantic: *Redbook,* September 1932, pp. 22–23, 97.
Putnam: Stabler, interview.
"Putnam would never speak": Bradford Washburn, interview, October 5, 1984.

153 Wheelbarrow ride: Canavello, correspondence.
Entertaining: *Globe,* July 21, 1963.
Party, December 30, 1932: PSC, Scrapbook #9: Walter Trumbull, "New York Lights" column, unidentified newspaper, December 31, 1932.
"Amelia Earhart Putnam": *U.S. Air Services,* June 1932, p. 13.

Chapter 14. Queen of the Air

155 "It's a routine now, Bert": Winfield Kinner, Jr., interview, October 27, 1985.
156 Franklin Institute: *PEB,* June 11, 1930, p. 2.
"After some bickering": Cochran Papers, DDEL, Ninety-Nines Series, Box 2, Official Correspondence, 1933 (4).
Dorothy Leh: ibid.
"The First Lady of the Sky": *Vogue,* January 15, 1933, pp. 30–31.
Anne Lindbergh: Lindbergh, *Locked Rooms and Open Doors,* 5.

157 Dinner party: *NYT,* January 24, 1933, p. 21; Putnam, *Soaring Wings,* 180–83.
Flight over Manhattan: *NYT,* January 24, 1932, p. 21.
Flight to West Coast: *Pioneer Press* (St. Paul), January 29, 1933, sec. 1, p. 1.
Northwest Airways tour: PSC, Scrapbook #10: *Tribune* (Bismarck), January 30, 1933; *Independent* (Helena), January 29, 1933; *Spokesman Review* (Spokane), January 31, 1933; *News Telegram* (Portland), February 1, 1933.

158 Training program for women: Samuelson, "Equality in the Cockpit."
159 "If women were drafted": PSC, Scrapbook #10: *Post Intelligencer* (Seattle), February 4, 1933.
"So far as sex is concerned": PSC, Scrapbook #9: *Daily Province* (Vancouver), February 4, 1933.
Lecture fee: PSC, Scrapbook #13: *Register* (Des Moines), October 19, 1933.
Paramount films: PSC, Scrapbook #10: *LAT,* February 8, 1933.

"the world's only regular airplane commuters": PSC, Miscellaneous: Mortimer Franklin, "Amelia Earhart Looks at Films," *Screenland* (June 1933): 28.

Helen Weber: Cochran Papers, DDEL, Ninety-Nines Series, Box 3, Official Correspondence 1933 (4).

"much more intense": SLRC, 83 M-69 F. 10, February 14, 1933.

160   "I join with the National Women's Party": *Evening Star,* September 22, 1932, p. 1.

Separate political party: Putnam, *Soaring Wings,* 137–38.

Minimum wage for women: PSC, Scrapbook #10: *Sun* (New York), March 7, 1933.

"I loathe the formal kind": SLRC, 83 M-69 F. 10.

Vacation: PSC, Scrapbook #10: *Daily News* (Sandhill, N.C.), February 21, 1933.

161   "women like to do such things": Transcript of CBS radio script, Canavello, correspondence, January 22, 1985.

Three important women: PSC, Scrapbook #9: unidentified Poughkeepsie newspaper, November 20, 1932.

Committee for the Recognition of Soviet Russia: Swarthmore College Peace Collection, National Council for Prevention of War, DG23, Series 4, Box 32; *NYT,* March 25, 1933, p. 12.

Eleanor Roosevelt flying: Lash, *Eleanor and Franklin,* 368.

162   D.A.R.: PSC, Scrapbook #10: *NYWT,* April 21, 1933.

"be made to do the dirty work": *Yale Daily News* article, November 10, 1933, from Whitelaw Reid, interview, October 10, 1984.

"A woman with Miss Earhart's fine courage": *NYT,* November 14, 1933, op-ed page.

163   Resigning: Letter from Earhart to Bingham, May 6, 1933, Earhart Collection, NASM Library.

"a promoter": PSC, Scrapbook #10: *New York Sun,* May 8, 1933.

Disagreement over NAA magazine: PSC, Scrapbook #10: *NYWT,* May 4, 1933.

"too dissimilar": Letter from Earhart to Bingham, May 6, 1933, Earhart Collection, NASM Library.

Honorary membership: Letter from Bingham to Earhart, May 17, 1933, Earhart Collection, NASM Library.

Air meets: PSC, Scrapbook #10: *NYWT,* May 4, 1933; *New York American,* May 7, 1933.

Amy and Muriel: SLRC, 83 M-69 F. 10, February 14, March 6, April 20, June 8, August 4, and September 17, 1933.

164   Ninety-Nines: Cochran Papers, DDEL, Ninety-Nines Series, Box 2, Official Correspondence (6).

Vogue: ibid., (6)(1).

All-woman air race: *Sportsman Pilot,* July 1933, p. 47.

165   Letter to Cooper: Letter, June 24, 1933, Earhart Collection, NASM Library.

World's Fair: PSC, Scrapbook #10: *News* (Chicago), June 10, 1933.

Takeoff: *NYT,* July 2, 1933, p. 1.

166 End of race: *NYT,* July 3, 1933, p. 5; *The Ninety-Niner,* July 15, 1933, Earhart
Collection, NASM Library.
Boardman and Thaw: *NYT,* July 4, 1933, p. 1.
Nichols: Nichols, *Wings for Life,* 226–30.
Pickford and Arnold: *NYT,* July 5, 1933, p. 10.
Pickford's divorce: *NYT,* July 3, 1933, p. 1.
Amelia with Pickford: Ninety-Nines Archives: *Herald and Examiner,* July 7,
1933.
Broken hatch: PSC, Scrapbook #10: *Newark Sunday Call,* July 9, 1933, p. 1;
NYT, July 8, 1933, p. 8.
167 New record: ibid.

Chapter 15. The Queen and the Minister of Finance

168 "She loved flying": Harry A. Bruno, COHC, vol. 6, pt. 1, p. 16.
Mollisons' flights: McDonough, *Atlantic Wings.*
169 Mollisons' crash: *Hartford Courant,* July 25, 1933, pp. 1–3.
Mollisons in Rye: Putnam, *Soaring Wings,* 233–34.
Lunch with the Roosevelts: *NYT,* July 30, 1933, pp. 1, 3–4.
Publicity with Mollisons: PSC, Scrapbook #10: *Midweek Pictorial,* August 12,
1933, p. 5; *Atlantic City Evening Union,* p. 1; unidentified clipping.
170 "49.5 Club": *International Herald Tribune,* August 2, 1983, edit. page.
G. P. and Douglas Fairbanks: *Pictorial Review,* December 1932, pp. 12–13.
Northwest Airlines: PSC, Scrapbook #10: *Tribune* (Bismarck), January 30,
1933; Scrapbook #16: Drew Pearson and Robert S. Allen, "Merry-Go-
Round," unidentified newspaper, July 1, 1936.
171 Vidal's appointment: Vidal, "Love of Flying," 15–20.
"To Eugene Vidal": Vidal Collection, Box 4.
Amelia in love: Vidal, "Love of Flying," 15–20.
Investment: Haggerty, *Aviation's Mr. Sam,* 22–28.
Air service operation: ibid.
National Airways: Mudge, *Adventures of a Yellowbird,* 38–40.
172 Checking each stop: Collins, *Tales of an Old Air-Faring Man,* 134.
Contract: ibid., 135.
Stockholders: *NYT,* August 6, 1933.
"You will see me often": Mudge, *Adventures of a Yellowbird,* 50.
173 Marcia-Marie Weber: Canavello, correspondence.
Press coverage: *NYT,* August 21, 1933, p. 19.
Winter operations: Collins, *Tales of an Old Air-Faring Man,* 135.
Completing flights: Mudge, *Adventures of a Yellowbird,* 54.
174 Amelia on airline: Collins, *Tales of an Old Air-Faring Man,* 135.
"members of the code agree": Ninety-Nines newsletter, September 15, 1933,
Ninety-Nines Archives.
Kodak: *House and Garden* (April 1933): 62–63.
"Everyone is very cordial": SLRC, 83 M-69 F. 10, October 15, 1933.

175 Theo Otis: Morrissey, interview, April 20, 1983.

"I tried to forget": SLRC, 83 M-69 F. 36.

"If you can stand it": PSC, Scrapbook #13: *Evening Telegraph* (Alton, Ill.), October 22, 1933.

Toledo to Lansing: *News Bee* (Toledo), October 20, 1933.

Mary Yvonne Scales: PSC, Scrapbook #13: *Banner* (Logan, W.V.), November 7, 1933.

176 "a fellow who will get an idea": PSC, Scrapbook #13: Lucinda Reed, "Mrs. and 'Mr.' Earhart," *Family Circle* (December 8, 1933).

Functional clothing: Putnam, *Soaring Wings*, 205.

New York firms: PSC, Scrapbook #11: *Women's Wear Daily,* December 11, 1933.

177 AP interview: Arne, "She Breaks Precedents," 7.

Separates: *New York American,* April 6, 1936, p. 12.

Franklin Institute aviation hall: *NYT,* December 18, 1933.

Smithsonian Institution: *PEB,* October 31, 1979.

Rotary Club luncheon: PSC, Scrapbook #11: unidentified clipping, January 22, 1934.

178 Cheap hat: Morrissey, interview, April 20, 1983.

"one of the hardest strains" SLRC, 83 M-69 F. 3.

One-week tour: PSC, Scrapbook #13: *Constitution* (Atlanta), February 3, 1934; *New York American,* February 4, 1934.

Watch: Putnam, *Soaring Wings,* 112–13.

Secretary of transportation: PSC, Scrapbook #12: *Christian Science Monitor,* March 6, 1934.

179 Airmail contract: Smith, *Airways.*

"As a result": PSC, Scrapbook #13: *Daily Record* (Boston), March 17, 1934.

"Airlines should stand": *NYT,* March 21, 1934, p. 1.

"She was just one of the gang": PSC, Scrapbook #14: *Wyoming State Tribune,* n.d.

180 "I held out": Earhart, "Flying and Fly-Fishing," 16–17, 62.

"We'll have to pack in": PSC, Scrapbook #14: *Wyoming State Tribune,* n.d.

"Woman's Day": *Airwoman* 1, no. 11 (September-October 1934), in Ninety-Nines Archives.

"Amelia Earhart Night": *News* (Bangor), August 13, 1934, p. 1.

Ralph Mills: Mills, "Dad's Flight with Amelia Earhart," 72.

181 Groucho Marx: *News* (Bangor), August 14, 1934, p. 1.

"a gracious hostess": *Daily Kennebec Journal,* August 15, 1934, p. 1.

Boycott: *Airwoman* 1, no. 11 (September-October 1934), in Ninety-Nines Archives.

Marsalis: Cochran Papers, DDEL, Ninety-Nines Series, Box 2, Official Correspondence 1933 (1).

Women in air meet: Allen papers, A&M 2252, Box 8: *NYHT,* February 4, 1933.

Elimination of women from meets: Letter from Amelia to Helen Rogers Reid, August 14, 1933, Reid Family Papers.

Flying Mary Pickford: ibid., August 31, 1934.

Allen's move to *Herald Tribune:* C. B. Allen, unpublished manuscript, Earhart
    Collection, NASM Library.

182   School of Aeronautics: Reid Family Papers, September 27, 1934.
    Purdue University: PSC, Scrapbook #12: Notes by Edwin C. Elliott.
    Burbank: *LAT,* November 7, 1934, pt. 2, p. 1.
    Fire at house in Rye: Morrissey, *Courage Is the Price,* 88–89; Putnam, *Soaring
        Wings,* 94–95; *Rye Chronicle,* November 30, 1934.

183   Restoration: PSC, Scrapbook #14: *Minneapolis Star,* November 30, 1934.

Chapter 16. Across the Pacific

184   Relationship between Amelia and G. P.: Edna Gardner Whyte, interview,
        January 24, 1984.
185   Natal to Africa: PSC, Scrapbook #12: *Washington Post,* October 4, 1934.
    San Francisco to Honolulu: PSC, Scrapbook #12: *Chicago Tribune,* October 4,
        1934.
    "on vacation": *LAT,* November 7, 1934, pt. 2, p. 1.
    Honolulu to San Francisco: Putnam, *Soaring Wings.*
    Kingsford-Smith: *LAT,* November 7, 1934, pt. 2, p. 1.
    Mantz: Col. Vincent Ford (USAF, ret.), interview, February 26, 1983; Don
        Dwiggins, interview, October 25, 1985.
186   Mantz's planes: *The Ninety-Niner,* March 2, 1934, Ninety-Nines Archives.
    Mounted camera on plane: Ford, interview.
    "I am not a stunt pilot": Frank Pine, interview, January 11, 1984.
    Army Air Service: Greenwood and Greenwood, *Stunt Flying in the Movies,*
        91–92.
    Citation: Dwiggins, *Hollywood Pilot,* 79.
    William S. Hart's ranch: Putnam, *Soaring Wings,* 234–35.
    "He wanted someone to back him up": Pine, interview.
    Work on Vega for flight: *Airwoman,* July 12, 1935, Ninety-Nines Archives.
187   Charting course: Rowena Willis, interview, October 23, 1985.
    Experimental radio work: *NYT,* November 22, 1934, p. 9.
    Third-class operator: PSC, documents. License dated December 22, 1934.
    Amy moves in: Morrissey, interview, April 20, 1983.
    Bobbi Trout: Trout, interview.
    T. P. Ulm: *AYB* 1935, p. 329; 1929, p. 158.
    Best-dressed: PSC, Scrapbook #14: *Post* (New York), December 20, 1934.
    Lurline: PSC, Scrapbook #12: *SB,* December 24, 1945.
188   Apology and instructions to Amy: SLRC, 83 M-69 F. 10, December 26, 1934.
    Chris Holmes: *SB,* December 27, 1934, p. 1.
189   Confidential memo: *SB,* December 28, 1934, p. 1.
    Denial of plans: ibid.
    Hawaiian sugar interests: *News* (San Francisco), January 4, 1935, p. 1.
    "an opportunity to emphasize": Pan Pacific Press Bureau, undated release,
        Ninety-Nines Archives.

"Anything I can do": PSC, Scrapbook #12: *NYT,* January 13, 1935.

"I suppose . . . tomorrow": SLRC, 83 M-69 F. 10, December 26, 1934.

190   John Williams: *SB,* December 29, 1934, p. 1.

Lt. Leroy Hudson: National Archives, RG 237 835, Commerce.

Editorial: *SB,* January 2, 1935, p. 6.

"Army experts": *SB,* December 29, 1934, p. 1; December 31, 1934, p. 1.

Dole race of 1927: *NYT,* January 7, 1935, p. 7.

Businessmen reconsidering: Morrissey, interview, April 20, 1983.

191   University of Hawaii: *SB,* January 3, 1935, p. 1.

Standard Oil: Letter from Putnam to Mantz, January 24, 1934, Don Dwiggins,
       personal files.

"Put it away": SLRC, 83 M-69 F. 10, December 26, 1934.

Letters: Putnam, *Soaring Wings,* 260–62.

192   Stephens's forecast: Dwiggins, *Hollywood Pilot,* 92.

Gas tanks: Letter from Putnam to Mantz, January 24, 1934, Dwiggins files.

Before takeoff: *SB,* January 12, 1935, p. 1.

193   Fire engines: Earhart, *Last Flight,* 21.

Takeoff: ibid., 50.

Seven hours out: *NYT,* January 12, 1935, p. 1.

194   Tired of the fog: Earhart, *Last Flight,* 27.

Swollen eye: *NYT,* January 13, 1935, p. 1.

Pierce: Examiner (San Francisco), January 13, 1935, p. 1.

"I know she felt it unbelievable": Vidal Collection, Box 19, p. 95.

Fatigue: *NYT,* January 13, 1935, p. 1.

195   "I want to sleep": *SB,* January 12, 1935, p. 1.

Dinner and article: PSC, Scrapbook #12: unidentified clipping, January 13,
       1935.

House on Valley Spring Road: *NYT,* January 14, 1945, p. 17.

196   "how easy and little fatiguing": *NYT,* January 15, 1935.

Cables from the Roosevelts: PSC, 1935 Postflight Correspondence.

Mines Field: National Archives: RG 237 835, Commerce.

Dinner in Oakland: PSC, Scrapbook #13: unidentified clipping.

Letter from Roosevelt: PSC, 1935 Postflight Correspondence.

Selling *Lady Southern Cross:* SB, January 14, 1935, p. 1.

Kingsford-Smith lost: Lockheed Publications Office, 07-60, 9, A-1 x7-6490,
       press release dated June 2, 1976.

Newsweek: PSC, Scrapbook #12: *Newsweek,* January 19, 1935.

"Flier in Sugar": *The Nation* 140, no. 3630 (January 31, 1935): 21.

197   "A Useless Adventure": *The Aeroplane,* January 16, 1935.

Chapter 17. The Flying Preacher

199   Telegram to G. P.: Telegram from Dr. Petra Dahl, February 15, 1935. PSC,
       Hawaiian Flight, Postflight Correspondence.

Letter to Mantz: Letter from Putnam to Mantz, January 24, 1934, Dwiggins files.

Instructions to Amy: SLRC, 83 M-69 F. 13, February 11, 1935; SLRC, 83 M-69 F. 10, February 11, 1935.

200   Midwestern tour: *NYT,* March 2, 1935, p. 12.

Woman's National Press Club: PSC, Scrapbook #14: *Washington Post,* March 6, 1935; unidentified clipping, March 4, 1935.

Buckminster Fuller: PSC, Scrapbook #14: *NYT,* March 8, 1935.

Radio broadcast: PSC, Scrapbook #14: *NYHT,* March 15, 1935.

Towns on tour: PSC, Scrapbook #14: unidentified newspaper, Battle Creek, Mich., February 13, 1935; *Tribune* (Chicago), February 16, 1935; *World-Herald,* February 19, 1935; *News* (Indianapolis), February 21, 1935; *Free Press,* February 24, 1935.

Amelia driving Dymaxion: Reid, interview.

Lunch with Sam Solomon: Haggerty, *Aviation's Mr. Sam,* 48–49.

201   Hungry all the time: PSC, Scrapbook #14: *Boston Transcript,* March 11, 1935.

"fed everyone for a time": *NYT,* March 13, 1935, p. 23; *NYT,* March 15, 1935, p. 16.

"We all thought Lindbergh": SLRC, 83 M-69 F. 100, March 8, 1935.

Mexico City to Newark: *NYT,* March 17, 1935, p. 24.

Radio homing compass: PSC, Scrapbook #14: *NYHT,* March 31, 1935.

"dollar-a-year" expert: *Air Commerce Bulletin* 6 (April 15, 1935): 224.

Autographed covers: Curley, "Amelia Earhart," 16.

202   Charted course: Earhart, "My Flight from Hawaii," 596.

Trailing antenna: Williams, "Charting A. E.'s Course to Mexico."

Takeoff: *NYT,* April 20, 1935, p. 3.

Flight to Mexico City: *NYT,* April 21, 1935, p. 1.

203   Preparing for flight to Newark: Earhart, *Last Flight,* 33–34.

Putnam's arrangements: Earhart, *Last Flight,* 35.

New York City to Mexico City: *AYB* 1936, p. 457.

Takeoff: Earhart, *Last Flight,* 35–37; *NYT,* May 9, 1935, p. 1; *Newsweek,* May 18, 1935, pp. 34–35.

Across the Gulf: Earhart, *Last Flight,* 30.

204   Vidal at Hoover Airport: *NYT,* May 9, 1935, p. 1.

Newark: ibid.

"the arm holder started": Earhart, *Last Flight,* 38.

"the lowliest peons in Mexico": *NYHT,* May 10, 1935, p. 8.

Vega: *NYT,* May 10, 1935, p. 23.

Message from Vidal: Telegram from Eugene Vidal, Director of Air Commerce, to A. E., May 9, 1935, National Archives, RG 237 805.0.

Editorial: *NYHT,* May 10, 1935, p. 8.

Douglas Dolphin: PSC, Scrapbook #14: unidentified clipping, May 15, 1935.

205   Conference in Chicago: *NYT,* May 24, 1935, p. 5.

"Skies fine between Atlanta and New York": Reid, interview.

Stamp deal: SLRC, 83 M-69 F. 106.

Newsweek: Newsweek, May 11, 1935, pp. 15–16.

Walter Curley: Curley, "Amelia Earhart," 16.

"There isn't that much money": *Newsweek,* May 11, 1935, pp. 15–16.

206   Indy 500: PSC, Scrapbook #14: *NYHT,* June 3, 1935.

Lectures in Indiana: SLRC, 83 M-69 F. 10, May 22, 1935.

Appointment at Purdue: PSC, Scrapbook #14: *NYHT,* June 1, 1935.

"A Flyer's Husband": *Forum and Century* 93 (June 1935): 330–31.

Parachute jump: *NYHT,* June 3, 1935, p. 1.

Note to Vidal: Letter from G. P. to Vidal, June 3, 1935, Vidal Collection, Box 19A, p. 95.

Alf Landon: *Globe,* July 21, 1963, memorial sec., p. 1.

Uncle Theo: SLRC, 83 M-69 F. 100, June 17, 1935.

Louise Bode and Luanna Hartsock: SLRC, 83 M-69 F. 36, September 1937.

207   "the kids found her there": *Globe,* July 21, 1963, p. 1.

New Jersey school: Stabler, interview.

G. P.'s grandchildren: Sally Putnam Chapman, interview, September 21, 1985; David Putnam, interview.

"We are still hoping": SLRC, 83 M-69 F. 10, May 22, 1935.

Surgery: SLRC, 83 M-69 F. 10, June 25, 1935.

Pleurisy: SLRC, 83 M-69 F. 10, July 5, 1935.

Amy's vacation: SLRC, 83 M-69 F. 10, July 5 and 28, 1935.

208   Oceanside article: PSC, Scrapbook #14: *Oceanside Blade-Tribune,* July 12, 1935, p. 1.

Birth announcement: PSC, Scrapbook #14: *LAT,* July 7, 1935.

Photograph session: *National Aeronautics,* July 1937, p. 18.

Ingalls: *AYB* 1936, p. 440.

Turner and Gilmore: Harvey Christen, interview, October 26, 1985.

Post: *National Aeronautics,* July 1937, p. 18.

Plans with Mantz: Memorandum of agreement, September 1935, Dwiggins files; SLRC, 83 M-69 F. 10, July 28, 1935.

209   Luggage: PSC, Scrapbook #14: *Star Ledger* (Newark), August 31, 1935.

United Air Services agreement: Memorandum of agreement, September 1935, Dwiggins files.

Updating will: Morrissey, interview, April 20, 1983.

Premonition: Haggerty, *Aviation's Mr. Sam,* 49.

"This Amelia": PSC, Scrapbook #14: unidentified clipping, August 4, 1935.

Post broke: Bruno, COHC, vol. 6, pt. 1, p. 16.

Crash: Johnson, *More Than My Share of It All,* 42.

Roger's airsickness: Vidal Collection, Box 11, Speeches #1.

210   Post's obituary: Earhart, "Wiley Post," 196.

Cable to G. P.: PSC, Scrapbook #14: Telegram from A. E. to G. P., August 29, 1935.

Menasco and Mantz: Don Dwiggins, interview with Mantz, May 13, 1964.

Came in fifth: PSC, Scrapbook #14: unidentified clipping, September 3, 1935.

"It is my ship": Putnam, *Soaring Wings,* 172.

Fall lecture tour: Dwiggins, *Hollywood Pilot,* 95.

Future of aviation and Russia: PSC, Scrapbook #14: *Akron Beacon,* February 14, 1935.

211   ICC: *NYT,* August 7, 1935, p. 17.

Pacificism: *Home Magazine,* August 1935, pp. 22–23, 59–60.

Chatauqua: *Courier Express* (Buffalo), August 10, 1935, p. 1.

Helen Richey: PSC, Scrapbook #14: *NYT,* November 7, 1935.

Never taking a man along: PSC, Scrapbook #14: unidentified Ft. Wayne newspaper, March 21, 1935.

Defending Richey: PSC, General Correspondence File, Telegrams, November 9, 1935.

"terribly feministic": Cochran Papers, DDEL, Ninety-Nine Series, Box 4, President's Correspondence, January 6, 1936.

Problems of career women: PSC, Scrapbook #14: *Sun-Tribune* (Chicago), October 13, 1935.

212   "there was never enough time": Morrissey, interview, April 20, 1983.

Facing discrimination: PSC, Helen Schleman, "Dedication of a Portrait," April 13, 1975.

"Surely we must have something": Goerner, *Search for Amelia Earhart.*

"wages should be based": PSC, Scrapbook #16: *Post Dispatch,* April 3, 1936.

Equal rights amendment: *Equal Rights* 22 (November 15, 1935): 1.

Purdue: PSC, Schleman, "Dedication of a Portrait."

Frances Merrit: PSC, Scrapbook #12: *News* (Indianapolis), November 27, 1935.

Marian Frazier: *Star* (Indianapolis), November 24, 1935, sec. C, p. 1.

213   "She came home dead tired": SLRC, 83 M-69 F. 4.

Dinner with the family: SLRC, 83 M-69 F. 10, November 23, 1935; ibid., F. 13, November 26, 1935.

Zanesville interview: PSC, Scrapbook #14: *NYWT,* December 2, 1935.

Dorothy Fleet: Fleet, *Our Flight to Destiny,* 116.

Dinner party at Lotus Club: *NYT,* December 23, 1935, p. 13.

"with nearly everything else": PSC, Scrapbook #14: *Herald* (Miami), December 24, 1935.

Children's book: Betty Huyler Gillies, interview, January 10, 1984.

214   Blanche Noyes: Noyes, COHC, vol. 1, pt. 3, p. 13.

Vidal giving Noyes a job: Letter from A. E. to Vidal, May 8, 1936, Vidal Collection, Box 19.

Mantzes' divorce: *LAT,* March 3, 1936, "City News," p. 1.

"I ran outside": Dwiggins, *Hollywood Pilot,* 77–78.

215   Letters to Amy: SLRC, 83 M-69 F. 11, March 18 and 23, 1936.

Car accident: PSC, Scrapbook #14: unidentified clipping ca. February 16, 1936.

"leaving my ship": SLRC, 83 M-69 F. 11, February 26, 1936.

"it would take months": ibid., April 1, 1936.

Chapter 18. A Threatened Partnership

220 "a reasonable partnership": Putnam, *Wide Margins,* 283–84.

"I'd like to find a tree": *Pioneer Press,* October 6, 1935, sec. 3, p. 5.

Communications between G. P. and Mantz: Letters from Putnam to Mantz, January 4 and 7, 1936, Dwiggins files.

221 Amelia wanted an Electra: ibid.

Special equipment: Letters from Putnam to Mantz, March 24, 1936, Dwiggins files.

Cracked brackets: Dwiggins, *Hollywood Pilot,* 96.

222 Plane's total cost: Letter from Putnam to Mantz, September 30, 1936, Dwiggins files.

Amelia's messages: Letter from Putnam to Mantz, March 24, 1936, Dwiggins files.

Uniqueness of flight: PSC, Scrapbook #11: Carl B. Allen, in *NYHT,* February 21, 1937.

Ignoring regulations: National Archives, RG 59 841.413, October 17, 1932.

Five-hundred-dollar fine: Richard S. Allen, personal files.

Richard Southgate: National Archives, RG 59 800.79611.

"a thorough field test": National Archives, RG 237 835, October 15, 1936.

223 Instrument flying rating: ibid., October 20, 1936.

Pacific weather data: ibid., November 6, 1936.

Honolulu takeoff: Letter from Putnam to the secretary of the Navy, October 16, 1936, Dwiggins files.

Eleanor Roosevelt: Columbia University Rare Book and Manuscript Library Manuscript Collection. Meloney-Putnam, November 5 and 9, 1936, and January 15, 1937.

Practice refueling: PSC, World Flight 1, Preflight Correspondence, November 10, 1936.

President's help: ibid.

Navy's cooperation: Franklin Delano Roosevelt Library, Hyde Park, NY, National Archives and Records Service. General Services Administration. Memos re: Earhart, November 17, 18, and 20, 1936.

224 Howland Island: National Archives, RG 237 800, May 13, 1935; December 8, 20, and 24, 1936.

Scratch-grade runway: Richard C. Black, COHC, pp. 33–34.

Electra's colors: Letter from Mantz to Putnam, May 7, 1936, Dwiggins files.

Other commitments for plane: Letters from Putnam to Mantz and from Mantz to Putnam, September 30, 1936; ibid., October 24, 1931 and November 14, 1936.

225 Announcement of purchase: PSC, Scrapbook #14: *NYHT,* April 20, 1936, p. 30.

"flying laboratory": *NYT,* January 16, 1930, p. 23.

Denial: PSC, Scrapbook #14: *NYHT,* April 20, 1936, p. 30.

"all applesauce": SLRC, 83 M-69 F. 11, April 1, 1936.

Announcement and confirmation: PSC, Scrapbook #15: *LAT,* May 14, 1936; *NYT,* May 14 and 22, 1936.

Department of Commerce: *NYT,* September 4, 1936, p. 8.

226   Cruise for Amy: PSC, Scrapbook #16: Eleanor Roosevelt, "My Day," unidentified Baltimore newspaper, n.d.

Advice to Amy: SLRC, 83 M-69 F. 11.

Family relations: SLRC, 83 M-69 F. 23, July 1, 1937, August 24, 1937; SLRC, 83 M-69 F. 34, June 25, 1941.

227   Frances Putnam's death: PSC, Scrapbook #17: *NYT,* July 1, 1936.

"All the while poor Fannie": SLRC, 83 M-69 F. 11, July 1, 1936.

First flight in Electra: *LAT,* July 22, 1936, p. 1.

Electra bill of sale: Roy A. Blay, interview, Lockheed Corporation Publications Office, Burbank, California.

Commerce license: Allen, files.

Practice run: PSC, Scrapbook #15: *Examiner,* August 3, 1936.

228   Los Angeles to New York: PSC, Scrapbook #15: unidentified Kansas City newspaper, August 21, 1936.

Bendix race: PSC, Scrapbook #15: *Cleveland News,* September 4, 1936.

Finishing fifth: *NYT,* September 5, 1936, p. 1.

"too much Hollywood ballyhoo": Allen, A&M 2252, West Virginia University Library.

Flying the Electra to Purdue: PSC, Scrapbook #15: *Indianapolis Times,* September 20, 1936.

229   Democrat voter rally: PSC, Scrapbook #16: *New York Daily News,* September 27, 1936.

Seconding speech: *NYT,* September 5, 1936, p. 1.

Endorsement of Roosevelt: Letter from Vidal to Mary Dewson, September 29, 1936, Vidal Collection, Box 19.

"I am deeply interested": *Equal Rights* 22 (November 15, 1936): 1.

Lecture at naval academy: *NYT,* November 6, 1936, p. 22.

Vincent Bendix: PSC, Scrapbook #16: *Tribune* (South Bend, Ind.), November 22, 1936.

230   Gene Vidal: Letter from Vidal to Mary Dewson, September 29, 1936, Vidal Collection, Box 19; PSC, Scrapbook #15: *Times* (Indianapolis), September 21, 1936.

Gore Vidal: Vidal, "Love of Flying," 19–20.

231   Jacqueline Cochran Odlum: Mrs. James E. Bassett, Jr., interview, January 14, 1984.

Cochran's childhood: Cochran Papers, Cochran, *The Stars at Noon,* 11–12.

Relief tube: Letter, August 14, 1987, Richard S. Allen.

Friendship with Cochran: Cochran Papers, DDEL, Article Series, Box 1, pp. 1–3.

Psychic powers: ibid., Box 8, final draft of *The Stars at Noon,* chap. 5, pp. 8–9.

232   Powers attributed to Amelia: PSC, Scrapbook #16: *New York Daily News,* February 16, 1937.

Amelia at Indian Palms: Cochran Papers, DDEL, Speech Series, Misc. Aviation, Box 1. Speech to the Ninety-Nines.

Bruce Odlum: Putnam, *Soaring Wings,* 232–33.

G. P. and Cochran: Cochran, COHC, p. 25.

Chapter 19. Crackup

234   "caught up in the 'hero stream'": Railey, *PEB.*

Mantz as instructor: Dwiggins, interview with Paul Mantz, May 13, 1964.

Johnson as instructor: Johnson, *More Than My Share of It All,* 43–45.

235   Assistance from Roosevelt: PSC, World Flight 1, Preflight Correspondence,
       January 8 and 11, 1937.

Margot DeCarie: SLRC, 83 M-69 F. Box 2, F. 53, February 7 and 21, 1939.

Interview: Boykin, "Amelia Earhart at Home," 46–47.

California home for Amy: Morrissey, interview, April 20, 1983.

236   Instructions to Amy and Muriel: SLRC, 83 M-69 F. 11, January 31, 1937, and
       February 8 and 23, 1937.

News coverage: *NYT,* February 11, 1937, p. 19.

LaGuardia: *NYT,* February 17, 1937, p. 18.

237   Oklahoma arrest: PSC, Scrapbook #17: *Blackwell Daily Journal,* February 21,
       1937, p. 1.

Deal with *Herald Tribune:* PSC, World Flight 1, Preflight Correspondence,
       March 15 and 16, 1937.

238   Endorsements: PSC, Scrapbook #17: *NYHT,* March 7, 1937.

Feature film: Morrissey, interview, April 20, 1983.

"Amelia Earhart kitchen": *NYT,* February 13, 1937, p. 3.

William T. Miller: National Archives, RG 237, 835.0, March 9, 1936, January
       16 and 29, 1937; February 8, 10, and 11, 1937; January 11, 1937, March
       1, 1937.

239   "quiet but nice": Sims, Vivian Maatta, interview, March 29, 1987.

Emergency signal kite: Vidal Collection, Box 19A, unidentified clipping,
       March 3, 1937.

"what is easy for Amelia": PSC Scrapbook #17: *NYWT,* March 19, 1937.

Harkness Davenport: Harkness Davenport, interview, September 22, 1985.

240   Instrument rating qualification: National Archives, RG 237 835, March 11,
       1937.

Davenport's instrument rating: Davenport, interview.

Written and radio tests: National Archives, RG 237 835, March 14, 1937.

Autographing cacheted covers: Carl B. Allen, unpublished book review, NASM
       Library, p. 1.

"I've got to get away": ibid., p. 8.

G. P. and Mantz: Putnam, *Wide Margins,* 287.

241   Mantz on Cochran: Dwiggins, interview with Paul Mantz, May 13, 1964.

Cochran on Manning: Cochran, COHC, p. 33.

Mantz on Manning: Letter from Mantz to Putnam, February 11, 1937, Dwig-
       gins files.

Fred Noonan: PSC, Scrapbook #17: *Plain Dealer,* March 14, 1937.
"had her doubts": Sims, interview.
G. P. wanted Noonan: Bassett, interview.
"two hitchhikers": *NYHT,* March 14, 1937.

242 Cachets: *NYT,* March 18, 1937, p. 1; PSC, Scrapbook #17: *Sun* (Baltimore), March 18, 1937.
"Never jockey the throttle": Dwiggins, interview with Mantz.
Mantz's takeoff: National Archives, RG 237 835, March 17, 1937.
Flight and landing: Dwiggins, interview with Mantz.

243 "I'm terribly tired": *Evening Star,* March 18, 1937, p. 1.
Holmes' party: Dwiggins, *Hollywood Pilot,* 102–3.
Contaminated gas: ibid.
Propeller bearings: PSC, Scrapbook #17: *NYHT,* March 21, 1937.
Noonan drunk: Basset interview.
"So many things can happen": PSC, Scrapbook #17: *NYHT,* March 18, 1937.

244 "It seems as if I hit a wet spot": *NYT,* March 21, 1937, p. 1.
Left tire blew out: PSC, Scrapbook #17: *Boston Globe,* March 21, 1937.
Other versions: *NYT,* March 21, 1937, p. 1.
Mantz's version: Dwiggins, interview with Mantz.
Capp's opinion: Edna Whiting Nisewaner, letter from William C. Capp.

245 Five-hundred-dollar fine: R. S. Allen, files.
Electra's repairs: National Archives, RG 237 835, March 23 and 24, 1937.

246 Electra moved to docks: Bell, "History of the Hawaiian Air Depot."
Arrival at San Pedro: *LAT,* March 21, 1937, p. 1; *LAT,* March 26, 1937, p. 1.

Chapter 20. The Vortex

247 Ben Howard: Howard, COHC, vol. 2, pt. 2, pp. 64–67.
Talking about the accident: "The Amelia I Knew," *The Ninety-Niner* (1949), Cochran Papers, DDEL, Article Services, Box 1, p. 2.

248 Williams's criticism: PSC, Scrapbook #17: *NYWT,* March 31 and April 6, 1937.
G. P.'s defense: PSC, Scrapbook #17: *NYHT,* April 7, 1937.

249 Raising money: Bruno, COHC, vol. 6, pt. 1, pp. 13–14.
Byrd's donation: Morrissey, *Courage Is the Price,* 199.
Kraft Music Hour: PSC, Scrapbook #17: unidentified clipping.
Cachets restamped: Curley, "Amelia Earhart," 19.
Additional one thousand covers: PSC, Scrapbook #17: *NYHT,* advertisement.
Muriel's radio interview: SLRC, 83 M-69 F. 23, March 23, April 15, and June 14, 1937.

250 "American's Great Women": *McCall's,* May 1937, cover.
Loss of Miller and Manning: Letter from Miller to "Vivian," May 5, 1937, Dwiggins files.
Jacques de Sibour: PSC, World Flight 2, Preflight Correspondence, de Sibour to Putnam.

251 Letter of authorization: National Archives, RG 237 835, May 10 and 14, 1937.
Albert Bresnik: Albert Bresnik, interview, January 27, 1988.
Noonan's car accident: *San Francisco Chronicle,* March 30, 1937, p. 7, and April 5, 1937.
Margo DeCarie: SLRC, 83 M-69 F. 53, April 20, 1940.
Noonan as navigator: Letter from Mantz to Putnam, June 8, 1937, Dwiggins file.
"without dumb luck": Cochran, COHC, p. 33.
Amelia at Indian Palms: Claudia M. Oakes, interview with Cochran, May 20, 1979.

252 "some inner compulsion": Cochran Papers, Speech Series, misc., Aviation, Box 1, p. 2.
Tired of G. P.: Vidal, "Love of Flying," 18–19.
"sweet giftie": Vidal Collection, Box 19A, Item 10.
Jockey shorts: Vidal, "Love of Flying," 18–19.
Burbank to Oakland: C. B. Allen, unpublished book review, Earhart Collection, NASM Library.
Trailing wire: Dwiggins, *Hollywood Pilot,* 106–7.
Shakedown cruise: C. B. Allen, unpublished book review, p. 11, Earhart Collection, NASM Library.

253 Edna Gardner Whyte: Edna Gardner Whyte, interview, January 24, 1984.
Near crash landing: PSC, Scrapbook #18: *Miami Daily News,* May 24, 1984.

254 Denial: ibid.
Fuel-flow gauge: Telegram from A. E. to Mantz, May 24, 1937, Dwiggins files.
Morse code key: C. B. Allen, unpublished book review, p. 12, Earhart Collection, NASM Library.
Shortened aerials: Letter from Putnam to Mantz, June 3, 1937, Dwiggins files.
Revised plans: *NYHT,* May 30, 1937, p. 1.

255 Bruce MacIntosh: Clint and Marian Morrison, correspondence, August 5 and 6, 1987.
Interviews and photographs, PSC, Scrapbook #18: *Miami Herald,* May 30, 1937.
Lunch with Harvey Firestone: PSC, Scrapbook #18: *NYHT,* May 31, 1937.
Extraction: Goerner, *Search for Amelia Earhart,* 169.
Flag to Cochran: Cochran Papers, "To the Ninety-Nines," Speech Series, Miscellaneous Aviation, Box 1, p. 2.

256 "It's not a premonition": Allen, unpublished book review, p. 9, Earhart Collection, NASM Library.

Chapter 21. Just One More Flight

257 "for fun": *Sunday Star,* July 7, 1937, p. 1.
Fans at airport: *NYHT,* June 3, 1937, p. 1.

258 Gas fumes: PSC, World Flight 2, notes for book on world flight.
Chief means of communication: Note from Kelly Johnson on drawing by

Elgen M. Long, December 3, 1980, Earhart file, Lockheed Publications Office.

Error in navigation: PSC, World Flight 2, notes for book on world flight.

Navigating by instinct: Earhart, *Last Flight*, 114.

Anne Lindbergh: *NYT*, June 14, 1931, sec. 2, p. 1.

259   Joseph Gurr: Letter from Joseph Gurr to Frederick A. Goerner, May 3, 1982, p. 5, Earhart Collection, NASM Library.

1935 flight: *NYT*, January 13, 1935, p. 1.

St. Louis: Earhart, *Last Flight*, 121–23.

Eleanor Roosevelt: PSC, Scrapbook #18: *NYWT*, June 8, 1937.

260   Bad weather: *NYT*, June 9, 1937, p. 27.

Dakar to Gao: *NYHT*, June 11, 1937, p. 1.

Gao to Assab: *NYHT*, June 13, 1937, p. 1.

Arrival at Karachi: *NYT*, June 16, 1937, p. 25.

261   Karachi to Calcutta: *NYT*, June 18, 1937, p. 23.

"ardent feminist": *Equal Rights* 23 (June 15, 1937): 82.

Telegram from G. P.: PSC, World Flight 2, telegram, June 18, 1937.

"personnel trouble": Collins, *Tales of an Old Air-Faring Man*, 147.

Across Bay of Bengal: Earhart, *Last Flight*, 170.

Akyab: *NYT*, June 19, 1937, p. 6.

Trying for Rangoon: *NYT*, June 20, 1937, p. 25.

Race to Singapore: *NYHT*, June 21, 1937, p. 1.

Circling the field: *NYT*, June 21, 1937, p. 25.

262   Bandoeng for repairs: ibid.

Malfunctioning instruments: *NYHT*, June 27, 1937, p. 1.

Landing at Koepang: *NYT*, June 28, 1937, p. 1.

"I will rise at 4 A.M.": Earhart, *Last Flight*, 187.

Radio broadcasts: *NYHT*, June 27, 1937, p. 1.

263   Communications with *Itasca:* CG Log.

266   "I think will have recovered tomorrow": PSC, World Flight 3, June 10, 1937.

"personnel trouble": Collins, *Tales of an Old Air-Faring Man*, 147–48.

Noonan to Collopy: August 28, 1937, Dwiggins file.

"every aid to locating it": C. B. Allen, unpublished manuscript, p. 11, Earhart Collection, NASM Library.

Gyroscope: Lt. Cmdr. Thomas Zinavage (USN, ret.), interview, December 20, 1986.

Meteorological reports: Rear Adm. Richard B. Black (USN, ret.), COHC, p. 36.

267   Government charts: *LAT*, interview with Elgen Long, June 28, 1987, pt. 2, p. 9; *San Diego Union*, interview with Grace McGuire, December 21, 1986.

Inadequate radio skills: August 28, 1937, Dwiggins files.

Takeoff: Collins, *Tales of an Old Air-Faring Man*, 147–48.

Harry Balfour: ibid.

268   Broadcasting fees: SLRC, 83 M-69 F. 23, June 30, 1937.

Radio contact with *Itasca;* CG Log, pp. 39, 40, 41.

269   "a quick drawl": Dwiggins, interview with Mantz, May 18, 1964, Dwiggins file.

Radio contact: CG Log, pp. 42, 43, 45.

270   "When I go": PSC, Scrapbook #15: G. P. Putnam, article in unidentified newspaper.

Epilogue

272   Schlesinger: *Washington Post,* September 18, 1986, sec. D, p. 4.

Letter from Eleanor Roosevelt to Mantz: May 14, 1938, Dwiggins file.

Mantz's belief: Dwiggins, *Hollywood Pilot,* 119.

Cochran's pain: Claudia M. Oakes, interview with Cochran, May 20, 1979.

Cochran's psychic powers: Cochran Papers, DDEL, Speeches, Box 10, December 17, 1969, Aviation Hall of Fame.

Letters from Cochran to E. Roosevelt and Mantz: March 11, 1938, Dwiggins file.

273   Vidal's opinion: Vidal Collection, Box 19, p. 97.

Collins's opinion: Collins, *Tales of an Old Air-Faring Man,* 153.

Johnson's opinion: Johnson, *More Than My Share of It All,* 46.

Allen's opinion: Letter to Robert Highham, July 3, 1971, Earhart Collection, NASM Library.

Evidence of Japanese capture: PSC, Scrapbook #18: *Washington Star,* November 26, 1961; *Christian Science Monitor,* July 2, 1960.

Masataka Chihaya: Masataka Chihaya, letter, November 12, 1986.

INDEX

311

O'Keeffe, Georgia, 187
Oldham, Mr. and Mrs. D. H., Jr., 122, 123
Omlie, Phoebe, 84
Ontario (Coast Guard cutter), 264, 265, 267, 268
Orenstein Trunk Corporation, 209
Otis, Alfred E., 4, 5, 7, 8
Otis, Amelia Harres, 3–5, 8, 9, 12
Otis, Carl, 8
Otis, Harrison Gray, 23
Otis, Mark, 5, 12, 125
Otis, Theodore "Theo," 125, 175, 206
Owen, Elise von R., 41, 164
Owens, Jessie, 145

Pan American Airways, 203, 222, 241, 248, 254, 255, 263
Pan Pacific Press Bureau, 189, 197
Paramaibo, 258
Paramount News, 135
Paramount Pictures, 137, 159, 232
Paris, Neva, 95, 96
Parsons, Louella, 75, 159
Payson, Phillip F., 172
Pearson, Drew, 232
Peary, Robert E., 143
Perkins, Frances, 200
Perkins, Marion, 42, 44, 47–49, 53, 55, 57, 64, 70
Perry, Margaret, 93
Phipps, John S., 47
Piccard, Auguste, 157
Pickford, Mary, 145, 166, 170
Pierce, S.S., 194
Pitcairn, Harold F., 120
Pitcairn-Cierva Autogiro Company of America, 120
Pope Pius XI, 138
Pollack, Gordon, 16
Port Darwin, 262–64
Post, Wiley, 88, 203–4, 208–10, 222
Postal covers and stamps, 201, 202, 205, 238, 241, 242, 249, 252, 255, 260, 261
Prajadhipok, King, 124
Pratt & Whitney: aircraft motors, 221, 243; S1D1, 186
Purdue University, 182, 206, 211, 212, 220–25, 228–30
Putnam, Binney, 208
Putnam, David Binney, 48, 114, 118, 133, 141–45, 149, 157, 161, 173, 208, 255, 257

Putnam, Dorothy Binney, 68, 73, 87, 112
Putnam, Frances, 113, 114, 116, 117, 227
Putnam, George Haven, 113, 154
Putnam, George Palmer I, 153
Putnam, George Palmer (G.P.), 46–48, 53–61, 64–70, 72–75, 77–79, 81, 86, 87, 109, 111–21, 123, 124, 126, 129–33, 137–40, 142–45, 147–54, 156, 157, 159–62, 165–80, 182–85, 187–89, 191–93, 196–201, 203–10, 213–15, 219–25, 227–30, 232, 233, 235–41, 245, 246, 248–55, 257, 259–68, 271
Putnam, George Palmer, Jr., 118, 165
Putnam, Nilla, 208, 255, 257
Putnam, Palmer C., 113

Radcliffe College, 14
Railey, Capt. Hilton H., 45–47, 60, 63, 64, 66, 113, 133, 135, 143, 153, 178, 234
Ramsdell, Powell, 29
Rand McNally maps, 202
Rangoon, Burma, 261
Rasche, Thea, 55, 92
Ray, James G., 120
Raymond, Allen, 63, 64
Raymond, Gene, 159
Real Airplane Luggage Company, 209
Red Sea, 260
Reichers, Louis T., 131
Reid, Helen Rogers, 115, 153, 169, 181, 182, 200, 204, 205, 237, 238
Reid, Ogden, 115, 153, 169, 200, 204
Reid, Whitelaw, 162, 205
Richey, Helen, 148, 211, 213, 228
Rickenbacker, Lt. Edward "Eddie," 26, 169, 179
Ritz Carlton Hotel (Boston), 70
Riverside (launch), 141, 151
Rockwell, Norman, 182
Rogers, Will, 90, 93, 115, 119, 209, 210
Rogers, Capt. William, 54
Rogers, Emory, 26
Rogers Field (Los Angeles), 23, 24, 36
Rogers Field (Pittsburgh), 74
Roosevelt, Eleanor, 161, 162, 168, 171, 187, 196, 200, 201, 222, 223, 226, 259, 268, 272, 273
Roosevelt, Elliott, 153
Roosevelt, Ethel Du Pont, 269
Roosevelt, Franklin D., Jr., 269
Roosevelt, Franklin Delano, 161, 170,

DATE DUE

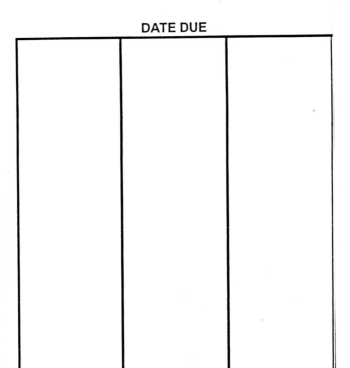